SHOW DG

The Charmed Life and Trying Times
of a Near-Perfect Purebred

SHOW DG

JOSH DEAN

!t

itbooks

AN IMPRINT OF HARPERCOLLINS PUBLISHERS

FIRST EDITION

Designed by William Ruoto
Illustrations by Alexis Seabrook
Frontispiece photograph by Kerry Kirtley
Title-page photograph by Kate Lacey

Library of Congress Cataloging-in-Publication Data has been applied for.

ISBN 978-0-06-202048-2

12 13 14 15 16   OV/RRD   10 9 8 7 6 5 4 3 2 1

FOR GILL AND CHARLIE,
AND ESPECIALLY MY MOM,
WHO LOVED SO MANY THINGS,
INCLUDING WORDS AND DOGS

CONTENTS

Preface xi

1   Wildwood 1

2   Hello, Jack, Meet the World 25

3   Jack's Mom, Human Variety 33

4   The Road to a Championship Starts with a
Single Point 44

5   White Plains: Meeting the Menagerie 53

6   Heather and Jack 64

7   Fantastically Rich People Do the Darnedest
Things: A Brief History of Dog Shows 72

8   Westminster: Welcome to the Big Time, Kid . . . 79

9   How the Hell Does a Wolf Become a
Pekingese? A Brief History of Purebreds 95

10   York 114

11   Pardon Me While I Fondle Your Dog's
      Testicles: Show-Dog Judging Explained 122

12   Edison 132

13   And Now a Brief Interlude Featuring the
      Perez Hilton of Dog Shows 145

14   The Campaign: I'll Take Thirty-four
      Consecutive Back Covers of *Dog News*, Please . . . 153

15   Meet Ron Scott, Show-Dog Investor 160

16   Harrisonburg 169

17   Like Walking Energy on a Leash 174

18   Welcome, Halle B 182

19   Stayin' Alive (Often with Great Effort):
      Breeding Ain't Always Pretty 192

20   Delaware and Beyond: The Slump Begins 205

21   Oyster Bay 212

22   Freehold 221

23   Ludwigs Corner 225

24   Do Dogs Actually Like Dog Shows? 230

25   New Paltz 241

26   Jack and Summer 246

27   Bel Alton 249

28 Bloomsburg 257

29 August: All Is Not Lost (Yet) 262

30 Hey, Puppies! 274

31 Deep into the Heart of Texas 278

32 Bloomsburg (Again) 290

33 Philadelphia 305

34 A Quick Lesson in Poor Sportsmanship: The
    Battle for (and Insanity over) Number One . . . 314

35 Go West, Young Jack 322

36 Wildwood: Once More, with Feeling 336

37 Last Stop, Westminster 350

38 The End. For Now. Maybe? 364

Acknowledgments 371

Appendix: Finally, a Thoroughly Random
Collection of Purebred-Dog Marginalia 375

PREFACE

· ·

This is an expensive sport, and there is little financial
reward.

—DAVID FREI, DIRECTOR OF COMMUNICATIONS FOR, AND THE FACE
AND VOICE OF, THE WESTMINSTER KENNEL CLUB DOG SHOW

Like everybody else in the world, I got started by buying a
dog and getting talked into going to a dog show and winning
a ribbon and getting hooked for life.

—PAT HASTINGS, TOP DOG-SHOW JUDGE, HANDLER, EXPERT

· ·

The American Kennel Club history books will know him as Grand
Champion Wyndstar's Honorable Mention, but you can call him
Jack. That's what his mom calls him. Not his biological mother, of course.
That would be Champion Wyndstar's Enough Said—or Gracie—and
she's a dog.* Nor his mom Kerry Kirtley, the California woman who bred
and nurtured him in his earliest days, or Heather Bremmer, the professional handler who trains and cares for him when he's making the rounds
of America's East Coast dog-show circuit. No, I mean his mom Kimberly
Smith, who first glimpsed a brown-eyed ball of spotted fur on a Web site
during a low moment in her life and decided, That's it. That's him. That's
my dog. She's the one who named him Jack.

_____

*Actually, she's a bitch.

Jack is a purebred Australian shepherd, America's twenty-sixth-most-popular breed and neither a particularly new or old one in the grand scheme of things. He is a resident of Pennsylvania and, sometimes in spite of himself, an exemplar of a very special kind of dog: a purebred who participates in the sport of conformation, which you and I know more colloquially as a dog show.

If you, like me, are an outsider to this world, it's easy to laugh at people who meticulously groom their dogs and put them on display, and to dismiss their "sport," as they call it, as a subculture that occupies only a tiny slice of America's attention—something akin to Renaissance fairs or sci-fi conventions—but the numbers suggest otherwise. There are more than eleven thousand dog shows sanctioned by the American Kennel Club, and an estimated 2 million of the 20 million purebred dogs in the United States participate in them. So yes, dog showing may be a subculture, but it's a mighty big one.

For at least the last five years, the notion of telling a show dog's story has nipped at my ankles. These most-doted-on specimens are so much like the dogs that amble around our lives—unconditionally lovable, irrepressibly mischievous—and yet at the same time so different—well traveled, hypertrained, pampered beyond imagination. They are, as I would find out, just regular old dogs with a lot of fancy trappings.

The real problem with embarking on such a project was that I didn't have the slightest idea how to focus on one specific individual. Out of 2 million dogs and 167 AKC-recognized breeds,[*] many of which I had never heard of, the thought of selecting one was daunting; it felt a little like singling out one flower in a field of thousands. Yes, it's beautiful and smells great, but so do all the others. What makes this one so special?

And that's where I was when I wandered into the 2009 Westminster Kennel Club Dog Show, with no clear plan, without even the vaguest notion of how it all worked—the elaborate point systems, the cham-

---

[*]That was the total in 2010; three more joined in 2011, with another three to come in 2012.

pions, the grand champions, the nuances of bone and structure that would give me night sweats over the months to come—and at an early press conference I met a Sussex spaniel named Frank. It was the first I'd ever heard of a Sussex spaniel, and this one just happened to be featured because his owners were New Yorkers and thus a good match for the local reporters in attendance.

SUSSEX SPANIEL

A Sussex is like a stocky cocker spaniel, with a thick head, long floppy ears, and a beautiful red coat. Members of this breed have the rare ability, Frank's owner told me, to sit up on their haunches, with the top half of their torso upright, front limbs dangling, for as long as an hour at a time. I'm not sure why this is a useful skill for a dog, or how the hell it ever developed in the first place, but hers demonstrated. The trick was impressive, not to mention adorable, to witness.

Two days later the Sussex spaniel was a famous breed, after an eleven-year-old named Stump emerged from retirement to become the oldest champion in Westminster history, winning the Best in Show title (BIS) in front of fifteen thousand spectators at Madison Square Garden and eventually landing on the cover of *AARP* magazine. He had droopy ears and droopier eyes, and I couldn't help but imagine the voice of the cartoon character Deputy Dawg as Stump lumbered around the show ring, winning the biggest prize in the sport over more heavily favored, styled, and coddled dogs like a standard poodle, a giant schnauzer, and a Scottish terrier.

To this point I'd been stressing over how to choose a dog. Stump answered that for me. It didn't matter. Any one of them can be a good story. You just never know. As you'll see with Jack.

The truth is, I had no idea what to expect when a series of connections led me to Heather Bremmer and Kevin Bednar, a husband-wife handling team, who in turn led me to one of their client dogs, a not-even-two-year-old Australian shepherd owned by a single mother from Pennsylvania.

Jack was, I thought, a good representative of what I'll call the accessible show dog—undeniably beautiful and special even among other top dogs in his breed—but also a family dog first and foremost. My hope was that his story would be more representative of the experience of the average dog-show enthusiast, the person who loves the sport, and all that goes with it, but doesn't have the bank account to run ads and jet around the country piling up points in pursuit of Best in Show ribbons at major events like Westminster.

On the other hand, it also wasn't impossible that Jack could develop into a star dog in his own right; even without a major financial backer behind him, he stood a very good chance of becoming one of America's best Australian shepherds, and also just maybe a contender in the Herding Group, one of the seven groups into which show dogs are divided.

Part of the fun in choosing an unknown dog was exactly that: the unknown.

Over the many months I spent reporting this book, one question in particular seemed to arise whenever the subject came up: Will it be like *Best in Show?* That Christopher Guest film, released in 2000, had a profound effect on the way Americans view the dog-show world—people seem to think that, having seen it, they are intimately familiar with this world, which they will almost certainly call "crazy" or some variant of that adjective ("nuts," "freaky," etc.). The more surprising thing for me, though, was that so many dog-show people wondered the same thing. Some as a toe-in-the-water measure of what I was up to: Did I mean to make fun of them and expose them as a community of weirdos? Others merely to suggest that it was maybe a touch mean-spirited but that it was also spot-on. Doug Johnson, a breeder of rare spaniels who has twice won Westminster—he bred Stump—perhaps said it best. "It's so close to the truth that it's not even funny."

Earlier on the day of Stump's surprise triumph, I met a handler who was about to show an American Staffordshire terrier that had been bred in Thailand but whose owners had dispatched him by air freight to the United States to achieve his AKC championship. Dog showing is a global phenomenon, and Asia is the fastest-growing region for the sport. But America, he said, was still the promised land; the only true measure of a purebred's greatness is for him to succeed in America. This handler proceeded to tell me he had heard that owners of a few of the previous year's top dogs had spent at least half a million dollars in expenses, and probably more. "This is crazy, the things people do for show dogs," said the handler of a dog flown in from Thailand— alone—in pursuit of ribbons. When I told him about my book project, he laughed. "It's probably going to be called *Why Are We So Crazy?*"

Clearly there's something about dogs that brings out the best and worst in us. Over and over I found myself explaining to outsiders the obsessive and occasionally psychotic behavior of dog-show participants by comparing it to the way we act in regard to our children. Go to a Little League game and watch the parents. Emotion makes us irrational—we suspend good sense—and the only thing besides a child that can make an otherwise normal adult human act this way is a dog. We created them, after all, and there are today more pet dogs in the world than there are babies—more than 500 million at last count. I may not have a dog at the moment, but I do have a son, born while I was working on this book, and although he's still not coordinated enough to swing a bat or throw a ball in its intended direction, I'd be lying if I said I didn't sometimes catch myself projecting great athletic ability upon his wild swats and tosses.

There are people who claim that dogs are our greatest invention. Having spent more than a year observing, reading about, and generally obsessing over them, I find it hard to argue this point. Spaceships and mainframes make for awkward bedmates, and there is no other thing that so willingly—and happily—does what we ask, even when what we are asking is seemingly unpleasant. There's a story that stands out in my mind because it says so much about dogs, and about us.[*] The story goes that a man decided for whatever reason that he needed to get rid of his dog. So, being a devious and deeply flawed human,[†] he urged the animal into a rowboat, paddled out into a lake, and cast the dog overboard in an attempt to drown it. In the process of perpetrating this atrocity, the man fell overboard, and because he couldn't swim, he began to drown. If you have a dog or have spent much time around one, I probably don't need to finish this story. You know exactly what happened. The dog saved the man's life.

My point? Dogs are awesome. And that's the real reason people enter them in dog shows.

I am a dog person without a dog. I grew up with a mutt named Heidi and had Percy, an English setter, in high school, but I haven't lived with a dog since college, when I shared a run-down student apartment with an adorable and utterly untrained mutt named Whitney, who smelled like a compost bin, regularly crapped on our living-room carpet, ran around campus with a pack of other unruly mutts owned by drunken Hacky Sack enthusiasts, and then vanished into the Rocky Mountains when her owner, my former roommate, moved west. The fact that my intervening fifteen years have been dogless has nothing to do with

---

[*]It's a fairly widely told story, and likely (unfortunately) apocryphal, but I saw it in Jeffrey Moussaieff Masson's *Dogs Never Lie About Love.*

[†]Which I guess is a redundant way of saying "a human."

Whitney and everything to do with New York City. Small apartments, late nights, frequent travels—all these things conspired against adoption, but I've lingered around the fences of New York City's dog parks for years, envious of the relationships inside. It's very possible this book is a direct result of that.

—JOSH DEAN, SEPTEMBER 2011

SHOW DG

CHAPTER ONE

Wildwood

Show dogs are just pets that get to go to dog shows. The
ring is just a small part of their lives.

—BILL MCFADDEN, DOG HANDLER

The parking lot outside the Wildwoods Convention Center in
Wildwood, New Jersey, greets visitors with a sign that reads NO
CAMPERS, RVS, BUSES. But that hasn't stopped the lot from filling up with
all three. The dog show has come to town.

If you were to arrive between Memorial Day and Labor Day, this famously kitschy Jersey Shore town would be packed with sun-scorched
families gnawing at clouds of cotton candy as they prowl the boardwalk from musty fun house to rickety carnival ride, between stops for
funnel cakes and old-timey photos. But in early February it is a ghost
town of more than two hundred shuttered-for-the-season fifties-era
doo-wop motels and motor inns with names that seem to have been
plucked from whatever list casino builders use: Lu Fran, Star Fire, Jolly
Roger, Sand Dune, Sea Chest, Ala Kai, Beau Rivage, Tangiers, et cetera.

Though the town's population can swell to 250,000 or more over
the Fourth of July weekend, the year-round residents number just 5,436.

And if dog-show week is any indication, 5,400 or so of those must fly south for the winter along with the birds. Wildwood in winter is so deserted that the city actually turns off the streetlights, and you could take a nap in the middle of the main beach road and probably have to get up only once or twice a day to let a car roll by.

So there's more than enough room in the convention center's parking lot for the SUVs, vans, box trucks, and RVs that ferry around America's show dogs and their human attendants. To walk the parking lot at a dog show is to see every possible seven-letter-or-less dog-related word applied in license-plate form: DOGRUN, DROOLRS, PAWSRUS, LAB LVR, FIDOFUN, DOG MOM . . .

If the plate doesn't give it away, you can almost always discern a vehicle owner's breed of choice by the silhouette stickers that adorn it—hulking Great Danes, elegant Afghans, the wispy Gremlin ears of a papillon. The lot is also a good place to tour the taxonomy of America's recreational vehicles, many hooked up to power—usually in limited supply, and only by advance reservation—and most adjacent to sawdust-lined pens that serve as combination exercise area and dog potty. (Dog shows have official, shared-use versions of these fenced areas, by the way. They're known as "ex-pens" and are used as indoor bathrooms. They are unisex, though at bigger shows there's sometimes one reserved exclusively for bitches in heat.)*

Other vehicles come emblazoned with the names of professional handlers, or of kennels, or of the many businesses that chase show dogs and their owners around. For instance, Lil' Pals, "a pet portrait studio that comes to you," offering the sort of high-concept photography displayed on the side—say you'd like to see your Pomeranian with angel wings, or your bichons frises imagined as a blissful couple on their wedding day, complete with tux and veil.

The convention center itself can't be more than a few years old. It's a concrete-and-steel leviathan parked on the precipice of Wildwood's

---

*Indicated, to my great amusement, by signs that read BITCHES IN HEAT ONLY.

famous 2-mile boardwalk, and you have to imagine that a few doo-wop motels came down to make room for it.

Inside, it's vast and sterile, and the most complimentary thing you can say about its architectural design is that there really isn't any. Outside, on dog show week, the beach was still covered from the last unexpected snow, and people inside were muttering into cell phones about contingency plans if the local weathermen were right and a giant storm that newscasters had already dubbed both "the Snowpocalypse" and "Snowmageddon" were to arrive.

People will often refer to a dog show by a singular name—in this case "the Wildwood show"—but that's actually a little misleading. Each day is its own show, sponsored by a different kennel club, and so even a single weekend combines two shows into what has become known as a "cluster," a trend that arose in the 1970s in response to the Arab oil embargo. Prior to that initiative, exhibitors had to pack up and move to a new location every day, but the gas crisis caused the AKC to ask local kennel clubs to work together so that two or three or four of them from a particular region would meet and stage shows at a single, central location. Hence the cluster.

The five-day Wildwood cluster was, then, actually five separate events, meaning that a dog entered all five days could win five purple Best of Breed ribbons—or lose five times and get nothing.

It's common practice to enter a particular dog in all the events and then pick and choose which ones to actually compete in. Experienced owners and handlers, for instance, tend to know which judges favor which types of dogs, so if you have a slighter dalmatian and you know that Saturday's judge has a particular fetish for larger dogs, you might opt to skip that day.

Being new to the game, Kimberly Smith tended to follow the lead of Heather Bremmer, her handler, and so she sent her new champion Australian shepherd, the twenty-month-old Jack, off to the Jersey Shore, unsure of how many times she'd actually have him shown. He was entered all five days—the fees of seventy-five dollars a day must be paid at least eighteen days in advance, so on Heather's advice she hedged her bets—and for sure she planned to let him show Wednesday, Thursday, and Friday. But if he were to struggle those days, she was unlikely to throw him to the wolves over the weekend, when the field would swell with the entries of owner-handlers whose day jobs preclude participation during the week. Momentum would dictate events.

Heather Bremmer and her husband and handling partner, Kevin Bednar, tend to arrive at a location just about the time it opens, so they always have prime real estate as near as possible to the show rings. Once a beachhead has been established, Kevin—who carries at least two hundred pounds on his square-shouldered, six-foot frame—will begin the manual labor. He'll roll in the crates and kennels and assemble them so that the smaller boxes, for the smaller breeds like corgis, sit atop the jumbo boxes, which house big dogs like the Bernese mountain dogs, bullmastiffs, and Akitas. Next he'll set up two or three grooming tables, plug in the generators that power the industrial cool air hair dryers, and make sure each crate has a towel and a water bowl.

All around them other owners and handlers do the same, so that within hours the convention center is transformed into a warren of crates and tables and supply boxes—a quick-rising temporary dog town with all the supplies necessary to feed and house a thousand animals, most of whom will also sleep on-site in their crates.

The actual competition rings don't open until 8:00 A.M., but by 6:30 in the morning of the first show, everyone will be showered and dressed and at work bathing and blow-drying the first breeds on the schedule.

Depending on the size of a show, Heather and Kevin will have at least ten and sometimes twenty or more dogs in their care. To make their lives easier, they specialize in working, sporting, and herding dogs—dogs like Jack the Aussie; Rita, a Chesapeake Bay retriever; and Tanner, a Bernese mountain dog, plus assorted other golden retrievers, corgis, and mastiffs. These breeds require pretty minimal grooming, as

compared to Malteses or especially poodles, which have such outland-
ish and time-intensive hairstyles that poodle handlers work exclusively
with that breed. These specialists arrive early and toil furiously, with
the help of trusty assistants, on however many poodles they have in
their care, and they aren't distracted by other dogs that might have to
be shown in the meantime, as breeds are scattered across the day. A
complete poodle grooming can take upwards of two hours, and you'll
rarely find poodles competing first thing in the morning; organizers
aren't that cruel.

The most famous poodle handler in all the land—in fact, the world—is
Kaz Hosaka, an immaculately coiffed Japanese man who moved to
America at age nineteen speaking no English and who now handles anywhere from five to twenty-five poodles, including, for 2010, Walker, the
nation's top-ranked toy poodle. Walker, like many of the country's best
dogs, handlers, and owners, was in Wildwood for his last tune-up before
the Super Bowl of dog shows, the Westminster Kennel Club show in New
York City. Both judges and crowds love poodles, toy and standard, and if
you can get past the ridiculous hair, it's not hard to see why: More than almost any other breed, poodles exude an air of confidence in the ring. You
don't want to give too much credit to an animal's awareness of what's going on at a dog show, but it's easy to watch poodles trot around and think
they are very consciously performing for the crowds.

It certainly seems as if good show dogs know what's expected of
them. To see Kimberly Smith's dog, Jack, under normal conditions is
to see an animal that takes great joy in tackling life. If he's not sleeping, he's playing, and he radiates energy to such a degree that his hair
almost stands on end. But once Heather snaps on his show lead—a gold
choke collar at the end of a thin piece of blue kangaroo leather deco-
rated with silver and blue glass beads—Jack transforms into something
else: a willing, almost subservient participant in a game he seems to
enjoy. That is, when he's focused.

Jack loves a challenge, and this clearly is one. It probably takes every
ounce of composure to suppress his urge to jump up and kiss the judge

or to romp with a ring full of his peers, but you wouldn't know it to look at him when he's at his best in the ring. He follows Heather's direction, eyes locked on her hand, and when it's time to move, he moves smoothly, with no hitches. Some of this is learned, sure—and both Kimberly and Heather would tell you that Jack was still a puppy and has learning to do—but there also seemed to be something less tangible at work here. Could it be talent?

K imberly wasn't able to take off from work, so she missed the first day of the Wildwood cluster. Jack was no worse for it. He was selected Best of Breed out of twelve champion Australian shepherds, beating a solid field of competitors, including a black dog named Shocka (full registered name: Ch* Heatherhill Shock N Awe) that won the breed at Crufts, the world's largest dog show, held mid-March every year in England, as well as a sturdily built red dog named Striker (Ch Schaefer Vinelake Impulsive) who had beaten him back-to-back days at some recent shows in Westchester County, New York.

The losses to Striker, Kimberly felt, were indicative of a potential problem for which no handler can correct. Striker is a solid, blocky animal, with "more bone" than Jack, who has a lithe and athletic build that would seem to be an asset for an animal designed to be agile while herding around uncooperative flocks of sheep. But individual preference for size is a bias you can't overcome, and much to the frustration of Kimberly and Heather—who runs into this issue in all the breeds—some judges just prefer it. Once you've learned that about a judge, the strategy is simple: You do your best to avoid him or her.

To beat Striker, then, was a nice start to the weekend. "I'm a pessimist," Kimberly said when informed of the result. "I always expect him to lose." While this was a common refrain for her, she, like any owner, wanted very much for her dog to win.

---

*"Ch" is an abbreviation for "Champion."

Heather and Kevin's team was off to a good start. Tanner, who had finished 2009 as the number-one-ranked Bernese mountain dog in America, also won his breed, as did Rita the Chessie, Trader the Akita, and Benny the bloodhound, who really only had to show up and not fall over in the ring, considering he was the only bloodhound entered.

Technically a judge doesn't have to reward a dog just for showing up; if he decides that dog just isn't deserving of a ribbon, he can withhold it, and this rare event is just about the biggest humiliation any owner can experience and should probably be taken as a sign that your dog—and, by proxy, you—might want to look for another hobby. Benny had no such issues; he is 145 pounds of droopy, bloodshot eyes and sagging, drool-laden jowls, the sixth-ranked bloodhound in America and a few generations removed from Ch Quiet Creek's Stand By Me, the bloodhound that played the part of Hubert in the movie *Best in Show*. Benny enjoyed a few minutes of his own in the spotlight the previous Thanksgiving when he and Kevin won the breed and placed fourth in the Hound Group at the National Dog Show, held in Philadelphia and aired to a national audience on NBC.

Less popular breeds quite often end up with little or no competition, so anyone looking to create champions and be competitive almost immediately could do worse than to pick a rarer breed like the puli or pharaoh hound or komondor, all of which dwell near the bottom of the list of most popular breeds, published annually by the AKC. As of this writing, the breed in dead last was the English foxhound, a hunting dog that looks very much like an overgrown beagle. Considering that the beagle is ranked fifth, this could be surprising until you realize two things: (a) There just aren't many English foxhounds in the United States; it's primarily a British dog owned by foppish men in jaunty caps and red coats. And (b) unlike beagles, which adapt to both country and city, foxhounds, say the breed club, "do best with acreage," which pretty much rules out city folk.

By the morning of day two, Kimberly and Jack had been apart for nearly forty-eight hours, and because Jack has a tendency to get overexcited and is difficult to bring back from that state, Heather asked Kimberly to arrive early enough that her dog could get their joyous reunion out of his system so that Heather could steer him back in the general direction of composure by ring time.

When Jack sees Kimberly after an absence, his eyes go a little wide, his head dips, and then he begins to vibrate, from back to front. These vibrations become tremors, which become earthquakes, until Jack's fifty-five-pound form is practically levitating. Because he was on the grooming table when she arrived in Wildwood and thus had a choke collar around his neck, connecting him to a pole, Jack couldn't really move very far, but that didn't stop his body from spasming around until he was released from the lead and could jump up and onto his mother for a good hug.

Hugging was a new thing for Jack. He loves affection and will jump up and paw at you repeatedly, as well as propel himself up and into your midsection over and over until you stoop down to his level and apply pats and rubs. But the full-on paws-around-the-neck hug was something he picked up from his new roommate, Summer, a young Australian shepherd that Kimberly had recently purchased from Mont-Rose Aussies in New York State to be his home companion as well as perhaps a future paramour should their respective traits prove to be a good match. Summer was a big hugger, and after a few weeks of watching her stand up and hug his favorite human, Jack began to imitate her. It was, for a time, one of his favorite things to do.

Heather looked sternly at both Kimberly and Jack and directed him back to the grooming table. At shows, Heather is in charge and everyone knows it. Being five foot three and not much over a hundred pounds, and looking more like the kind of person you'd find at the front of a kindergarten classroom than one you'd see reprimanding a rottweiler, Heather is easily outweighed by many of the animals at the show, but like any good handler she has the aura of an alpha dog. Many times a day, I would witness her silence a barking dog simply by saying its name once in a brusque manner, and sometimes just by staring it down.

Heather has a particular fetish for presentation, and she likes for Kevin's outfits to color-coordinate with hers. For Thursday it was turquoise. Kevin wore a turquoise shirt and turquoise accents in his tie, while Heather chose a turquoise blazer and a black skirt. On the spectrum of conservative to flashy, the two fall somewhere in the middle. You'll see some handlers in sequins and others in off-the-rack suits sized for a much larger person, a fashion faux pas that is sometimes a result of poor taste but often an unfortunate byproduct of the need for dress pants you can jog in.

"So we won yesterday," Kimberly said, beaming a little, as Heather put her blazer aside and replaced it with a black fleece she wears while grooming.

"He was a nightmare," Heather answered. Jack's handler was finding her star Australian shepherd to be an unfamiliar challenge. Some days she put on the lead and he was calm and focused; other times he seemed totally uninterested in playing along. On these days it took all her tricks to bring him in line. She felt that he still needed more experience. "I think if he did a whole month with us, it would make a huge difference," she said.

Because Kimberly wasn't able to afford a full-time handling plan on her own—which could be two thousand dollars per month or more—Jack was on an erratic schedule, and it seemed to Heather that one reason he tends to be unruly the first day of a show is that he forgets how to act like a show dog. Every time, she theorized, Jack had to work through his excitement anew. If you're a dog who loves dogs and people—let's face it, who loves stimulation of any kind—a dog show is pretty overwhelming, and so it's easy to see how Jack could lose his composure so easily.

Still, he had the win, due partly to his presence of mind that day and partly to his beautiful appearance. Aesthetically, Jack doesn't have many flaws. As a type of Australian shepherd known as blue merle, he has an exotic look, with black, gray, brown, and blue patches on his otherwise ivory white coat, but even those spots aren't really so random.

He does have what's known as a "rose ear," a condition in which one of his ears perks up ever so slightly instead of folding perfectly over in a mirror image of the one on the other side. Unfortunately, it's his left ear, and the left side is the "show side," or the side that faces the judge when the animals are standing still in the ring.

It's a weak muscle that causes the rose ear, though, and the issue is quite easily corrected. If this very minor flaw is recognized early enough, a breeder can painlessly glue the ear when the dog is two months old, and the problem takes care of itself in a few weeks. Since Jack is older, Heather's method, which she picked up from an e-mail that Kerry sent to Kimberly (including photos), was to apply some thick tape from one ear to the other, under his chin, for an hour or so before showtime in the hope that the ear would stay down for a while. Tape, however, poses problems. Most isn't strong enough to withstand Jack's violent attempts to shake it off, and the kinds that are strong enough— duct tape certainly is—pull out tufts of hair, leaving bare spots.

Kimberly had come up with an ingenious solution. She researched magnets online until she found a set strong enough to stay together when stuck one on either side of a hyper dog's ear but weak enough that they're easily pulled apart by humans and don't actually hurt the dog. She wrapped two dime-size magnets in electrical tape, and connected them to another pair using speaker wire, which is both pliable and strong, and covered the whole thing in more black tape. It's a surprisingly tidy contraption, and with Jack's thick white ruff,* you can hardly tell he's wearing them. Kimberly thought that the next step was to dip the ear holders in liquid rubber, and Heather had told her more than once that she should sell a more refined version at dog shows to owners of other breeds that tend to suffer from rose ear: Rottweilers, for instance.

Kimberly reached into a box and picked up the latest issue of the *Canine Chronicle*. The *Chronicle* is a glossy, oversize monthly magazine

---

*That's dog lingo for the mane.

with a smattering of editorial hidden inside hundreds of pages of vanity ads promoting top show dogs, including, in this edition, a two-pager for Tanner and another for Rita. Virtually every inch of the *Chronicle* is for sale, including the cover, on which appeared the nation's top-ranked boxer, Scarlett, who was also the fifth-ranked dog among all breeds in all the land. She was in Wildwood for the weekend.*

When Kimberly boasted that Jack had beaten a former Crufts winner, Heather smacked her lightly on the arm with a grooming brush. "I keep telling you, you have a good dog," she said. "He's crazy, though. He saw somebody yesterday who looks like you"—indicating me, a human he'd previously met only once—"and he went nuts."

"He remembers people," Kimberly said.

Heather pointed to some new styling she was trying on his rear. To help even a slight slope in his "top line"—that's his back, which is supposed to be as close as possible to level, even though very few dogs have this—Heather had fluffed up his fur using water, hair spray, and a blow dryer. The effect is a less extreme version of what teenage girls once did to their bangs in the 1980s. Kimberly laughed. "I'll have to call him 'poufy butt.'"

It's worth nothing that, technically, much of the grooming you see at a dog show is in violation of rules. Technically, a dog should appear in the ring au naturel. You can wash and brush him, but—technically—you're not to apply powder, thickener, hair spray, dye, or any other product that can artificially alter a dog's appearance. But stroll around the handling area of a dog show and you will see all these things in open use. By the time a bichon is through grooming, he will have swollen in size by a third, with the use of enough hair spray to style the cast of *Jersey Shore*. Most black dogs have had any nonblack spots, however tiny, blacked in with dye (in the case of fur), makeup (for snouts and whiskers), and even markers (for touch-ups—all of which you'll find

---

*In 2009, Scarlett won twenty-one Best in Show titles, defeating more than 34,400 dogs in the process. She has four different, unrelated owners.

among the hundreds of canine beauty-modification products you can buy from concessionaires on site at any dog show. Products of this sort were being deployed on every table in the building.

So, you know—technicalities.

N ot to pick on all-white breeds, but to look at a dog ring full of Samoyeds or bichons frises as an abject amateur is to be thoroughly baffled. They look identical—white and fluffy and . . . well, mostly white and fluffy. I have no idea how a judge can tell them apart, let alone which is best.

In the case of Aussies, a typical ring offers great variation. There are four recognized color patterns, the most common known as the black tri. These dogs are mostly black with some white and red around their necks and faces, and they often have white circles around their eyes that look like reverse panda masks. Red tris have a similar look, only in place of all that black the dogs have a rusty red coat. Jack, as previously discussed, is what's known as a blue merle—a striking pattern that is haphazardly spotted in gray, black, brown, and white, with gray and white being the most dominant colors. The final type is the red merle, which has the same type of pattern as the blue, only instead of gray patches it has red. Truly, it's rare to find even two tris that you couldn't tell apart, even though their markings are fairly consistent, but you will never have issues distinguishing any two merles. Such apparent randomness as you see in their coats is typically a quality we associate with mutts, but you don't have to know anything about Australian shepherds to know that when you see a beautiful merle, like Jack, you are looking at a special kind of animal.

BLACK TRI AUSSIE

By the time Jack was due to show on day two, the judge had already cast aside a good dozen lesser dogs from the lower classes that precede the Best of Breed competition. Being so new, I couldn't help but obsess over aesthetics—I was searching for the dog whose appearance looked best to my untrained eye—but Kimberly pointed out that the more knowledgeable observer of Australian shepherds keys on movement. "Jack is a good mover," she would say over and over (and over). And as he stacked up behind the Crufts dog, noticeably larger in juxtaposition, she patted my shoulder. "I have butterflies."

The common belief about dog shows is that they are beauty pageants, but that's only sort of right. A beauty pageant as we humans do it is a competition that sets out to judge some entirely subjective idea of beauty—hair, eye, and skin color hardly matter; height and weight do, to some degree, but what's perfect, exactly, is never clear. What matters, really, is that the judges—using gut instinct and fuzzy logic, plus their own inclinations—decide that one human is more "beautiful" than the others, whatever that means.

In a dog show, it's a lot more scientific, at least in theory: The judge sets out to identify which of the dogs assembled best represents a very specific ideal that is articulated quite explicitly in print by the parent club of a particular breed and then backed up by the American Kennel Club. It's known as the breed standard, and you can find it on the AKC Web site as well as in Web and print materials published by each breed's parent organization. It's not necessarily which Australian shepherd, then, is the most beautiful, but rather which one looks the most like the theoretical perfect dog as defined by the small group of humans who founded the breed and maintain its definition.

How a breeder knows that a puppy will grow up to be perfect, or at least potentially so, is pretty fuzzy, too (no pun intended). It's not at all a science and is at best a mix of instinct and guesswork. Basically, that breeder is looking for clear markers of future flaws that would disqualify a show dog. In the case of Aussies, one would be white splashes "between withers and tail."

Some of these markers are apparent early—those white splashes, or some badly splayed back legs—but often it's more like an educated guess, and if a statistician were to get ambitious and track an appropriately giant sample set to match predicted success with actual success, we'd probably find out that breeders are wrong as often as they're right. Go to a dog show and talk to enough people and you'll find plenty of examples of people who "had no idea" their dog would become a champion, and each year at Westminster the PR machine trots out examples of dogs that were abandoned, or left for dead, or considered too ugly or lame or stupid who grew up to become top show dogs. Kimberly chose Jack, for instance, primarily to be a house pet, as well as an occasional agility competitor.

Each breed also has a standard for movement, and because Aussies have such disparate looks and the breed was created to be agile, movement is especially critical in judging. Kimberly explained it this way: "You need to move fast enough so you can get that flowy movement but not so fast that you lose foot timing." "Flowy movement" is a bit of an amorphous idea, but it's more or less an elegance of motion that looks both athletic and effortless. Foot timing refers to the four feet being in perfect alignment, so that one front and one rear work together, as if joined on a string. "That's all the handler," she said.

When directed by the judge, a handler will lead her dog straight ahead and then back. This is known as "down and back" or "coming and going," and if you hang around show people, you will often hear them say things like, "I wish he were better coming and going." Handlers will next run their dogs around the outside perimeter of the ring to give the judge a look at the "side gait." These are two different measures of perfection in movement, and judges of different breeds weigh the value of each pattern differently.

One tip-off that a judge doesn't like a dog is when she stops watching before it has completed the movement—she might watch it down but will then turn to analyze the next dog by the time it's coming back. Very often the judge will watch only half of the run around the ring and then turn back to the next dog in line.

Before the test of its movement, though, a dog must "stack." This is that statuary pose you'll know if you've ever watched Westminster on TV. The dog stands dead still, front legs under its chest, back legs slightly splayed, staring straight ahead at the fixed palm of its handler, which may or may not contain treats, known as "bait." Treats come in many varieties, the most popular being hot-dog chunks, Purina Carvers, and freeze-dried liver. Some dogs love mozzarella sticks.

Unlike movement, stacking is not a natural act for a dog, and each one must be taught. Some pick it up easily. In Jack's case, he was already good at tricks and obedience and was adept at something called "targeting"—putting a paw on a fixed object—so Kimberly just had to teach him to set all four paws in a stance and "stay." Once he got it, he got it.

Nearly all dog behavior is relatable to wolves (after all, they are just evolved wolves), and if you think of all dog activity in the context of their wild ancestors, you will realize that standing stone still is not so natural; it's hardly biologically advantageous in a world where other things want to stalk and kill you. And yet it is a critical ability of any show dog—not just to stand still but to stand still in a very precise way that accentuates structure, and to do so for an extended period while an unfamiliar human molests you.

Plenty of dogs flunk conformation before they've attended a single show, because they are unable to master this seemingly simple skill. And plenty of others owe their aptitude at impersonating a statue to something called Happy Legs, a contraption devised for the very specific purpose of teaching dogs how to stand-stay in a correct show pose. Basically, the Happy Legs looks like a box with four "stilts," or paw-size platforms, on which a dog balances. After some time and ample treats, a dog will come to see this as a trick he can do on command, like fetching or rolling over. Happy Legs come in three sizes, costs two hundred dollars, and if the "barkimonials" on the Web site are any indication, purchasers see results within minutes.

Happy Legs* is the invention of Mr. and Mrs. Happy Legs, aka David and Susan Catlin of Kennesaw, Georgia, an exurb of Atlanta so conservative that local lawmakers—in reaction to a nationwide movement for increasingly stringent gun legislation—passed a town ordinance in 1982 mandating that all residents own "a firearm together with ammunition."

Happy Legs "has revolutionized the way that people teach the stand for examination," Mrs. Happy Legs told me.† She said it is such a staple of the show world that it is now "standard equipment, just like a grooming table or a brush."

Happy Legs works for the same reason any obedience trick does—

---

*Ironically named? You decide.

†Colorful but unverifiable biographical detail about Mrs. Happy Legs: "I believe [people] are recycled. Susan might be a new entity, but my energy has been around for millennia. Certainly in a past life I had to have been a horse-livestock person. My mother was scared of anything. She didn't like animals."

and for the same reason that Jack will gladly do things: for the satisfaction of successfully completing a challenge. Susan said that in the very early days there were people who accused her of dog torture. "People said it was cruel. But dogs think it's a game. It's muscle memory. And it's a quick, easy game. You stand up on these four things that won't tip over and you've won. They're like, 'Really? You're happy, I get food, and you'll pet me? That's it?'"

Prior to its invention, she said, "We just yelled at the dogs." Which in addition to being cruel is actually detrimental, because one common flaw in purebred dogs is an insecure temperament, and if you yell at an insecure dog, it's only going to intensify his shyness around humans. "So we would slowly but surely lose the show attitude," Mrs. Happy Legs told me. "You tried to teach them this concept that they never really got. A certain amount of dogs are so correct in structure they can't stand any other way. Others are ever so slightly off. We simply lost dogs much, much sooner."

On her contribution to the service of show dogs, Mrs. Happy Legs isn't modest. "It has changed the face of the show scene," she proclaimed. "I would argue that point with any high-profile judge or handler."

In Jack's case, he was both structurally sound and willing to play the game of standing still. There was no need for Happy Legs, even in the beginning. And he looked good in the ring on Wildwood's second day, but, for whatever reason, the judge preferred the Crufts dog that day. Judges have no obligation to explain themselves. If you ask nicely, some will gladly elucidate their rationale; others choose to keep their reasons private.

"He showed well today," Heather said as she walked out and handed the dog to Kimberly. Within minutes she'd be on a new dog, in a new ring. "I could tell she liked big dogs. And she didn't want them to move too fast." Both things did not favor Jack.

Kimberly seemed to be accepting of her fate. "I said before I got here that because he won yesterday, the weekend is a success no matter what happens," she said, but I didn't totally buy it.

• • •

At 9:23 A.M. on Friday, day three at the Wildwood show, a PA
crackled to life and a tinny female voice addressed "all the rumors and stories about the storm."

"The show will go on," the voice droned, for once wielding this
tired old cliché in proper context. "This building will not close. We
are open twenty-four hours for your and your dogs' safety." There was
more murmuring that I couldn't pick up, and the woman finished with
this defiant line, using, for the second time in one PA announcement,
a cliché in a way that was not only appropriate, but accurate. After a
dramatic pause, as in a stump speech, she bellowed, "Together we will
weather this storm!"

Kimberly had gone home for the night and returned with Summer,
to start the process of getting her second dog used to the chaos in case
Kimberly decided to show her, too, even though whether or not she
ultimately would was very much in question. Lately the young bitch
had been growing into her looks. If you'd asked Kimberly in January,
she would have said she thought that Summer was "sweet, but not so
smart" and that despite the fact that she'd appeared to be "show quality" as a puppy, she looked likely to grow up to have overly short legs
and subpar movement. Lately, however, Kimberly was starting to look
at her differently.

The more Jack won, the more valuable his sperm would become.
And Summer (whose AKC name is Montrose Sheza Hot Shot), could
ultimately be a good mate. Because Jack is a blue dog who is "red fac-
tored," meaning he has red genes in his pedigree,* theoretical litters
from a theoretical mating with a red dog like Summer could, theoretically, produce puppies in all four color variations, an attractive result in
that there's something for everyone. This was an angle that Kim had

---

*Red genes that could result in red tris and red merles, each of which is less common
than the black/blue version.

considered from the outset, and it's the reason Summer is a red tri and not a red merle.

To protect the gene pool, breeders of Australian shepherds have learned that it is not advisable to breed merle to merle—no reputable breeder would ever do it. The reason: There's a 25 percent risk of blindness and/or deafness in the resulting puppies. "What it does is produce too much white," Kimberly explained as we waited for smooth-coated collies to clear the ring and make room for the Aussies. Lest you think the breed standards are too capricious and nitpicky—and *I* certainly thought that—consider that they have very specific reasons for being. In the case of Aussies, the standard dictates where and how much white a dog can have. In particular, white hair around the ears and eyes is considered a serious flaw. This isn't because someone decided it looks bad, but because white around the eyes is an indicator of increased potential for future blindness. Similarly, if the ears should be all white, there's a good chance that dog will be deaf. In the end nearly any specific stipulation of the breed standard is there to protect the gene pool. Because showing dogs is really all about breeding.

Ditto movement. The fact that a judge dismisses a dog for having a less-than-perfect gait really stems from the same place. Ultimately the question the judge should be answering is this: Can this Australian shepherd do his job? If he's built right, and moving right, and can turn quickly, and be light and agile, he can do his job—he can herd sheep. Similarly, this is why you'll see judges pull on the terriers' tails. Terriers need sturdy tails that can be yanked and tugged, because that's the way you pull them out of a hole should they get stuck while chasing rats or rabbits or gophers. If one barks or snaps or recoils when the judge pulls, he's probably going to be a bad terrier.

AUSSIE MOVEMENT

Jack's performance on Friday would dictate Kimberly's schedule for the rest of the weekend. If he won, she'd likely enter him the next day, because two wins in a row add up to momentum, and you never stand in the way of that. If he didn't win, however, she was likely to take him home and skip the weekend. Having a pessimist's view on Jack's progress, Kimberly tended to take a loss as more than a loss—she saw it as a sign that her dog wasn't good enough after all, even though anyone who's been in showing dogs for a long time will tell you not to draw any conclusions from a single result, or even a string of them. Even the world's best dog will sometimes lose to a clunker.

But a problem seemed to be brewing. Because Jack's judge was now running twenty minutes late, there was a chance Heather wouldn't be able to handle him at all. So tightly packed is Heather's schedule at a big show like Wildwood that she can't really accommodate delays without bumping another dog from the slate. Only the few top dogs on yearlong contracts, such as Tanner and Rita, get priority ensuring that the proper handler (Heather for Tanner, Kevin for Rita) will be on the leash. In situations where there's an intractable conflict with newer noncontract dogs, like Jack, it's up to Heather to make a judgment call as to which one has a better chance of doing well with a substitute handler, and in that case she'll recruit a friend to take over.

This informal system of handlers helping other handlers is a critical component of the so-called all-breed professionals who take a truck full of dogs to the show, because there is almost never a weekend, or even a day, when a handler doesn't need a last-minute substitute. A secondary and no-less-critical effect of this system is that it encourages handlers to be good sports and to maintain friendly relations with one another, because gossip is rampant at dog shows, and if you alienate one member of the club, you're much less likely to find a free hand when you need it.

Kimberly watched the clock and fretted, first over the possibility that she'd driven up, paid for a hotel, and spent the whole day watching other people's dogs, all for naught. Then seemingly over whatever else popped into her head. "One of the things I'm getting worried about is that many of the Best of Breed winners out there are so much older," she said, apropos of nothing. "Jack isn't two yet, and Aussies don't fully mature until they're three." She said she was constantly asking Heather if she should wait for him to grow up a little.

Heather's answer?

"No. Every time no."

Perhaps, at least, this could explain his irrational exuberance, as well as his tendency to get distracted.

"That's my fault," she answered, and explained that because she'd bought Jack as a companion foremost, she'd taught him tricks and commands that were essential (sit, stay) or else fun and cute (do a handstand, find your baby), but because he was bought at show quality and Kimberly was afraid he might get sick or injured, she'd neglected to socialize him with other people or dogs—to teach him, for instance, when it's appropriate to jump on a person. (The answer: only when encouraged to do so.) "It's something I need to work on," she said. "But he's smart; he knows. He can learn."

The judge, meanwhile, had finally arrived. She was a plump, elderly woman who both hunched and shuffled. Because she would also judge the Herding Group later in the afternoon, a win for Jack in the breed ring would be extra nice. But Kimberly's natural defense against disappointment, pessimism, was getting the best of her, and she had already decided that it was a lost cause, even if Heather did show up, which she was certain wasn't going to happen anyway.

Now that Jack was a "special"—as champion dogs that continue to show are known—and competing only against other champions, Kimberly was having to adjust her expectations. "Everyone keeps telling me I was spoiled," she said of the early days when she was working on Jack's championship. "It's harder now that we are competing against other champions. They are all nice dogs, and most are more mature than Jack."

I pointed out that no dog can possibly win every weekend and that Tanner's owner, Dawn Cox, was a good person to consider as a model. Tanner, America's top Bernese mountain dog, had lost earlier in the morning, to an unfinished dog out of the puppy classes, which is sort of ridiculous, and Dawn had just shrugged it off. In part because that's Dawn—whose response to Tanner's defeat was, "I'm more worried about what time I'm having my first glass of wine"—and in part because that same judge had also failed to pick the country's number-one-ranked boxer and the top-ranked Doberman, the two dogs that had bested Tanner in the prior day's Working Group, which that judged had declared "the finest Working Group she'd ever judged in her career." So Dawn just laughed. "This is why you can't get mad. It means absolutely nothing."

Kimberly shrugged. She understood, at least in theory. "I know if I really want to be successful, I have to accept failure. You win and lose."

This day's competition was formidable, with ten specials entered, including the Crufts dog, Striker, and even Jack's own father, Honor (who ultimately did not show up). Kimberly's expectations, she told me, were low. "I figure we have a one-in-ten chance."

Back in the ring, if the judge didn't hurry and clear the collies, Jack might have no handler. Finally the class dogs entered, and a man with gray hair tinted an unpleasant shade of yellow rode over on his red motorized Rascal scooter and parked directly in my line of vision. He pointed at a black tri. "Two more points and she'll be our thirty-fifth champion," he said, and swigged from one of two cups of coffee parked in the scooter's front basket, along with a pack of Kool menthols.

Just as the last of the class dogs* were exiting the ring, Heather darted out of the crowd and, smiling, snatched the lead from Kimberly. And Jack seemed no worse for the lack of time to practice with his handler outside the ring. While the red tri next to him fidgeted and had to be reset, Jack stacked perfectly. "He's her dog," Kimberly said, her mood brightening. "Look at that focus." Almost instantly her pride and confidence swelled. This was a whole different spectator from the one I'd been waiting with just minutes before. "Jack's face is so distinctive that you have to look at him," she said. "He dares you to look away."

A nervous countenance returned briefly as she watched the judge stare at Jack and Heather on the down and back, then stare even harder when they ran around. The judge thought a minute, pointed to Heather, and said, "One," and then to a red bitch and said, "Two"—the second dog picked is always Best of Opposite Sex, which in this case meant the best bitch in the ring—and the whole lot of them trotted around the ring in their perfunctory victory parade.

"Whee! I'm so excited!" Kimberly said, and punched me in the arm.

Jack was two out of three headed into the weekend, and as the storm swirled up the coast, preparing to bury Wildwood and knock out power and water to the convention center, Jack won again Saturday and Sunday, capping his triumphant weekend, just ten days

---

*Dogs that are not finished champions, competing in the classes in search of points.

before his Westminster debut, with a pair of fourth-place showings (known as "Group 4s" in show parlance) in the Herding Group, a set of results that was likely to land him in the rankings of the top Australian shepherds in America for the first time. Jack the Aussie was on the rise.

CHAPTER TWO

Hello, Jack, Meet the World

. . . .

I used to also call them the dog world's best-kept secret.
Now everyone loves Australian shepherds.

—KERRY KIRTLEY, JACK'S BREEDER

An Australian shepherd, it seems to me—
Is the best dog that ever could be!
They're intelligent, handsome and loving, too.
Patient, alert, persevering, on cue!

—FROM "THE MOST WANTED DOG" BY MARCIA DE VOE

. . . .

Nearly two years before Wildwood, before Jack was a champion dog squaring off against the country's best Australian shepherds, he was just a work in progress, starting his life as a tiny lump at a kennel in the dusty hills above San Bernardino, California.

Since it's in the high desert, most nights at Wyndstar Kennels are cool and clear, with star-speckled skies, and it was no different the night the spotted pup that would grow up to be Jack plopped onto the concrete floor. There, an eight-year-old black tri named

Ch Wyndstar's Enough Said—or Gracie—had hunkered down for the arrival of the puppies that had been gestating inside her for two months.

It was April 2, 2008, sixty-three* days since Gracie had bred with Ch Millcreek's Medal of Honor—aka Honor—and because her temperature had yet to drop below a hundred (once it hits ninety-nine or lower, the puppies are less than forty-eight hours away), Kerry Kirtley, Gracie's owner and the proprietor of Wyndstar, felt comfortable heading up the hill to bed at a little before midnight, satisfied that the puppies she'd been anticipating for two months wouldn't be coming for at least another day.

If it's particularly hot or cold, Kerry will do the whelping (as the delivery of puppies is known) in her sprawling ranch house, but in the milder months it tends to take place in a small whelping room near the entrance of the tin-roofed, concrete-floored, sixteen-stall kennel that houses her Australian shepherd flock—numbering anywhere from ten to twenty-five, with wide variances depending on recent arrivals.† On this particular night, though, she was secure in the belief that the puppies weren't done cooking, and she was still in an early-morning fog when she rose at 6:00 A.M. and trudged down to the kennel to let the dogs out for their morning constitutionals.

The light was only beginning to filter in from the outside, and Kerry had to rub her eyes to be sure that what she was seeing was real. There, in the pen, was Gracie, happily nursing five puppies in the

---

*Canine gestation is remarkably dependable; it is nearly always sixty-two or sixty-three days—variations are only a day or two in one direction or the other—and considering that wolves in the wild tend to breed in February and March (at least in the Northern Hemisphere), all wolves conceived and born in a particular year will be almost exactly the same age. May is a big birthday month for wolves.

†But never more than fifteen adult dogs, the maximum a kennel is allowed to have unless it is certified as "commercial." Wyndstar is what you call a "hobby kennel"— meaning that Kerry can legally have up to fifteen dogs on the premises (puppies under four months don't count). To have a professional kennel, which allows for up to a hundred dogs, a breeder needs to have a minimum of five acres. "But I'd never do that," she says. "I feel sorry for these guys already."

plastic igloo that provides further shelter in each kennel for dogs who desire it. To a woman who cares for her dogs every bit as passionately as a mother does her children, the realization that she had missed not only Gracie's birth signs but also the birth was a shocking moment for Kerry.

She hollered for her husband, Don, scooped the pups up in her arms and ran Gracie and "the kids" up the hill and into the alternate whelping room inside the house, where she let them all resume their first day in a more comfortable nest of towels while ensuring that all parties were healthy and able-bodied. "They were all breathing, and no one was bleeding," she recalls. "Everything was fine."

Over her three decades of breeding at least one litter a year, and sometimes two or three ("never more than three"), Kerry can count on one hand the whelps she's missed, and in every other case she missed them due to traveling for work. For those dozens of other whelpings, Kerry has been there, with Don, for however long it takes ("from four hours to twelve"), using dental floss to tie off umbilical cords and then applying iodine to sterilize navels and prevent infection, clearing out nasal passages with a bulb syringe, and deploying heating pads for any puppy who appears to need it.

When her prized Phoebe, a dog who had once been the second-ranked Aussie in America, began to drop puppies from her first litter a week premature, Kerry tucked one of the tiny preemies into her bra and another into her armpit and rushed them to the incubator while helping Phoebe safely deliver the third and final pup. Once everyone was stabilized—the survival of premature puppies is extremely tenuous—Kerry carefully placed them all together in the house whelping box and basically lived on an adjoining mattress for the next sixteen days, making sure the three puppies, none of which weighed more than five ounces, survived by tube-feeding them every two hours for the first three days. The pups, she recalls, "were no bigger than my index finger, and I didn't think they would live." Complicating matters was the fact that Phoebe was a new mom and "didn't know squat." Half of the reason Kerry couldn't leave was to keep the mother from accidentally stepping on her pups. And all three survived to day sixteen, when tragedy struck. Kerry left the whelping room to take a work call, and Phoebe lay down on the sole boy, suffocating him. "I thought I was going to die," Kerry recalls, and she's still emotional at the memory. "I worked sixteen days to keep them alive. It was heartbreaking."

The two remaining puppies, both girls, survived and thrived and are today two dogs that will never leave Wyndstar. One, Flav, is now a champion and will likely soon have a brood of her own.

Having endured such an experience, and heard of worse from other breeders, Kerry was always on edge around due dates. So you can understand why the memory of missing the arrival of Jack and his siblings would trouble her—and continue to bug her for months and even years after. She couldn't shake the feeling that she'd let Gracie down, even though the puppies arrived safely.

Gracie, however, was no worse for the experience. She was an old pro; this was the fourth of four lifetime litters, and she'd managed just fine on her own. Because the birth went unwitnessed, we'll never know where Jack appeared in the order of arrivals, but the total count was four boys and one girl, ranging in weight from 11 to 15 ounces. Two of the boys were blue merles. Jack was the biggest (at 15.1 ounces); his brother was 2 ounces lighter.

However it happened, they'd have arrived one by one, in sacs, which Gracie would have punctured to free the pups, then licked their faces to stimulate breathing. With no human around to cut the cords, Gracie just chewed through them and ate the evidence, the way canine mothers have for millennia. And then Jack and his siblings would have settled in for the first meal of their lives.

When Kerry and Don Kirtley, her second husband, bought the property that is now Wyndstar in 1982, the year they married, it was just a single barren acre with nothing on it but dirt and rocks. For the first three years, the Kirtleys lived in a travel trailer on the only flat spot on the property, until Don, an electrician, and Kerry built the house themselves, but only after they'd built the barn to contain the desires of the missus—an animal lover who fantasized about a menagerie of horses, goats, dogs, cats, and chickens. Today the property has grown to three acres and is well shaded by vegetation hand-planted by Kerry and Don, with peach and plum and pomegranate trees, flowering hedges, and a grove of cottonwoods that harbor a constant thrum of hummingbirds so numerous that Don has to refill the feeders twice a day.

Five miles up the hill, the Angeles National Forest starts, meaning that the Kirtleys share these highlands with all manner of varmint. Coyotes are a constant threat to small pets. Eagles are capable of snatching puppies. Mountain lions have been darted and relocated to higher, less populated altitudes. Then there's the constant threat of fire, fueled by the area's notorious Santa Ana winds.

Once she and Don were settled in, Kerry began to search for a dog that complemented her outdoorsy lifestyle. She wanted something she could bring out with the horses, and take hiking and fishing, and her research led her to a then-somewhat-new breed known as the Australian shepherd. Aussies, as they were commonly called, were said to be active and energetic and smart—in almost every way, the perfect dogs for outdoorsy people—as well as very friendly and loyal. They were said to be good family dogs that fit in with most personalities and lifestyles, to have a protective instinct, the will and energy to run for days, and the propensity to grow so attached to owners that one of the breed's nicknames is "the Velcro dog."

Most every kennel owner's story begins the way Kerry's does, with a statement like this: "I started with one." Growth thereafter is exponential. From the outset Kerry's preferred style was the red merle, and in 1985 she got her first, a female that unfortunately turned out to have a congenital heart problem, putting her at high risk of sudden death, particularly when so much of her time would be spent chasing after horses. Kerry returned the puppy a day later and "searched far and wide" for another. When she couldn't find a red merle, she took the next-best thing, a red tri from New York State, and Annie, as she was named, became the first of many Australian shepherds to enter Kerry's life. A year later she added a second dog. Then two dogs turned into three, and then four. By 1987, one of the dogs had a litter of puppies, and by 1991, with the arrival of a beautiful bitch named Hailey, Kerry was breeding officially. Wyndstar—so named because "we live in the wind tunnel of the world" and because "they were all going to be stars in my world"—was born.[*]

Today there are generally fifteen adult dogs, plus babies, spanning the age spectrum, and everybody gets a turn in the house. Though they spend parts of their day—and most nights—in kennels inside the barn, Kerry is adamant that hers are not just kennel dogs. For one thing, each dog's enclosure is large—twelve-by-twelve inside and open to a twelve-by-twenty-four-foot outdoor area that can be closed off to protect small dogs from coyotes and eagles. Those spaces in turn connect to three acres of "turnout areas," where the dogs can run and play freely, and beyond that, on many days when Don and/or Kerry is home and the front gate is shut, some portion of the dogs are given the run of the entire property.

It's hard to figure out how Kerry, now in her mid-fifties, has time to look after so many dogs, but she does. In her capacity as a veterinary-product representative, she works for a company that sells more than thirteen thousand different items ("from ears to rears"), ranging from disposable syringes to a hundred-thousand-dollar digital X-ray machine. Every day she visits some of the eighty accounts that must be serviced biweekly, then returns home to her dogs, maintaining a constant chatter with Aussie owners around the world on her BlackBerry.

Not surprisingly, she is very thin, and often tan, and with her high

---

[*]The reason it is "Wynd" and not "Wind" involves a business and branding dispute too convoluted to explain.

energy and reddish hair with blond highlights, she has, like so many dog owners, taken on a little of the appearance of her animals. She looks, in fact, a bit like a human iteration of her favorite dog, a red merle.

Dogs come and go at Wyndstar—they're born and get placed, but they also drop in for breedings, to diversify the gene pool in whatever way Kerry feels is necessary, and sometimes they arrive because she can't help herself. Just as often they go. A few dogs are permanent, but the majority are itinerant; puppies stay until they're sold but are welcome forever, with one rule: "Everybody has to get along. If anybody's pushy, they don't stay." Kerry pairs them up for companionship, so that everybody has a buddy. And they all get her attention and affection. As she likes to point out, she does not have kids. "These are my children."

E ven for an experienced breeder, it's difficult to look at a ten-week-old puppy and know that it's going to be a show dog. Puppies are like adolescent children, all potential in an awkward package. So Kerry often ships her dogs off into the world having no idea what they'll become. One thing Jack had from the beginning, though, was presence and attitude, relatively rare qualities that can't be instilled. "He had that 'Here I am! There's a spotlight over my head!'" Kerry explains. And a dog that seems to crave attention automatically has a leg up if your goal is to win dog shows.

To become a top show candidate, it is essential that a dog have this attitude, plus perfect structure, or "conformation," as it's known in the show world. Most times one thing or another is lacking. And on rare occasions you get everything in one package. Breeders know from experience to be cautious. One problem of attaching expectations to a dog is that you set yourself up for disappointment. The main reason Kerry prefers to keep her best show candidates for at least a year, as opposed to selling them as pups, is that people expect a dog labeled as "show quality" to be a surefire winner. Too many times she's seen good puppies come home to her. "A dog loses once and people are calling saying, 'Why didn't we win?'" she told me. "You know what? You lose more than you ever will win."

Nonetheless, Wyndstar has produced many champions over the years, the most successful being Phoebe, whom Kerry showed in back-to-back years starting in 2006. The first year she covered the expenses, including the cost of a professional handler. The second year, when Kerry had a backer to help cover the costs, Phoebe was the number-one Aussie for most of the year, taking two Bests in Show[*] and many Group Firsts, and in the end the beautiful blue merle missed being the number-one Australian shepherd in America by a measly seven points.

Given his "exuberant energy," Kerry saw some parallels in Jack and had high hopes for him from the beginning. He was, she recalled, "my pick in the litter. A real standout—what a sweet boy he was." Kerry was due for a successful male. She'd been unfortunate in that her last two big winners had been girls, which complicates matters for a breeder in that a female dog can't both show and breed. Whereas a stud dog can take a day here and there for breeding or, better yet, can have his semen frozen, which doesn't just save on travel and stress—it provides protection, God forbid, should anything happen.

It was for these reasons, and more, that Kerry had very high hopes for Blue Merle Boy #1, the dog we now know as Jack.

---

[*]The correct but oft-mistaken plural, by the way. Like "attorneys general."

CHAPTER THREE

Jack's Mom, Human Variety

Humans don't just like dogs, we cannot do without them.
—JON FRANKLIN, *The Wolf in the Parlor*

K erry wasn't immediately sure whether she'd keep this young male or offer him for sale to the right home. As she always did with new arrivals, she posted photos of Jack and his siblings on her kennel's Web site to test the waters, and that's where Kimberly Smith first saw him, while banging away on her laptop in search of a companion from her Pennsylvania home, nearly three thousand miles from Wyndstar.

By day Kimberly is the director of Phonebet and player services at Parx Racing & Casino, a horse track north of Philly. In that capacity she serves as senior management, overseeing all wagering, both live and by phone. Even when there's no actual racing at Parx, there are simulcast races from places like Dover and Santa Anita to attract the bored, the elderly, and the addicted, so Parx is a 364-day-a-year business. (Even bettors pause to open Christmas presents, ideally cash.) After steadily climbing the management ladder for fourteen years, she technically works a nine-to-five day but has great flexibility in her schedule.

Kimberly is also a single mother to a teenage son named Taylor, who in mid-2008 was nearing his sixteenth birthday and in the home stretch of his adolescence. The sole provider for most of Taylor's life, Kimberly was already feeling the bond between them straining, as her son increasingly felt around for his independence. He was, of course, just being a teenager, but when you're a teenager, it's not cool to hang around with your mom anymore. And that new reality is never easy for a mother to accept.

She told Taylor she was going to get him a dog for his sixteenth birthday, and his reaction was, "Yeah, right. You're getting a dog for yourself." Which of course she was, considering that he'd never once asked for one himself.

Kimberly, then forty-five, had recently parted ways with her live-in boyfriend, a man with three children of his own. Together they'd adopted a yellow Lab named Sandy, and because he was the one who'd chosen the breed, and because he had three children who would be heartbroken at the loss of the dog, he got Sandy in the split. The problem was, Sandy was very much Kimberly's dog. She was the one who'd raised and trained her.

Unrelated to her work at the track, Kimberly has been in thrall to horses for most of her life. After her mother found a book in which she'd drawn in crayon about caring for horses (or how she imagined this to be, based on movies and TV), she bought Kimberly a set of riding lessons. Kimberly loved the sport, bought her first horse at fifteen with a small inheritance, and has ridden in her spare time ever since. At various times she's owned nearly a dozen horses over the years, and for a period even showed a Congress champion, Eric (A Carolina Star) on the American Quarter Horse circuit.

Sandy would accompany Kimberly every time she went to the stables to ride her quarter horse, Eric, and would run in circles inside the ring as Kimberly and Eric trotted around, often getting so close that the horse would gently nudge the dog out of the way so as to not step on her. The two animals became close, as dog and horse rarely do, and it wasn't unusual to see Eric grooming Sandy when they were both at rest in his stall.

Needless to say, it was a big blow when Sandy disappeared from Kimberly's life. Knowing that she was only a year from having an empty nest, and also seeking to assuage the loneliness of a breakup with a guy she once thought she'd marry—and who took their dog!—Kimberly very quickly began looking around for a puppy, specifically an Australian shepherd. Aussies, along with border collies and Welsh corgis, are common around the horse community, for the simple reason that they are energetic and aren't afraid, and the horses seem to sense that and like them for it.

She'd gotten particularly attached to an Aussie named Gucci, owned by her horse trainer, Keith Miller. Gucci was sweet, smart, and well behaved, with a pretty face that was more expressive than that of other dogs she'd spent time around. Gucci traveled to most shows and was such a barn fixture that she might as well have been the stable's mascot.

Making the very logical assumption that good dogs come from good breeders, Kimberly located a ranking of top Aussie show dogs and used that as a metric, working backward to find those dogs' breeders, which are always listed under the dogs' names in show catalogs and listings. That's how she ended up at the Web site for Wyndstar Kennels, a lavender-hued outpost featuring a star pulling a rainbow with the distinct look of a Web site designed in the 1990s (a common trait of breeder Web sites, for reasons unclear). There, on Kerry Kirtley's site, Kimberly glimpsed a face that she would not be able to get out of her mind. Among the shots in the site's "puppies" section was one of a paint-splattered fluff ball lying in the grass, an unmistakable glint in his eye.

When Kimberly inquired about the puppy in late May, Kerry told her that her he was "show quality," as opposed to "pet quality," and wasn't officially for sale, especially to someone with no history in showing dogs. If Kerry were to give him up, she wanted the puppy to go to a person with a track record of showing dogs, because a breeder is only as good as her pool of champion animals, and when a good one is whelped—a puppy that displays all the hallmarks of show quality—the goal is to pass that dog on to someone who can make it into a champion, furthering the valuable bloodline and thus increasing the value and desirability of future litters. As is often said, "Showing is all about breeding."

For several weeks after their first correspondence, Kimberly found herself clicking back to this puppy's photo. He had tan cheeks and what looked like black splotches under both eyes (his "football smudges," she calls them now); his fur was fluffy and multicolored, and he was undeniably beautiful and unique. Kimberly had no interest in buying a dog she couldn't meet in person—and this one was an entire continent away—but she found herself back at Kerry's Web site more and more frequently. If you believe in love at first sight involving two-dimensional images posted on the Internet, this was it, and Kimberly was increasingly certain that this was her dog. "I was looking for that dog that tripped my trigger, that called to me," Kimberly would later recall. This little blue merle was the one.

For nearly a month, Kimberly and Kerry e-mailed back and forth and occasionally spoke on the phone. Kerry slowly warmed to the idea of parting with the puppy. What ultimately sold her on Kimberly was that she did have at least some experience showing animals. Granted, hers was with horses and not dogs, but the general idea of conformation is the same, so much so that the dog-show world is full of onetime horse people. (The former is also much cheaper than the latter.)

To help ease her concerns about Kimberly's lack of dog-show history, Kerry offered to co-own the puppy. For a reduced price of a thousand dollars, instead of sixteen hundred (plus shipping and expenses), Kerry would retain a stake, granting her a vote on things like naming and show selection, as well as limited breeding rights in the future—meaning that she could, and would, recall him to California for the occasional love vacation.

With that, Kimberly agreed to buy a puppy she'd never actually seen or touched. Kerry obtained the proper health certificates, packed him into a crate, applied duct tape and zip ties to prevent tampering or theft en route, said good-bye, and booked the ten-week-old blue merle puppy a Delta Airlines flight from Ontario, California, to Philly, with a connecting stop in Atlanta.

Up until the minute he left, in the wee hours of June 19, there was some doubt whether or not the trip would work out, because the maximum temperature at which pets can fly in cargo is eighty-four, and temps were rising back east. Kimberly was scared to death that her new dog wasn't going to make it out, and the anticipation of it all was driving her nuts. She clicked obsessively on online weather forecasts and then also on the flight tracker, but the flight was fine and the puppy saw his new owner for the first time in a dusty cargo office through the slit openings in his crate. She'd been there, waiting in the office, for more than an hour.

Once Kimberly figured out how to actually liberate the dog from his well-secured crate—luckily she had nail clippers in her purse strong enough to cut the zip ties, and good old-fashioned grit worked on the tape—she stared at that familiar face in three dimensions for the first time as the puppy sized her up and stumbled out into his new world, so many miles from where he'd started the day. The puppy looked no worse for the long trip and, much to Kimberly's surprise, hadn't soiled his cage. She expected at least a little mess, if not a nasty coat matted with his waste. Instead both crate and coat were spotless. It was a good omen.

Kimberly hugged the puppy, took him on a short walk, and then held him in her lap in the driver's seat of her car, where he slept for the hour-long drive home to her town house. A friend who'd come along to keep her company tried to insist that Jack be put back into his crate, because it seemed a little unsafe for Kimberly to drive with a puppy in her lap, one that could pounce on her brake foot at an inopportune moment. But she was having none of it. "I wanted him to bond with me," Kimberly said. "I wanted to be the person who rescued him from this terrible flight. That's how I've been with him ever since. We're buddies."

· · ·

Choosing a name was going to be important, so Kimberly took some time thinking about her options. Seeing as this was a show dog, his name would have added significance—because it creates an impression and appears in printed catalogs and show programs—but first and foremost the puppy was to be a part of the family, so Kimberly felt the need to get Taylor involved in the process. She threw out Zeus, a little presumptuous and arrogant-sounding—what if he turned out timid and runty, nothing like a Greek god?—and also King, which felt almost rote, but really in her heart she was hoping for Major, as shorthand for He's Got Major Moves, which she thought made a nice show name. Show dogs have both a fancy formal name (registered with the AKC and writ in stone; you cannot change it) and a day-to-day name that is the one people actually use. But Taylor insisted on a human name. He said, "He's a Jack. Let's call him Jack."

And so he was. Kimberly named him Jack.

Jack wasn't actually the first Aussie at the Smith home. Bailey, a sixteen-year-old Ocicat,* had lived there her entire life, and the Oci is the rare breed of cat, oddly enough, that is both doglike and Velcro. It took a few days for Jack to assert his status in the home. He was wary of the cat, which followed him around and acted like a dog, even borrowing and playing fetch with one of his toys, but soon enough Jack was chasing her away and also thumping up against Taylor's legs in an attempt to push around his sole rival for the master's attention; it was friendly play, but also a statement of where Jack saw himself in the house pecking order: one step below Kimberly.

Where Kimberly went, Jack went. "He was very quickly my shadow," she said, and her Velcro dog lived up to the name. "Get an Aussie and never go to the bathroom alone again."

Within weeks owner and dog had settled into a happy routine.

---

*Pronounced "Aussie cat."

Jack's days would begin on a pillow on Kimberly's king-size bed. He slept well on the pillow, "hogging the fan" that spun at bedside, and tended to spend most of the night there, after he and Kimberly had snuggled while watching TV. Then she would say, "Good night, Jack," and that was his signal that it was time to head for the pillow. They wouldn't speak again until morning, when the day started anew with a big belly rub.

Once she realized how intelligent her new dog was, Kimberly began to revel in training him. And "good night" was just one of many phrases in Jack's growing vocabulary. By his first birthday—between agility and handling classes, at-home trick lessons, and basic obedience—he could respond to at least thirty-five words and understood the nuances between such apparently similar commands as "wait" and "stay." The latter means to sit still and not move until told to do so by his master, who is Kimberly, or someone else he respects, which could be Taylor or Heather. "Wait" is more of a temporal concept; it means Jack needs to sit there for an unspecific amount of time, enough so that Kimberly or Taylor or maybe Summer can complete a task—say, open a door or fill a bowl—at which time he can, as Kimberly says, "self-release."

A good example of waiting can be seen on a day when it's too cold out for Kimberly to take Jack on a walk just to pee. For such occasions she has a single long lead tied up outside the back door, just off the kitchen of her two-bedroom town house. Because Summer was younger and not yet totally on board with the housebreaking thing, she got first crack at the yard. In that case Jack would sit and wait his turn to relieve himself outside. If he acted antsy, Kimberly simply said "wait," and he did.

Kimberly learned not to open her eyes in the morning until she was definitely ready to get up, because without fail the first thing she'd see was Jack's face, staring in wait for his opportunity to dive in for the "morning cuddle," a two-part process that starts with the dog snuggling in under her arm before rolling over onto his back for a belly rub. After the cuddle, Kimberly and Jack head downstairs to hit the yard for a morning pee, then breakfast. For most of his life, Jack has eaten Purina One, your run-of-the-mill grocery-store pet food, which "show people would scoff at," Kimberly says. If it's a show week, she might up the quality to the more expensive, Heather-approved brands (Taste of the Wild especially) or sprinkle in some supplements or a scoop of yogurt to help settle Jack's sensitive stomach, which can get seriously aggravated when he's nervous or excited. If there's time, and he's feeling frisky, he might squeeze in a quick morning romp around the house with Summer, a short but wild bout of play Kimberly calls "a rip 'n' tear."

Then it's off to the shower.

Jack has a conflicted relationship with the shower. He loves to be in the room when Kimberly is in it, because he has only limited time with her before work, and a good chunk of it is wasted in the shower. But he also distrusts the sound and sight of that water, since that's where his baths happen. Most dogs hate baths, and Jack is no exception. Because he can't ever know when, exactly, he might be asked to enter the steamy, wet, glass box, he waits in the hall until he hears the shower door thud close. Then he enters and parks himself just outside the glass, staring suspiciously at the activity inside. Some extra sense tells Jack when Kimberly's about to turn off the shower, because every time she's about to, she looks out and Jack is gone; he's left the room to avoid the risk of being swept through an open shower door.

During this interlude Jack moves to the bedroom, where he awaits a safe, dry return to the bathroom with no risk of being dragged into the torture box. Once Kimberly is dried and dressed, she sits down on the tub and does her makeup, using a small vanity mirror on the sink. Jack, by now, will return to the room and wedge himself into "this little bitty cubbyhole—a one-foot space between the counter and tub." And there he lies until the makeup application is complete. So consistent is Jack in his movements that "I could draw you a picture of all of his positions in the morning," Kimberly said. "Somehow he knows when I take my mascara out. As soon as I take it out, when he appears to be sleeping, he gets up and leaves the room again. He knows that after mascara I blow my hair dry. He's not afraid of it; it's just his thing."* (Summer has no interest in the morning's minutiae; she's typically downstairs on the back of the couch, keeping an eye on the yard.)

These things happen daily, without fail—before and after work. Kimberly finds it all endearing. When she arrives home from work, Jack is inevitably there, in the window, and by the time Kimberly has opened the door from the garage, he's there, too—with a toy in his mouth. "When he gets excited and all wiggly, he likes to have something in his mouth," she explains. "If he's not at the door, I know he's gone to get a toy."

Jack's favorite toy of all is the Frisbee; it's blue and the size of a dinner plate, and though he loves to chase it, that's not really critical to his enjoyment of its tasty, tooth-bitten plastic. He's just as happy to pick it up and carry it around, and many mornings the first thing Jack thinks when he wakes up is not, "Damn, I have to pee," it's, "Where's the Frisbee!?" If Jack looks stressed, a good first guess at the cause is this missing disk.

After the Frisbee his favorites come and go. For a while it was his chicken—a squeaky toy with rubber legs that stretch and pull. Like many of his toys, it's actually for children. Jack is less hard on his toys than your average dog, so Kimberly can shop for them most anywhere; her universe of options is so much larger than the pet store. She finds yard sales to be particularly fertile ground; that's where she discovered a little purple gorilla that Jack carefully chewed for over a year until it finally came unstuffed. It took him a full two years to chew the legs off his favorite stool—a stool she used to teach him to do handstands—and it still lives on in his collection, somewhere in the basement. For a time

---

*It's probably more irritating than she realizes. Dogs are vastly more sensitive to high-pitched noises than we are. To reach the level where they hear the sound of a piano, you'd need to add forty-eight extra notes to the right side, says researcher Stanley Coren. This high-frequency hearing goes back to wolves—it enabled them to find mice, voles, and rats, which emit high-pitched squeaks and rustling sounds.

he was partial to a rubber bug, and there was always room in his heart for his ball and the duck—"all noisy things," Kimberly says. "The only thing he likes that doesn't make noise is his Frisbee."

Naturally, Jack loves new toys, and they enter and leave his life with some regularity. He recognizes the color and shape of bags from the high-end pet store where Kimberly shops, and he wiggles with exaggerated frenzy when one enters the house. For Easter she made him a basket, as well as ones for Summer and Taylor, who likes to say to her, "You love Jack more than me." To which Kimberly replies, "I love all of my children equally." (For the record, of all the children, Jack unpacked his basket most carefully, taking the time to check out and play with each new toy before tearing into the next.)

Like all Aussies, Jack loves a challenge, and learning words—and the tasks that go with them—is a challenge, so his vocabulary is ever-growing. One of his favorite games is to retrieve toys by name (say "rope" as opposed to "duck"). He loves it when Kimberly says, "Get your duck," and he will search the house high and low until he finds the correct toy and then bring it back and drop it at her feet. Sometimes the toy isn't on the floor where he's looking, and Kimberly will say, "Look upstairs" (if he's downstairs), and Jack does just that. It feels at times as if she can actually speak to him.

Jack can spin clockwise (that's "Turn around, Jack!") or counter-clockwise ("Jack, twirl!") and maybe his coolest trick is the modified handstand, which he can't quite do to full extension—you know, using a wall—but which he's now capable of doing on anything up to the height of a hassock that Kimberly keeps in the living room. The handstand evolved from a popular dog-agility drill known as "targeting," wherein a dog has to locate and touch an object (most often a light-switch cover, though no one knows why this is) with either a paw or, in the more advanced version, a nose. Jack can now target with both front and rear legs. (Rear targeting, by the way, is pretty advanced stuff and is the way Kimberly taught him the handstand—he targeted with his rear legs on increasingly tall objects, starting with a pillow.)

He also loves to jump, almost as much as he loves his Frisbee, so a favorite game of his is for Kimberly to order him to "table-sit," which is pretty self-explanatory and is a standard part of an agility test. Then she'll put her hand (which now stands in for the light-switch cover) in the air at shoulder or head height and say, "Jack, touch." And Jack will jump up and touch her hand with his nose, then hop back on the table and do it again.

It is occasionally tiring to own a dog as smart as Jack.

"Sometimes he comes to me with this look, like, 'Okay, let's work,'" Kimberly says with an exhale. Really he means, "Let's do tricks for treats." If Kimberly doesn't immediately bite, he'll bait her, by putting all four of his feet on a stool or by doing a handstand on an ottoman, or even by putting a single back leg up on a wall as if demonstrating, "Hey, I might do one on this wall!"

"He's comical," Kimberly observes. "It's like he's saying, 'Aren't I cute?'"

CHAPTER FOUR

The Road to a Championship Starts with a Single Point

Dog shows are the trade shows where you bring your product and put it on display for other people to see and learn from and take advantage of in their breeding programs. That's the entire premise of dog shows.

—AKC FIELD REPRESENTATIVE (AND FORMER PRO HANDLER) SUE VROOM

As Kerry Kirtley said, breeders never really know what they have in a particular puppy. They can make assumptions based on coloration or bone structure or the early indications of graceful movement, then hope he'll be good, but the only real test is to get a dog into the show ring and see what happens.

Kimberly Smith, never having shown a dog in her life, didn't know what to expect. She promised Kerry that she would at least attempt to show Jack, but she had no idea if he would be good. She didn't even really know what being good meant. Certainly there were periods when she was worried—in particular an awkward teenage stage round about nine months when his frame was so gangly and his coat so ratty that she e-mailed Kerry expressing concern that he wasn't going to live up to his potential. Give him time, Kerry told her; all Aussies have an awkward stage. Sure enough, Jack began to fill out.

And a few months after his first birthday, Kimberly decided to give it a shot.

The first goal for any show dog is to achieve the "Champion" title represented by the "Ch" you see prefixing certain names. The Champion designation itself is actually short for "Champion of Record," and achieving this title is known as "completing his/her championship" or "finishing" your dog. It validates a dog as special and increases its breeding value and for that reason is the end goal of the average owner-handlers who make up the majority of entries in America's dog shows.

In addition to attaching a measure of prestige, the Ch prefix affords a dog direct entry into the Best of Breed competitions at a given show; before he's earned it, he has to first win his "class"—meaning the judge selects him from all contenders in a particular group of like animals. Every breed shares a handful of classes—specifically, puppy six to twelve months, twelve to eighteen months, bred by exhibitor (which means the person handling the dog is also its breeder), American bred (a dog whose parents were mated in America), open dog, or open bitch. The winners from each of those classes then face off before the same judge for the selection of Winners Dog (or Winners Bitch, as it were), and those two dogs—one male, one female—both receive points toward their championships. They also earn entry into Best of Breed.

To "finish," a show dog needs fifteen points, including two "major" wins, and the dog must have received points from at least three different judges to eliminate the possibility of simply following around a friend who judges. Only Winners Dog and Winners Bitch get points, and you get one point for a small show and two, three, four, or five points by beating a big enough pool of dogs—anything over three points is a major. The overwhelming majority of wins are worth one point, and at many of the dinkier shows it's not uncommon to have just two or three dogs vying for that point.

In the case of Aussies, there must be at least seven dogs of your dog's sex entered in order to earn a major,* and to get a five-point major you're talking upwards of twenty dogs. Those are hard points to come by, and dogs have been known to stall at twelve to fifteen points for months while waiting for a major to come along.†

Kimberly never really considered handling Jack herself. And it took only two attempts to be certain that her hunch that this would be a bad idea was spot on. The first time was at a show put on by the Australian Shepherd Club of America (ASCA),‡ and Jack was a disaster—too excited at the prospect of socializing with all these dogs: "So! Many! Dogs! Hooray!"—to actually follow orders. The second time he was even more distracted. Due to the initial fiasco, Kimberly was terrified to try again and walked around for an hour attempting to calm her nerves. She was the last person to pick up Jack's number—assigned to each dog before a show and attached to the handler's arm with a rubber band—from the judge's table, just seconds before the steward called for the dogs to enter the ring.

When she finally steeled herself and walked into the ring, Jack was hyper and seemed more interested in sniffing around his competitors than beating them. Kimberly finally corralled him into line and reached under to pull his back end into alignment in the stack when she was greeted with a rather rude surprise. Jack was—let's say—excited. The reason he'd been so hyper was that somewhere on the premises there

---

*At least at the time of writing—this changes annually based on the total number of AKC registrations for a particular breed.

†Especially in the most popular breeds, like golden retrievers or Labs, which require huge entries to make a major.

‡An Aussies-only group that does not affiliate with the AKC and is less prestigious in the larger dog-show world. Many Aussie owners, however, choose to participate only in ASCA. This split will be explained further a bit later in the book.

was a bitch in heat. But when Kimberly reached under and found the surprise, Jack was as shocked as she was. The dog yelped as if a bear trap had just closed on his tail, and she was humiliated and convinced that everyone around her thought she'd smacked her dog.

The next day Kimberly asked a friend to take a turn. The poor guy, a college student who moonlighted as a handler for Summer's breeder, didn't know what he was in for. Jack jumped all over the ring, and when I ran into the young man a year later, he was still traumatized. "Maybe I'll show Jack again someday," he told me, and laughed nervously. "Like when he's nine."

It was time to find a professional handler, and for that Kimberly turned to the AKC Web site. Not all top handlers have AKC accreditation; the process is onerous, taking five years and numerous annoying inspections of home and travel facilities, and some handlers have no problem building impeccable reputations without it. But Heather Bremmer is not the sort to cut corners on anything, so she endured the process, followed the many rules,[*] and as of this writing was one of 116 on the AKC list. (Her husband, Kevin Bednar, has not yet worked long enough to apply. He will after five years and in the meantime enjoys residual luster by association.)

The job of professional dog-show handler isn't one that gets much attention in the general public, and if it weren't for the movie *Best in Show,* most of us probably would have gone through life oblivious to its existence. It is a very odd and specific job—caring for and preparing dogs to be judged at dog shows—and isn't the kind of thing you can learn in school. Dog handlers emerge one of two ways: Either they're born into it—many of the top handlers are second- or third-generation show participants who learned from their parents—or they studied the pursuit and its nuances the way all tradesmen used to, by apprenticing under a master.

---

[*]Because regulations require one, she even installed a fenced pen outdoors, even though she almost never keeps dogs on the premises. For the rare occasions she does, they have large indoor kennels and a fenced yard. Three years after the pen's installation, she'd yet to use it once.

Kimberly wasn't thinking about a handler's history; her method was hardly that scientific. She just wanted to hire someone she could trust, who would take good care of her dog, and who lived within driving distance of her home so she wouldn't have to leave Jack overnight for extended periods—plenty of owners have no issue leaving their show dogs in the care of handlers for weeks and months at a time—and whose facilities she could personally inspect. Because Jack was her pet first and a show dog second.

Two handlers met her distance criteria, and she sent off e-mails to both. One of them, a woman named Shirley who works alone, wrote back very quickly, and Kimberly ventured out to meet her the next time a dog show came through the area.

It was a broiling July afternoon, and she left Jack in the car, with the A/C running, while she went to meet Shirley. And there they were, chatting alongside a gigantic, drooling bullmastiff that the woman was working with that day when who should appear at the feet of this hulking canine but Jack, a blur of furry black and white buzzing its ankles. Kimberly had forgotten to lock the windows, and Jack had lowered one and liberated himself when he got bored of watching from behind glass.

Putting Jack in Shirley's hands was a marked improvement. American Kennel Club rules state that dogs can't officially enter shows until they are six months old, at which time they're eligible to enter the six-to-nine-month puppy class. And on July 11, 2009, Jack made his AKC dog-show debut at the Twin Brooks Kennel Club in Morristown, New Jersey. It was an auspicious beginning. The fifteen-month-old dog won his class and was also named Winners Dog, earning two points toward his championship. He won again the next day, at the same site, earning another two points, and there was every reason to expect that Shirley could deliver a championship, but Kimberly was having doubts. She was uncomfortable with the fact that the handler's setup was a van full of cages and fans. Jack was, she often said, her "baby," and she couldn't bear the thought of him sleeping in a cage inside a van.

When Heather finally responded to her e-mail, two weeks later, Kimberly went for a visit, to both the show setup and to her house. She loved the house, where good dogs were not caged, and especially her climate-controlled truck, where dogs spent hot days cooling in the A/C. What's more, she liked that Heather didn't automatically accept dogs and needed to evaluate Jack first. When the young handler told her that she'd love to have a chance to show him, Kimberly decided to make a change.

She paid Shirley in full for her services and threw her dog's lot behind the young, spunky blonde. And a few days later, Heather and Kevin were enjoying a rare weekend off at the beach when her cell phone rang. It was Shirley, and she was pissed. "I spent hours going back and forth with Shirley and Kimberly trying to smooth things out," Heather told me. "Kimberly didn't tell me that she'd booked Shirley for more shows and that she'd signed a contract.* So when Shirley found out, she had a conniption. It was a whole goings-on!" (For the record, Kimberly recalls that the transition went far more smoothly.)

Several hours into it, Kevin pulled the cell phone out of her hand. "Really, Heather?" he said. "This is a class Aussie.† We're on vacation. We don't need this."

Heather agreed, but she was too far committed to quit. She and Shirley smoothed things out, and the next weekend Heather and Jack were officially a team.

Based on first impression of his structure and overall appearance, Heather was excited to take this new Aussie on, and during a trial run in Lackawanna, Pennsylvania, she won two more points. This despite the fact that he sat during the down-and-back ("We get extra points for that, right?" she joked to the judge) and that overall she found him to be a total handful. "He could barely walk on a leash without killing himself," she recalled. It seemed almost as if he hadn't been trained, but

---

*Nonbinding, as it turns out.

†Meaning an unfinished dog who could end up winning nothing.

Kimberly swore he'd been through handling classes, and the reality was that once Heather had him in the ring, Jack tended to settle down. He was somehow both totally wild and obedient at once.

Any professional handler has worked with bad dogs—including dogs that bark and/or bite at very inopportune moments—but this was something new. With a misbehaving dog, as Heather explains it, there's an added complexity to her job that she describes as "putting together the pieces of a puzzle." The majority of show dogs are very good at their job of following instructions and, within a few shows, are almost robotic in their ring behavior. They don't make mistakes. Handlers actually like this, because if they have no worry about whether or for how long a dog will stack, they can focus on the little things that enhance the presentation. "My job is to pull it all together and make it perfect," she says. Jack seemed to have the ability to be both a willing and an unwilling show dog, depending on his mood. "Jack is almost too smart for his own good," she explains, and the notion makes her chuckle.

Even to a handler who'd worked with thousands of dogs, it was a real head-scratcher—not to mention a very intriguing challenge.

Some dogs take years to earn their championship. Jack took four months.

Conformation shows are a process of elimination, starting with a pool of hundreds or thousands of dogs and ending with one that is named Best in Show. Once a dog wins Best of Breed or Variety,* as Jack did on September 10, 2009, at Pocono Mountain, Pennsylvania, he goes on to the Group Stage. There are seven groups in total: Sporting,

---

*A variety is a subset of a breed based on one of three factors: coat, color, or size. The varieties compete separately in the group. There are three breeds subdivided by color— cocker spaniels, bull terriers, and English toy spaniels. Three breeds are divided by coat: dachshunds (longhaired, smooth, wirehaired), Chihuahuas (smooth or long coat), and collies (rough—which means longhaired—and smooth). And three are split up according to size variation: beagles, Manchester terriers, and of course the poodle, which comes in small, medium, and large (pardon me: "standard," "miniature," and "toy").

Hound, Working, Terrier, Toy, Non-Sporting, and Herding, the newest of the groups (added in 1983) and the one that includes Australian shepherds. Four awards are given out to the top four dogs in each group, but only the winner goes on to the final—in which a judge selects among the seven group winners for Best in Show.

Pocono, then, was Jack's first appearance ever in the Herding Group—facing the winners of all twenty-four herding breeds—and that, too, went well. He took a Group 2, meaning he was judged to be the second-best herding dog in the entire show—one spot away from qualifying for the Best in Show competition. Two days later he won the breed again, and also a Group 4.

Had Kimberly been willing to put Jack in Heather's hands every weekend, he'd probably have finished his championship sooner, because everywhere Jack showed up in his early days, he seemed to win. He was Winners Dog in Philly, and then, at the Northeastern Maryland Kennel Club show in West Friendship, Maryland, he took it again, emerging from his class to win the breed and capturing three points for his final major. On November 20, 2009, Jack won the title of Champion—just in time to make the deadline to qualify for Westminster, one of the few shows that admits only champion dogs.

Being a newbie, Kimberly didn't realize that so much success so fast was unusual. It's impressive and not the norm for a new dog to achieve a championship in a few months; it's especially impressive when that same dog also wins several Best of Breed ribbons, over finished champions, and then group placings, out of the puppy class. It didn't necessarily mean that Jack would always do so well, but it certainly showed that this was no ordinary show dog either.

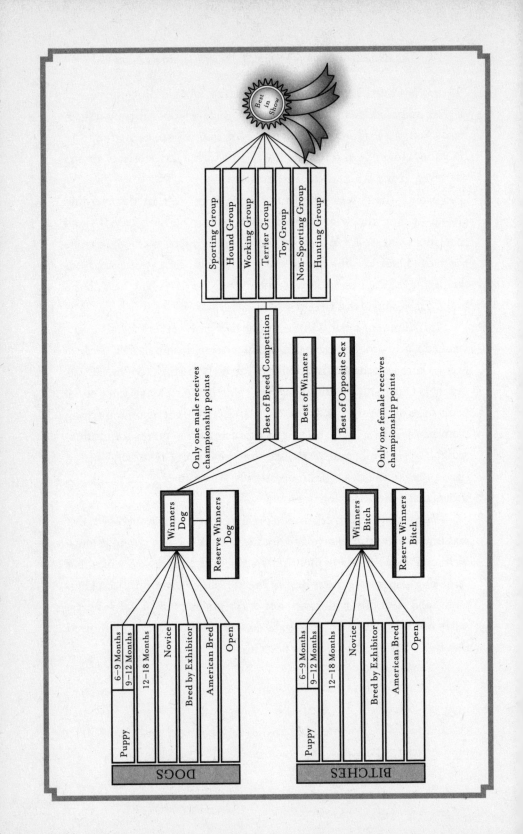

CHAPTER FIVE

White Plains: Meeting the Menagerie

Conformation: formation of something by appropriate arrangement of parts or elements; . . . correspondence, especially to a model or plan.
—*Webster's New Collegiate Dictionary*

I met Heather and Kevin and Jack and Kimberly for the first time on January 9, 2010, in White Plains, New York, a few months after Jack had become a champion and in the very early days of the next step of his experience as a burgeoning show dog: testing his mettle against other finished Australian shepherds to see if he had even greater potential—to be one of the best dogs of his kind in America.

New clients headed for their first show are likely to be bewildered by the sea of setups in which handlers operate. Heather always tells people to "look for all the pink stuff," pink being Heather's favorite color, and that's how I found her—standing with a pink dryer and a pink brush in front of a pink tackle box, grooming Jack, who stood calmly atop a pink towel on a grooming table, which along with a good cool-air blow dryer is a handler's most critical accessory.

Heather is a small person with a large personality. She is petite with white-blond hair, bright blue eyes, and bangs nearly always pulled tightly back by barrettes. She wore a purple satin Tahari suit (Tahari being her designer of choice, bought in multiples when found on sale) and black shoes that were about as stylish as possible when you're looking for sensible flats you can stand on without breaks. Dog-show handlers expend great effort to find shoes conducive to ten or twelve hours of nonstop standing, and in the case of a handler like Heather, who also cares very much about her appearance,[*] shoes present a particular challenge. Of late she'd been happy with a pair of Geox, which come with air soles.[†]

Heather has only one mode—focused—and during working hours has little time for idle conversation. She is very friendly and always smiling (unless she's mad at Kevin, and even then you'd have to be standing nearby to notice) but tends to speak in clipped sentences that closely resemble her e-mails and text messages, and she always seems to have one eye on the clock, which is understandable once you realize how frantic a day in the life of a successful dog handler is.

Depending on a particular show cluster's duration—if it's two, or three, or five days—Heather and Kevin pack up the dogs and the gear and head out first thing Wednesday or Friday. If it's a winter show, they'll more likely than not take the Chevy Astro van, because for that period it's too cold to sleep in their twenty-six-foot trailer (the pipes tend to freeze). During those months Kevin and Heather sleep in what-

---

[*]This is not always the case with dog handlers, believe me.

[†]The book *Dog Show Judging: The Good, the Bad, and the Ugly* says that "buying comfortable, sturdy, and attractive shoes designed for both walking and standing (judges do a lot of both!) can be more difficult than finding the right dog!" but then goes on to list a number of brands recommended by judges, including Clarks, Dansko, Easy Spirit, Arcopedia, Rockport, and Cole Haan Nike Air. It also recommends orthotics and insoles, including a brand called Happy Feet!

ever motel happens to be dog-friendly,* and, failing that, she has a Service Dog pass that allows her to get select sensitive dogs—or dogs that are particularly babied by their owners, like Jack—into others. In the summer, though, they sleep in the trailer and the dogs are in the truck, so the whole lot of them have no need to leave the show premises.

If you are the sort to panic when circumstances get chaotic, you wouldn't want to consider a career in show-dog handling; circumstances are often, if not always, chaotic. On a given weekend, Heather and Kevin have at least ten and sometimes up to twenty dogs under their care. The mix changes regularly—they'll show any dog they've checked out and decided is ringworthy, which means manageable and not difficult to handle, not necessarily that it is actually going to do well. It's eighty-five dollars per dog per day for the handling, plus fifteen dollars for transport. If your dog should win, it's an extra twenty dollars to show him or her again in the group competition, and should he/she win that, it's one hundred seventy-five for the Group One, plus the additional handling required in the Best in Show ring. At that point, though, you're thrilled to be writing the check.

Jack was what you'd call a semiregular client. He was a step above the day-rate dogs that come out here and there but a step below the dogs on monthly retainer, which Heather calls "the bread and butter." Those dogs go wherever Kevin and Heather go, and their owners pay a flat rate of at least two thousand five hundred dollars per month for that privilege.

Kimberly was actively looking for a financial backer so that she could elevate Jack to such status, to help him rise above Trader the Akita or Benny the bloodhound or a group of golden retrievers known as the Golden Girls, to reach the level of Kevin's top dog, Rita the Chesapeake Bay retriever, and Tanner, Heather's A-number-one client dog and Jack's big black teddy bear of a buddy.

---

*One place you can always count on: Super 8, the official partner motel of the AKC (as well as of the Cat Fanciers Association, so cats are also welcome).

BERNESE MOUNTAIN DOG

Ch Blumoon Tanzenite V Blackrock—or Tanner to those who know and love him—was America's top-ranked Bernese mountain dog by the end of 2009. He was four years old then and a hundred-plus pounds of black, brown, and white fur, a gentle, mild-mannered beast who loves nothing more than to stand on his rear legs and throw his prodigious body into you for hugs. If you sit, Tanner will sit—and then lean into you. If you are giving him love and happen to be distracted—say, you've started up a conversation—he will tap you in the back or on the shoulder with a gigantic paw until you've resumed paying attention to him. Even for a breed known for temperament, his is exceptional, causing Heather to often declare, "Tanner should be the spokesdog for the breed."

This gentle, affectionate nature is very much in the breed standard for Berners, which were first bred in the Alps to pull farmers' carts down from the mountains to market. It's a job that required strength and patience, but also the wherewithal to regularly encounter strangers along the way. Similarly bearish dogs, like the Great Pyrenees and the kuvasz, aren't quite so docile, mainly because they were bred to guard flocks of sheep. In that capacity a friendly nature is sort of counterproductive.

Tanner belongs to Dawn Cox, a boisterous and athletic-looking woman who, like her dog, is both physically impressive (in her case tall and buxom) and tremendously friendly. A lifelong lover and breeder of Bernese, she got her first dog when she was thirteen, after her father took her to a local kennel and she was awestruck by the large and friendly black dogs. "I'd never seen anything so beautiful," she recalls. Unable to afford a puppy, she was told that several retired show dogs were available for adoption at no cost. So Dawn and her father picked out and took home a seven-year-old named Birdie, and, except for a break for college, Dawn has been breeding dogs ever since.

She and her husband, Newell, have two kids, a twenty-three-year-old son, Andrew, and a twenty-year-old daughter, Meredith, a two-time Pennsylvania Class AA high-school-basketball Player of the Year in 2005 and 2006 who went on to star in the sport at Georgetown University. For more than twenty years, Dawn has been breeding Berners, and puppies from each litter are named for every letter in the alphabet, counting upward. When Dawn finished A through Z, she started over again with AA. "The next one is KK," she said in the early days of 2010. "I'm wondering what happens when I get to triple-K—that wouldn't be so good."

Tanner, though, is her pride and joy, her first dog ever to reach number one in the breed, a feat that surprised everyone considering that 2009, the year he did it, was supposed to be more of a warm-up for 2010.

In fact, it could have happened even more quickly. Tanner finished at fourteen months and would have done it sooner, but, Dawn reports, "We had to break for surgery." One day before his first birthday, Tanner was more sluggish than usual. Dawn took him to the vet, who ordered an X-ray, noticed a blockage, and cut him open on the spot, removing this mysterious clump from his digestive tract. After surgery he showed Dawn what he'd taken out and said, "Recognize this?"

"Yep," she told him. "That's the pool cover."

Tanner and his Bernese buddies have a knack for eating inedible things. "They're big chewers," she said, "and sometimes I think they're chewing on something like a stuffed animal or a shoe and they just think, 'Hmm, it's in my mouth—I may as well swallow this.'"*

Dawn couldn't have gotten Tanner to the top of the breed without the help of his backer, Georgeann Reeve, another Bernese breeder and friend who retired from a career in the air force and now lives on a ranch in western Virginia with her husband, also retired from the military. In return for her investment, Reeve receives not only joy and pride but also breeding rights. A top dog's sperm is a valuable commodity and, thanks to cryogenics, is a gift that keeps on giving. Tanner had sired eight litters already, most the old-fashioned way, but he's also had his little guys—his "pupsicles," Dawn calls them—frozen.

That's probably a good thing, because as much as Tanner loved the ladies, he wasn't yet an accomplished lothario. "He's really not the most successful stud dog," Heather told me, and explained that he tends to think he's tied with a female ("tied" being locked in the mating position, the only way a pregnancy can be naturally achieved) when he actually isn't. It's not that Tanner isn't interested per se—if you want to get him excited, and I use the term relatively, because excited for a Berner is something like sleepy as compared to asleep—you stand to the side, hold some sort of food, and say in an animated voice, "Tanner, where's your girlfriend?" This is a surefire way to get him to look wherever necessary. He will immediately perk up his ears and pay attention.

Second banana in the truck was Rita (Ch Cabinridge's Mega Margarita), a mild-mannered but strong-willed four-year-old Chesapeake Bay retriever owned by Cindy Meyer, a school administrator from Allentown. As Tanner was to Heather, Rita was to Kevin: the dog atop his priority list. Meyer got her first Chessie as a pet with her late husband in

---

*Eating themselves to death is one hitch in dogs' evolution that has yet to select itself out. A common killer of all pet dogs is antifreeze, which is very toxic but also brightly colored and sweet and which dogs love to lick off of garage floors.

the latter 1990s and, at the urging of some friends, stayed afterward at puppy kindergarten to participate in a handling class. "I told them, I'm not handling my dog. It's a pet," she explained. "Next thing I know, I'm in the ring showing my dog. Then it gets addictive."

Rita entered her life in 2006, shortly after her first dog had died of cancer. Cindy handled Rita, then only a year and a half, for a friend at the breed's National Specialty Show* and was surprised and thrilled when her friend offered to let her keep the dog. Over the next six months, Rita matured into a spectacular specimen, and when Cindy realized that her full-time job made it impossible to show her as widely as was necessary to find and win the majors she still needed for her championship, she decided to hire a handler. But only until the dog was finished.

Heather and Kevin worked hard for Rita, chasing points all the way to South Carolina, where they finally found a field large enough to win a major, and on the way home Heather called and asked, "Now what?" Cindy's reply was, "What do you mean? I have a finished champion. I'm done."

Heather told her that she and Kevin saw great potential in Rita and asked if Cindy would be willing to let them try her out against the breed's specials. Cindy agreed, and Heather's hunch was right. Within a few months, not only was Kevin winning breed competitions, he'd begun to win group placements. At that point, heading into 2008, Cindy decided she wanted to see her dog at Westminster. So Kevin entered Rita, and while she didn't win any ribbons, she made the cut out of a large field, and once again on the drive home Heather called again with a familiar question: Now what?

Kevin felt he could make Rita a top-ten Chessie. Cindy thought he was crazy. But winning was fun, so she gave him permission to try. And Kevin fulfilled his prophecy. Rita was a top-ten dog for 2009. At which point it took very little pressure to keep Cindy hooked. She signed a

---

*An annual event in which dogs from only a single breed gather to compete.

contract for 2010, and Rita (and her crate full of well-chewed plush ani-mals) was a fixture in the camp.

The rest of the menagerie varied by week but usually included an Akita named Trader, several Welsh corgis, a couple golden retrievers, a Rhodesian ridgeback, and numerous Bernese mountain dogs, not to mention their human mothers and fathers who make camp in the mar-gins around the grooming tables, filling the day's many lulls with con-versation and gossip and snacks. A dog show is at least as social for the humans as it is for the dogs.

Every dog requires some grooming, so even though Heather and Kevin choose to work only with breeds on the low-maintenance side of the spectrum, Heather never sends a dog into the ring without at least a little primping. Jack, having a fluffy coat and large expanses of white, requires about ten to fifteen minutes of hair spraying, blow dry-ing, and chalking of his legs and feet.

Once she's finished touching up a dog, Heather typically hands it off to the owner, if present, and asks him or her to await her arrival at ring-side. This is because she is showing many dogs in a day—sometimes ten herself, with another ten on Kevin's schedule. So once Jack was suf-ficiently sprayed and brushed and poufed, he was handed off to Kim-berly, who took him to the ring—and that's where I found her in White Plains. She was, like a proud mother, excited that I'd taken an interest in Jack, and she told me that she'd already thought of the headline for his first dog-magazine advertisement, should she decide to buy one to start building him a reputation as a show dog to watch.

"'He's Got Major Moves'—that's the headline," she said, smiling wide. "I wanted to call him that, Major—but he's too frisky to be a Major." When she chose Wyndstar's Honorable Mention instead, Kerry didn't immediately cotton to it, considering that this was an animal at-tached to high hopes. "Let's hope he doesn't live up to his name," she said.

With only ten total dogs entered—evenly divided between males and females—it wasn't enough for a major, not that Jack needed the points. He'd been finished since late 2009 and would have been finished sooner, Kimberly told me, if they hadn't had to wait around for his final major win. He got his first thirteen points in two months, then waited another two for a major to arrive. Because dogs have to be registered three weeks in advance, which includes a nonrefundable fee, Kimberly "lost a lot of money" seeking out those final points. She just kept paying and withdrawing when the entry was revealed to be too small, because it's considered bad etiquette for a dog awaiting his final major to show up and take points from newer dogs with owners who need them. There are dogs with fifty points that aren't finished, she said. These would be rude dogs. (Or rude owners.)

Jack comes from good stock. His father, Honor—hence the "Honorable" in Jack's name—was ranked the number-twelve Aussie in America after just three months of showing. And Jack is Honor's first AKC champion. Though Kimberly was new to the game, she was excited about his chances but had no experience of her own on which to base expectations. "Heather thinks he could be one of the top Aussies in America," she told me. "She wants to take him to Canada." (To pursue his Canadian championship, which can often be accomplished in a week or less.)

Because Kimberly didn't have the means to pay for a campaign, which involves weekly showing, she was working on Kerry—trying to talk Jack's breeder into helping pay his way. And Kerry was considering the notion, depending on results. Wins, more than anything, would dictate her willingness to spend money to promote him.

Heather came by and took Jack into the ring, and, as she would at nearly every show going forward, Kimberly had butterflies, she told me.

Out in the ring, Heather kept Jack's focus by waving a hand in front of his face. In that hand was a piece of liver (or something tasty), and this "baiting" is how you get a dog's attention. Heather's preferred bait is what she calls "cookies," actually a leathery dog treat known as Purina Carvers. For certain dogs she uses hot dogs torn into chunks. Some handlers will store these treats in their own mouths to keep the dog's focus up and to keep the treats wet and tasty. Heather, who is a meticulous woman, does not.

Truthfully, particularly attentive dogs don't even need treats; handlers will sometimes use an empty hand formed into a fist, and Heather often does just that with Jack, who seems to get reward enough from the satisfaction of playing along. Many dogs, however, require food. With one mastiff Heather had to stuff several pockets full of liver or he'd lie down and quit on her in the middle of a judge's evaluation.

Kimberly pointed at the row of dogs, all standing in the same precise manner—"foursquare" is one way to describe a good stack—facing the judge. She said that one unique thing about show dogs is that they don't sit, and once you're aware of this, it's very obvious. If you look around the room at dogs waiting to show, they are almost invariably standing, because this is paramount among their skills and because even undercarriages are groomed, and lying down could muss a coat. To keep larger, lazier dogs from taking a load off while being groomed or waiting—Tanner was often guilty of this, the big lug—Heather sometimes puts an empty water can underneath their bellies.

Not being at all attuned to the minutiae of a dog show, I didn't yet follow what was happening, and a few minutes after Jack and Heather walked into the ring, it was over. Jack had lost. "I don't see it, but that's okay," Kimberly said, biting her lip a little after a red merle took the Best of Breed ribbon. The merle, she said, had "more bone," and she lamented that this trend was gaining popularity among breeders and also judges. "But they're herding dogs. They need to be agile and turn on a dime. When was the last time you saw a big, heavy herding dog?"

She wasn't even a half year into showing, but, Kimberly said, "I've gotten to like winning. So it's a little disappointing to get nothing in a small show like this." She felt a bit better when the Aussie who beat Jack finished second in a strong Herding Group that included a number of

2009's top dogs, including a Cardigan Welsh corgi, a border collie, and the eventual winner, a bearded collie named Roy who looked like an old wizard. "It's the beginning of the year," Kimberly said with a wry smile. "It's a long year."

BEARDED COLLIE

CHAPTER SIX

Heather and Jack

The best handler is invisible. If you don't notice the handler, it's a good thing.

—DAVID FREI

If money were no object and she could bear to part with her surrogate child so often, Kimberly could easily have Jack on the road fifty weeks a year, for a total well in excess of 150 days. The only two weeks a year when the dog-show world hits the pause button are Christmas and New Year's; otherwise there's always a place to anchor the RV and set about grooming the menagerie.

Kimberly is a woman of modest means. She's comfortable enough to drive a late-model Subaru and watch TV on a large, wall-mounted flat-screen, but she doesn't have the kind of money you'll find behind the country's top show dogs, which either have owners who can foot six-figure bills or are owned by multiple interested parties so that the dog is both an animal and an LLC.

When Kimberly writes a check, she feels it. But if she was going to show, she wanted to do it right, and that meant she needed professional help. In the upper echelons of the show world, the majority of dogs are handled by a professional. These handlers bear a whole list of responsibilities: Most basically, they prep the dogs for the ring and then guide them through the process so that they not only endure the experience of being scrutinized—of having their ears poked and their genitals fondled—but actually excel at it. Handlers also feed, bathe, and transport the dogs. In many cases they house them, too, at least for the days immediately before and after shows, but often full-time, as in the case of top dogs such as Sadie—aka Ch Roundtown Mercedes of Maryscot—the Scottish terrier who finished 2009 as the top dog in all the land. In Sadie's case her "owners" served primarily as financial backers, and during her prime show years she lived exclusively with her Mexican-born handler, Gabriel Rangel, at his home in California. She didn't return home to live with her owners until she was retired.

Many more dogs, however, are like Jack. They are serious competitors, ranked in their breeds, but they live more normal existences (relatively speaking, of course). Two nights before a show, Kimberly drives an hour north to drop Jack off with Heather and Kevin. The handling ranks are stacked with married couples such as Bill and Taffe McFadden, Michael and Michelle Scott, and Diego and Eve Garcia; it makes sense when you consider that their lifestyle is essentially itinerant. All these people have homes, but they rarely stay in them. For the better part of a year, they live in motel rooms and RVs, some of them as plush as any you'll find carting around famous pop stars.

Heather and Kevin were high-school sweethearts who broke up for a spell before reuniting in college at Kutztown University in Kutztown, Pennsylvania. Heather has been showing dogs since she was a teenager. Before that she showed horses and had the country's top-ranked pony when she was ten. But being serious about horses was all-consuming, and Heather decided in the eighth grade that she wanted to have more in her life than school and the barn. "I wanted something else," she says. So she gave up horses, and her mom bought her a dog.

That dog was Griff, a Bernese mountain dog from champion stock, and because she'd grown up showing horses, it seemed only natural for Heather to show her dog. A professional handler named Ross Petruzzo taught her the basics of grooming and handling, and Heather began to show Griff on weekends, enjoying success almost immediately. Griff finished his championship before he was a year old, and he and Heather became regulars in the Best of Breed ring.

Heather treated the new job like a sport, training in the evenings and on weekends and reading everything she could get her hands on. She apprenticed with Petruzzo, and also with Jennifer Schamp. At age sixteen she won Best in Breed at Westminster with Griff, becoming one of the youngest handlers ever to do such a thing. "I thought, 'This is easy,' " Heather said. "I got really used to winning."

The teenage Heather became a fixture at Pennsylvania dog shows, and busy handlers like Michelle Ostenmiller (now Michelle Scott, a two-time Westminster winner) and Carol Knox began to use her as a supplemental handler, to take dogs into the ring when they had conflicts, such as two Bernese mountain dogs competing in the same class on the same day. That led to some client work, and once she turned eighteen and was no longer eligible to compete in Junior Showmanship, Heather began to accept payment. Throughout college and then grad school, weekend handling jobs put spending money in her pocket.

With degrees in both elementary education and special education, as well as a master's in classroom technology, Heather worked as a schoolteacher, handling dogs on weekends and during the summer, but five years into a teaching career she enjoyed, she had a kind of epiphany: It was too much to handle both the kids and the dogs, and when it came down to it, she preferred the latter. "You can always get a teaching job," Kevin, who was then a salesman for Pepsi, told her. "You should try this while you can."

Being conscientious, Heather called her mother and stepfather at their vacation condo on the Caribbean island of St. Thomas to break the news. "You paid for my education," she told her stepfather. "I feel guilty telling you this, but I don't want to teach anymore. I want to pursue my passion. I want to handle dogs—"

Her stepdad cut her off. "You can stop there," he said. "Your education is your education. You'll always have it. Your passion is something different. Follow your passion."

This sounds like a convenient story for a book, but I heard it the same way from both Heather and her mom. And the whole lot of them look smart now. Heather's handling business took off so precipitously that six months later Kevin, who loved dogs but had no interest in dog handling, quit his job at Pepsi to help out, meaning that Heather's unconventional passion consumed them both in less than a year. The alternative, Heather explains, was to hire a full-time assistant and to accept that she and Kevin would be living separate lives, a prospect that seemed untenable. "I was going to be on the road all the time. If I didn't have a husband who was into this, I couldn't do it."

H eather and Jack had an immediate and special bond that Kimberly attributes to a certain mysticism that good handlers possess; "It's a kind of magic that Heather has," she told me.

German dog trainers have a term to describe the ability of a dog to pick up on our mood. The word is *Gefühlsinn,* and it means, more or less, "a feeling for feelings. " The dog-show personality Pat Hastings, a retired handler who now judges and travels the world giving seminars, told me that it is absolutely true that the dog's comfort level relates to the handler's and that the lead is a kind of wire that transmits that energy from one animal to the other. A dog can feel his handler's tension going down the lead and can also smell it, in the form of adrenaline. "When we are nervous, our dogs can sniff it on us," she told me and said that, "one way to help counteract this is to carry breath mints and pop one when you walk into the ring."*

Heather may be small, but dogs—even big ones—respect her. "It was always large dogs," her mom, Sue Bremmer, told me. "She gravitated to large dogs, and large dogs took to her. As tiny as she is, they just know." Sue recalls taking Heather to a weekend clinic put on by the handler George Alston. She remembers there being "at least a hundred people there," along with Heather and her dog, Griff, who was still a puppy. Heather was given the clinic's Best in Show award, and Alston approached Sue at the end and told her that "your daughter has the best hands I have ever seen on a child." He told her that Heather could work for him anytime she wanted.

When you hire a top handler, what you're really doing is paying to present your dog in the best manner possible. In Jack's case a big part of that is keeping him from leaping up and sticking his nose in the judge's ear. But there's much more to presentation than that.

"The reason top handlers do the majority of the winning, particularly on circuits and at clusters, is because their dogs are usually well rested, in good weight, and feeling good physically and mentally," Hastings told me. "They are eating, drinking, and eliminating as they should; they are not stressed from the heat."

And Heather is as organized as they come. "Heather's personality is a lot like mine: She's quite emotional, quite demanding, and everything has to be a hundred percent perfect," says her mom. "She might not win, but those dogs go in that ring looking immaculate, and both she and Kevin look picture perfect." That is one thing that you can control,

---

*Hastings has some other homespun handler tricks: To keep flies out of your kennels, plant marigolds. Flies will not fly over or around the scent. "One of the easiest ways to improve coat condition is to use a humidifier in whatever room your dogs spend the most time." If you have a male that is ultrasensitive to bitches in season, put vanilla extract (which is long-lasting and nonirritating) on his nose and whiskers. Coconut macaroons can help to eliminate stress-induced diarrhea. And if your dog is eating too fast, slow him down by adding a billiard ball to his food dish. "It's too heavy and slick to pick up, so they have to keep moving it around to get to the food."

she said. "You and your dog have to look phenomenal. Beyond that, it's one judge's opinion."

It's an absolute certainty if you attend dog shows that you will hear owner-handlers complain that they have no chance, that in today's game it's all about professional handlers. Here's how Tom Grabe, a former professional handler and now the publisher of the industry magazine *Canine Chronicle*, sees it. "If I was a bicycle racer and I rode my bike fifty miles a day every day and you went out on weekends and want to be a bike rider but have a job during the week, odds are, unless you're incredibly talented, I'm probably going to beat you during the race. Pros are showing ten to thirty dogs three to four days a week. Owners can't practice as much as professional handlers." This is not illogical.

Presentation, then, is probably foremost. If your dog isn't well fed, properly exercised, and groomed in a way that best accentuates his positives—and, if necessary, disguises any negatives—it won't matter how well he moves or handles himself. If you hire the right handler, that part is never a worry. The second part, of course, is how well the dog plays along. And the reason that handling, done well, is so effective is that dogs are genetically attuned to observe us. Provided we give them the right messages, they want to comply.

Dogs can, better than any other species, respond to human gestures. Recent research has shown that they are born knowing how to read our faces. Dogs display something called "left-gaze bias," meaning that—when watching humans—they look to the right side of our face, which psychologists have proved to be the side that best reveals our true intentions. Wolves do not seem to do this, nor do dogs do it to other dogs, so the best theory is that dogs have learned, by living at our side for thousands of years, how to read us.

Dogs can also read and respond to head and arm cues, nods, and even quick glances of our eyes—something neither chimpanzees nor three-year-old kids are very adept at. Brian Ware, a researcher at Harvard, discovered that dogs could interpret fairly subtle signals, even a glance, indicating the location of hidden food four times better than monkeys can and twice as accurately as young children. "When faced with a manipulation task that they can't solve," reports the dog-cognition guru Stanley Coren, they "will stop, look at the face of the person with them, and try to discover clues as to what to do from the person's actions." Wolves, notably, do not do this.

The psychologist Alexandra Horowitz, the bestselling author of *Inside of a Dog* and one of the world's foremost authorities on dog cognition, says that dogs are inherently adaptable to different situations, "especially if you make them encounter those situations when they're young." She says that early exposure to dog shows certainly benefits a potential show dog—and the AKC stages puppy shows to give experience to both human and dog newbies—but that a well-adjusted dog from a loving home "is just going to be adaptable to all situations as long as there's the constant of a person there. That's the interaction which is salient to them."

A dog wants to respond to and please you, the constant, Horowitz says. But for this to work well, "you have to become more skilled in clearly telling your dog what you expect of [him]." For instance, "'You're standing still now while I'm blow-drying your hair.' Or, 'You stand with me and then run by my side, and here's the little bit of food that will remind you of that.' If you're clear about it, they will listen." The problem, she says, is that "most owners are not clear about what they tell their dogs," and the result is that "we feel like the dog's behavior is all over the goddamn place." The fault is ours, "because we're just not explicit with them with what we want them to do. They're very responsive if you're explicit."

What you're buying in a handler is an ability to be explicit in a way that gets through to dogs. An effective handler, she says, is one who doesn't give unnecessary cues. "They give consistent cues—cues that are quickly timed for behavior so that behavior happens and it's the positive behavior. You reinforce it quickly. Dogs are on that—if you give them the opportunity to listen to you, they will."

This isn't just about the dog's ability to understand you; it also means being able to read the dog's signals. Handlers have an "ability to see the dog's behaviors" in a way we regular pet owners probably don't—which means to "be so observant of your dog that you're seeing when a behavior starts, a behavior that you desire to reinforce or a behavior that you want to discourage." The vast majority of us, she says, are very slow at reacting to our dogs. "We're kind of clumsy compared to the dog's pace of acting."

One of Horowitz's favorite areas of study is canine play. She will videotape two dogs playing and then meticulously watch and log every cue and movement—in such detail that twenty seconds of video take six hours to analyze. In a single minute of dog play, she says, "there are thousands of little things happening"—starts and stops and warnings and signals and behaviors—most of which we never pick up on. Horowitz has never studied handlers, but she's pretty sure the good ones are the ones who can pick up on nuances in posture and signals and other behaviors so that "they start seeing when behaviors start and stop and they'll be on it and will be able to reinforce it and catch the behaviors they want and discourage the behaviors they don't."

CHAPTER SEVEN

Fantastically Rich People Do the Darnedest Things:

A Brief History of Dog Shows

So enthusiastic is the average fancier today over the beauty and the wonder of his own dog that he sees him for the most part as the exponent of a breed unique among all other breeds; to him, other breeds may not even exist.

—JOSEPHINE Z. RINE, MID-TWENTIETH-CENTURY DOG WRITER

D og shows first appeared on the scene in England during the Victorian era, and you can still see that period's patrician influence in the floppy hats and natty attire that the sport's old guard love to trot out for big events like Westminster. The first dog show ever held seems to have occurred on June 28, 1859, when a group of hunters gathered in the town of Newcastle upon Tyne and picked over sixty dogs from just two classes: pointers and setters. It wasn't that they were being choosy; these were just the only dogs anyone involved owned at the time. Winners were given guns in lieu of trophies.

A second show was held in November of that year in the town of Birmingham, and its organizers expanded the field by a full one-third, tossing spaniels into the mix. A year later the Birmingham show welcomed hounds for the first time, and we were off and running. The National Dog Show Birmingham, as it was called, survives to this day, with far more company for those hounds and spaniels. It is considered to be the world's oldest dog show and is held every year in May at the Staffordshire County show ground with a field that typically features more than ten thousand dogs. More than three times the size of Westminster.

In those early days, there weren't really standards for the breeds; the dogs' owners probably couldn't have told you exactly what breed their animals were, because no one asked such questions. He was, for instance, probably just a red-colored foxhunting hound, and since the progenitors of shows were hunters, the real measure of that dog was how well he performed at his particular job.

Things began to formalize in 1874, upon publication of the first Kennel Club stud book, which included a code of rules that dictated how a dog show should be conducted, as well as a calendar of events that listed a full year's worth of shows—all two of them.

Here in the United States, we were too busy spearing each other with bayonets to make time for something as frivolous as selecting the finest dogs, so it wasn't until the end of the Civil War that things got moving. And we owe it all to Mr. P. H. Bryson, a furniture dealer from Memphis, Tennessee,* credited in a history of the Memphis Kennel Club as "the First Advocate of Dog Shows in America" (their caps, not mine). Like most able-bodied men of his day, Bryson served in the war, and he survived his service, but just barely. He was so badly wounded that when army doctors discharged him from a military hospital, it was to "go home to die so that he might have a decent burial." Once home, Bryson went to see his family doctor, the honorable D. D. Saunders,

---

*And to the late Baptist minister and dog-show judge Dr. Braxton B. Sawyer for uncovering the very rare source materials that revealed this story.

and when the doctor got a look at the skeletal presence in his office, a 110-pound weakling who "could not walk a hundred yards without pausing to rest," he told Bryson his only hope of carrying on was to try to rebuild his strength, and he prescribed exercise—in particular hunting, with the help and companionship of a bird dog.

Bryson went out and got himself a gun and a dog, a "bobbed-tail Pointer," and commenced killing birds. The exercise, and the dog, saved his life. His vigor returned, and he put on a hundred pounds. Bryson and his brother would move on to setters, importing top specimens from England, and founded the Bryson Setter Kennels. But hunting and breeding weren't enough for old P. H. Bryson. He wanted to show his dogs. Bryson began a campaign to get the sport off the ground, lobbying via a series of articles in the magazine *Turf, Field & Farm,* which despite its name was not a periodical about sod. Apparently people were reading, because before the Bryson brothers could even put together their own show, the Illinois State Sportsmen Association beat them to it, staging America's first-ever dog show, in Chicago, on June 4, 1874. It featured just twenty-one dogs, all of them setters and pointers.

Lacking any template or rules, organizers were making things up as they went along. Instead of a winner, the three judges merely pronounced critiques of the dogs presented. All the dogs were complimented by the judging panel, but the best review seemed to go to Exhibit 5, J. H. Whitman's Frank and Joe—a pair of three-year-old "black and steel mixed Setters, bred by Hilliard, from imported Gordon Setters." The judges' report proclaimed that "the committee, among so many well appearing dogs, find it hard to make an award, but incline to the opinion that this pair of animals are entitled to the highest marks of credit as the best pair of Setters exhibited." It wasn't pithy, but it was kindly received.

America's second dog show was to be held a few weeks later, in Oswego, New York, but this one didn't go off quite so well. "As there was no competition, there being but two dogs and one bitch entered, the committee deemed it advisable to return the entrance money to the exhibitors, Mr. A. L. Sherwood and N. W. Nutting," said a report. (Though it should be noted that "the committee desires to express the highest commendation of Mr. Sherwood's orange and white pair of Setters," which I guess were the two dogs that entered.)

A third, better-attended show took place in October in Mineola, on Long Island, and that one at least aspired to be organized. It was carried out according to English Kennel Club rules, and dogs were judged according to four categories: Irish setters, Gordon setters, "Setters of Any Breed,"* and pointers.

The Bryson brothers, then, would stand fourth in the historical record. On October 8, 1874, the two, along with old Dr. Saunders, staged a Field Trial and Bench Show in Memphis that would, for what is believed to be the first time in America, present a Best in Show award—pitting the Best Pointer against the Best Setter. And who should qualify to compete in the final two but Mr. P. H. Bryson, with his setter, Maud, and May, the pointer of Dr. Saunders, the physician who told him to get a dog in the first place. After much deliberation the judge made the difficult decision and let the record state that the first Best in Show in American history was awarded to P. H. Bryson, the man who'd started the whole dog-show conversation in the first place, by a hair over the doctor who'd saved his life by prescribing a dog.

America's oldest surviving show happens to be its most famous: the Westminster Kennel Club show, so named because it was born at the bar of the Westminster Hotel in 1877. Originally called the "First Annual New York Bench Show† of Dogs," it was open only to sporting dogs but is now a juggernaut broadcast live over two nights on national TV (the only show to get such treatment) and is the second-oldest continuously held sporting event in America, after the Kentucky Derby, which predates it by a single year. Among the top attractions of that debut show

---

*Excepting Irish and Gordon, one presumes.

†A "bench" or "benched" show being a then-common type of show in which dogs were on display, in cages on benches, for the entirety of the show.

were two staghounds from a pack owned by (the then-dead) General George Custer, two deerhounds bred by Queen Victoria of England (reported to be worth fifty thousand dollars each), and a two-legged dog said to be "a veritable biped, and withal possessing almost human intelligence." It was the place to be for New Yorkers on the scene. A *New York Times* story reported that "the gentlemen who served as ticket sellers could not make change fast enough to suit the impatience of the throng that was continually clamoring for admittance."

Just a year later, benched dog shows had become such a hit that *Field & Stream* wrote the following: "We doubt if even the 'Bench Show of Intellect,' suggested by *The World,* and in which it is proposed to exhibit all classes of poets and literary people in general, would call forth more interested, aristocratic, or cultured throngs than the dog show audiences." And then, a year later, concern for dog shows' spread prompted this in the same magazine: "We think there are too many Bench Shows. This opinion is not alone our own, but is pretty generally expressed by the public. We believe that during the year there should be held only two great shows in the country, and no more." The proliferation of shows, the editors felt, could only diminish the luster of existing events.

Field & Stream's plea fell on deaf ears, and the dog-show juggernaut rolled on. The American Kennel Club was formed in 1884, in Philadelphia, when the heads of twelve distinct clubs gathered with the goal of creating a "club of clubs" to rule them all. A month later they met again in New York City to write a constitution and bylaws and formally adopted a reliable "studbook" that set breed standards. It took a while for the AKC to inculcate the nation's dog fanciers with formalized rules and standards for conformation, but by 1909 the organization had created the fifteen-point requirement for achieving a dog's championship (and even then an exhibitor needed those points to come from at least three judges). By 1920 the AKC was officially sanctioning shows, and in 1924 the two existing groups—Sporting and Non-Sporting—were split into five: Sporting (which included hounds), Terrier, Toy, Non-Sporting, and Working (which included herding). That same year 154 conformation shows were held across America, up from 11 in 1884, the year the AKC was founded.

Because of the close association with hunting, dog shows began as a high-society affair in America, too. All the wealthiest families had kennels on their estates, and the handlers who ran them worked tirelessly to improve the quality of their stock. The conformation record books are filled with titans of American business—the names Belmont, Morgan,* Whitney, Gould, and Rockefeller were all commonly glimpsed in the show programs[†]—and shows were regularly featured in magazines and newspapers alongside news of other popular sports. "Everybody," wrote a *New York Times* reporter of an early show's attendees, "was fashionably dressed and wore an air of good breeding." (I'm fairly certain no pun was intended.)

To give you an idea of just how prized a top dog was to society folk back then, consider that in 1908, a Ford Model T cost $825, while, according to Mark Derr, in his fascinating and fact-dense *A Dog's History of America,* "the most desirable purebred dogs routinely started at $1,000 and ran to $5,000."

The country's top dogs were featured in *Popular Dogs* magazine, a weekly filled with profiles and new stories as well as promotional ads for champions, show listings, classifieds, and small boxed advertisements for products like Vermicide Capsules and the delouser Pulvex, which, according to its slogan, "Actually kills fleas instead of stupefying them!"

No show got more play, of course, than Westminster, which even then was world-famous. And the January 11, 1929, issue of *Popular Dogs* offered the following important news: "For the first time, perhaps, in

---

*J. P. Morgan loved dogs—and once offered thirty-two thousand pounds for a top-winning Pekingese owned by the Englishwoman Clarice Ashton Cross, who politely turned him down.

†In England the Prince of Wales, who became Edward VII, and his wife, Alexandra, were patrons of the Kennel Club—and showed borzois, gifts of the Czar Nicholas II of Russia.

the history of dog shows, canine reciprocity will be the order of the day, meaning that special precautions are to be taken lest the dogs endanger the people and the people annoy the dogs. There will be no biting of spectators at the Garden show this year, nor will there be any sticking of fingers in dogs' eyes by a too interested public." New wire cages, it reported, "will make accidents impossible, unless, of course, the spectator goes out of his way to make trouble for himself."

CHAPTER EIGHT

Westminster: Welcome to the Big Time, Kid

It takes all your time, all your money, everything you got.
If you're lucky, you might win enough money to get across
the George Washington Bridge.

—OWNER OF A CHOW CHOW, IN THE BENCHING AREA AT
WESTMINSTER, 2010

The Westminster Kennel Club Dog Show, held every February, is. and has always been the most famous and important dog show in America. It is a vast and overwhelming two-day affair that brings nearly three thousand dogs and exponentially more breeders, owners, handlers, salespeople, psychics, dog masseuses, and hairstylists to New York City, where they take over Madison Square Garden while living on takeout and Chablis across Seventh Avenue at the Hotel Pennsylvania.

The seventeen-hundred-room Pennsylvania, a slightly dowdy grande dame that is the city's fourth-largest hotel, transforms itself for the occasion into the world's most dog-friendly hotel, complete with "his and her relieving areas"—the boys' room is the one with plastic fire hydrants, in case you are confused—the world's largest "doggie spa," and a makeshift "Paw Mall" of vendors hawking treats, leads, combs, and dog-imprinted gear. The Pennsylvania's PR machine loves to promote all this, celebrating the "five-paw service" overseen by doggie concierge Jerry Grymek, who spends eleven months concocting puns that he wields liberally in person and in press releases. Jerry is fully to blame for all the quotation marks in this section.

The ostensible purpose of Westminster, according to the Kennel Club's bylaws, is "to increase the interest in dogs, and thus improve the breeds, and to hold an Annual Dog Show in the city of New York." All those things remain true. It's the one time each year that cabdrivers will talk about dog shows and will be able to explain the origins of the Norwegian buhund* between conspiracy rants, thanks to live coverage on the USA Network. The show has been on TV since 1948 but has really become a cultural touchstone since it began airing in primetime on USA, where it is one of that channel's most-watched specials. In 2009 David Frei, the club's director of communications and the voice of Westminster to millions of Americans—he's the droll one who explains the derivation of the buhund's name—celebrated his twentieth year on the air or, as the official press release called it, "140 years (oops, that's dog years)."

TV is one reason Westminster is such a big deal. The other is that it is a champions-only show and an invitational; the top five American dogs in each breed are automatically eligible to compete. The remaining entries are accepted via lottery and only finished champions are eligible to enter.

The nation's top dogs begin to arrive on the Friday before the traditional Monday start, and by midday there are stacks of crates teetering

---

*An all-purpose sheep, cattle, and guard dog. The name comes from the Norwegian word *bu*, meaning "mountain hut," and skeletons that appear to belong to buhunds have been found in Viking graves dating to A.D. 900. A newly recognized breed in the United States, appearing at Westminster for the first time in 2010, the buhund has been recognized at Norwegian shows since 1939; the first buhund ever registered, by the way, was named Flink.

on the sidewalk outside the Pennsylvania. Inside, bemused Europeans in orange clogs and unseasonably short pants snap pictures and ogle the various breeds wandering the lobby.

Placards advertise the Skybark VIP Pooch Event in the Skytop Ballroom ("VIP," by the way, stands for "very important pooches"). As noted, these and other puns are the work of Jerry Grymek, a thin Canadian with a small silver loop on his upper ear.

Jerry, whose hotel badge actually reads DOGGIE CONCIERGE, said that 460 dogs were scheduled to arrive, with another 360 due the following day, most during the 1:00 P.M.–to–3:00 P.M. dog check-in. In total he was expecting between 800 and 1,000 canine check-ins. Three of the last four Best in Show winners, he was pleased to report, had stayed at the Pennsylvania.

Jerry's tasks include managing the vendors, acting as liaison between owners and the hotel, and generally facilitating dog comfort, which often means handing out special cookies that bulge in his pant pockets like nuts in the cheek of a squirrel. Though it's not something he advertises, Jerry will occasionally fulfill more unusual requests for returning customers. "We don't have room service, but sometimes a guest I know really needs something for an upset dog," he said. "I've gotten meatballs with extra sauce, pizza slices, and cheeseburgers— hold the onions."

No dog is too big for the Pennsylvania—"We took a bullmastiff that was two hundred twenty pounds"—but handlers who bring multiple dogs will be asked to book more than one room.

"You see that bloodhound?" he said, pointing across the lobby to a dog waiting its turn on a stage where David Frei was running a satellite media tour for local TV affiliates. "That dog"—whose name, I later learned, is Harvey—"is a contender for the record of world's longest ears. His late grandfather, who recently passed, currently holds the title."*

---

*The number, because I know you're curious, is 14 inches, shattering the old record of 13.75.

Jerry led me down some stairs and into the Paw Mall (which, frankly, could use another pass by the pun committee), where we had just missed Annie Germani, the pet communicator, currently out to lunch. Jerry pointed out the "his-and-hers canine loo" (that's Canadian for "bathroom"), as well as the rather luxe display by the DogPedic memory-foam mattress company, which sells beds in three sizes, and can be purchased for two payments of $19.99 plus shipping and handling. If I came back in a day, Jerry said, I could meet Montel Williams, DogPedic's celebrity endorser and one of a surprisingly large and fervent community of famous dog-show enthusiasts.[*]

"We call this Dogtors corner," Jerry said, and I must have looked confused, because he clarified. "Like doctors. Only dogtors."

He meant that this would be your therapeutic zone, which included Annie Germani as well as masseuse Debbie Zimmerman, a graduate of the Ojai School of Massage and a specialist in animal massage, preventative sports massage, Veterinary Orthopedic Manipulation (VOM), as well as obedience and agility training, behavior training, and crystal healing. Debbie charges a dollar per minute and said that typical massages range from twenty minutes of sport work in the case of dogs prepping for agility competitions to a more comprehensive thirty- to forty-minute rubdown for the conformation dogs, meant to help them loosen up.

"I remind people that they need to stretch their dogs," Debbie said. Over the course of the weekend, she estimated she'd do eighty-five massages and that she could easily do more, "but I don't have enough hands." Because, like humans (including this one), not every dog finds massage all that relaxing, Debbie also wields Chill Out aromatherapy spray, a pleasant mist that includes essence of lavender and chamomile.

---

[*]The alpha dog of this pack is Bill Cosby, who's been participating in shows for years and whose Dandie Dinmont terrier—a low-slung breed that looks like a little schnauzer wearing a curly white toupee—named Harry, entered the 2007 Westminster show as the number-one-ranked dog in America. Harry won the Terrier Group but lost to a springer spaniel named Diamond Jim for Best in Show.

"It helps calm them down," Debbie said, and as if I had just stepped into a commercial in progress, a woman lingering nearby interjected, "It really works."

I wasn't sure what if any of this stuff Jack would use—though certainly the Chill Out spray is worth a test—but I could imagine that Kimberly might want to use the roomy bathing tubs, if not the whirlpool. He would definitely enjoy the Jog-A-Dog treadmills, which like all products targeting this market come in three sizes. An older golden retriever with wisps of gray in his face was plodding along effortlessly on the largest size, looking as if he could do it for days.*

How long have you been doing this? I asked Jerry.

"For a dog's age," he answered. "Easily seven years."

Obviously a single show can't occupy his entire year.

"Three hundred sixty days a year I'm in public relations," he clarified. "Five days a year it's pooch relations."

I must have had the look of someone who'd just been bludgeoned by one too many hits of bad wordplay, because he smirked and said, "I have so many more."

How many?

"How much time you got?" he said. "You know how I write them down?"

He reached inside his suit jacket and pulled out a pencil with a rubber dog head for an eraser.

I f you have ever been to Madison Square Garden for a basketball game, a circus, or a concert, you would likely not recognize it during the two days of Westminster. The arena's floor has been covered in green carpeting, on which six show rings have been roped off, all of them surrounded by the throngs of spectators who invade one an-

---

*Speaking of things that come in threes, I would be remiss if I did not mention the table hawking Sniff-brand pants for bitches in heat. The three varieties are "panties," "thongs," and "cummerbunds."

other's personal space for eight hours of Best of Breed competitions, commencing at 8:00 A.M. sharp.

But that's just part of the experience. Westminster is one of the last surviving benched shows, and thus all the dogs showing on a particular day must be benched—on display—with their breeds, from open to close, so that the fifteen thousand–plus spectators in attendance for the day session can cycle through, stare at, photograph, and, with permission, pet them. Not that people always ask for permission; it's pretty common to witness a dog owner scolding someone's child for reaching out and petting a dog's face. This seems mean, and certainly people could be nicer about it, but the owners are (mostly) looking out for the child's well-being. Dogs are often tense with strangers, and if you don't give them a chance to sniff some part of you first, to gain their trust, they might snap at an unfamiliar thing thrust into their face, especially when this takes place in a hot, crowded tunnel jam-packed full of humans and canines. Benched shows are very popular with crowds, but owners tend to hate them. Whereas once they were common, today there are only six benched shows a year.

Professionals like Heather and Kevin get a bit of a break. One section of the labyrinth under the Garden is set aside for multibreed handlers, so that they can have all their dogs in one location and not have to scramble through the crowds to retrieve dogs when the time comes to get them ready for the ring.

Heather's day started with Shumba, a shy Rhodesian ridgeback who practically cowered on the grooming table. This being Westminster, Heather was dressed a bit more formally than usual, in a sparkly ivory blazer with intentional crinkles in the fabric, a black skirt, and a pair of nice but sensible black Geox shoes.

Rhodesians were the second-largest entry in the field, after Aussies, and forty-three of these long, lean, tannish red dogs with the raised hair along their spines (that's the "ridgeback") were crammed into the ring for a first pass by Dr. Richard Meen, a solidly built man with slick gray hair and a bow tie, who looked like an Oxford economist or the guy who'd play the stern dean of students in a Hollywood movie about fraternities.

The rule of thumb is that a judge takes two minutes per dog over the course of a particular show, so seventy-five minutes had been allotted for the Rhodies, from eight-thirty to nine forty-five.

Shumba looked much less nervous in the ring and got the competition off to a good start for Team Bremmer. Meen chose a male, then pointed to Shumba as Best of Opposite, giving her a coveted second place in breed at the country's biggest dog show. At Westminster, second (or third, or fourth) is not a disappointment; on the contrary, it is a career accomplishment for most dogs.

J ack, meanwhile, had some time to kill. To save money, he and Kimberly had been staying at the Affinia, another nearby hotel that welcomes dogs, where they were sharing a room with two friends from Pennsylvania and their Pyrenees shepherd, as well as a junior handler who sometimes worked with them. It was a crowded house. The Affinia also hadn't embraced its four-legged guests with quite the élan that the Pennsylvania had—and with no Jerry of its own, how could it? Most notable, there were no sawdust-lined his-and-her canine loos, and Kimberly said that by the time she checked in at 3:00 P.M., the patch of rooftop Astroturf set aside for dogs "already reeked of pee."

So instead she walked Jack a few blocks to the Pennsylvania to use the potty. Jack, like many dogs, preferred a soft, "natural" surface to the concrete of Manhattan's sidewalks. They went back again the morning of the show, both to use the facilities and to get him on the Jog-A-Dog. This served two purposes. One, it allowed him to burn off some nervous energy and also to have some fun—Jack loves treadmills. Two, it helped speed up his digestion. "You really want them to have a BM before a show," Kimberly explained. (As opposed to during a show.) "He's had some issues," she said, then was quick to add, "They all do." She'd learned that one way to avoid the issue was to get him running shortly before the show. It's like clockwork. "You start moving and things get moving." So she took him to the treadmill, and sure enough he crapped.

This being Jack's first Westminster, expectations were low. No matter how well he'd been doing, even after the big weekend in Wildwood not even two weeks earlier, Kimberly wasn't so delusional as to think her dog was ready to contend for the claim of best Australian shepherd in America.

She hadn't necessarily even wanted to enter Jack—he was still so young (the second-youngest Aussie in the field), and the combined cost of entry and handling fees was over a thousand dollars—but Heather talked her into it. The idea being that he could gain valuable experience in the big, chaotic atmosphere of a major show, and anyway what the hell? He'd gained entry into the world's most famous dog show, so why not give it a shot? "I have to admit it's pretty cool to say my dog is showing at Westminster," Kimberly said as we stood ringside.

Are you nervous? I asked her.

"My stomach tells me yes," she answered. "But I don't feel nervous mentally."

I pointed out that it should help that expectations were low; she didn't come expecting to win, not with fifty-some Aussies, many of which had been campaigned for more than a year.

Kimberly started to agree and then stopped. "Heather would tell me, 'You always come to win,' but I don't expect him to win. If he makes at least one cut, I'll be happy. If he doesn't make any cuts, I'll be demolished."

I asked how Jack was taking to New York.

"You know how hyper he is? He walks around Manhattan so calm. He could be a city dog." She glanced up at a clock. "Okay, I have to go wash my dog's feet."

I think I'll wear pink tomorrow," Heather said as she fluffed the fur on Jack's rear in the moments before heading to the ring. "The sparkles are working well." So far she and Kevin had shown three dogs, and two of them had been rewarded with Best of Opposite ribbons. Already the show was a success.

Kimberly and I walked out toward Ring 4, where the Aussies would assemble. "Let's go up to the seats so I can just get rid of nervous energy," she said.

Because of some late scratches, the actual number of Australian shepherds entered turned out to be just over forty, most of them black tris assembled in front of Mrs. Lynette Saltzman, a regal woman with dark hair and a necklace of pearls. Kimberly pointed Jack out to a curious spectator sitting nearby and breezed quickly through his biography. "It took him two months to get to thirteen points, then another two months to get the major, because we couldn't find one. Then he showed once in December, then at Wildwood, and then here. He's not been around the block much." Jack was still maturing, she explained, and most of his rivals were a good year or two older.

There were a few familiar dogs, including Beyoncé, a female black tri who was America's number-one Aussie, and Spooner, Summer's father. To make the most of the limited space, Judge Saltzman split the dogs by sex, so that Jack first matched up against all the boys. The numbers were randomly assigned, but the randomness had been fortuitous for Jack, who was stacked in a group of black tris—three on either side of him, so that his unique look stood out even more than usual. Heather's black-and-white ensemble matched him perfectly. A man sitting just in front of us pointed him out to his son and said, "Look at that one. He's beautiful."

Told that the dog he fancied was Kimberly's, the man asked about his temperament. "He's a love," Kimberly said. "And he's great with kids. He herds kids. He tries to herd my son, who is seventeen."*

Behind us another guy chimed in. "That's a pretty dog."

---

*A perhaps apocryphal but totally believable story bandied about the Aussie community is that the dogs were also used as baby-sitters on farms, looking after kids during short stints when both parents might be required to complete certain jobs.

The judge must have agreed. Jack was the first dog picked out of his group, meaning he was in the top six males selected out of the larger pool of twenty-nine, including many top champions. Saltzman dismissed the dogs from the ring to make room for the bitches.

"I can go home happy now," Kimberly said. "Top six—out of the top twenty-nine in the country! And he's not even two!"

One of the men wanted to know what Kimberly's plan was for Jack, and I, too, was getting a little caught up in things. Here, on the country's biggest stage, her dog was already among the best in his breed. Kimberly was trying not to get swept away by the excitement. "My son's going to college," she said. "I have to have priorities. He already thinks I love the dog more. If I said, 'You can't go to college because I need to show Jack,' . . . well—then he might not love Jack as much." She smirked.

The odds are certainly better if you're showing a bitch. Once the boys had left, only females remained to face the judge, including Beyoncé and her handler, Jamie Clute. Beyoncé was the first girl pulled, and she led the group of five that would join the six males in the final judging of the show's biggest breed.

All around us buzz began to swell over Jack. A woman asked where he came from, then took out an envelope and wrote down the kennel name as Kim told her, "It's Wyndstar with a y." A man with a New York accent as thick as cream cheese said, "I love that dog." Kimberly didn't even try to disguise her pleasure at all the attention—not because it validated her, exactly, but because these people were affirming what she already knew to be true of Jack: He's a very special dog.

"Did I tell you my kennel name?" she said to me quietly, and I was surprised to hear it, seeing as she had never bred a single dog. "Jackpot. Because Jack is the cornerstone. I hit a jackpot with him. And if you buy one of my dogs, you hit the jackpot, too. And I work at the casino." She giggled. It's good, I said, but you're lacking two important pieces: puppies and the space to raise them.

It wasn't hard to tell which dogs Saltzman preferred, and after watching a down-and-back and then a free stack—in which Jack froze and fixed on Heather's hand as if he'd been doing this for years—Judge Saltzman was clearly favoring both Jack and a red tri from Louisiana, named Rowan. She reordered them for a final jog around the ring, putting Jack in front, which seemed to indicate that she was leaning toward choosing him. Kimberly was practically bouncing in her seat.

Then, when they were midway around, Saltzman reordered the dogs again, putting Rowan the red in front of Jack. Jack still looked great—confident, happy, beautiful—and he moved smoothly at the end of Heather's lead until she stopped him one last time for a final look by the judge. Saltzman fixated on the two males—back and forth, back and forth. Beyoncé seemed to be out of the running. Later Heather would tell us that the tension was palpable.

The judge made her decision: It was Rowan, a dog who'd been exhibited and advertised for at least a year. I don't know this for sure, but I have to imagine that when it comes time to break a difficult tie, you might tend to choose the dog you know from the advertisements. And you could hardly fault Judge Saltzman if that were the case.

Because second place always goes to the opposite sex, the Best of Opposite was given to Beyoncé, but it was clear to everyone watching that Jack was Saltzman's second-favorite dog. Anyway, he was given the first Award of Merit, in the largest group at his first-ever Westminster, and by hesitating so long to make her choice, Judge Saltzman had told everyone watching that either of these two males could have won Best in Breed.

At ringside, Kathy Glaes, a reporter from the breed's specialty magazine, the *Australian Shepherd Journal,* asked Kimberly if she could set up a time for an interview about this unknown dog who'd nearly won the breed. "He's an up-and-comer," said a woman who'd been eavesdropping. Jack was a total unknown—to date he had not appeared in a single ad—but people responded to him. He got a reaction. And to think that Kimberly had briefly considered not bringing him.

"You know what the lesson is?" Heather's mom, Sue, said as she congratulated Kimberly with a hug. "Always listen to Heather."

Handler and dog posed for their win photo and then joined us. "He was losing focus at the end," Heather said. "I was getting upset with him. When I had to free-bait the last time"—free-baiting is when the dog must stop and stack with no help from the handler, who is not allowed to touch the dog or reset its feet—"I was nervous. I was losing him. That other dog has been campaigned."

I pointed out that even though I still had no real idea what was going on out there, I could see that Jack had uncommon flair.

"That thing he has—he loves it—that's the best thing you can ask for with a show dog," Heather said. "But it's also his weakness. The more he's out, the better. Wildwood was huge, I think. To get those five shows under his belt—oh, my God, that was huge."

Kimberly looked dizzy. "I came here with no expectations," she said. And yet that's not entirely true. Yes, she didn't expect to win. If I'd told her Jack was going to win an Award of Merit before the forty-four Aussies assembled in the ring, she'd have laughed at me. But this is emotional business. It's not exactly like someone subjectively judging your child in a spotlit ring surrounded by spectators, but it's not far from that.

Because Heather believed in Jack and understood that Kimberly wasn't rich, she seemed willing to negotiate on price, but it wasn't just benevolence at work. Both of Heather's campaign dogs—Rita and Tanner—were scheduled to come off the books for the summer, and she was in the market for a new dog to take to the top. That dog, she hoped, was Jack.

"I can get him to top ten," she said. "I would say top five, but you just never know at that point. There's so much that goes into it."

Like those orange-jacketed attendants who direct pilots parking their planes at airport gates, show judges communicate mostly through gestures—two hands up, palms out, means stop. A sweep one way is meant to direct a down-and-back, and a twirl of the finger indicates once more around the ring. When a judge has completed an inspection, he'll give the dog a little pat on the side or rear to send it on its way.

Kevin showed Rita to a handsome blond woman who looked like a librarian. Despite some slipups—at one point Kevin tossed a treat to Rita and it bounced off her nose and onto the ground, where another dog snatched it up—it went well, and Rita was given Best of Opposite, continuing the couple's hot streak.

I found Kevin back at the stand, red-faced and wiping away sweat.

"Four out of six is a pretty good show," I said, meaning that Jack, Shumba, Rita, and Trader had all been among the top dogs at the world's best show. Any owner with realistic expectations would be thrilled with such a result.

"Not bad," he answered, and you can understand why as a professional he might see things differently. "But no wins yet."

Hopes of an appearance live on national TV, under the lights at night in the groups, rested on the final dog in the truck: Tanner, who stood quite happily on the grooming table while Heather finished up his primping. En route to New York, he had eaten an entire bag of Purina Carvers dog treats that Dawn had accidentally left near his crate and had slowly but surely been puking them up ever since. "Let's hope the last one doesn't come out in the ring," she said.

"No accidents yet," I said, and immediately realized that everyone was looking at me as if I'd just poked Tanner in the eye.

"You can't say that!" Dawn said, kind of laughing, but in a way that made it clear she wasn't actually amused. "It's like when the announcer says, 'He shoots ninety-five percent from the line. He never misses.'" She paused a beat. "He always misses."

When judging began, both Heather and Kevin were forced into duty. Heather with Tanner, of course. Kevin with Roxy, a young female bred by Dawn and one who was to become a featured dog in the coming months. She was at the Garden mostly for practice and was still quite green, something that became very apparent when, mere moments into the judging, she fulfilled prophecy and took a giant dump that neither the judge nor the ring attendants seemed to notice. The crowd, however, was fully aware, and as the handlers maneuvered around the steaming pile, a buzz grew.

"Do you get points off for that?" a man sitting nearby asked. The buzz spread to the desk where the ring steward sits, overseeing the schedule and the judge's book, and frantic pointing ensued as one handler after another just barely dodged the crap. Finally, a good four or five minutes later, the cleaning crew arrived and the two-man team— one with dustpan and broom, the other with a mop—took care of business, much to the delight of the crowd, which erupted in a huge cheer.

"It's like the Zamboni guy," said one young woman. To which her friend answered curtly, "Well, everybody poops."

Westminster is so different from the other shows that it can be a bit of an equalizer. It takes certain dogs way outside their comfort zones. They spend their day cooped up in stuffed aisles, show in front of a crowd of thousands, and then exit the building into a loud and intimidating city with virtually no grass.

Considering the lack of open space, David Frei told me it's "kind of amazing that we don't have more accidents in the ring than we do. And when we do, everyone in our world understands that's it's no big deal."

Unless it happens on national TV. He said that a few years back, in the Sporting Group, a dog "just stopped dead center of the ring with camera on him and took a dump." Frei, working the broadcast, said that the camera didn't linger for too long but that there's not much you can do to distract the thousands in the audience who are naturally going to fixate. "Roger [Caras, the show's announcer], on the house PA, said, 'Well, it is a dog show,' and everybody cheered and went on with the show."

Frei can't remember how that particular dog finished, but he distinctly recalls that after she was done, "she went flying around the ring like a different dog. She's like, 'Okay, I feel great. Let's go.'" No judge is going to punish the act, because they've all been owners and handlers themselves, "and it's happened to them," Frei said. "It's happened to me. Once the judge moved around to the back of my dog and was feeling down the haunches when my dog scooched up and took a dump, almost right in his hands."

Dawn probably has many of these stories herself, as Kevin and Heather surely do. Tanner, meanwhile, didn't even seem to notice Roxy's faux pas. He was cool and collected and trotted around the ring as if he were pulling a cart to market.

Heather's mom was a helpful cheerleader and led a boisterous rooting section that was buoyed by circumstance when the golden retrievers—quite possibly the most beloved breed of all—entered the ring next door. At that point the judge had set the dogs in the order that appeared to be her favorites, with Tanner in the lead, followed by a bitch named Dallas who was one of his main rivals. I looked over and saw Dawn leaning forward, practically chewing on her hands. She reached out to touch her son, Andrew, and then, just as the dogs were trotting around, the judge reset them and moved the bitch to the front. She pointed. "Best of breed!" Then, to Tanner, "Best of Opposite."

I could read Heather's lips as she looked up at Dawn. She said, quite clearly, "Shit."

Though no handler likes to have defeat snatched from the jaws of victory at the very last minute, for any other dog in Heather and Kevin's menagerie this would have *been* a victory. Tanner, however, was the country's top Berner. This was his ring to win.

Dawn looked deflated and walked down to the floor to greet her dog. "Tanner Banner!" she said, some light returning to her face. "What did you do?" She gave the big bear a hug.

"It's still Best of Opposite at the Garden," Heather said, trying to convince herself, quite unconvincingly, that this was okay.

"If this is the worst thing to happen . . ." Dawn said. "I mean, I hate to be mad. . . ." Neither statement was finished.

"She put him first," Heather said. "She loved him. I could tell. He moved well, he free-stacked well."

"She put him first, and I grabbed my son's hand and said, 'We're gonna do this!'" Dawn said. "And then she put the bitch first." She stomped a foot. "I hate this show."

By this time Tanner's co-owner, Georgeann, had come by to commiserate. "The judge did the same thing with the Great Danes," she said. "She likes the bitches. And that's a showy bitch."

Now Dawn was no longer pretending to be happy with her second place. "I'm immensely disappointed. Immensely," she said. "I'm a terrible loser." She nodded at Heather. "She's devastated."

Heather rejoined the circle, removing her sparkly jacket. "She put me in front, and I'm thinking, 'I need to go back to the hotel! I need a new outfit! Maybe I'll get a new outfit!'" She shook her head. "Never do that!"

"That's the thing with dog shows," Dawn said. "There's no point in getting your hopes up." A friend asked Dawn about her Best of Opposite ribbon—if she was really going to keep this one, implying that she typically does not. She shook her head.

Do you really throw them away? I asked her.

"Yes. I told you I'm a terrible loser." She laughed one of her hearty Dawn laughs. "I need a drink."

CHAPTER NINE

How the Hell Does a Wolf Become a Pekingese?

A Brief History of Purebreds

The domestication of the dog from its wolf ancestors is perhaps the most complex genetic experiment in history, and certainly the most extensive.

—ELAINE OSTRANDER AND HEIDI PARKER, *Journal of the Public Library of Science: Genetics*

It's not that hard to see where an Australian shepherd comes from. The dogs are low-slung and agile, with fluffy, multicolored coats, and they look, by and large, like something that evolved from a wolf. If you encountered one in its more natural environment (or what is supposed to be its natural environment, the one the breed was meant to inhabit), on sheep ranches in the western United States, you'd find some more ratty and smelly specimens, and you might mistake them for border collies, but the two breeds, while similar, have very different ways of going about their jobs.

A border collie employs a technique known as "strong eye" to stare down a flock's leaders and force them to comply using intimidation. Aussies are more "loose-eyed"; they don't so much intimidate as work low and use their presence as a deterrent. They can and will stare down a sheep when necessary but prefer not to. They'll also bite a sheep or a cow on the nose if the larger animal is being especially uncooperative, which is a breed hallmark. This requires great agility, since a cow bitten on the nose can get a little angry.

BORDER COLLIE

On a more personal, companionate level, you might say border collies don't have an off switch while Aussies can quite easily clock in and out of work. As one lady at a dog show explained to me, "Aussies ask; borders do." The former love tasks and will eagerly complete them but is also happy to lie around the house for much of the day. The latter are so obsessed with jobs that if you don't provide them, the dogs will just create their own. So if you if should come home and find all your shoes herded into a hole dug in the plush carpet, it's your own fault for leaving.

Herding is a fascinating skill that is impressive to behold in person. The AKC runs a series of herding contests in which Aussies and other dogs typically herd geese or ducks, and they're worth checking out, especially if you like nervous waterfowl. The act of herding is pretty awesome to think about—it is predatory behavior modified over time to omit the killing, and it's a remarkable adaptation when you consider that these animals have been bred to disregard what is surely an over-powering natural instinct to kill and eat the animals entrusted to their care.[*]

Herding behavior, then, provides a pretty easy link to the Aussie's lupine heritage; and when you combine that with the dog's physical appearance, you can certainly see where the breed comes from. (With some of the wilder and more erratic coat patterns to be found, and with the long and snipey faces that show up in some litters, Aussies can sometimes look downright wolfish, except for the coat, which is fluffier, and the ears, which droop instead of prick up.)

Ultimately, though, all dogs descend from the same source, and it's hard to walk around the floor at a dog show looking at poodles and Pomeranians and think, "Okay, that used to be a wolf." More likely you're thinking, "There is no fucking way that used to be a wolf."

But it was. All dogs come from a single ancestor: the wolf, or *Canis lupus* (as opposed to *Canis familiaris,* the dog). *Which* wolf exactly has historically been subject to debate. These days most scientists agree that all dogs come from the gray wolf, a wide-ranging species that you know as the kind we have in the United States—in Yellowstone Park as well as Michigan, Minnesota, Washington, Wisconsin, and especially Alaska, where they are so numerous that they are hunted freely from helicopters by vice presidential candidates.

We owe the specificity of this knowledge to a project led by the UCLA geneticist Dr. Robert Wayne, who used mitochondrial DNA

---

[*]It's worth noting that this modification of behavior is pretty unique to the herding breeds; you would get very different results if you tried to herd using some type of terrier—say, a rat terrier, a rather cute variant with an ugly name that's bred to hunt and kill vermin with great efficiency. There are many tales of terriers killing hundreds of rats in contests regularly held at English pubs.

to pinpoint the dog's origins. Wayne collected and studied blood and tissue samples from sixty-seven different dog breeds, as well as from wolves around the world and other canines such as coyotes and jackals. What he found was pretty surprising—whereas the mitochondrial DNA of wolves and coyotes differed by 6 percent, samples from wolves and dogs differed by just 1 percent. That means a Pomeranian is closer to a wolf than a wolf is to a coyote, and it's kind of mind-blowing if you've ever seen a coyote, an animal that many people mistake for a wolf. It sure as hell looks more like a wolf than a Pomeranian does. So close are dog and wolf, in fact, that a Pomeranian is more similar, genetically, to a wolf than a white human is to a black or an Asian human.

Some of the most common head butting among dog scientists is over the issue of when wolf became dog. You will find a wild span of estimates on the matter—some suggesting that domestic dogs existed as far back as 130,000 years. The latest guess is one from German researchers studying a fossil found over a century ago in a Swiss cave. The Germans began to study the so-called Kesslerloch dog after a zoological archaeologist stumbled on the 1873 fossil and subsequently dated it to between 14,100 and 14,600 years old. Because the skeleton was found in a cave with human remains, and because the jawbone was noticeably smaller than that of a wolf, the scientists deduced that the animal must have been a domesticated dog.

This settled nothing. For a long time, it was thought that gray wolves were first domesticated in Europe or Asia, but another Robert Wayne–led study published in 2010 suggested that the first dogs actually appeared in the Middle East at least 13,000 years ago.[*] Wayne thinks our estimates about when this happened are far too conservative. He cites archaeological evidence of "dogs"—canines noticeably different from wolves—in 31,000-year-old Belgian fossils, and he says that in those 15,000-year-old fossils "they already look more like Great Danes than

---

*Canine remains have been discovered in burial sites dating back that far, including in one grave that contained a human buried with a puppy cradled in its arms—or at least that's how it appeared when the skeletons were found.

wolves." His best guess, then, is more than double the 14,000-year-old number most often cited. "I'm thinking forty thousand or fifty thousand years."

Whenever and wherever the first proto-dogs, as they're often called, appeared on the scene, it was likely because wolves had been sniffing around the periphery of human civilization for some time, scavenging on our garbage, which made for a much easier meal than chasing down and killing an angry animal with horns. Over time the tamer wolves got closer and closer to people, who began to welcome them into their homes, perhaps for warmth or hunting assistance, or perhaps just for companionship and someone to throw spears with (and certainly, in the case of early man's angry youth, *at*).* Slowly but surely the dog became earth's first domesticated animal—and the one that enabled all those that followed.

The merging of human and wolf cultures was a mutually beneficial situation. The wolf-dogs got security and easy food; their new masters got help in tracking and killing game, as well as a loyal and fearsome assistant once other animals were domesticated and it became necessary to protect sheep and goats and cows from predators, including their recent ancestors, wolves.

As they got closer and closer to humans, these animals grew further and further from their wolf forebears as the combined effects of artificial and natural selection went to work. Humans would have recognized the friendlier animals from the beginning and would have bred them together, as well as those that displayed other desirable characteristics, such as hunting ability and loyalty. The early dogs in turn would

---

*There is a model for what this might have looked like; it's the relationship between aborigines and dingoes in Australia, first observed by the Norwegian explorer Carl Lumholtz in the late nineteenth century. Lumholtz observed that the aborigines treated these animals "with greater care than they bestow on their own children. The dingo is an important member of the family; it sleeps in the huts and gets plenty to eat, not only of meat but also of fruit. He caresses it like a child, eats the fleas off it, and then kisses it on the snout. When hunting, sometimes it refuses to go any further and its owner has then to carry it on his shoulders, a luxury of which it is very fond." Here, I guess, is a primitive version of the modern-day dog that rides in a stroller, a not-uncommon sight around New York City.

have begun shedding many of their natural characteristics that were no longer necessary in human company and taking on a different, more human-friendly appearance: shorter snouts, bigger eyes, multicolored coats (wolves are solid in color), floppy ears, and drooping tails.* This was magnified by human preferences—even in our spear-chucking days, we couldn't resist cuteness; the more adorable face was always going to win out over the homelier one.

The dog essentially became a wolf trapped in its juvenile stage. Scientists call this "neoteny," meaning that the wolf got stuck at the point at which it was cutest and most enthusiastic, traits that would be very useful in endearing a pup to its family. Once a wolf becomes sexually mature and no longer has to rely on its parents for survival, it also becomes an adult in appearance.† But because a dog will always rely on human love and care, it behooved the species never to stop being cute. In a sense, dogs are just wolf puppies, writ (mostly) large.

These changes took root in what Wayne calls the second phase of the dog's evolution—when the proto-dogs moved into the homes of humans who had begun to live in settlements. Here artificial selection takes over and "diversity takes root," he says; the dogs would have become "morphologically very divergent," with different sizes developing. Mostly these would have looked like the mongrelly "village dogs" you see in the Third World today—dogs that are no longer subject to selective breeding; in fact, when dogs become feral, they tend to gravitate toward this dingo-like appearance. (Case in point: dingoes!)

The German scientist Helmut Hemmer has suggested that the key

---

*In the case of these last two, the changes reflect the dog's devolution from the wolf—both pricked ears and upright tails are critical in wolf-to-wolf communication, but not so much in dog-to-human.

†Neoteny—nature's trick for getting adults to care for the helpless newborns. I'm not sure how to reconcile this very logical-seeming theory with birds, though, which in most cases are born far uglier than they'll be as adults. They look like dinosaurs until they fill out and grow feathers. Picture in your head a beautiful scarlet-and-yellow macaw or an African gray parrot. Now Google a chick of that species. Yikes, right? If human infants were similarly freakish, we'd live in a world of single mothers.

factor in wolf domestication was the suppression of the animal's *Merk-welt*, which roughly means "perceptual world." To quote an essay by the eminent British biologist Juliet Clutton-Brock on this very subject: "This means that, whereas a high degree of perception combined with quick reactions to stress are essential for the survival of an animal in the wild, the opposite characteristics of docility, lack of fear and toler-ance of stress are the requirements for domestication." This resulted also in a change of appearance in the animal, as well as reduction in the size of the brain, less acute sight and hearing, and the retention of juvenile characteristics and behavior into adult life.

In other words, it is the preservation of likable traits that unwilded the wolf.

T he selective breeding of dogs into specific types is an art at least four thousand years old, and—over what is a very short time in evolutionary terms—it has "resulted in the most morphologically di-verse species of mammal on the planet," according to the anthrozoolo-gist Hal Herzog. So diverse, in fact, that Charles Darwin of all people refused to accept that the species had a single forebear; he was sure that all wild canines played a part in the dog's creation.

What's most remarkable, though, is just how fast this tree is branch-ing.

Juliet Clutton-Brock has written that "most of the main breed types of dogs that exist today were well-defined" by the Roman period, but the key word there is "types" The Romans had mastifflike dogs for fighting and shepherdlike dogs for herding, as well as thin, fast dogs for hunting and even smaller house dogs, but they wouldn't have had the desire, nor the time, to craft the kind of remarkable divergence you see today.*

The majority of the four hundred or so breeds extant today were

---

*And the Middle Ages were a boom time for hunting dogs, because hunting was the best way to procure dinner—and distinct hounds bred for specific game appeared: deer-hounds, wolfhounds, otterhounds, and so on.

crafted by humans in the past two hundred years, and their work is nowhere near done. (Hybrids, such as Labradoodles, are further confusing matters.) But by far the most explosive period in dog diversity was the Victorian era, which UCLA's Robert Wayne calls the "Age of Novelty." He estimates that 70 to 80 percent of the modern breeds were born in this period of parasols and bowler hats.

Human meddling in dog genetics has led the canine family tree to branch in many, many weird and wonderful ways, to give us dogs with webbed feet that instinctually leap into water and save drowning humans and that have the strength to tow boats (the Newfoundland); dogs with warm, silky coats optimized to fit inside the sleeves of a Chinese nobleman's robes in the times before central heating (the Pekingese—which gave us the word "lapdog," by the way); and long, skinny, feisty dogs bred to burrow into holes and ferret out badgers (the dachshund, whose bold and dangerous purpose caused it to develop a temperament defined by its parent club as "courageous to the point of rashness" and explains why, if you give a dachshund a chew toy, he or she will almost certainly destroy it forthwith).

"Dogs range in size from a Chihuahua to a Saint Bernard, a 100-fold difference," wrote the retired professor Ray Coppinger, in *The Domestic Dog*. So extreme was our monkeying with the species, he notes, that an "adult Boston bulldog has a skull the shape of a newborn puppy and eyeballs the same size as an adult wolf. Its brain volume is that of a 12-week-old wolf puppy." But while the wolf pup "has its baby teeth, . . . the Boston bulldog has permanent adult teeth stuck into a puppy jaw."

One thing I've always wondered is which breed is closest to the wolf. Is there a modern-day rendition of the proto-dog? Based on appearance you might think this would be the husky or malamute—both of which look very much like gray wolves. Robert Wayne swiftly stomps on that opinion, warning that appearance isn't helpful in this regard. "You can't use modern-day phenotype to judge whether a breed is wolflike," he said. "It's mostly a human construct."

Certainly you could make a case for the basenji, an African breed that has never taken on two dog adaptations: Like a wolf, it does not bark. Also like a wolf, it has only one heat cycle per year* and can bear only a single litter in a year. I've also heard an argument for the Canaan dog, a herding breed originating in Israel that is really just a feral dog that was domesticated in the 1930s. Because these were essentially wild dogs interbreeding for thousands of years in the Middle East—which is now thought to be the birthplace of dogs—might these not be the closest we have to proto-dogs? This is still unclear.

A slightly easier question, however, is which breed is most different from the wolf. Not genetically, of course; they're all equally different (or, rather, similar) to wolves, but if we're going on aesthetics alone, a strong case could be made for the Pekingese, an ancient Chinese breed that in its dog-show coat looks like a Pac-Man ghost bred to angora goat, and its closest relative by appearance would seem to be Cousin Itt from *The Addams Family.* Juliet Clutton-Brock calls it "the most highly bred" example of a dog and says, "with its soft fur, large eyes and 'infantile' face," the breed "must represent ideal baby substitute and the complete antithesis of the wolf."

Not content to quit there, she goes on, "The development of the skull of the Pekingese from that of the wolf must rank as one of the most extraordinary examples known of morphological variation within a single biological species."

There you have it: Pekingese = antiwolf.

There are three principal ways that breeds can develop. The first is what Darwin called "sports," which was his confusing term for mutants that appear in a litter. Maybe it's a dog born with unusually short limbs. You then breed that to another short-limbed relative and within a few generations you have mostly (and then entirely) dogs with short legs. "That's the principle way that many fancy breeds came

---

*It is monoestrous, in scientist-speak.

into existence," explains Robert Wayne. To make themselves feel better about messing with nature, humans would attach functional significance after the fact. "Dachshunds, the folklore says, are bred to chase badgers down holes," Wayne says. "But actually the nature of the mutation restrained what the breed looked like." What he means is that because they had short legs, they were able to go into holes, not vice versa. But when we explain their appearance, we explain it backward—that is, they go into holes, and thus they are short-legged.

The second way you get a breed is by crossbreeding. You mate two distinct types—say, mastiff and dachshund—and the genes that cause the phenotypes you're looking for (toughness; or large, square heads; or short legs) begin to sort out, and you select the puppies that display them. You then breed the short-legged mastiffs back to regular mastiffs to transfer the genes, and through generations you start to see those dogs more and more. This crossbreeding followed by selection has, over time, moved certain phenotypes (stubby legs, barrel chests) "all across dogdom," says Wayne. The dog genome is so malleable that to transfer dwarfism, for instance, to a whole new part of the family tree takes only a few generations. It's the reason you now see merle coats, like Jack's, in so many breeds, and the trait has become so widespread that we don't yet know where it first appeared.

Method three is what's known as "idea-driven selection." We start with an idea of what we want—a variety of cattle with a low ratio of fat to meat, say—and over many generations select out the individuals in which this quality appears. "That's the one that Darwin chose as the analog for what happens in nature," says Wayne, and is the reason "we have miraculous cattle and high-yielding corn." But it doesn't happen with dogs very often, because it takes so long and such a large pool of animals. The only examples he can think of where this might be true in dogs, oddly enough, are with the herders, which may have been "progressively selected" over many, many years.

One place this was done with canines—though not dogs—was in Siberia, where the Soviet scientist Dmitri Belyaev began a fascinating experiment in the 1940s that continues to this day under the supervision of his successor, Lyudmila Trut. Belyaev wanted to observe domestication and artificial selection in progress and so started with a massive farm of silver foxes. Over many hundreds of generations, he selected out for docility; considering that these were wild animals, with a very active fight-or-flight instinct, in the early stages this was measured by "flight distance." This was not, as I first interpreted it, which foxes were fine with being picked up and stroked but rather how close Belyaev could get to a particular animal without it freaking out.[*]

The most docile foxes were bred together until, slowly but surely, aggression would fade. Belyaev's theory going in was that the key factor in domestication was that the least-most-afraid animals started the process, and he was right. He was able, over many years, to create a domesticated fox that would coexist happily with humans, and that's just half of what he found out there on the frozen tundra of far eastern Russia. As the foxes became tamer, they underwent the exact transformation that wolves did—their snouts shortened, their ears drooped, and their solid coats began to develop spots; in other words, they, too, began to freeze in adolescence. Some fox-dogs were even sold as pets.

That's all well and good, but where did Jack—as, one could argue, a Grecian ideal of the Australian shepherd—come from? Everyone in the Aussie community agrees that the dogs are not actually, despite their name, a product of Australia, but beyond that there's little agreement. What is likely is that the breed as we know it arose semi-organically on sheep ranches in the Midwest and West of the United States.

Part of the problem is one of nomenclature between the British Isles and the Americas. All (or nearly all) of the breeds extant in the Aussie's

---

[*]Because that would have provided him a pool of zero foxes to work with.

lineage are what would generally be called "collies," which in England simply means herding dogs and thus is synonymous with "shepherd dogs." The confusion lies in the definition of "collie" in America, where it has come to mean a long-snouted and silky-coated tan-and-white dog of the sort made famous by the TV character Lassie.* The "collie" you find in the AKC registry is exactly this.† It's this domination of the term that always confused me about border collies, which look far more like Australian shepherds than Lassie dogs. Now I understand—it's because of the terms' interchangeability in the UK.

The best guess of what happened is that a variety of shepherd dogs were working out west, interbreeding with whatever other herding dogs happened to be working nearby. The gene pool further diversified when dogs from the East began to arrive in the late nineteenth century along with reinforcement flocks meant to replace sheep that had originally arrived with the Spanish but became lunch during the Gold Rush and the Civil War. These dogs were lower and rangier and accompanied sheep that may have been imported from Australia. Which is one good guess as to how the name arose. Other shepherd dogs in the West originated in Spain—these were larger dogs—and since many shepherds were of Basque origins, there is a prevailing wisdom that Australian shepherds are more Spanish than anything. Blurring this distinction between countries is the fact that the dogs that did come from Australia were originally from Europe anyway; Basque herders, who followed the dwindling shepherd jobs around the world, took them to Australia and then from there to America.

In truth the breed is almost certainly all of the above. Americans living in the West generically called the dogs the British would refer to as collies "English shepherds," even though there was no such

---

*Who was actually first portrayed by a male dog named Pal, and later by several male heirs.

†Though it comes in both "rough" (or long-haired) and "smooth" (short-haired) varieties.

breed in England.* And because the newly arriving sheep had Australian provenance, it's quite possible the same naming logic applied to the dogs that came with them. As Linda Rorem wrote in an article about the breed's history that appeared in a 1987 issue of *Dog World* magazine: "People seeing sheep from Australia being unloaded at their destination may have noticed merle dogs accompanying the flocks. They then associated that color and general appearance with similar herding dogs in the area, irrespective of the actual background of individual dogs, calling such dogs in general 'Australian Shepherds.'"

Slowly but surely the name began to stick, and soon all these American stock dogs would be known as Australian shepherds. Rorem writes:

> Over time, references to the Australian Shepherd began to appear more often. An article about a shipwreck on the Oregon coast in 1881 relates that a half-grown Australian Shepherd pup was found alive on the beach near the bodies of the lost crew. An Australian Shepherd appeared in a dog show in Idaho in 1905. Lost and found ads mention, among others, a blue Australian Shepherd dog with one-half stub tail lost in Woodland, California in 1911 and a black and white Australian Shepherd pup lost in Reno, Nevada the same year. In the 1910s and 20s there are Australian Shepherds listed for sale in newspapers in California, Nevada, Montana, and even Alberta, Canada, with mentions of these kinds becoming more frequent as time went on. In the late 1920s and early 1930s an Australian Shepherd named Bunk appeared in movies with cowboy star Jack Hoxie, and was in some non-Westerns as well, such

---

*When breeders finally got together enough to start treating Aussies as an independent breed, the very first registry was in fact a subdirectory of the International English Shepherd Registry, or IESR. The first dog, Hart's Panda, entered in 1958.

as the 1928 versions of "Shepherd of the Hills" and "Little Shepherd of Kingdom Come."*

The reality is that it's impossible to reconstruct an exact history of the breed. Among the many surprises I found while doing my research is that specific breeds don't tend to have a succinct, annotated history; while many were very specifically engineered from a traceable set of ancestors, others—like the Aussie—just sort of happened by circumstance. The Australian shepherd isn't simply Australian, or English, or Spanish. It's all of the above. Though the very best answer is that it's American.

I t's due only to better record keeping that the history of the Australian shepherd begins to crystallize between the world wars. Prior to that, dogs that appear to be Aussies were doing their jobs— accompanying Basque herders tending to the sheep flocks of the West and then being adopted by American ranchers who admired their work ethic—all over the West. It didn't matter to his owner where a dog came from or who his sire was; it mattered only that he was good at his job. Very often you will find these dogs referred to as "little blue dogs" or "little blue bobtails," and it's pretty clear that the two defining physical characteristics of the Australian shepherd, as it developed organically, were a blue coat and bobbed tail. Which makes Jack, accidentally, a perfect exemplar for the breed's look.

The characteristic that led to the dog's becoming a formal breed, however, was its ability to "work" livestock—at first sheep, but also horses, cows, ducks, chickens, or any other animal a farmer might need to tend to, including his children.

That's how Ernest Hartnagle came to the breed. And no family has

---

*How's this for kismet: The earliest photograph of an Aussie-like dog I found was a 1904 picture of an "early bobtailed collie" named—you got it—Jack. (Jack Tailless, to be more accurate.)

had more influence over the Australian shepherd than the Hartnagles of Colorado.

After World War II, the family patriarch, whom most people call Ernie, was working on his uncle's ranch on the steep slopes of what is today the Vail Ski Resort. He had border collies and Aussies, and only the latter were consistently capable of driving the cattle from lower elevations to the rich summer pastures near the mountaintops, then back down again, in any conditions.

His first Aussie, acquired in 1953, was a female named Snipper, and Ernie was so thrilled with her that he began seeking out others like her, laying the groundwork for what is called the "foundation stock" of the breed as we know it today. Ernie selected dogs for working ability, and in the process selected for the traits that accompany that—genes being a messy and complicated business.

Ernie met and fell in love with Elaine Gibson, who just so happened to grow up among Aussies herself. Her godmother, Juanita Ely, according to *The Total Australian Shepherd,* a book Ernie wrote with his youngest daughter, Carol Ann, was a "salty ranch woman from Idaho" who got her first Aussie, Teddy, in 1928. Juanita began breeding and was one of the eight original members of what became known as the Australian Shepherd Club.

Colorado was the hub of breed activity, mostly because it was a center for American livestock. The Hartnagles' Las Rocosa kennel—which would become to the first kennel awarded Hall of Fame status by the Australian Shepherd Club of America—provided many of the foundation dogs you'll find in the Aussies of today. Other key contributors were the dogs of Jay Sisler, renowned rodeo star (more on him later) and Dr. Weldon T. Heard, a Denver veterinarian whose Flintridge line is all over the family trees of America's top Aussies.

Jeanne Joy Hartnagle, another of Ernie's daughters and probably the most recognized authority on breed history, told me that Heard's dogs were especially important in the lineage of Aussies that succeeded in the conformation show ring—especially his two foundation sires,

Fieldmaster and Dutchman, the latter of whom was the very first Champion of Record in the ASCA record books.

Whereas Ernie Hartnagle was in pursuit of the perfect herding dog, Dr. Heard was chasing a different sort of perfection, focused more on structure and appearance, that translated well into the conformation ring.

Heard's impact was huge. "Of all the foundation bloodlines," the Hartnagles write, "the Flintridge line exhibited the greatest influence on the modern Australian Shepherd."

If you were to pinpoint a birthday for the Australian shepherd breed, it would probably be May 5, 1957, when the Australian Shepherd Club of America was formed, in Tucson, Arizona, after, according to the Hartnagles' history, "a notice was posted that a meeting would be held for all who were interested in the Australian Shepherd." Prior to that date, owners and breeders had to traverse the country to participate in rare-breed shows, but ASCA's formation unified the dog's breeders and provided a network of shows at which they could compete against one another in search of titles and find better breeding stock.

In 1975 the Colorado affiliate club, led by Ernie Hartnagle—with the participation of his wife and five children—was appointed by ASCA to "draft a professionally written, concise breed standard in order to create more uniformity in type and standardize the breed." It was a long, contentious, and tedious process, partly because every breeder had strong opinions and was willing to argue them and partly because the methodology was as scientific as it could be. Starting with each affiliate club's ideas for what an Aussie "is," as well as the AKC guidelines for drafting a breed standard, the committee went out and recorded the size of Australian shepherds all over the country, finding that the majority fell into a bell curve between eighteen inches (for a female) and twenty-three inches (for a male). "That's how they decided the size," Jeanne Joy Hartnagle told me. "It wasn't arbitrary." Committee members also considered such important questions as "What is the function of the head?" Meaning, why is the head shaped the way it is? Each facet of the dog's structure was broken down and analyzed, then debated and honed.

Two years later, in 1977, the standard was approved in a majority vote by the club's members and the Australian shepherd as we know it today was born. The registry began with just a few dogs, but by 1989 there were fifty thousand entered.

Because the AKC has and will always be the gold standard for America's pedigreed dogs—an imprimatur of quality, deserved or not—ASCA's members sought inclusion in that club's stud book from a very early point. It just seemed that a breed wasn't really a breed until the AKC said it was.

Ernie Hartnagle wrote the first letter requesting admission to the AKC stud book in 1976, saying essentially, "Hi there. We're out here," and received a polite rejection. The reason was simple: There weren't enough dogs. Nowhere in the AKC bylaws is there a precise minimum, but apparently 1,518 weren't enough. ASCA tried again a few years later, when the registry was over 5,000 and was rejected (politely) again. In 1984, at a contentious meeting in Las Vegas, the members voted not to pursue recognition a third time, but according to Jo Kimes, ASCA's longtime executive secretary, the discussion continued, and it's very likely the group would have applied yet again and surely would have been accepted.

They weren't given the chance. In 1984, Kimes received a call late at night from the club's then-president, and when she growled at him for calling so late, he responded gravely, "We've lost the Aussie."

His choice of words may have been overly dramatic, but his news was shocking indeed. That a breakaway faction of ten ASCA members—calling themselves the United States Australian Shepherd Association (USASA)—had secretly prepared and applied for AKC membership separately from the club was upsetting enough; that they were accepted was gutting.

"The next thing we knew, the breed was AKC-recognized," Kimes says. Those ten members "wanted it very badly"—so badly that they weren't willing to wait for ASCA to back them. "For some reason they broke a hundred years of tradition," she said, solemnly. "They thought it was best for the Australian shepherd."

And just like that the breed's community, which was only a decade old to begin with, was suddenly and violently cleaved, never to reunite. It's not unprecedented for a breed to have more than one parent club, but it's unusual, and ASCA today is the largest single-breed registry in America. To this day ASCA and the AKC-affiliated parent clubs operate independently of one another. They run their own registries, and accreditations, and dog shows, and though some breeders, owners, and dogs participate in both, many don't.

"The remaining ASCA members "were very bitter, and rightfully so," explains Kimes. "Someone comes and takes your toy and doesn't ask you. They just take it and go." Times heals most wounds, of course, and the majority of Australian shepherd puppies born today are double-registered with both groups—as Jack and most of Kerry's dogs are—but resentment lingers. Some ASCA-allied kennels refuse to sell puppies without a promise that the new owner won't register with the AKC, while other, USASA kennels consider the rival outfit to represent a different, lesser version of the dog.

Kimes, who has two Aussies that work cattle on her South Texas ranch, says that a few years back she was in the process of buying a puppy from Slash V Kennels—an ASCA Hall of Fame Kennel known for its working dogs—and the proprietor, Terry Martin, asked her if she was planning to register the dog with AKC. "I said, 'Probably not,'" Kimes recalls. To which Martin replied, "That's not good enough."

Kimes was happy to comply.

"I love my dogs. But I also love my friends."

Of all the dogs under Heather and Kevin's care, only Jack represents a breed with two parent clubs and two competing sets of events. If he'd been raised by Kerry, who is herself an ASCA judge, he'd probably have shown mostly at ASCA events. But as long as he was with Heather, he'd be an AKC dog. And the reality is, AKC events, which don't match dogs only against others in their breed but against others in their groups, are a far bigger deal. Jack would be an AKC dog first, with perhaps the occasional dalliance in ASCA. And everyone seemed just fine with the arrangement.

CHAPTER TEN

York

The first requisite of his service is that he must be alive,

for little pleasure can be derived from a dead dog.

—MCDOWELL LYON, *The Dog in Action*

The weeks following Westminster make up one of the slower periods of the year. There's the inevitable hangover, whether or not you won, and, for a significant percentage of the dogs and owners who don't live close by, the sheer logistics (and expense) of traveling to New York for the show makes it a difficult week. Thus not a lot happens immediately in its wake.

Kimberly and Jack took a few weeks to relax. She helped her son, Taylor, weigh his college options and sort out the financial details of how they'd pay for the one he was leaning toward—a local branch of Penn State, which was just fine with Kimberly. Going there would allow him to live at home, cutting out a huge chunk of the cost, and would also, at least in theory, help to keep him out of trouble. "Most kids party the first year," she said. Living at home would complicate that at least a little.

The daughter of a close friend was staying with the Smiths, occupying the spare room and helping keep tabs on Taylor while also pitching in with the dogs. Her name is Megan and she had become Jack's designated running buddy—leading regular mile-long jogs around a local lake.

That was fortunate, because in Heather's estimation Jack was getting fat. "He could lose a pound or two," was one of the things she often said about Jack (and other client dogs), and sometimes she was even more blunt. "Your dog is fat," was how she put it to Kerry. When Kimberly heard this, she thought it funny, and she was not at all offended. In her view he wasn't fat, and depending on how you look at it, both of them were right. If, like Heather, your perspective is canine excellence, then every extra ribbon of loose skin mars the perfect presentation, even if that fat is largely invisible to the casual observer. If, like Kimberly, you *are* that casual observer, then Jack looked fine. One adjustment of ceding control to a handler is learning to adhere to the handler's dictates, even if you don't fully agree with them. For Kimberly that would take some getting used to.

Kimberly was also struggling with the economics of keeping Jack out on the circuit. With her regular bills—including boarding for a horse she was desperately trying to sell—and Taylor's college looming, there wasn't really enough disposable income left to pay Heather a full month's handling fee, which could approach two thousand dollars, not including entry fees and travel expenses. It wasn't yet a critical issue, fortunately, because Jack's early and unexpected success was enough motivation to keep Kerry's interest. For Kerry, who occasionally did this for owners of promising dogs, the hardship of coughing up an extra thousand dollars or so a month was outweighed by the possibility that a potentially great dog could be retired because his owner didn't have the financial wherewithal to keep him out on the circuit. So Jack's breeder and co-owner agreed to pay his fees at least temporarily, to allow Heather to show him for the entire month of March. After that, the two agreed, they would reassess.

The month's results, meanwhile, were keeping her riveted from afar. An unsuccessful weekend in Harrisburg—Jack was shut out both days—was quickly forgotten by a milestone moment in York, Pennsylvania, home turf to Tanner and Dawn, who sits on the board of the local kennel club.

York was a five-day cluster, and the first days of those tend to have significantly smaller entries, so Kimberly's expectations, which waver from high to low with great frequency anyway, tended to be higher then. At work she sat and stewed, an anxious owner on pins and needles wishing she could be there and wanting at the least to know how her dog was doing at a fairground less than an hour's drive away.

It was frustrating to Kimberly that Heather and Kevin didn't have time to stay in better touch, and she'd been wishing they'd implement a more immediate notification system, say, a method of sending out short texts or e-mails throughout the day for anxious owners. But due to the logistics of Heather's workday, which rarely even allows time for eating (not that she would eat anyway), she has made it a policy to make all the calls to owners at once, at the end of the day. There were no exceptions, and from a business standpoint this makes sense: Return one call or text and you have to return them all.

For an owner who couldn't attend the show, however, this was excruciating, and Kimberly would fixate on the slow-moving clock hands, wondering how Jack was doing and checking in regularly with Facebook, where owners attending the show would often post results out of pride—or disgust. (Kimberly often provided this service herself.)

On Wednesday, the first day of the York cluster, Heather finally called at 8:00 P.M., and the news wasn't great. "We didn't win," she told Kimberly, who sank down into her couch. Jack had shown well, Heather said, but faced stiff competition, including a nice-looking dog she hadn't seen before—a blue merle named Bentley handled by the respected professional Jessica Plourde. Heather reported that he had a look similar to Jack's, though in her opinion he was a bit less "pretty." But she noted that Plourde is known for handing Aussies (in the way that Heather is known for Berners), and once a handler has a reputation within a certain breed (or breeds), judges tend to pay her an extra measure of respect, in the form of an extra-long look or a touch more forgiveness for a miscue. (Because, the logic goes, a specialist knows a quality dog.)

Bentley won the breed and also took first in the Herding Group. And then won again on Thursday.

But Kimberly learned from Facebook that Plourde wasn't entered for the weekend, and this lifted her spirits.

Kimberly took Friday off and headed out for York but got caught up in traffic caused by an accident, which meant she was barely going to make it for Jack's ring time. It definitely wouldn't allow her to greet him, and they'd been apart for three days. Sure enough, Heather asked her to stay away. "He's been a real handful," she told Kimberly, adding that despite the fact that he'd been showing well in the ring, it was requiring extra diligence on her part to focus him. Under these conditions a celebratory romp with his owner was out of the question.

The problem was, Kimberly missed her dog. She hadn't seen Jack in four days and then arrived to learn she would have to wait at least another couple hours. She stalked the room carefully to locate the Aussie ring without being seen by Jack and found a hiding place with a semiobstructed view. From there she saw a huge field of nineteen good dogs, and her low expectations lowered further when she spied Jessica and Bentley, who hadn't left after all. Facebook had been wrong.

Kimberly's deflated feeling quickly subsided, however, as Jack turned on his sparkle and won the breed easily, at least if the swiftness and confidence of the judge's decision was any indication. Heather, having a date with Tanner at the Bernese specialty being held in the building next door, hustled quickly out of the ring and, spying Kimberly in the crowd, waved her off as she rushed Jack back to his kennel. Only then did she walk back and explain what was happening. "I know you want to see him," she said. "He was really good. Such an improvement! But I don't want you to see him until after group."

It was 10:30 A.M. And the groups wouldn't begin until 2:30 or 3:30, meaning that Kimberly had four to six hours "to hang around the show and not see my dog." Despite the fact that she was sure he knew she was there, because "he's got such a keen sense of smell. But Heather's Heather, and she's the boss when it comes to this."

The hours crept by, and Kimberly passed the time by perusing vendors, downing Diet Pepsi after Diet Pepsi, and chatting with the occasional acquaintance, and then she carefully sneaked back to the ring to find a place where she could watch the group with no danger of being spotted by her dog.

The Herding Group was to be judged by a European judge about whom Heather knew nothing. With familiar judges, professional handlers often have a good sense of their chances, but with this wild card, Heather said, "I have no idea." What's more, European judges are known for making unconventional choices, as they are largely uncolored by the influence of advertising or any prior knowledge of a particular dog's reputation.

And from Kimberly's secret vantage point, his actions indeed seemed a little unorthodox. Her position afforded her a good view of the down-and-back and from her spot she could see very clearly that this judge was barely watching most of the dogs. He seemed more interested in judging the spectators. But she did notice that he "seemed to definitely be looking at Jack. And someone commented that he seemed to like Heather."

The judge concluded the movement portion and then asked the handlers to stack the dogs. He walked the line once, briskly, and pointed first at Jack, pulling him out. Kimberly wasn't sure if this meant he was the group winner or merely the first dog in a first cut from which the judge would further winnow. It was the former, and Jack leaped up on Heather as the judge raised an index finger to indicate that he had been given his first-ever Group 1 over several nationally ranked herding dogs. Kimberly yelled and nearly hugged the strange woman she'd been hiding behind. She was ecstatic. The joy wasn't quite Westminster level, but it was pretty close.

The group broke up, and Kimberly headed to meet her dog and handler, but once again Heather—who at this point was basically sprinting back and forth between buildings, so that both Tanner and Jack were attended to—whizzed past with her hand up, and a tight hold on Jack's lead. Kimberly still needed to stay away—and there were still four groups to go before Jack got his chance at Best in Show. It would be at least six o'clock before Kimberly could actually greet her beloved dog.

Granted, circumstances provided a nice salve, even though he didn't win the big event. "Seeing how things played out at Westminster was exciting," she explained later. "Watching that judge go back and forth between Jack and Rowan. That was a highlight for me, because it's so prestigious. But he gets nothing for rankings." What she means is that an Award of Merit at Westminster is great but provides no points. The Group 1 at York, on the other hand, would be a massive boost to his all-breed ranking, even though he didn't win Best in Show. The two Group 4s at Wildwood, after all, had catapulted him toward the top twenty, and winning the Herding Group at a show as large as York would add several hundred points to his total. It might be enough to crack the rankings for the first time.

Kimberly was very much a newbie in the Australian shepherd community, having no history in a breed that is rich in owners who've been at it for years, and the fact that she showed up out of nowhere with a dog who immediately started winning made her very cautious of gloating too openly. No matter how excited she might feel after a win, she was treading very lightly. "I don't want to seem boastful," she told me. "I don't want to be hated." Thus, after York she was proceeding carefully. She went out of her way to congratulate all the dogs in a Facebook post she wrote after getting home. In return she received many kudos in the comments.

When he finally got home on Sunday night, Jack trudged in the door, had a drink of water, walked to a corner—which wasn't his usual sleeping spot—lay on a heating vent, and crashed.

· · ·

I suppose you could dismiss Westminster as a fluke—or, as I did, as a good omen of things to come—but Jack's success in York was the first sign that he'd officially crossed the line from unknown to contender-on-the-rise, and it would explain why Kimberly was exhibiting some hesitation for the first time when it came to bragging more openly about his exploits. There's a fine line among show people between friend and foe, and an owner is constantly tiptoeing along it. The hive mentality that brings together owners who are all emotionally and financially invested in this somewhat arbitrary pursuit (and thus irrationally inclined to overreact) coalesces around the reality that most dogs out there lose far more than they win. And you take consolation in other losers who share your disappointment and tend to feel better about losing when you can blame that losing on something, or someone, else. Especially a dog and owner who win.

Kimberly obviously wanted to win, but she also wanted to be liked; she genuinely appreciated the camaraderie she'd found in shows and the kindness of other, more experienced owners who shared advice and supplies and even hotel rooms. Unlike the smug owner who'd invested tens of thousands in crafting a top dog, Kimberly mostly got lucky that she happened to stumble upon and fall in love with the right random puppy online, so it was going to be a difficult balance for her to push Jack forward while maintaining her place in the larger community of average owners.

On March 23 she sent me the following e-mail.

> Hey!!! Check this out. Jack is on the top 20 All Breed list. He's number 20, but he's on the list!!!! Hopefully our Group 1 last weekend helps us move up! We aren't on the Breed rankings yet but if my calculations are right we would have had 40 points as of Feb 28th. Friday entries were 19 and Sunday was 30. Cross our fingers that we hit the Breed Top 20.

The distinction between the two rankings is this: The top-twenty breed ranking is based purely on the number of Australian shepherds defeated. Each time Jack is named Best of Breed, he gets one point for every dog entered that day (nineteen on Friday, for instance, and thirty on Sunday). All-breed rankings, on the other hand, factor in group wins and placements. If a dog wins a group, as Jack did for the first time in York, he gets a point for every herding dog defeated—if there were twelve collies, say, he gets twelve points, and so on for all the herding breeds entered. A single group win, or placement (because if a dog is given a Group 4, he gets all the herding dogs, minus the three that beat him), carries great weight and can shoot an Aussie up the all-breed ranking, but to build breed points you need to consistently win Best of Breed.

Kimberly provided a link to the rankings in the *Canine Chronicle*, the monthly magazine that prints them and also keeps them updated online, and there he was, at number twenty, Ch Wyndstar's Honorable Mention. (Beyoncé was solidly entrenched at number one.) The dog at number twenty in the breed rankings was the Westminster Winner, Ch Copperridges's Fire N Bayouland (aka Rowan), and at seventeen I noticed a familiar name: Ch Heatherhill Shock N Awe (aka Shocka), the Crufts winner we met at Wildwood.

I wrote back, "Wow, he's nationally ranked! I bet you never expected that when you bought a puppy from a stranger in California."

I received her response a few seconds later. "He's done a lot of things I never expected," she wrote. "I love that boy!!!"

CHAPTER ELEVEN

Pardon Me While I Fondle Your Dog's Testicles:

Show-Dog Judging Explained

Perfection in a dog doesn't exist. We can—and should—
strive for ideal structure, but every dog will have some
flaws. That's life.

—PAT HASTINGS

What is a perfect Australian shepherd anyway? As with any breed, this question has a very specific answer: the "breed standard," crafted and lorded over by each breed's parent club. A breed standard is somewhat fluid and changes over time, sometimes dramatically in the case of newer and less common breeds, over which a few determined breeders wield tremendous influence.

The Australian shepherd would be considered a midsize dog. Its general appearance, according to its standard,* "is well balanced,

---

*To simplify matters I'm quoting from the AKC standard, drafted by USASA. ASCA has

slightly longer than tall, of medium size and bone, with coloring that offers variety and individuality." Unlike the standards for many of the fussier looking breeds, which focus largely on physical characteristics, the Aussie's official definition is as much about its personality and agility. "He is attentive and animated, lithe and agile, solid and muscular without cloddiness. He has a coat of moderate length and coarseness."

Among the many (many) traits a great Australian shepherd must have is compact, oval feet "with close-knit, well-arched toes," "well-sprung" ribs neither "barrel-chested nor slab sided," and coloration that can vary, within reason: "White on the head should not predominate, and the eyes must be fully surrounded by color and pigment." (We know why this is.) He has a "smooth, free and easy gait" and "should be able to change direction or alter gait instantly."

Trust me when I say that this barely scratches the surface of the great specificity with which a human is supposed to judge an Australian shepherd dog during conformation. To watch this process, however, is to be wholeheartedly confused; it's mind-boggling to look at a ring holding, say, twenty Aussies (or, in the case of Westminster, forty-five!) and even begin to comprehend selecting out the finest specimen.

Nonetheless, that's what the judge must do.

What's clear is that judges work hard to earn this right. For a start, a prospective judge should already be a dog-show person—a breeder, owner, or handler who has a vise-grip lock on the specificities of at least one, if not several breeds. The prerequisites for judging vary by country and change frequently, but the current criterion in the United States is that a prospective judge must have "been involved in dogs" for at least twelve years and "bred at least five litters that resulted in at least four champions." Beyond that he should be an expert in a particular breed in order to be approved to judge it, and once approved for two breeds a prospective judge can apply for two more. The maximum number

its own standard, and while it is largely identical in content, the wording differs slightly. I'm not quoting AKC here because it's more accurate but because Jack showed more often at AKC shows.

of breeds a first-time applicant can apply to judge is fourteen. To make it worthwhile for a judge (and the kennel club paying his/her way) to travel to a show, it makes sense for judges to be as well rounded as possible. The best judges can assess toy poodles and miniature pinschers one day and Great Danes and bullmastiffs the next.

If today's prospective judges should ever feel overburdened by the road to certification, they should consider William Lort's path to the profession. It's always unfair to compare your autobiography to one from the nineteenth century, when anyone who merited notice from historians seemed to lead a life worthy of a motion picture, but Lort's story is a standout even in that context. A father of twelve children, the British-born Lort was a surgeon by profession, but like so many young men he decided to take a backpacking trip to first sow some wild oats and headed off for the then-extremely-wild Rocky Mountains of the United States, where "with only his knife and gun he lived off the land with the fur traders." After making some "important geological discoveries," he was named an Associate of the House by the U.S. Congress, and then it was off to South America and then Canada, where he dabbled in whale hunting. On one particularly turbulent voyage, he jumped ship during a storm to rescue the captain from drowning, then took command and sailed the damaged vessel safely through the storm. He later became a champion swimmer and in his retirement explored the Arctic. In between he joined England's Kennel Club, created the stud book for pointers and setters, and was one of the first breeders of Irish setters and field spaniels. He would not have been a boring dinner companion. Lort was not necessarily the first conformation judge, but he was one of the first to gain notice. According to Ann Hier, author of the excellent compilation *Dog Shows, Then and Now,* he was "a compelling force who successfully established the authority of the dog show adjudicator." In an age before written standards existed, he judged the dogs "at a glance." Bully on you, Lort, old boy.

Today there are more than three thousand AKC-approved judges, and most of them can judge numerous breeds. It should go without saying that you can't start judging the group competition at AKC shows until you're certified to judge all the breeds in that group (otherwise how can you possibly judge a giant schnauzer against a bulldog?). But once you can judge one group, you can judge Best in Show—the thinking being that by this point every dog has passed two rounds of judges and is so good that there is no wrong choice. "We always joke, how hard is it to judge Best in Show?" Westminster's David Frei told me. "Close your eyes and point—you're going to hit a great dog."

At the very top are the all-arounders. Less than 1 percent of the three thousand–plus AKC judges around the world are jacks-of-all-trades, eligible to judge every breed.

Simply put, a judge is looking for the dog that best approximates a perfect specimen as laid out in the breed standard and measured in any number of ways. A dog that is known to be a good representation of the standard is said to be "typey," because "type" is what makes an Aussie truly an Aussie. As the dog writer Tom Horner once wrote, "Type is the sum of those points that make a dog look like its own breed and no other." (There is such a thing, however, as being too typey. This would mean generically attractive in an entirely uninteresting way; to use an apt but extremely dated analogy, it is like Richard Grieco as compared to Johnny Depp.)[*]

In analyzing the "structure" of a dog, the judge is assessing it as something between a fashion model and an architectural installation. Several unfamiliar terms come from horses: "withers," for instance, is the term for the high point of the back, after the neck, and is the point from which height (to floor) is measured. Other terms are more familiar and make the poor animal seem like a side of beef; they are terms shared, in fact, with actual sides of beef sliced apart by butchers: Brisket, flank, and hock are all terms used in show judging.

---

[*]As opposed to Luke Perry and Jason Priestley, both of whom are too typey.

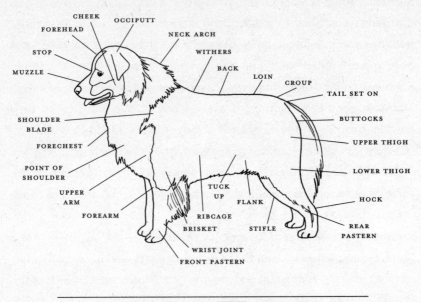

ANNOTATED ILLUSTRATION OF

A DOG'S STRUCTURE

One thing working in judges' favor is that all breeds have roughly the same number of bones—between 319 and 321,[*] depending on the length of the tail (or, in the case of Aussies, a dog that's either docked or naturally tailless). That simplifies things a little. Good judges also hone this "eye" over time, first in the breeds they know best and then slowly in other breeds the more they study and judge them, so that they can survey a row of stacked dogs and immediately rule out or focus on certain specimens. This is a difficult thing to imagine for those of us who haven't spent a lifetime obsessing about canine perfection, but the general idea isn't so hard to grasp; it is the ineffable sense that all humans feel when something just looks right—or wrong.

---

*Humans, in comparison, have only 206.

Pat Hastings is one of the most familiar names in dog showing. She is a former professional handler who began showing dogs in 1959 and is today an accomplished judge. Though she had no recollection of him when I spoke to her by phone, it so happens that she judged Jack in his first show as a finished champion, way back in Lackawanna, when he was basically a rookie. Hastings chastised Kimberly, who had impulsively chosen to handle him that day because of a conflict in Heather's schedule, for putting too much product in his hair, but she still pulled him out as one of the two best dogs, giving him a hard look despite Kimberly's faux pas before making him runner-up, as Best of Opposite, to the bitch that Hastings had selected as Best of Breed. That bitch was a finished champion with a professional handler.

Hastings, who resides in Washington State, is somewhat unique among judges in that she makes her full-time living in dogs. Most are either gainfully employed or retired. But Hastings, who retired from a career as a professional handler after her husband and handling partner, Bob, died in 2002, writes for magazines, sells books, evaluates litters of puppies, and travels around giving seminars about breeding, handling, and judging—these travels in turn increase her exposure and facilitate far-flung judging assignments.

Currently she is approved to judge "almost four groups"—Working, Herding, and Non-Sporting—plus "twenty-two of the twenty-seven terriers." And she admits what seems obvious: "There is absolutely no way in the world anyone could memorize all standards." A good judge, then, just has "an idea in mind of what this breed should look like—its proportions and angles and head." Foremost, she says, a judge should be able to recognize a breed by its head and silhouette. "If it was behind a fence and all you can see is the head, can you identify it? And if it's on a hill, with the sun behind it? That's where I start."

It is absurd to expect judges to suppress their own tastes. Preferences are clearly an influence. "It shouldn't have an effect, but get real," says Hastings. "Judging is one hundred percent relative."

To Hastings the most important thing is that the judge look at the breed standard "as a blueprint that allows that breed to do the job it was bred for. That's what it was written for." She thinks it's crucial for a good judge to go and watch "these dogs doing when they're meant to do." In the case of Aussies, watch them herd. "But all standards are open to interpretation. Plus, everybody uses one side of the brain more than the other. If you're analytical, you're more influenced by structure and motion; if you're an emotional, artistic type, you're much more influenced by cute and pretty and hair and face, and you are who you are. Which is why a dog can go Best in Show one day and get beat in breed the next."

As I heard Helen Lee Jones, an AKC judge whose background is in poodles and dalmatians, explain it, "Every breed standard is determined by the function of that dog and calls for very specific characteristics." To use an example of a breed that outsiders sometimes confuse with the Aussie, a border collie moves in a crouched position that looks a little sneaky, but if an Aussie were to move that way, he'd be judged as shy or tentative—either of which would be a major problem in that dog's ability to do its job.

Likewise, the Aussie is slightly longer than tall, befitting its agile nature. By contrast, a Doberman pinscher is a square breed—a sound one has the same length from chest to rump (or, rather, from forechest to buttocks) as from the withers to the ground. Most breed standards keep these things at least a little vague and general, but in some standards the authors have spelled out distances exactly. A good example is the golden retriever. The America's Sweetheart of dogs according to its AKC breed standard, is "measured from the breastbone to the point of the buttocks is slightly greater than the height at the withers in a ratio of 12:11."

Tails vary greatly and have purposes that can be generalized. If you know that a breed is supposed to work in water, its tail serves as a rudder, so a water dog that holds its tail upright is going to lack that rudder and be a less good swimmer for it.

Once a judge has eyeballed a dog and employed whatever personal tricks are helpful for assessing certain elements—say, using the thumb and index finger in the "I crush your head" position to approximate a particular distance—he next must "put his hands on the dog." Something you inevitably hear when people are talking about how a new, exciting dog looks is, "Did you put your hands on him?" There are several reasons for this. For one thing, hair gets in the way. On coated breeds it's very difficult to assess a dog's chest by sight, and many breeds— Aussies, for instance—emphasize chest size in a major way because a shallow chest would inhibit heart and lung capacity. An Australian shepherd with a chest that stopped above the elbows, for instance, could never do its job.

The two most intimate parts of the exam are the inspection of the teeth and, in the case of male dogs, the testicles. Most breeds have very specific requirements for teeth, as well as the depth of the jaw and the way the jaw fits into the neck. Testicles are gently squeezed for a very simple reason: A dog with one nut or none can't breed, and breeding is the whole point.

Once all the visual and tactile information has been downloaded, the judge turns to movement. Which, Helen Lee Jones says, is meant to answer this question: "Did your evaluation and the information it gave you really fit with the way that dog moves?" And if you're still not sure, she says, "move it again and find out."

An honest judge knows he can't be perfect—and, more than that, that no dog is either. Ed Bivins, a veteran Best in Show judge, described judging as "an articulation process," meaning that a judge should "elevate those things about which you feel most positive. You take the dog that possesses the greater number of positive characteristics to the higher degree and elevate him to the first position."

Despite the fact that conformation shows were created to help single out those dogs most capable of functioning properly— doing their "jobs"—a constant and underlying tension has arisen between showing and working. True working-dog enthusiasts, those who breed and own dogs specifically to perform jobs, think that the nature of judging dogs in the ring creates a beauty pageant, even though it's not supposed to. People are people, and they are drawn to what's most attractive, even it's not correct to the ideal of the standard. In the case of the Aussie, this tension is most apparent in the matter of movement.

We know that the Australian shepherd is a "movement breed"—it is the dog's mantra (or one of them)—and that means that how a dog moves is paramount over how it looks. But it's actually more complicated than that.

A major bugaboo for the Hartnagles—a family that literally wrote the book(s) as well as the standard on the breed—is that the way the Aussie's movement is judged in the ring isn't even proper. Show dogs are bred for "reach" and judged in what is called a "two-beat trot," an easy, effortless-looking run that is smooth and flow-y and pretty to look at. The correct terminology for this movement is "at the trot," a phrase that never stops sounding awkward.

To create the flowing trot movement, breeders strive for a structure that includes what Jeanne Joy Hartnagle (using the lingo coined by her father, borrowing from the automotive industry) calls the "trotting drivetrain." The particulars of this involve angles I never fully understood, but the point, Jeanne Joy says, is that "dogs with this trotting drivetrain—show dogs—take a half-stride more to get into a gallop."

Now, that would seem to be the very definition of nit-picking but consider that a true working Aussie jogs, sprints, jumps, and makes quick cuts over varied terrain in close proximity to hooves and horns and a half-step could be the difference between a corralled sheep and an escapee, or worse—a hoof to the head or one that is dodged. "That really is a huge, huge difference," she told me. "A lot of people showing don't understand that."

Hartnagle pointed out that a working Australian shepherd should instead have "a sprinting drivetrain." The fault, she says, comes from McDowell Lyon, author of the 1950 movement and structure bible "The Dog in Action." Lyon, whose book is still revered, strongly "believed that a dog with a long-striding trot could work all day long." He thought this was the most efficient movement.

"Herding dogs are different," Hartnagle explains. They have to follow stock—and a single dog can be responsible for 2,000 head of sheep. A dog needs to round-up, gather, settle, and then direct those sheep wherever they're needed and to do this requires a variety of movements. "Sometimes trotting, sometimes walking," Hartnagle says. "If something breaks away the dog has to be able to sprint and turn on a dime, chase them through arroyos. That dog has to be able to change gaits"—and the most effective way to do that is to have "a sprinting structure. But in show ring it's free-flowing trot, which is pleasing to the eye."

If technical detail helps you picture this, Jeanne Joy Hartnagle explains that "the greater angulation of the trotting drivetrain produces fewer strides per 100 feet than the sprinting drivetrain does at the same gait." Why? "Because the trotting dog spends more time in the air due to his longer stride which produces a slower reaction time. The sprinter, with his shorter stride, is more agile."

The sum total of misunderstanding this has changed the breed, she said. "Now you see Australian shepherds that don't move anything at all like the original dogs."

By the time I finished chatting with Jeanne Joy Hartnagle I was more convinced than ever that the job of judge is not only impossibly subjective, it's nearly impossible to do correctly. Which, I think, is why the people who've been exhibiting dogs the longest are the least fazed by the ups and downs and seemingly inexplicable wins and losses.

CHAPTER TWELVE

Edison

The five-second rule does not apply at dog shows.

—DAWN COX, AFTER SOMEONE DROPPED A DORITO ON THE FLOOR AT
EDISON AND FOR A SECOND CONSIDERED EATING IT

For the final weekend of March, Heather and Kevin's carnival decamped for Edison, New Jersey, home of the New Jersey Exposition Center. In the pantheon of depressing convention centers, the Expo Center is certainly formidable. Located several miles into a complex consisting exclusively of industrial and office-park buildings, it looks like the fulfillment center for curtain rods or terra-cotta pots or any other anodyne product you might purchase from QVC, and it's tucked among other buildings even less aesthetically appealing, if that's possible.

On the inside . . . well, it still looks like a fulfillment center—one that pulled up stakes and left in the middle of the night. The NJEC has concrete floors, concrete walls, and an industrial ceiling of exposed beams and ducts painted black. On this particular occasion, it also smelled like shit, literally. But that wasn't the building's fault. It was the work of 2,069 dogs in 154 breeds, plus 4 entered in the Miscellaneous category, a catchall for provisional breeds not yet officially accepted by the AKC.

I found Kimberly outside Ring 5, where Jack would soon show, and she was fretting. "I'm having handler issues," she stage-whispered. "We need to talk later."

It was a typically large group of Aussies, numbering twenty-three, including Striker, the red merle who was becoming a consistent winner himself, and a young black tri female named Aster, who had beaten Jack in a Herding Dog specialty show held the night before and would turn out to be a top-five dog by year's end. "She's a real nice bitch," Kimberly said. "I would breed Jack to her, and I'm picky."

As was often the case, Aussies made up one of biggest entries in the show, trailing only goldens and Rhodies. To give some sense of how dramatically you can skew your odds by simple breed choice, consider the four breeds showing in the ring after the Aussies: Pyrenees shepherds, Norwegian buhunds, Beaucerons, and the Xoloitzcuintli,[*] a bizarre, hairless Mexican breed that had only provisional status with the AKC.[†]

At Edison there was just a single dog entered in each of these four breeds, meaning that unless these dogs were to show up lame, or fall asleep, or maul the judge, they were guaranteed passage into the Herding Group. To do the same, Jack would have to beat twenty-two dogs. The flip side is that your Beauceron better be some kind of specimen to even merit consideration for group placement.

---

[*]The Xoloitzcuintli (CHO-lo-eeks-QUEENT-ly), or Xolo, is often referred to as the Mexican hairless dog because it is both of those things. The dogs date back at least thirty-five hundred years in the Americas and are one of the few breeds thought to have evolved naturally, without the meddling of humans. They were considered sacred by the Aztecs, a fact that didn't stop some of them from seeing Xolos as a food source. If you were to compile a list of dogs best suited for neurotics and germophobes, the Xolo would top the list: It doesn't shed or produce dander and, because it has no hair, is impervious to fleas. The downside is that it will almost certainly frighten children.

[†]In 2011 it was to be officially accepted by the AKC, however, completing a remarkable comeback, because the Xolo was the first and only breed ever dropped from the stud book, in 1959.

XOLO

Like many of the best all-breed handlers, who find themselves in demand precisely because they are among the best, Heather and Kevin were always scrambling from ring to ring, handing off one dog so that they could dash to show another. And in Edison the schedule wasn't looking good for Jack. "I think there's a conflict," Kimberly said coldly, meaning that Heather might not make it in time and had dispatched Kevin to take Jack just in case. The thing was, if delays were to arise, Kevin would have a conflict himself, and if that were to happen, Kimberly would either have to show Jack herself or recruit another handler to take him as a favor.

The only way for her to ensure Heather as handler was to sign on for a full-year contract, which would put Jack just behind Tanner on Heather's depth chart, but considering the realities of her finances, that wasn't actually an option. If Kimberly wanted Heather to handle Jack, stress and worry were going to be part of the package. Her choices were either to deal with that or not.

These were the sorts of thoughts bouncing around her head when, at the eleventh hour, Heather came fast-walking down the aisle between rings, wearing a melon-colored suit that (sort of) matched Kevin's orange tie—there seemed to be no limit to the colors in their complementary wardrobes—grabbed the reins from him, and prepared to take Jack in front of a stern-looking woman with white hair, wearing a brown suit and kerchief.

Jack, having passed from one boss to another and, in Kimberly's view, not spending enough time at ringside getting his game face on, looked a little antsy out there. As the dogs and handlers trotted around the ring, he was fidgety and pulling in close to Heather's legs so that he was practically head-butting her knee. "He's a noodge," Kimberly said. "She hates when he does that."

As the Aussies free-stacked, Heather tore a chunk from the limp hot dog strapped to her arm with a rubber band and dangled it in front of Jack's nose. Considering that he isn't a dog who needs food to be focused, the act was telling. She was concerned with his concentration. Once in place, however, he didn't budge. And by the time the judge arrived at his side, the nervousness was gone. He looked attentive.

After the judge moved on, Heather motioned for a tissue. "I don't know if it's for his mouth, his butt, or her nose," Kimberly said, and then Heather took the tissue and blew her nose and the mystery was solved.

Jack looked good, but the judge picked Striker, who to my eye looked a little bulky.

"I thought he showed great," Kimberly said to Heather, who agreed.

"You did good, Jack," she said, and leaned in for a kiss that was enthusiastically delivered.

"Now he just needs to start winning," Kimberly said.

Elsewhere, Kevin was out at Ring 6 with Tico, a Tibetan terrier. Sometimes called "the Holy Dog of Tibet," the Tibetan terrier was bred to work in tandem with the gigantic Tibetan mastiffs, and if the two breeds were to star in a buddy cop movie, it would play the role of the comedian and would probably be voiced by Chris Tucker. Basically its job was to be alert and bark, something it does well; that bark served as a signal to the mastiffs, which are bigger and lazier and prefer to lie around sleeping until there's a person to attack rather than patrol and look for problems on their own. Once the terrier barked, the mastiff would awake, yawn, and take care of business, while the terrier backed off and watched safely out of range of ninja swords.

Tico was a semiregular of Kevin's. He wasn't on a monthly plan, but I'd seen him around quite a bit lately. This afternoon he stood vigilant near the table at Ring 6, home to one of my favorite new dog-show regulars: the Candy Lady. The Candy Lady is Dottie Davis, an elderly woman with a warm and pleasant visage who serves as a ring steward, meaning she keeps order for the judge, calling out entries and breed types from a sheet of paper with the help of a pair of glasses that dangle from a chain around her neck.

"Everyone loves Dottie," Kevin said. "She loves dogs and shows and has been in dogs for like fifty years."

And her candy is for anyone?

"For exhibitors only," he said, and grabbed a piece. "But you can have some."

One thing the Candy Lady does not offer is dog treats. There were plenty elsewhere in the room, though—for instance, in the pocket of every handler in the house—but the real mother lode of dog treats was found at a kiosk known as Best Puppies on Earth. BPOE is a one-stop shop for dog goods. It has chains and leads and bowls and beds and rugs and a diverse inventory of clothing that includes your standard raincoats and sweaters but also tutus and prom dresses (mostly in pink) with feathers and satin and sequins. There are infant-style onesies, quilted sleepers, vests, and camo jackets. (And all the most outrageous stuff seems to be made by Cha-Cha Couture, a brand whose slogan is hardly a match for its goods: "Fashion & Beds for Pets.")

BPOE has a human-high wall of baskets and bins filled with animal parts dried for canine consumption: duck trachea (which looks like a ribbed straw and comes three for $1.00), duck feet (also three for $1.00), elk bones ($6.00, or two for $11.00), beef kneecaps ($2.00), pig ears ($1.50), smoked hoofs ($1.25, and isn't it "hooves"?), bacon-wrapped beef ribs ($3.00), beef knuckle bone: ($5.00), Achilles tendons (species not specified, $3.00), buffalo knuckles (appropriately gigantic, $5.00), and pork jerky bone ($3.50). It would be a disservice to the show's canine-general-store competitor White Dog Bone to suggest that BPOE's treat wall is any larger or more thorough. It is not. The only difference as far as I can tell is that White Dog Bone uses slightly cutesier nomenclature—for example, Porky Bone ($2.25) and Meaty Knuckle ($3.50). The alpha treat at WDB is the fourteen-inch Monster Femur (from a cow), which costs $9.00 and looks like something you'd find on Fred Flintstone's plate at the dinosaur steakhouse.

One major event was about to affect the team. Dawn and Georgeann had decided to send Tanner off to Europe, to spend the summer breeding with top Bernese mountain dogs on the Continent as well as to compete for championships in various countries under the care and handling of a Norwegian friend. His summer would culminate with an appearance at the World Dog Show, to be held in Copenhagen in August. I was going to miss the old galoot, who was relentlessly happy and utterly dominant in his breed ring despite the fact that he mostly looked like he was just out for a stroll. But I wouldn't miss him as much as Heather, who'd be losing her favorite dog.

Heather and Kevin wouldn't be lacking Berners in Tanner's absence. Georgeann had contracted to keep a dog out all year, and Dawn was experimenting with one or two of her own, including Echo, a giant young male who was very sweet but also quite dumb and had become the house outcast. Everyone in her house, Dawn said, hated him. "My husband says, 'Tanner is number one. Echo is number zero.' The other day he came in with this sad face and he reeked of cat pee," she told me. "I said, 'Echo what did you do?' And he just has this look—it turns out the cat peed on him. He's like, 'Nobody likes me; even the cat peed on me.' That's the ultimate insult."

I'd also miss Tanner because of Dawn, who was planning to enjoy some rare weekends away from the dog shows with her husband, Newell (who loves Tanner and sometimes comes to shows, even though it's not really his world),* while her favorite dog was off on a European vacation. Dawn is the kind of person who overpowers any conversation and who always has the right amount of perspective, allowing her to step back and observe that this world to which she's devoted a major portion of her life is sometimes, if not often, ridiculous. You can count on her for a good story. And in Edison she had a doozy.

We were discussing the matter of a recent controversy involving Trader, a top Akita handled by Kevin who'd recently been given a ban for allegedly attempting to bite a judge. Kevin swore that the judge misinterpreted the situation and that Trader did not attempt to bite anyone, but the judge reported the action and Trader was at least temporarily banned from competition.

The owners in Heather and Kevin's camp tended to believe Kevin, an honest guy of great integrity, and the talk of politics led Dawn to share an experience we'd somehow all missed back in York. As part of her duties as a board member for the York Kennel Club, Dawn had to sit on a panel adjudicating any violations of rules or decorum, and on the show's second day, Dawn said, she and her fellow board members had to mete out some punishment of their own. They actually kicked a handler out of the show—because this grown woman had decided to relieve herself in the ex-pen.†

---

*He is very supportive and friendly to all of Dawn's dog-show friends but refers to them one and all as "dog people," as in, "Phone for you, honey. It's a dog person."

†It is in Edison, by the way, where I realize that the "ex" is short for "exercise." Now, that's euphemism at work if ever I've seen it. A mastiff or Great Dane or Saint Bernard can barely turn around in one of these things, let alone run.

It seems that this owner of a field spaniel had a sudden and uncontrollable urge to pee just at the moment when her dog was scheduled to enter the ring with a chance to earn its final, elusive major. The restrooms were occupied, so this owner, almost certainly having spent too much time in the company of dogs, ducked into one of those sawdust-lined, fenced enclosures and dropped her pants.

Someone reported the incident to someone else, who reported it to an AKC official, who said it was the first time in all his years he'd ever heard of such a thing happening. He reported it to Dawn and the board, and their reaction was equal parts shock and disgust. "What the hell were you thinking?" Dawn said she asked the woman during an impromptu hearing called to address the situation.

I had only two options, the lady told her: to pee myself or pee in the ex-pen.

"I said, 'Stop—that is not an option. You had thirty-two options, and that's not one of them," Dawn recounted, her voice rising. "The other one also isn't really an option either.' I'm basically yelling, and the chairman says to me, 'Aren't you being a little harsh?' And I'm like, 'Are you kidding me? NO! This woman peed in the freaking ex-pen."

And not just any ex-pen. It was the one for puppies, which has a short door intended to keep out larger dogs. The woman, Dawn said, had to crunch into a ball and crawl to get in, and then—to add to the indignity—she got stuck on the way out. Within a few minutes of her ungainly exit, someone had hung a sign that said DOGS ONLY.

"The ex-pen is never an option!" Dawn howled, coining a phrase that should one day grace a T-shirt. She exhaled. "These are the things that make us look nuts!"

Kimberly had it easy, relatively speaking. Because while there's only occasionally drama between rival owners of Australian shepherds, owners in many other breeds struggle to maintain even a modicum of congeniality. There's inevitable resentment in losers and jealousy of winners, no matter the dog, but in the most highly competitive breeds the atmosphere can be downright nasty. You will rarely see, for instance, more than a couple of rottweiler owners heading out for drinks together at the end of a day. Of all the owners in Heather and Kevin's camp, it was Cindy Meyer who had the hardest time. The Chesapeake Bay retriever isn't a terribly popular or competitive conformation dog, but for whatever reason tensions run consistently high among the humans who love and show them, and Cindy had long since given up hope of having both a winning dog and a collection of good friends who share this highly specific interest.

This was clear on the second day in Edison, after Rita lost to a dog handled by her owner, a prominent breeder. "We didn't lose to the dog," Cindy hissed. "We lost to *her*." Within seconds, though, she'd hugged her dog and moved on. Every loss stings, even if an owner tries to shrug it off, but Cindy had seen it all and, like Dawn, had acquired the ability to get over it quickly.

"Kim called me last week to ask me how I deal with it," she told me. "I said, 'Kim, get used to it. There's always another day.'"

Like tomorrow.

Cindy thought she'd be done with dog shows by this point. Her plan for most of 2009 had been to retire Rita after Westminster in order to breed her, but her Best of Opposite was such a good result that, with some cajoling from Kevin (who loved Rita and her winning), Cindy had a change of heart. Dog shows, I was finding, seemed to be popular among humans in large part because they are addictive. There's a very obvious element of the gambling psychology involved, wherein each ribbon won triggers the same reward center as does a major payoff at the blackjack table. Similarly, the drive to satiate this reward center overwhelms good sense and allows people to say the kinds of things gamblers are wont to say—for example, "Tomorrow's the day I win for sure!"

Cindy had just bought a new stuffed toy to replace the red-and-green "baby" that Rita adored and had almost literally loved to death.

She'd torn it open repeatedly, and the fact that it lived on to Edison was thanks entirely to Cindy's heroic sewing.

"I am so in debt over this dog," she said as we watched Rita chew on her new baby.

Nearby a young woman laughed loudly. "That's all of us."

"I was going to pull her," Cindy explained. "Then the rankings came out."

"Where are you?" the woman asked. Told that Rita was number three overall and number-one Chessie bitch in the country, the woman's eyes lit up. "That's good!"

"Good for them!" Cindy said with a smirk, nodding toward Kevin.

The tricky thing about Rita was that the dog was stuck in a bit of a cycle. Cindy wanted to breed her and knew that that window was closing fast, but Rita couldn't go into heat until she was taken off a medication she'd been put on to prevent false pregnancies—a medication necessitated by her life on the road. You see, poor Rita had been plagued by false pregnancies, and they weren't good for her psyche. It's a wicked trick nature plays, letting a dog think she's pregnant, to the degree that Rita was nesting on Cindy's bed and then took to carrying around her "baby" as if it were a puppy when no real puppy arrived.

"That's why she has that toy in her crate," Cindy said, and my heart broke a little for her. "She got depressed. She's five. I should have bred her by now."

J
ack was approaching his second birthday. He was now sexually mature. And he was starting to show it. After seeing how Shumba the Rhodesian ridgeback's hormones were affecting him, Heather asked Kimberly to take Jack home at night rather than keep him in the trailer with the gang. Like any teenager experiencing the first flutters of sexuality, Jack wasn't exactly in full control of his faculties.

This was quite apparent on the grooming table, which was frustratingly close to Shumba's crate. Technically she was out of heat at this point, but even the dwindling effects of her reproductive status were still giving Jack fits. His gums tensed and seemed to vibrate, a phenomenon known as "chattering," which indicates that he's ready to service her, if necessary. ("That means 'I'm here for you,'" Kevin said with a grin.) Jack picked up one paw after another, as if walking on hot sand, and his mouth curled up a little so that he looked to be smiling.

"He wants some of what he's not getting," Kimberly said.

Soon enough Jack would have his moment, but it was unlikely to be satisfying. A few days before the show, Kerry sent me an e-mail that said she was planning to breed "one of my nice bitches" to Jack. "I'm hoping for her to come in season in the next month or so." Kerry wasn't likely to ship this nice bitch out east and nobody wanted to pull Jack off the circuit to mate the old-fashioned way, so sometime soon Kerry and Kimberly would have to arrange to have a sample of Jack's sperm extracted and shipped to California. No one was thrilled at the prospect, including Kimberly. "Kerry may be missing the excitement of seeing Jack win," she told me. "But I'm going to miss the excitement of the birth of his first litter and watching the puppies grow. Hopefully, I can find an appropriate bitch around here so I can experience it, too."

The logistics of canine lovemaking were a lesser concern at the moment, however, as Kimberly and Heather were butting heads more and more over Jack's spot in the pecking order.

Once Tanner left for Europe, Heather wouldn't have a ranked dog, and she was well aware that her reputation in part is based on her ability to win often. And when she surveyed her kennel in search of dogs with star potential, few stood out more than Jack.

The issue reached critical mass on the last day at Edison, when Kimberly and I were standing with Jack at ringside, mere minutes before he was to show.

She looked nervous, and I noted this.

"Nervous that I have no handler," was her reply.

Due to slow judging, Heather was unlikely to make it in time, and despite the fact that she had vowed never to show Jack herself—and that she and Kerry had agreed it was better to scratch him than to have her do it—Kimberly strapped Jack's number onto her arm with a rubber band and sighed. She approached the ring steward.

"Can you move me back?" she asked, meaning in the order of examination.

How far?

"To the end of the specials?" By doing this, Kimberly would buy herself time. With eight specials entered, her turn wouldn't come for at least ten minutes, and as long as the judge hadn't begun his hands-on examination of Jack, she could still pass the number off to Heather.

The steward conferred with the judge, who looked like a redder, rounder-faced Ed Begley Jr. He acceded, but not happily.

Out of the crowd appeared Rachel, a cute, freckly twelve-year-old apprentice who was assisting Heather for the weekend. She was nearly out of breath and managed to say, between gasps, "Jesse is going to start, and then Heather will take over." Jesse was a young, good-looking handler whom none of us had ever seen before, and Kimberly handed Jack off to this strange man a little tentatively. She wasn't happy. "I don't want to stress out about my dog every weekend."

Just in case, Kimberly gave Jesse a quick primer. Most important, she told him, is a firm hand. " 'Yes' is a praise word. I use that more than 'Good boy,' " she said. And because praise is positive reinforcement, a dog is happy to hear it, and when Jack is happy, he is bad (for dog shows). "We're practicing baby talk at home so he doesn't get so excited," she said. "Because sometimes judges talk to them that way, and that will set him off. It's a problem in the ring. Sometimes his back end starts going."

I scanned the crowd nervously as Jesse led Jack into the ring, and I spied, in the distance, a flash of melon. It was Heather.

Hold on! I said, and Heather was nearly sprinting as she reached the ring, jumped into line, popped Jack's number under her armband, and calmly began to trot him around the ring as if nothing had happened.

Kimberly was always silent at ringside, but she was especially stoic now. "Too much drama over my dog," she muttered coldly. "I'd be surprised if he wins."

And Jack did seem antsy. "See that?" said Dawn, who'd come over to show her support. "That little edge is what makes them show dogs. They're not blah."

"They're a little bad," Kimberly added. Or in Jack's case a lot bad.

In my entirely unscientific sample of shows attended to date, I found that it was always a positive sign when Kimberly said this. And sure enough, despite Jack's obvious jitters, the judge was giving him a good look. It was quite apparent he was going to choose either Jack or Striker, Jack's old nemesis. In the end it was Jack.

Heather said whatever it is she says to Jack when he wins,[*] and he jumped up and kissed her, then jumped up again onto a chair near the entrance and almost knocked over the steward's table.

Success has a funny way of assuaging troubles. When Heather handed Jack's lead to Kimberly, both were all smiles. With the weekend's success, Jack had solidified a spot in the top twenty rankings, and any thoughts of switching handlers had faded, at least for a while.

---

[*] "Good boy, Jack!" will do it.

CHAPTER THIRTEEN

And Now a Brief Interlude Featuring the Perez Hilton of Dog Shows

All knowledge, the totality of all questions and answers, is
contained in the dog

—FRANZ KAFKA, "INVESTIGATIONS OF A DOG"

I t's a little unfair to compare Billy Wheeler of Memphis, Tennessee, to Perez Hilton of Los Angeles, California, but I can see why
the latter is sometimes used as a reference point. While he's not at all
mean-spirited or even judgmental (he has, in fact, an explicit "no hat-
ers" policy), Wheeler's blog, Dog Show Poop, is pretty much a must-
read for America's handlers, judges, and show-dog owners.*

When I reached him by phone at his Memphis home, it was just a

---

*Aesthetically as well, the two couldn't be more different. Hilton is gay, flamboyant, and
prone to wearing mauve hair and things with sequins; Wheeler is straight, somewhat
reserved, heavyset, and white-bearded. Hilton was punched by the tour manager of the
Black Eyed Peas; Wheeler is a retired management analyst who once advised the Cat
Fanciers Association.

few days after he'd celebrated his fortieth wedding anniversary. "Forty years in the dog-show game and forty years with the same woman," Wheeler told me, his husky voice a little fatigued thanks to the weekend's celebration at a local casino. In the background a bird squawked. That was Julio, his double yellow-headed Amazon parrot. "He likes to get in on the conversation. He imitates my wife and daughter to a tee." Julio used to have unclipped wings and the run of the place, and each morning he'd wake up in his cage and fly upstairs to crawl into bed with the Wheelers. Then one day Mrs. Wheeler's poodle attacked him, and he's been caged ever since. Which is probably a good thing, since the Wheelers now have terriers, one of which has already shown an aptitude for killing birds outdoors.[*]

When he's not blogging, Wheeler is often showing dogs himself. His local kennel club, in Memphis, is a very old one. He says it has disbanded and re-formed several times but that "there is solid documentation that they had the first dog show in the country." His club, I discovered later, was the one that rose from the ground laid by our old friend P. H. Bryson, the 110-pound weakling who started this whole business in the first place. The show Wheeler was referring to was the one in which Bryson beat the doctor who saved his life.

Wheeler caught the show bug in 1968, at age nineteen, when he attended a show and saw Michele Leathers Billings—"one of the doyennes of the judging circles"—handling an Afghan hound named Gabe. "It was a very glamorous couple," he recalled. "A beautiful woman with a beautiful dog. It hooked me."

He and his wife skipped around the country a little, often showing Maltese, before settling in California, where they stayed for twenty-five years. There he bought his first terrier, a Sealyham,[†] and took him out

---

[*]That Cairn terrier, Dee Dee, killed her first rat when she was just twelve weeks old. In the past year, Wheeler said, she'd killed two birds, three squirrels, and two rats.

[†]A small white terrier that, in its show coat, has long bangs and lengthy muttonchops that hang from its jowls, making it look a little like Chester A. Arthur, our twenty-first president, in his latter years.

to shows, where he found California to be a hotbed of top handlers. "I never got a single point," he says. Not that this mattered. "I have no aspirations of winning. I just go for the company and human drama. What's really cool about the sport is that it transcends social structure. You'll be sitting there and talking to somebody and not realize they're fabulously wealthy."

Wheeler says that thanks to dogs he's had many, many brushes with greatness, including lovely talks about Pekingese with Jackie Onassis and Liz Taylor, whom he calls "the most beautiful fat woman I've ever met."

I had only mentioned Jack by his everyday name via e-mail, and with virtually no other details, but already Wheeler was keeping an eye on him. "Research is my game," he said. "He's a blue merle, right?" he asked rhetorically. "So he's got those eyes that look right through you."

Wheeler's blog is famous for its nonstop coverage of show results and also for its rankings of the nation's top dogs, updated weekly. Wheeler provides the rankings in two forms. One is the so-called traditional top ten and is uncolored by algorithm—it's just a straight-up ranking of the most dogs defeated. ("There are couple things wrong with that," he noted. "The person who shows at two hundred fifty shows a year is competing against the person who shows a hundred shows a year. Who has the better dog?") The second ranking is his own and uses two factors: group placements and the number of Bests in Show won. But Wheeler has a background in mathematics and has further tweaked the ranking by weighting for the size of the show.

"There are a lot of technical issues behind how the placings work," he said when I asked what it would take to get Jack onto this list. He said it would be "unlikely" that an Australian shepherd would make the top ten (at least at that particular point in time). This didn't surprise me, even if I didn't totally understand the reasons. Despite the fact that the Australian shepherd is an ascendant breed currently in vogue and is always one of the largest entries in a particular show, it does not win big awards often. In fact, as of mid-April, only one Best in Show in all the shows held to date had gone to an Aussie (and it wasn't Beyoncé).

Wheeler thinks that there are two main factors working against the Aussie. One is that "the quality is not that good," meaning the overall quality of the entries, not the quality of specific top dogs (such as Jack, or Beyoncé). This is because the breed is a popular family pet, and many of the exhibitors are showing pets for fun and not dogs bought expressly for showing. And the same would be true for other popular family dogs, such as Labs and goldens. The other hurdle for Aussies is that "a lot of the dogs are multiple titled." What he means is that because the dogs are such tremendous athletes, their owners tend to enter them in other disciplines—herding, obedience, dock jumping, Frisbee, et cetera. And, says Wheeler, "If you want to be good in something, focus on it. Michael Jordan found out he couldn't play baseball and basketball at the same time."

When I asked Wheeler to name the most commonly rewarded dogs, his first response was, "Terriers, without a doubt." And why terriers? "Terriers have the quintessential show personality," he said. "I own a Cairn and a Scottie, and my wife just absolutely hates the fact that they will not listen to her. They do what they damn please. Unlike Dobermans or gun dogs, they're bred to work by themselves. They see human interference as interfering with their jobs—to go out and kill something." He was right. Terriers never look bored or distracted. They always look like they're about to bite your ankles.

Wheeler asked me which dogs I thought won most. That was easy—and it was the same answer I'd have given if he'd asked me before I attended a single show: poodles. I'd since seen them win often and had observed the crowds that collected along the edges of poodle rings like metal shavings around a magnet.

My preconceived notion of dog shows was pretty common: that they were beauty contests that rewarded some weird and artificial concept of canine aesthetics that wasn't at all representative of reality on the street. And the dog that most represented that faux beauty was the poodle, a dog with preposterous hair that can be fairly portrayed by a clown with a knack for making balloon animals. They were so silly-seeming that I never gave them a chance to be smart. (In truth they're one of the cleverest breeds. Poodle proponents can stand near the front of the line of dog people who deserve my apologies.)

STANDARD POODLE

Wheeler was not surprised by my answer. "I had written early on in my blog something called 'The Standard Poodle Dog-Show Cliché,'" he said. "That dog is really a dog show icon. It's amazing year after year after year how many great ones you see."

He was, quite quickly, developing a status as the very loud voice of reason among dog-show enthusiasts. Even though that was never his goal. "Five years ago I had a heart attack," Wheeler said. "And I retired from my job. It was a long, slow recovery. My wife bought me the Scottie as a pet to help me through rehab. And after I recovered sufficiently I decided to get a show dog—something to help get me out of the house, to get me into the world."

Wheeler said he wanted a bulldog but that he went out to a local show and ended up chatting with "this very elegant little southern woman who looked like she walked off the set of *Designing Women*. She had a Cairn terrier on a leash." The woman told Wheeler that she was sitting on a litter of puppies sired by a son of the top-winning Cairn terrier of all time. "I jumped on it. For people to sell you a high-quality dog is very unusual." (Kimberly, again, got very lucky with Jack.)

This was August 2008, and Wheeler thought he would start a blog to write about his puppy. He thought it would "just be your typical personal blog," interesting to no one. Then he found himself mesmerized by that year's race for America's top dog—a race that was exceedingly close, especially between the top two, the giant schnauzer Ch Galilee's Pure of Spirit (who finished the year with seventy-one BsIS and 117,954 dogs defeated), and the pointer, Ch Cookieland Seasyde Hollyberry (with ninety-six BISs and 117,199 dogs defeated).

This interest began to show up in his prose, and slowly but surely the race itself became the blog's focus. And suddenly the handlers of top-ten dogs were sending in photos and updates and asking Wheeler to post the standings. He did this, more regularly than any other Web site, and also began his own rankings, including a feature called "Dogs-2Watch" that highlighted up-and-coming dogs. By the time Westminster rolled around, Dog Show Poop was a phenomenon. He hosted a "Garden Party" during that event, and twenty-five thousand participants ambled through the chat room, chewing over the show in real time.

Today Wheeler devotes more than eight hours a day on weekends and Mondays reporting on every all-breed show in the United States: "about fifteen hundred a year." His in-box overflows with photos and tips. Just the day before we talked, he said, at one of the big shows, "I had a lady standing at ringside giving me results by cell phone as I was typing. I broke the story on the president's dog six weeks before anyone else. They made the announcement in April; I broke the story in February."

How did he know about Bo? "I had my contacts."

According to Wheeler, some in the Portuguese water dog community tried to stop the sale of the First Puppy to the Obamas. "They did not want the president to have a Portuguese water dog. It's like the

Westminster effect—once the president has one, everyone tries to buy one. And there are a lot of negative aspects to that. But I wrote to a board member of the Portuguese Water Dog Club of America and said, 'He can run the free world and not own one of your dogs? He has a six-acre lawn.' "*

And it's all a labor of love. Wheeler estimated that he'd made "no more than seventy dollars" on the few micro-ads he's accepted. People often offer to pay him for placement of their dogs, and Dog Show Poop could easily become a revenue generator simply by taking the sorts of ads that pack the main industry magazines like *Dog News,* but he won't do that. He cares about his objectivity. He is the rare—perhaps the only—blogger with a strict moral compass. And that's because he just really loves dog shows.

"The sport is dying," he said, and that surprised me. A recurring theme of his editorializing, he told me, was a focus on what he calls "endangered species; the British Kennel Club calls them breeds at risk. I owned a Sealyham terrier once. There are fifteen thousand polar bears in Canada, and there are not five hundred Sealyham terriers in the world. And you can't have a polar bear sleep on the end of your bed." I'm not sure that's a fair comparison, but I suppose the point is taken. While breed popularity ebbs and flows from year to year, some breeds have fallen drastically out of favor and are in danger of disappearing entirely. Only breeders, reacting to demand, can save them.

"The rarest dog in the AKC registry is the American foxhound," Wheeler says. "That's a breed developed by George Washington." He

---

*One doubts there was a similar "bulldog effect" in response to Pete, Teddy Roosevelt's choice for White House pet. Mark Derr reports that Pete "terrorized the White House between 1905 and 1908" and "caused an international incident when he treed the French ambassador, who had come to play tennis with the president." A little over a decade later, Warren Harding's Airedale Laddie Boy made a less offensive grab at political notoriety by giving interviews and taking his own chair at cabinet meetings, and the Roosevelt family redeemed their canine heritage when FDR's Scottish terrier, Fala, "nearly achieved cult status," according to Derr.

pauses a moment for the thought to sink in.[*] "Do you want to be responsible for losing that iconic American symbol?" Wheeler said that more than a third of the 160-plus recognized breeds are at risk and could very easily disappear over five years.

And helping to stall that slide is one of his obsessions. "When the AKC published its top ten most popular breeds list last year, I published the bottom ten and went through each one and said, 'How come people don't own these?'" Just to return to the one he knows best, he marveled, "I don't know why people don't own Sealyham terriers. They've won Best in Show at Westminster three times. Alfred Hitchcock had one.

"My point is that the game is getting more and more difficult. It's expensive even at the entry level. Just gas—you have to drive around the country to shows. And from the get-go, the average exhibitor only stays in game for five years.

"Honestly, I try to preach this whole thing of balance. There are things in life other than dog shows. When people complain to me about politics, I say, 'You are taking this shit way too seriously. This is not life. This is a dog show.'"

---

*I think this is not exactly true, by the way. What seems to be true is this: George Washington kept a large pack of hounds at his Mount Vernon estate. He loved these hounds and was indeed an eager participant in further refining their traits. And his hounds are considered to be some of the foundation stock for the American foxhound breed. So there you go—the Father of Our Country was a dog breeder.

CHAPTER FOURTEEN

The Campaign:

I'll Take Thirty-four Consecutive Back Covers of Dog News, Please

Of course we've evolved. We've made it a big business. It's a multimillion-dollar business.

—SUE VROOM, AKC

For Jack to succeed on a national level, to rise to a point where he is among the handful of dogs that judges immediately look to when Aussies assemble in a major show ring, many things would need to happen. Foremost among these, he must win. That part was going pretty well so far. But winning isn't as simple as just being the best dog on a given day. A successful show-dog career is built on the smart decisions of his handler and to a large degree on the depth of his owner's pockets.

When an owner and a handler begin a dog's "campaign," which is what you call a pursuit of titles with the goal of a national ranking in both breed and group, they must spend money—toward travel expenses and entry fees, obviously, but also toward advertising the dog.

A show-dog advertisement is similar to those "For Your Consideration" Academy Awards ads that the studios buy for films they deem Oscar-worthy. These films are said to be "campaigned," just as dogs are, and I suppose both ideas borrow from politics. You place a flattering photo or two against a colorful background, make a brief and compelling pitch for why the film/candidate/dog is worth your consideration, and top it off with some witty or otherwise memorable slogans. You then place those ads in the highest-profile space you can afford; for a studio that might be the *New York Times*. For a dog it's *Dog News* or the *Canine Chronicle*—and the more money you're willing to spend, the more desirable the placement you'll receive, right up to and including the front cover.

The best of these ads, for the country's top-ranked dogs, are lushly photographed and well-designed spreads—two pages of full color with beautiful photos and artful typography positioned prominently in the magazines. Jack's first ad, which appeared in the April issue of the *Canine Chronicle,* was a little more modest and low-fi and fell more in the middle of the magazines. To use more popular magazines as a reference point, it's the sort of real estate where you might find the ads for Pam cooking spray as opposed to TAG Heuer watches.

Seeing as how Jack comes from modest means, with owners who have very little if any expendable income, he was only able to procure a slot in the discounted monthly section provided to Heather and Kevin for helping to distribute the *Canine Chronicle* in their area. And his debut show-dog advertisement was a basic one, with a cute close-up of his face taken at Westminster by the photographer Miguel Betancourt, with an inset of Jack's win photo showing him, the judge, and Heather, along with the purple Award of Merit ribbon. Across the top was the line "He's Got Major Moves!" over his show name. Below that, "Westminster 1st Award of Merit," with his call name "Jack," and the two sell lines, which speak in the lingua franca of dog shows to people who understand—judges.

One line was two simple words, "Movement—Expression" (citing, in most basic terms, his strengths), and, below that, "Multiple Group Placings in limited showings," a pithy phrase that actually says a lot. It means that when Jack shows, he does well, and the only reason he's not ranked higher is that he's not out there every weekend. For all the readers (i.e., judges) know, maybe his owners are just testing the waters or have a bigger-picture strategy.

A top-ranked dog is almost never a one-year project; typically you spend a year (or two) building a reputation and accumulating a list of judges who are proven to like your dog. Then you target those judges the next year, along with others you feel will like the dog, build some momentum, and help fuel it further with strategic advertising—or, if you can afford it, a promotional blitzkrieg.

The other critical factor in a campaign is scheduling. The dog world is small enough that most people who've been at it for a while—and though Heather and Kevin, both in their mid-thirties, are on the young side, they have experience beyond their years—can look at a list of dog shows and handpick a schedule that maximizes their animals' chances of winning. Judges are always chosen in advance, and certain ones are avoided; others are sought out. The size of the field can be a factor, as can the location—a site could be too hot, too cold, or too cramped for a handler's liking.

There's also the simple logistics of travel. If you're not the type of handler whose owner has a private jet, you can't show in Boston one weekend and Seattle the next; if you're like most people, you can't even really afford to show every weekend, though plenty do. I met many owners backstage at dog shows who have full-time jobs and yet somehow manage to show their dogs up to fifty times a year.

Kevin and Heather are on the road more or less forty-five weekends a year, mostly up and out the door by 5:00 A.M. and not finished until after 9:00 P.M., but they rarely travel so far that they can't get home in a day. No matter how you look at it, it's a grind.

Once Tanner had left for Europe and there was no longer a single dog important enough to build the schedule around, Heather and Kevin seemed to choose their shows based mainly on location—nothing too far from home, which still allows for quite a selection when home is Pennsylvania—and on general impressions of judges. Those who'd been kind to them before got preference.

By contrast, the dogs at the top of the all-breed rankings were speeding around America. And by April two dogs in particular had begun to distinguish themselves: a smooth fox terrier named Dodger and a Pekingese named Malachy.

Very rarely does a dog just emerge with a new championship and go on to compete as a nationally ranked special.* Most often a special campaign is a two-year process at a minimum. The first year is all about winning breeds and placing in groups and gathering those win points and photos in the form of ammunition that can be deployed in ads. The second year, having won over judges, you can start to focus on dominating a group.

Tom Grabe says that for anyone new to the specials game it typically follows a specific pattern. Few people set out to spend thousands upon thousands of dollars, but success begets success and the feeling is addictive. "First people want a championship, then to special the dog," said the man who benefits greatly from this addiction. "Then you win breeds and place in groups and you want to win a group," and once that happens—and this is exactly where Tanner is and has been—"you want a Best in Show. And then you want the next BIS, because that one's over already." And the next thing you know, you're advertising fifty-two consecutive weeks in *Dog News*. "I think that's how you get into anything."

If Billy Wheeler is the counterculture, Tom Grabe is the culture. Grabe publishes the *Chronicle* as well as its sister magazine, the *Equine Chronicle*, along with his wife, Amy, out of a modest office in Ocala, Florida. The *Equine Chronicle* is the largest show-horse magazine in the country, and the *The Canine Chronicle*, Tom thinks, has the same status

---

*That's industry jargon for a champion dog that's being campaigned. It serves as both noun (Jack is one of Heather's "specials") and a verb ("to special" is to enter in Best of Breed week in, week out).

among dog-show magazines, although because none are audited for circulation, it's impossible to say for sure.

The *Chronicle* was founded in 1975 by Ric Routledge and was a newspaper for the first fifteen years of its existence. Not long after its launch, the AKC board summoned Routledge to New York and said they didn't like the *Chronicle*. "They felt that it served only to attempt to influence AKC judges," Pat Hastings told me. "To which Ric said, 'Gentlemen, if your judges just judged dogs, I'd be out of business tomorrow.'" The implication: If buying ads didn't really help sway judges, Ric would have no customers. The AKC promptly shut up.

In the 1990s, Tom and Amy Grabe were professional dog handlers—their résumé, it turns out, includes the best-winning Aussie of all time, Bayshore's Flapjack—who never aspired to own magazines, but they regularly bought ads for their various dogs, and after a few years of flirtation with a woman who'd bought the publication from Routledge, they bought her out, moved to horse country, and changed careers.

The *Chronicle* has three primary competitors: *ShowSight, Dogs in Review,* and *Dog News* (a weekly), and none publishes its circulation or really even cares to sell subscriptions or drive newsstand sales.

The *Chronicle* prints fifteen thousand copies a month, most of which are distributed for free at shows, but the most important are the copies mailed directly to the more than three thousand AKC-approved judges, plus a few hundred more shipped internationally to the "all-arounders"—or judges licensed to judge all breeds (and thus those most likely to be hired to judge in the United States—in Canada, Australia, Mexico, and Japan). A judge need not ask Tom for a subscription; once he or she is approved for duty, a subscription goes out automatically. This is expensive, but it's smart business. Because exhibitors know that judges get (and flip through) every issue, they want to be in the pages. The way advertising works in traditional media is that a business buys a page in hopes that some percentage of the readers who pick it up will be interested in their product; in this case the target audience is 100 percent pure.

Premium placements are the most sought after—and anything in the first 125 pages is considered premium at the *Chronicle*—and the best of those (the inside front cover and its facing page especially) are essentially impossible to purchase if you are not a client with a long history of advertising. Fortunately for Tom and Amy, there is no shortage of those types, and to keep them happy the magazine rotates different advertisers in and out of the most coveted spots throughout the year.

The *Chronicle's* rates are reasonable: $400 for standard color (color photos on a white page with black type) or $450 for deluxe color (color photos on a color page with color type). The front cover runs $4,500, and the back is $3,500. The inside front is $1,600, and the inside back $1,400.

Premium spots are typically booked at least a year in advance. The truth, Tom admits, is that it's hard for any new client to buy a spot in the first fifty pages (the superpremiums!), because those belong to a core group of advertisers who've been with the *Chronicle* for years and have worked themselves into preferred customers, and who are rotated around in that area to be fair to all. A specific dog can appear on the cover only once in a year.

Tom says that "most of the top dogs" advertise with the *Chronicle*, but not necessarily all of them. "Everyone's got their favorite magazines. We put out a product, and people who like us like us. People who don't, don't."

Just for example, I picked up an issue that happened to be sitting in a pile on my desk. On the cover was Dodger, the smooth fox terrier who was the country's number-one overall dog. On the inside cover and facing page was Walker, the toy poodle handled by Kaz Hosaka and who had (at that point) collected forty Bests in Show and 153 Group Firsts; and after that, Beckham, the nation's top cocker spaniel, the number-two sporting dog, and the sixth-ranked dog overall; followed by America's number-one English sheepdog; then a top-ranked German wirehair pointer; and then Malachy the Pekingese, America's top toy dog and the furry little footstool that would duel Dodger for number one up until the final days of 2010. Not every dog in the first 125 pages is a major national contender, but most are, and if not, they're likely at least handled by one of the very top handlers or backed by an owner with a history of substantial show-dog investments.

The first Australian shepherd appears on page 54, and it is of course Beyoncé, in a two-page spread announcing her back-to-back wins at the Australian Shepherd National Specialty show at the Purina Farms complex* near St. Louis, Missouri.

The first editorial content appears on page 74.

When you consider that some owners campaign more than one dog a year, it's not hard to see how they can run up quite a tab. The maximum for a single dog in one year—factoring the inside front and facing cover every month, plus one cover—would be a bit under forty thousand dollars. "Unless you did a foldout ad," Tom says. "That runs forty-five hundred." The *Chronicle*'s average advertiser spends about thirty thousand dollars a year, but some clients have as many as five dogs advertised at a time. For the Westminster issue—the year's largest at nearly five hundred pages—there were two owners with seven different dogs. "You start adding that up and you can easily spend a couple hundred thousand," he says.

Though showing has historically been a preoccupation of the tweed-and-Ivy set, Tom says that the business has become more populist over time. He's seeing "more and more people who are self-made. Not old money, but new money. You don't see the kennels anymore owned by Firestones and Rockefellers." (Which isn't to say that old money has vanished entirely. One of the two backers of Malachy the Pekingese, I would later learn, is Iris Love, a Guggenheim.)

"It's much more of a microcosm of our society now," Grabe says. "That's the good thing about dog shows as opposed to horse shows—if you've got a dog, and a car and a leash, you can go show."

---

*The world's first dedicated dog-show facility, based at the pet-food brand's headquarters.

CHAPTER FIFTEEN

Meet Ron Scott,
Show-Dog Investor

· ·

Many years ago I asked one of our major backers of dogs
why she did it. She said, "Do you realize that most art in
museums is sponsored?" I didn't. She said, "I have a lot
of friends who sponsor art; I don't like art, I like dogs.
I would rather sponsor dogs for the world to see than a
painting on a wall."

—PAT HASTINGS

· ·

I f the dog-show world's top backers were imagined as our solar system, Ron Scott would be one of the larger planets—at least Saturn,
if not Jupiter. He will tell you that the white-hot sun that scorches all
earth is Victor Malzoni, a São Paulo–based construction magnate who
backs six or seven dogs a year in the United States plus another handful
in Europe and at least that many at home in Brazil. "He's a very wealthy
man whose passion happens to be dogs," Scott told me while finishing
up breakfast at his home in Pennsylvania. "He has a Gulfstream big
enough to fly back and forth from São Paulo to New York City." But

Malzoni is an interloper, and it's more typical of the current landscape and instructive to anyone curious about how backing works, most often, to stick with someone more local. (Though it does serve notice that the emerging economies, increasingly influential in most segments of business, are becoming a force in dog showing, too.)*

Scott, sixty-eight, is a retired entrepreneur who sold his forklift company in 2007 and now backs dogs along with his "partner in all things," the former professional handler Debbie Burke. He is the former chairman of the Harrisburg Dog Show and a thirty-plus-year participant in shows, but his greatest legacy will probably be his partnership with the Japanese poodle maestro Kaz Hosaka. For the past fifteen years, Scott has served as the backer to Hosaka's top dog—or dogs—paying not only handling and travel fees but also for the hundreds of pages of advertisements that promote them.

It is frequently said that competition in poodles is especially fierce. "There is nothing that takes more work or money than poodles," Pat Hastings told me. "It's probably the hardest breed to win in as an owner-handler. The average owner simply cannot compete against professionals when it comes to scissoring and coat care. People have real lives." I don't know if this is the main reason the breed has become a magnet for wealthy backers or if the breed just has a cachet. Probably both things are true. As is this: Poodles win dog shows, proportionally more than any other breed. That's what attracted Ron Scott.

Scott's background was in Yorkshire terriers, a breed he fell into through his ex-wife. One dog turned into a breeding and showing hobby that metastasized into an all-consuming passion. Ron came to love the competition, and especially winning, but soon winning breed ribbons wasn't enough. He wanted groups, and then Bests in Show. And he found that it was "very difficult to win Best in Show with Yorkshire terriers."

---

*Which I guess makes sense, since purebreds, like luxury cars, are a symbol of wealth among the nouveau riche.

"Some people want to continue to improve breeding stock, and finishing dogs is one way to prove to themselves that their stock is getting better. Some people say, 'I have a dog that I think is really good, and I'd like to special it.' They go out every week or most weekends and try to get enough breed wins that the dog is in the top ten for that breed." The former would describe Kerry, the latter, Kimberly. Neither of these things was the appeal for Ron Scott.

"I just decided that if I was going to continue, I needed a breed that could be competitive in the Best in Show ring on a regular basis," Scott explains. Looking around, he found that the choice seemed rather obvious. "Poodles do very well," he explained. "There are probably more Bests in Show in one weekend by poodles than all the flat-coated retrievers would have in an entire year. And you could say that about a lot of breeds. It's just the way it is."

Scott didn't exactly tiptoe into the poodle waters;* he cannonballed. By throwing his money behind a new arrival from Japan—a toy poodle named Spirit, handled by Kaz Hosaka, the master of the genre. "I loved his ability to transform a dog into something so beautiful and train it so well," Scott says. "I had the best of all possible worlds—a really good dog and a person to make that dog the best it could be." Spirit didn't disappoint. He won twenty-five Bests in Show as well as Best of Variety at the 1998 and 1999 National Poodle Specialty shows. "And it really got me hooked on poodles."

The partners combed the world for the absolute best poodles and piled up show wins. They won Westminster in 2002, with a miniature poodle named Spice Girl that Kaz himself bred. Their standard poodle Justin was the number-one Non-Sporting dog in America in 2005, and then the two men discovered Vicky, "this little toy poodle bitch at Smash Kennels in Japan." Vicky went on to be the number-one dog

---

*An apt metaphor, methinks, because the poodle is a water dog—thought to have originated with German fishermen who used the dogs to swim out and retrieve nets. The various poufs and pom-poms, if you believe poodle people, are not exclusively decorative. They are there to keep key joints and organs warm in the water.

in America, all breed, in 2007 and then the top winning toy poodle of all time, with 108 Bests in Show. "She was just an extraordinary little animal to watch."

Scott had found his poodle source. "Our deal is simple," he explains. The proprietors of Smash Poodles, a mother-son team in Fuji City, Japan, offer Scott first pick of every litter born and send the dogs off to America to be campaigned by Kaz. Scott pays nothing for a dog but picks up all the expenses and then returns it home to be bred once retired. By charging nothing for a dog that comes back to them a year or two later, the breeders have in essence shorted the dog like a stock. And while Scott pays nothing for the dog, he pays plenty to campaign it. "I'm too old to be breeding dogs." And this arrangement, he says, is ideal. "I get to pick the best dogs, show them, and send them back to be reintroduced to the breeding program, where hopefully a better one comes out. We've been doing that for ten years."

You can count on a top dog from Ron Scott every year, as dependable as the tides.

So here's the eight-hundred-thousand-dollar question: What's in this for Ron Scott?

I had this theory that people backed dogs for the same reason they owned all or part of racehorses—for the luster this association provides. Scott said no, that's not the case. And he would know. He also owns racehorses. "Racehorses are much less personal, for one thing," he said, and I think he means that you can't really cuddle or toss Frisbee with a Thoroughbred. "The second thing is, racehorses make money. You do not make money by showing dogs. It's nothing about making money. It's all about spending money. You do it for other reasons."

The most important reason for Ron Scott is that he loves the dogs. He and Debbie don't have a pet anymore—their last house dog, a Lhasa apso, passed away in 2009—and yet twenty-five to thirty weekends a year they travel by RV to visit Kaz and the poodles at show grounds around the East. "We carry them and pet them and play with them," he said. "So there's the cuddle factor."

There's also the thrill of competition and the addiction that comes with success. "My goal is pretty high every year," he says. "My goal is to have the number-one poodle in the variety that I show"—whether that's standard, miniature, or toy.

And to accomplish that goal, he spends a lot of money.

All told, Scott says the range of campaigning a dog over a year varies. "You're dealing with a hundred thousand dollars to half a million." Some people, of course, campaign multiple dogs.

And even then you don't know.

"People have spent millions and millions to win the Garden and have never won. Lots of people," Scott said. "The stars have to align. The year we had Vicky, we won sixty-nine Bests in Show, but the judge we had was going to put the beagle up, and he did." That beagle was Uno, the 2008 champion who is probably the most famous Westminster winner in history. So in retrospect there's little shame in that loss. The year they did win, with Spice Girl, "that was the year the gods lined up well." A Kerry blue terrier named Mick was "by far the number-one dog, almost unbeatable. And we beat him that day." Which just goes to show that "you never know."

"It's all about winning," Scott says. "Most people who show dogs or have racehorses or play golf or do whatever they do in sports, they do it to win." And certainly he has. He has won Westminster, Eukanuba, Morris & Essex, Montgomery County, and over three hundred total Bests in Show. "I've had multiple Winkie Award winners.* More Bests in Show than I've dreamed of. It's been a wonderful journey for me. And I hope for Kaz."

S cott will be the first to admit that it is nearly impossible for the regular show exhibitor to compete for and consistently win groups and shows. He doesn't know Kimberly, or Jack, but they certainly fall into that category.

---

*Awarded to Show Dog of the Year every February during Westminster Week.

You have a frank conversation with Ron Scott and you start to wonder if a regular person, with a great dog, could ever have a chance at
regularly competing for show wins. I always asked this question, near
the end, whenever I talked to someone about backers. Pat Hastings,
who knows as much about dog shows as any human does, could recall
just a few recent dogs that did well despite lacking a wealthy backer. She
remembered a Yorkie, owned by a family that wasn't rich, and shown
by their daughter, that won Westminster.

I looked it up. That was in 1978 when Higgens became the first and
still only Yorkie to win at the Garden. Though handled by Marlene
Lutovsky, Higgens's care was a total family affair. Marlene's mother,
Barbara, reported that she was the one who got up every morning at
five o'clock "to clean his teeth, brush and oil his coat, change the wrap-
pers, and give him clean booties."

When I posed the same question to Scott, he thought a second and
pronounced that "it would be very difficult, but not impossible." Then he,
too, recalled that family—the name escaped him as well—only his story
had a telling conclusion. "There was a family that won Westminster with
a Yorkie, and their daughter showed the dog," he said. "The family went
broke. Lost their house, everything. We never saw them again."*

I think Ron Scott is generally right when he says that no one gets
into dog shows for the money. And really, most breeders would tell
you the same thing. But you also can't ignore the fact that certain dogs
are more valuable than others, and if you happen to own one, you can
make money from breeding it.

As with all segments of the economy, more and more of the money

---

*David Frei later corrected the record on this. The last low-budget dog to win BIS at
Westminster was actually Pepsi, an Afghan hound owned by Chris and Marguerite Ter-
rell, who won in 1983. Says Chris: "I guarantee we spent less than anyone who won
Westminster." The Terrells, he says, bought a grand total of two advertisements—one
at the beginning of 1982, and another at the end of the year, when Pepsi became the
number-one all-breed dog.

and influence are coming from the developing world—from places like Brazil, home to Victor Malzoni, and China, a country that is absolutely bonkers for purebred dogs. The Chinese Kennel Club regularly dispatches envoys to large American shows to hand out pamphlets and recruit participants, and money from China (and Brazil and Russia) is causing an absurd run on global dog values.

This frenzy hit its peak in early 2011 when a Chinese coal baron paid $1.5 million for an eleven-month-old Tibetan mastiff* named Big Splash, whose diet included such peculiarities as abalone and sea cucumber, neither of which is exactly indigenous to Tibet. Stories reported that the price was outrageous but not idiotic, considering that Big Splash could fetch as much as $100,000 for stud services.[†]

Stud fees for American show dogs are far more reasonable—typically a few hundred dollars up to a couple thousand for a truly special dog.

---

*An ancient, regal breed said to have been owned by both Genghis Khan and Buddha.

†It's ironic that Chinese aristocrats were paying obscene amounts for this particular breed, considering that it was nearly wiped out by Chinese soldiers who beat them to death with rifle butts on the streets of Lhasa during the Invasion of Tibet in 1950. So tough were these prized guard dogs (or at least their reputations) that the Chinese army passed a law that Tibetan mastiff owners had to kill their pets and then burn them publicly on pyres. Those who refused were thrown in jail. This wasn't just cruel, it was a forced violation of religious beliefs, since killing living things was a direct breach of Tibetan Buddhism. There's both delicious irony and poetic justice, then, to the story that this same breed is now the most valuable object in China. Speaking of good stories, that's not the only one about Tibetan mastiffs. The breed's popularity in the United States owes itself largely to the efforts of a woman named Ann Rohrer, who happened to be in Tibet during the horrific invasion. Vowing to help prevent the breed's extinction, Rohrer fought for the dogs throughout her life, leading the charge for AKC recognition and helping create the foundation stock, thanks in large part to a remarkable dog named Kalu. Born in Tibet, Kalu fled to Nepal with some farmers and ably defended their livestock in the Himalayas, surviving numerous fights with snow leopards. Some sort of drunken trade put him in the hands of American travelers who took him home, where he was locked up in a kennel after mistakenly biting one child while protecting another. A sleazy breeder adopted him and then chained him to a fence behind a barn and basically left him to waste away. Fortunately, a Good Samaritan spotted the flea-bitten, malnourished Kalu, saved him, and passed him on to Ann, who nursed the dog back to health and used him as the founding sire of the breed. Kalu is the first Tibetan mastiff entered in the breed's American stud book. (By the way, Ann is also responsible for bringing the Tibetan terrier into the United States.)

TIBETAN MASTIFF

Midway through his first year, Jack was only beginning to attract some interest, and Kimberly and Kerry had yet to settle on a stud fee, though a thousand dollars was looking like a reasonable starting point. If your dog's services are in constant demand, I suppose you can start to recoup your expenses, but that's definitely the exception rather than the rule.

And in the absence of a backer or a run on his sperm, Jack's team just scrambled.

Out in California, Kerry was patiently sending checks while hoping for a miracle. She saw great potential in Jack but knew that without a Ron Scott he had little shot at living up to it. "He needs somebody behind him," she said. "That's what you have to have."

"Judges have egos—they want to see their pictures," she said, meaning in advertisements, where owners often include win photos of dog and judge together from shows. "Or they want to find the next up-and-comer." She knew from experience that a well-executed campaign can work if you've got the right dog. She'd seen it firsthand in 2008, when her bitch Phoebe was neck and neck with a dog that had six owners at the top of the Aussie rankings all year. Late in the year, when it was really close, she'd enter three shows (paying three entries) and then choose the one that looked to be the biggest. "We were chasing points," she said. Over Thanksgiving she skipped the National Dog Show in Philly and instead sent Phoebe to Chicago, hoping only to win the breed points over a deep entry of Aussies. They did that—and went on to win their one and only Best in Show.

In the end Phoebe was number one in the all-breed rankings but fell painfully short in the more important breed ranking. She missed a year-end ranking as America's number-one Australian shepherd by a mere six points.

Jack, meanwhile, was stuck somewhere between these two worlds.

And Kerry was conflicted. "Unfortunately, a lot of big things comes with a lot of big dollars," she said. "He's so young he really wasn't ready to be doing the phenomenal winning to get to Westminster and be noticed. You need a year's worth of winning groups and being seen all over." Beyoncé, she said, "probably hit a hundred twenty shows last year and was advertised every week. I've gone down that road. You either get a backer or you sell your soul or you work to death." The lack of a true backer, she said, "would be the only thing that would hold Jack back."

CHAPTER SIXTEEN

Harrisonburg

That Beyoncé is one beautiful black bitch.
—OVERHEARD OUTSIDE THE AUSSIE RING

As April dragged on, the competition grew more intense. For much of the spring, Jack had been competing against the top dogs in the Northeast, but because regions tend to be fairly self-contained, the competitors from separate regions cross paths only a handful of times a year. And on the weekend of April 10, a show in Harrisonburg, Virginia, was one of those times.

Harrisonburg is smack in central Virginia, thus something of a halfway point between the Northeast and the Southeast. A day before the crew set out for the show, Kimberly sent a one-line e-mail to me and Kerry. It said, "Beyoncé is in Virginia." She included a sad-faced emoticon for emphasis.

Beyoncé is owned by her breeder, Sharon Fontanini, who lives in Iowa, and based in North Carolina, with her handler, Jamie Clute (who is married to another handler, naturally), and tends to prowl the shows of the Southeast, which more or less orbit around Atlanta. She was in her second year as a campaigned dog and was well seasoned, not to mention utterly dominant in the breed.

Fontanini operates Myshara Aussies in Waukee, Iowa. Like Kimberly and Kerry, she comes from horses and first discovered Aussies around the barns. She bred her first litter in 1994 and has been a board member of the United States Australian Shepherd Association for six years. (She was to become president in January of 2011.) Fontanini breeds maybe once or twice a year.

Beyoncé was her first number-one Aussie, and the fact that she's done well despite the lack of a backer—"I'm it," Fontanini says—speaks volumes about the difference between showing Aussies and showing poodles (or even Great Danes or rottweilers or boxers). An Aussie owner, at least at this point in time, isn't likely to be drawn into an arms race of ad spending. Which isn't to say that Fontanini is getting off cheap; even a modest full-time campaign (with handling fees, entry fees, and travel expenses) runs her several thousand dollars a month. "It's a very expensive dog I have out there," she said with a sigh but no apparent regret. "I don't know how these people have backers. I'd love to have one." When I told her about Ron Scott, she seemed surprised. "No one's ever approached me."

Fontanini has been spending her own money on Beyoncé because she recognized "from the very beginning" that this was probably a once-in-a-lifetime dog. Beyoncé's mother was a Best in Show winner, and her grandfather won multiple Bests. "Did I know she'd be this good? I never know that until they go out." Fontanini works exclusively with Clute—a chain-smoking redhead in his mid-thirties who apprenticed under the legendary handler Jimmy Moses—on her top dogs. She admits that when the time does come to retire Beyoncé, the hardest part will be convincing Clute to part with her. "When Jamie first saw her, he fell in love. I said, 'Take her out and see what she does.' She just came out like gangbusters. That first year she went out and won the National Specialty." Beyoncé was barely even two.

That beautiful black bitch hasn't stopped winning since, and for two years running, as of late 2010, had been the number-one-ranked Australian shepherd in America by a large margin. Fontanini had plans to breed her but was considering keeping the dog out long enough to make a run at the all-time record for Best in Show by an Aussie bitch. That number is seventeen. The breed record is over thirty. "That was Bayshore's Flapjack"—a dog that won many of those with Jimmy Moses on his lead as well as, for a period, the Grabes—"and I don't think that will be broken for a long time."

It was interesting to hear Fontanini explain what makes Beyoncé special; her answer, in a sense, was that she isn't. "She has beautiful breed type. She's a nice moderate dog. She's not extreme in any way." Words like "moderate" and "medium," you might recall, are key words in the Aussie's standard. "She has beautiful movement. On top of all that, the icing on the cake, she is just a show dog. Her heart is always in it. In her mind that's her place in life. To be in that ring and be showing off for people."

The name didn't hurt either. Fontanini didn't have names picked out in advance for that particular litter. But she was watching *Dreamgirls* on TV while waiting for the puppies to arrive, and "Beyoncé was the star of that movie. And when she [the puppy] popped out, the movie was on. She was *my* dream girl."

Here's where things get perhaps a bit apocryphal (as many backstories do). "She wanted to be first from the beginning," Fontanini said. "I could just tell. Even as a puppy, she was like, 'Look at me.' She would push her brother and sister aside and say, 'Hey, it was me you came to see.' She always had that attitude. The world revolves around Beyoncé."

Well, the Australian shepherd world anyway—where it appeared that life was imitating art.

Nothing is impossible. Every dog show is subjective. You just never know. After all, Jack pretty much beat Beyoncé at Westminster, in the sense that when the judge was picking between the two best dogs, Beyoncé wasn't one of them and Jack was. But that was wholly unexpected, and it certainly wasn't the kind of result Jack could hope to repeat so early in his own campaign.

And Kimberly's pessimism was not unfounded. Beyoncé won both days in Virginia, taking the Herding Group on Sunday and nearly taking it Saturday, when she earned a Group 2. Heather later reported that she had no complaints about Jack's performance and that Sunday's judge sought her out afterward to say that she "absolutely loved him" but that "he could be fitter." She added that Jack and Beyoncé were "by far" the two best dogs she'd judged all day. It was high praise, but the criticism was justified. Heather was right again.

"My treadmill is broken, and the weather hasn't been good, but we will start running again now that the weather is better," was Kimberly's response when I relayed the conversation.

Failing an upset, the most exciting thing about the Virginia shows for Kimberly was that Heather asked her to be the team's assistant. Being still new to shows, and easily the least experienced owner among the regulars around the setup, she was thrilled to feel included. Despite any tension that might exist in their relationship, the fact that Heather had asked her to participate officially was appreciated. It didn't matter that what this really meant was that none of their regular assistants were available and that she would be the gopher, doing the jobs that Heather and Kevin either had no time for or didn't wish to do. No matter—Kimberly was happy just to be asked.

She was also happy because the latest rankings were out and Jack was again on the rise. Ratings are released at the end of each month, and as of March 31 he was the number-nine Aussie in the all-breed rankings and the number-twelve Aussie overall. "Not a bad start," Kimberly wrote in an e-mail to Heather and Kerry. "I'm so lucky!"

It made the less glamorous reality of her apprentice work in Virginia that much easier to take. The first thing Heather said when she arrived in Harrisonburg was that the Cardigan Welsh corgi Thor was desperately in need of a bath; he'd gotten diarrhea in his crate on the drive down and was now a nervous, short-legged mess.

The task of rectifying such a crisis is ugly enough, but it was made worse by Thor's unwillingness to let Kim anywhere near his rear end, which he was protecting as if his ass were full of jewels. She did the best she could and then told Kevin that he might want to check that there wasn't something more serious going on. Kevin managed to calm the dog enough to get a look under the hood, and . . . well, here's what he found, according to Kimberly: "His balls were bright red and raw. They were so sensitive and almost sticky." The problem, it turned out, was that there were multiple bitches in heat at Thor's house and he'd had no access to them. So he'd just licked himself obsessively for days, in misery.

CHAPTER SEVENTEEN

Like Walking Energy on a Leash

> When a dog is sad or happy, the feeling occupies his entire
> being; the dog becomes pure happiness or pure sadness.
> —JEFFREY MOUSSAIEFF MASSON, *Dogs Never Lie About Love*

Jack's place is a neat, white-sided town house on a street of neat, white-sided town houses in the quiet hamlet of Chalfont, Pennsylvania. It's bucolic country, rolling and green and especially yellow-lit and flowery on a warm, sunny day in April, the kind of day that makes anyplace look and feel like California.

In two days' time, Jack would be off to Heather's again, and then to Harrisburg, Pennsylvania, where he'd face off against the deepest pool of champions yet this spring, thanks to rumors that the Saturday show would be broadcast on Animal Planet. Kimberly took Jack's lost weekend in Harrisonburg harder than I'd expected, considering he ran into the unstoppable number-one Australian shepherd in the country, but her spirits were buoyed the April rankings, which (at least on the all-breed list) put her dog in the country's top 10.

Also brightening her spirits was the news that Kerry had decided to ship Jack's first-ever girlfriend out to Pennsylvania for breeding instead of having a vial of his potential progeny FedExed out to California on dry ice. This meant that Jack would get to "live cover," the dog-world euphemism for having actual intercourse. Breeding isn't as easy or intuitive as you might think, especially for a young dog who's never so much as fake-humped anything livelier than a human leg. Some dogs just don't ever excel. And Jack might not. But at least he'd get his shot, and this made Kimberly happy.

It was Thursday, and Halle B, the chosen bitch, was already in day four of heat. There was little time to waste. Kerry planned to box her up and have her on a plane by Monday, so that she could arrive and get acclimated in time to be comfortable for her short window of fertility—days ten through twelve of the estrous cycle.

Since Kimberly had never bred dogs before, many questions were yet to be answered. Foremost among them, would Halle stay and whelp in Pennsylvania or be sent home after her love holiday? Of course, she needed the dog to get pregnant first, so Kimberly planned to study up and have her friend Maggie, a local owner and exhibitor of Aussies she'd met on the show circuit (and who had some experience breeding), over to assist. Lastly, she researched and found a good local reproductive veterinarian. The rest would be up to Jack (and Halle).

While she was at it, Kimberly planned to get Jack's sperm extracted anyway. "God forbid something should happen," she said. Dogs are subject to the same cruel fates as the rest of us. "And Kerry's already had someone asking if he was available."

First things first: We had to find out if Jack was even good at this. And then if his puppies would indeed be good stock. Until that was known, "he's not proven," Kimberly said. In terms of a stud fee, owners basically set their own price, though, like anything, it's only as much as the market will bear. Kimberly settled with twelve hundred dollars in mind as a starting point. Tanner, by comparison, was twenty-five hundred a pop, but Tanner is proven—he has produced finished champions, even if he hasn't managed to master the actual art of natural reproduction. Proven for Jack would be a two-part process: He'd need "to prove that he's studly," in Kimberly's words, and then that he can produce champions.

J ack had no idea what excitement was about to befall him. Instead he was at the window barking and going nuts as if I had just pulled up atop a giant wolf or been attempting to jimmy the door with a crowbar while wearing a mime costume and a Hamburglar mask. If you were to meet Jack at home, showing up unannounced, you would not think, "This is a top-ranked show dog." You would think, "This is a wild animal." And his pal Summer isn't much better. The two of them tend to greet visitors with great vigor that is not easily subdued.

Jack in particular will propel himself at your midsection in the style of a battering ram or a bull in Pamplona. The first time he did this, he actually collided with my genitals with great force, causing me to double over. At which time he jumped on my back. "He has taken out many a man," Kimberly said, and laughed.

By this point, four months into our friendship, I knew to bend my right leg (only because I favor it; either leg will do) and raise it in front of my crotch like a hockey goalie deflecting a puck, then push him in the snout when he bounced up. Then I would attempt to position a piece of furniture—say, a dining-room chair—between him and me until he was settled down.

When the excitement seems uncontainable, Kimberly has a secret weapon. She has a little A-frame metal fence that came with one of her travel crates. It's tiny, not even chest-high on Summer, but it works like a force field. It's so low that Jack could fall over it accidentally, but he wouldn't dare risk it. Kimberly could put it in front of a pile of raw meat, so that it blocked the way only in front but was open on the sides, and Jack wouldn't eat even if he were starving. It was kind of amazing to witness, especially if you understand dogs to be mostly id, with only gossamers of superego holding back those primal impulses. "He started off afraid of it, but now he just respects it," Kimberly said. And Summer has learned from him to respect it, too.

Jack is also easily distracted with tricks. "Jack, where's your Frisbee?" I asked him. He froze and cocked his head, always to the right.

"I think it's downstairs," Kimberly said, and he looked at her the same way, then trotted around the corner out of sight and skittered down the wooden stairs to the basement. A minute later he was back carrying a Frisbee, but not his Frisbee. This one was purple. "Jack's is in bad shape," Kimberly explained. "He broke it in half, and I had to tape it up, but it doesn't really fly anymore."

Kimberly had promised Heather she'd be resolute on the issue of Jack's weight. Every morning, weather permitting, she was throwing his Frisbee for ten to fifteen minutes, and since Jack does nothing half-assed, this was a fairly intense workout. He likes his Frisbee to be thrown with verve and altitude, so that he needs to jump to catch it. He'll then sprint back and drop it for the next throw. After ten minutes he'll be panting like a dog that's just run the thousand-meter hurdles, which he sort of has. At least three evenings a week, Kimberly or Megan would also take Jack for a jog, and if it was raining, there was always the treadmill, which was now (sort of) fixed.

"Jack loves the treadmill," Kimberly reminded me, then demonstrated by unfolding it from the wall of her living room. Jack immediately ran and stood on it, just as he is likely to jump up and stand on any table, platform, or ottoman that crosses his path. (This is a vestige of his agility training—the table sit-and-stay is part of any agility course).

"It's not really working that well," Kimberly said as she shooed him off while it whirred and thumped to life. Once the track was moving at a decent clip, she gave him the okay, and Jack set about trotting. He'd prefer the treadmill go faster, frankly.

To further distract him, Kimberly had a game. She put him on a stay in the kitchen and tore up a few sticks of Pup-Peroni, which she then hid all around the main floor of her house—and not in obvious places: on windowsills, under couches, behind throw pillows. She then released him, and he began his sweep, first with a quick dash around the floor, jerking his head to and fro to catch scents. Then he returned to the living room and searched more methodically, with his nose on the floor, seeking scent trails. When he found a treat, he gobbled it and moved on. A few treats in, he came and stood in front of her to see how he was doing. If she said, "Jack, did you find all your treats? Did you find them all? Where are they?" it meant that he had not and that he should continue. If she said, "Good boy," and patted him, he was done. Kimberly and Taylor had taught Jack to play hide-and-seek, and he loved that, too. Kimberly would put her hands over Jack's eyes and hold a stay until Taylor was well hidden, at which time Kimberly would remove her hand and Jack would always find him, thanks to his excellent nose.

Kimberly is convinced that Jack could be a champion tracking dog, too, even though this is not at all a strength of Australian shepherds. She once scared Taylor during a rebellious phase of his by saying she was thinking about training Jack to detect the odor of marijuana and said she is "a hundred percent sure" that if she were to drop the dog an hour or two from the house, "he'd find his way home" like a dog from the movies. "I know it." (Though she also had him microchipped, just in case.)

She thinks maybe when he's retired from showing, she'll try him in tracking, and dock diving,* and surely agility and obedience. Maybe he'll be the first dog to achieve a championship in every possible discipline. "There's just so much I want to do with him," she said. "He excites the shit out of me."

I think we need a plan for tonight," Kimberly said, laughing. I had come to take Jack to handling class, to get a feel for what it was

---

*A kind of doggie long jump in which dogs leap into the water after a tossed toy from a dock. Farthest leap wins.

that Heather was up against. For months I'd been observing their partnership and respecting her ability to bring a difficult, strong-willed animal under her control, but I'd yet to actually give handling a try. It seemed like a worthy exercise if ever I was going to appreciate this mystical art.

"So you think he's going to give me trouble?" I asked.

"Jack will be a basket case." Kimberly thought she'd bring Summer along in case I got too frustrated and we needed to sub in a more will-ing participant. I pointed out the irony of the situation: that a relatively untrained puppy with virtually no show experience could be easier to work with than the twelfth-ranked Australian shepherd in America.

We grabbed the tools—a bag of Pup-Peroni, which looks and smells suspiciously like the human analogue,* and the choke collar, which is properly applied when you loop one end through the other and make a P (and not a backward P, which can hurt the dog).

Class is held at the Sanmann Kennels, in a large room above a ga-rage. Sue and Eric Petermann have been breeding champion golden re-trievers here since 1979, and Sue augments those services with groom-ing, boarding, and training services. There were four of the Sanmann golden puppies in my class—all of them in that adorable awkward phase where they have the giant paws and gawky teenage limbs to go along with the short, infantilized snout and downy fur—as well as two rottweilers, two Bernese mountain dogs, an Irish setter, two terriers, and a spinone Italiano† wearing panties. (She was in heat, obviously—a fact verified by the beeline Jack made for her.)

Prior to this I'd never attempted to handle Jack on a lead. I'd only seen him work with Heather, who we know has a direct line to his brain's cooperation center. Kimberly warned me that the other dogs would surely excite him and that I wasn't to allow him to socialize. Being a good handler is like being a good parent—you have to be stern

---

*Note to self: Buy only artisanal pepperoni.

†A wiry, midsize hunting dog also known as the Italian pointer.

and consistent. If you allow a little slack, the dog will run with it. And Jack. Oh, Jack. If you can imagine what it would be like to put a leash on a wild dingo that had been starved for a week and then was allowed to jump into a swimming pool full of rib-eye steaks, that's a little what it's like to try to wrangle Jack on his lead (which is a choke lead, I should add). But I tugged on him and tried to be firm, and by the time Sue asked us to line up and stack, he'd at least calmed down to something resembling a trained animal.

Sue has clipped, bleached-blond hair and the carriage of a gym teacher. She's nice and chatty and prone to tangents, such as one about Bruce Springsteen that I was unable to follow because I was too busy attempting to get Jack to stack. Every time I set his front legs about where I thought they should go, he moved his back legs, and vice versa. Later Kimberly would tell me that he was actually being helpful. He is so familiar with the stack that he knows what it feels like to be wrong. (This is the operating principle of the Happy Legs, of course: Once a dog knows how a stack feels and has been rewarded for finding that zone, he will just do it.)

Similarly, when we did our first trot around the room—which should begin with three exaggerated walk-steps: step, step, step, trot!*—Sue asked us to move the dogs from our left side, the show side, to the right. This is to take the dogs out of their comfort zones for a moment. To emphasize this point, she asked us to stop and cross our arms. "Okay, now cross them the other way. Feels weird, right?" It did. It seems that we all have a familiar, comfortable way that we cross our arms—one arm always on top—and to do it the other way just feels wrong. This is how it feels for a show dog to run on our right, Sue said.

Once we were under way, Jack was remarkably kind to me. I know he knows this stuff down pat and he's not exactly just following orders,

---

*And "trot" is the proper and appropriate term. A fast walk is too slow and a run too fast. This does not apply to terriers and other short-legged dogs. In the case of these animals, the handler will always appear to be out for a leisurely stroll, which is funny when you look down at the dog and see his/her little legs chugging along in a blur.

but he was no longer acting like an uncaged dingo in a pool full of meat. For the most part, he ran when he was supposed to run and stood still when he was supposed to stand still, with brief lapses every now and then to jump on the head of a golden retriever puppy.

The real problem was me. Sue corrected me twice in front of the class. Once because I was too stiff. "Relax!" she yelled, which just made me stiffen up more. "And remember you're the boss. You're in charge. Not Jack."

The second time she took issue with my running style.

"Are you a runner?" she asked.

Sorta, I answered.

"Well, I'm not, but do you run like this?" And then she did an imitation of me that looked like a man who had suffered right-side paralysis; her right arm hung dead at her side. "You're allowed to move your arm," she said. "It actually works better if you do."

I went around the room again, making sure to move my right arm like a jogger. It felt wrong. "Much better," she told me. "You'll be in the ring at Westminster next year."

Kimberly spied me patting Jack on the side and grabbed me when I came by. "Don't praise him," she snapped. "Heather says she'd love to get to a point where she can praise him in the ring." But at this precarious point in his career, praise just made his butt wiggle—and that won't do in front of a judge. Focus was a constant battle for young Jack.

On the ride home, Kimberly told me that she hadn't told Heather about our experiment, fearing that her handler would worry that I might somehow cause Jack to regress. I said that Heather didn't need to fret. I could actually tell that he knew what he was doing on the lead and that the only reason he wasn't actually listening to me as intently as he should have been under the circumstances was that he knew I was out of my element. It wasn't until I attempted to work in tandem with Jack that I realized there was nothing random about his impertinence, and it struck me that whatever impatience he showed wasn't with the task, it was with me.

CHAPTER EIGHTEEN

Welcome, Halle B

. . . .

Show dogs come home with us and live on our couches and
shed on our black clothes and drink out of the toilet just
like any other dogs.

—DAVID FREI

. . . .

On Monday, Kimberly left Harrisburg, Pennsylvania, after a disappointing weekend of losses and drove to Newark Airport to
pick up a very special package: Jack's girlfriend, who was scheduled to
arrive from California via Continental Airlines at 6:52 P.M.

Part of her purview as co-owner was that Kerry could dictate which
bitches to pair with Jack. And she chose for his first mate a large black
tri named Ch Wyndstar's Agua Dulce Halebeari—sound that last word
closely and you'll get it*—aka Halle B.

Halle B had last bred with Jack's father, Honor, and the result, Kerry
proclaimed, "was a very nice litter." She was optimistic about a partnership with Jack.

When I asked her what specifically she was hoping to get, she said

---

*Still need help? Here's a clue: She won an Oscar (and flashed her boobs) in *Monster's
Ball*.

she felt that Jack's "lineage" would further enhance the excellent quality she'd seen in mating Halle and Honor. "Jack's mother, Gracie, is the prettiest mover and has reproduced that numerous times."

As movement is something Jack is said to do well, you could expect that these puppies would share the trait. Breeding is far from an exact science, but the basics of it are fairly simple: You want to reinforce the good traits of specific animals while eliminating flaws. Responsible breeders of a particular breed work in concert to eliminate problematic traits—in the case of Aussies, for instance, the eye condition PRA (or progressive retinal atrophy). Before Kimberly and Kerry could breed Jack, they had to test that he wasn't prone to this trait, and the results said that he wasn't. He also had his hips and elbows certified to signify that they were not prone to failures. Beyond that, breeders will tend to pick mates that correct for minor flaws in the other dog.

Kimberly arrived alone and waited a good hour for Continental to deliver the crate to the PetSafe desk. Halle, she said, was "sweet, but scared to death." This was actually the first time, in all her years of breeding, that Kerry had ever shipped a bitch out to be bred, and I got the sense that it was at least partly for my benefit, which I greatly appreciated. She was even considering the possibility of keeping Halle in Pennsylvania throughout her pregnancy, so that Kimberly could experience the whole process and maybe even keep a puppy. Provided Halle got pregnant, that is.

"Halle B is a great mother, and it should be fairly easy for all involved," Kerry said. "Otherwise I wouldn't even consider the idea."

Once home, it wasn't an easy adjustment. Halle was a kennel dog and, like all kennel dogs, was not accustomed to being polite in houses. So, combined with the rather traumatic experience of flying cross-country alone in a crate, the dog seemed to be "scared stiff," Kimberly reported. Halle just couldn't seem to relax inside and was constantly agitating near the door, wanting to go out. Eventually Kimberly put her on a chain and walked her, and "finally, after an hour, she relaxed enough to take a dump—in my living room."

Almost from the instant Halle arrived, Jack was courting her. "He actually mounted her twice the first day," Kimberly said. "He's just being fresh. And she's letting him be." Heather had warned Kimberly to be careful, that she might want to keep Halle muzzled during her interactions with Jack, because a bitch in heat can be very aggressive to an interested male.

Halle, though, was fine. She liked Jack, and he liked her. Seeing as she wasn't exactly trained in the customs of indoor living, Halle was left in a kennel during the day, and Jack would flirt through the bars.

The second day Kimberly's friend Maggie took them to the reproductive vet so that Halle's progesterone could be tested. A dog is in heat—the proper term, by the way, is in estrus—for two to three weeks, but despite the fact that only a few days of the period are actually viable for insemination, there's no harm in hedging bets by letting the dogs hump as much as they want. (It's also good practice.)

Jack's travel schedule was a potential problem. It was a busy time on the show circuit—in fact, one of the busiest weekends of the year, with forty-three all-breed shows in sixteen locations taking place across America, none bigger than the trio of shows in Timonium, a Baltimore suburb. And the math seemed to be indicating that Halle might be most fertile while Jack was to be away at a show that Kimberly wasn't planning to attend. "If I have to, I guess I can take her," Kimberly said. "And get them a room." She laughed, mostly because that wasn't actually a joke.[*]

A few days into the courtship period, the ongoing saga was stressing Kimberly out. Despite repeated and eager attempts to mount his new girlfriend, Jack had been unable to breed Halle, and Kimberly's first trip to the vet verified what Maggie had suspected: The bitch just wasn't quite ready.

The vet had tested Halle's progesterone, and it came back a two—

---

[*] It's a violation of AKC rules to allow dogs to mate on a show's premises; it's even a little uncouth to show up with a dog in full-blown heat, frankly.

she wasn't quite ready. Truthfully, the vet didn't even need that result to tell. "How do I say this . . . ? Her vulva looks very small," Kimberly told me sheepishly. Dogs don't exactly have genitalia as expressive as baboons do, which have vulvas that swell to the size of hot pink baseball mitts, but they do tend to swell somewhat to give the males a bigger target. One reason Jack wasn't able to dock the ship was that the harbor wasn't exactly open for business. As Kimberly put it, with a bit more subtlety, "It would be difficult for him to get in there."

Poor Jack. Surely his little balls must have been feeling mighty blue by the time he got some relief from a woman wearing rubber gloves.

O n a Saturday morning, I rose about dawn and cajoled my nearly nine-months-pregnant fiancée* to accompany me, in order to bring fertility karma—as well as to hedge my bets should she go into labor and I miss key portions of this milestone event because I was two hours away watching a dog get a hand job. We splashed some cold water on our faces, brewed up some coffee, and pointed the car toward Bucks County, Pennsylvania.

Jack was due at the Timonium show, but he had a late ring time, and Kimberly had arranged to first take him to see the doctor for another collection. The vet would also be testing Halle's progesterone, and, if it seemed possible, she'd do an artificial insemination (or AI). There was even a chance that if the circumstances worked out, and if Halle had advanced into a more fertile period, that we could try to get the dogs to mate in a less clinical fashion. That, I suppose, would be the rare trifecta.

A dog's sperm has a vital life of seven days and can live in refrigeration for at least three or four more if a substance known as extender has been added to the sample. The vet had declared Jack's first sperm "good" but thought that the sample could still be better. It was Jack's

---

*Now wife.

first time, and maybe all parties, even the microscopic ones, had under-performed.

Whether or not he'd be willing to try an actual live cover was a different story. Kimberly said that he'd been mounting Halle "right and left" until Maggie came over to help. "Then nothing. The whole time she was here, he wouldn't try it." Young Jack had stage fright. Five minutes after Maggie left, he was right back at it. It seemed that Jack didn't want to fool around in uncomfortable surroundings—and any married person who's stayed more than a few days with the in-laws can certainly relate.

If the morning's efforts were unsuccessful, Kimberly might have to take Halle along to Baltimore and then find them some space to get intimate. She'd discussed the matter with Heather and learned that the grounds were plenty large. "She said you'd definitely have to go away from the show, but that it's not a problem to walk far enough off the grounds to a quiet area." But this would be a last resort. Kimberly didn't want to go to the show. She had plans. Specifically, a date with a guy she'd been seeing. "He might not be happy if I cancel to go help Jack get laid again."

My fiancée Gillian and I were out in Pennsylvania by 7:45 A.M. and found Kimberly in the parking lot, idling in her Subaru, with the always eager Jack bouncing from seat to seat. Halle was in the rear, in her crate, and Kimberly had to coax her out and into the parking lot, where she assumed the slinky posture of a nervous animal.

As excitable as Jack is, Halle was that mellow. She was a fairly standard-looking black tri with only a little red on her chest and around her eyes, which were ringed in thin white circles and were, in Kimberly's estimation, a little too close together. "I think she looks like Beetle-juice," she said, chuckling.

Halle was quiet and affectionate and already very attached to Kimberly. She didn't resist a friendly pat, but she didn't reach for it either.

And when Kimberly turned away, she would gently stand up on her rear legs and put those giant white paws on her hips, as if to say, "Help. I don't want to make small talk with these strangers." Jack, meanwhile, was Jack—launching himself into my midsection and, when scolded to stay down, running around and thrusting himself between my legs from behind, where he'd sit between my knees in the ready position he'd learned in agility class.

The doctor was doing us a favor. She had come in on her off day and met us in the lobby, where a TV behind the desk played Animal Planet's dog show of the day. She asked us to reconvene in the large animal ward of the hospital—a concrete-floored room through some metallic double doors of the kind you'd see in a morgue. It contained a stall-like apparatus for hoisting horses and other large animals in distress, and the room felt sterile and industrial. Fortunately, Jack doesn't require ambience.

The vet arrived and assigned me a critical role. I was to hold Halle in place, she said, pointing to a spot in the corner. "And face her butt toward us."

I complied, feeling a little like a character in a lost chapter of the Kinsey files. To her credit, Halle cooperated gamely as the doctor prepared a large, clear condom with a collector vial at the end. Once ready, the vet crouched back behind Jack with her hands near his midsection as Kimberly urged him forward.

It was awkward and overly intimate—and very awkward (did I mention awkward?)—to be one of three humans assisting two dogs in getting into the mood, but the dogs didn't seem to care much. I remembered a line I'd just read in a book about breeding written by a vet named Dan Rice. "Avoid a circus atmosphere," he'd written, but then qualified himself, saying that "if both are inexperienced, help may be necessary." Help had arrived and was in position.

The more I'd read about breeding, the more I learned that Jack had nothing to be ashamed of. First-time breeders—dog virgins—are often pretty inept. Dr. Rice wrote that "younger males often begin by mounting the female's neck, and fumble their way back to the appropriate position." Jack at least knew which end to aim for.

If we may break temporarily to discuss the physiology of the situation, I think you can better sympathize with a young male's plight. A dog's penis is more different from the human variant than you might think. (Or certainly more than *I* thought.) It doesn't actually become erect until he's successfully penetrated the female, at which time it swells to lock things into place. How does a dog penetrate a female with a flaccid penis? Good question. And nature has an ingenious answer. The dog phallus has something known as the os penis, a thin bone that runs through the shaft and allows a male to aim at the target and achieve initial penetration. I can't think of a totally apt analog to help you picture this, but I suppose it's a bit like tying a rock to a rope that you need to throw over the high branch of a tree. Without the rock you'd never get the rope high enough, let alone in the right spot, but once the rope is over the branch, the rock is no longer necessary. That's the os penis.

There in the lab, Jack was initially a bit hesitant, but Kimberly nudged him forward until nature took over and the potent fragrance of dog pheromones overpowered the intrusion of all these humans all up in his business, and Jack's pelvis began to bounce—first just a little, in a series of test humps, then more enthusiastically, until young Jack had Halle by the hips and was air-humping like a jackhammer. From where I stood (fortunately), I couldn't really see much of what was going on underneath all this gyrating fur, but Gillian later told me that from where she stood on the other side of the room, she had a fully unvarnished view of the vet's handiwork. Her exact words, on the ride home, were, "And I might never get that image out of my head. Or the smell."

Whatever the specifics of the transaction, the mission was accomplished and the vet revealed a vial one-quarter filled with a few teaspoons of milky white liquid that she proclaimed "a good sample. That's all sperm."

The doctor left us momentarily to check the sample under her microscope and returned a few minutes later to report that it was good. She asked if anyone wanted to take a look, and I certainly did. Seeing dog sperm at extreme magnification is kind of like looking at TV static—there's light gray background with all these electric-black particles whipping around. If you focus out the noise and look closely, those particles are tiny black worms spazzing in their singular purpose: to swim like hell for the uterus.

The average dog ejaculation has 1 billion sperm, the vet told me. "And you need two hundred fifty million to get a breeding." Since she won't need all this to do the artificial insemination, the vet could freeze the remainder, as well as future samples, to help ensure Jack's legacy for many generations. She didn't yet know how well Jack's sperm will deal with this. "Some dogs don't freeze well."

Using frozen sperm, however, is somewhat trickier than a live cover or even an AI. For one thing, it has to be inseminated directly into the uterus, which requires surgery.

Halle's artificial insemination turned out to be a breeze. A vet tech appeared and held her while the doctor inserted a sterile plastic plunger into her vagina. It's uncomfortable, and many dogs hate it, she said, but Halle was a champ. "She didn't flinch," the tech announced, and patted her on the head. To enlist gravity to the cause, the vet held Halle's rear section up in the air for another five minutes, but the whole thing was over in less than ten.

"How's Jack doing?" she asked, and took a peek at his undercarriage. She was wondering if his penis had retracted back into its sheath, and it hadn't.* She noted that his erection "was a good one" and said that not only had his full penis come out but also that something known as the bulbus glandis, a pink lump at the base that also appears when a dog is fully aroused. This is what swells inside the bitch and locks the dogs into a tie. Once tied, the dogs will shift positions until they are butt

---

*"Likewise," reported the author Dr. Rice, "a male's penis will appear inflamed and swollen for a few hours following tie breeding, but injury is unlikely."

to butt for the completion of the act and cannot be separated until the male has ejaculated and the swelling goes away. I had a vague notion of the lesson that mating dogs should never be separated—it can really hurt them—but I managed to go thirty-six years without knowing that when they're fully engaged, they will be standing butt to butt and will stay that way for up to forty-five minutes.

I haven't spent much time observing the mechanics of procreation across different species, but you'd have a hard time convincing me that animal lovemaking could be less romantic than it is for dogs. It begins simply enough—a willing female, an eager male—and accelerates quickly as the male grabs hold and commences frantic pumping (and in that way isn't that different from human teenagers, I suppose) until he has connected, literally. That's where things get weird and impersonal. Once locked in place (again, literally), the dogs begin a bit of yoga. The male will bring one of his front legs over the bitch's back until they're standing side by side, still attached at the privates. Then one of the dogs turns itself so that their rears are facing each other and the male's penis is facing backward between his legs while still locked in place. This sounds painful but is apparently not. He then stands butt to butt with his mate for the duration of the session, which consists basically of two dogs staring wanly in the distance. If you were to walk by two dogs in a "tie," you would think, "Those two dogs are really upset with each other." When, of course, the complete opposite is true: The dogs are engaged in the most intimate act of all. The bang then ends with a whimper when, after an unspecific duration that could be five or fifty minutes, the male dog's equipment disengages and he simply walks away for a nap.

I tend to be one of those nonreligious people who see the holy/magic/mystical/what-have-you in nature. The natural architecture, nearly always, is perfect—everything carefully crafted and having a precise reason*—but I am fully confused by the process of dog mat-

---

*Bats possessing sonar, the precise geometry of every snowflake, hummingbirds migrating thousands of miles and then returning to the exact same spot, et cetera, et cetera.

ing, which is by extension wolf mating. It's tough to understand why it would make biological sense for two wolves to be connected to each other for up to a half hour so tightly that it would cause harm to one or both of them to break away suddenly. And not only that, but to be connected for up to a half hour while facing in different directions, so that if danger does arrive, the two animals are doomed.

Any mental image I have of wolves panicking and attempting to evade disaster while connected at the pelvis is gruesome.[*] Either the stronger one drags the weaker behind, backward, very slowly and awkwardly, or the two tear apart in a fashion so horrible and violent that it would chill Lorena Bobbitt. Or, in the Wile E. Coyote–est of outcomes, they each attempt to bolt and so precisely counteract each other's energy that they are stuck in a kind of stasis, running in place as if on treadmills.

The only biological reason that the tie makes any sense is to ensure that babies will be made. Which means that, for wolves, the biological imperative of passing on one's genes overpowers the one I tended to regard as most potent in the animal kingdom: the will to survive. Mother Nature is saying, "Sure, some wolves might get picked off by rivals while copulating, but the vast majority will emerge unscathed— and they will almost certainly have puppies." The pack is more important than the individual. Or two individuals, as it were.

Within a few minutes, Jack had sheathed his sword, and we returned to the cars, us to head home, Jack and Kimberly to go to Timonium for the shows—where he'd lose the first two days before ending the disappointing but eventful month on a high note with a breed win at the third and final show of the weekend.

There in the parking lot, Jack was as calm as I'd seen him. I could swear he was smiling. "Wouldn't you be?" Kimberly said, and drove off.

---

[*]Unless I imagine them as cartoon wolves, in which case it's kind of hilarious.

CHAPTER NINETEEN

Stayin' Alive (Often with Great Effort):

Breeding Ain't Always Pretty

It does not make much difference where the dog came from. . . . They have been molded into gadgets for us to use, admire or play with, afield or on a cushion.

—MCDOWELL LYON

I feel like my dogs are my canvas and I paint with genes. When the judge looks at my breeding he or she is looking at my creativity, my art form. And when I walk into the Bred by Exhibitor class I'm signing the bottom corner of my painting.

—PAUL CHEN, "CONFESSIONS OF A BREEDER-OWNER-HANDLER"
(FROM DOGCHANNEL.COM)

I f it weren't for humans, bulldogs would be extinct. The dogs can't reproduce or deliver young naturally, and so almost all pregnancies are achieved via artificial insemination and all litters are delivered via C-section. You could say it's more than a little messed up that we're sustaining breeds that can't sustain themselves, but there's also another way to look at it: If it weren't for humans, bulldogs wouldn't have existed in the first place.

Bulldogs, as well as pugs, boxers, and Boston terriers, are what's known as brachycephalic dogs. The term means, literally, "short-headed" and that seems self-explanatory. Beyond the reproductive complications that afflict them, bulldogs and the other brachycephalic dogs commonly suffer from respiratory problems—their shortened airways can cause breathing distress, and they will pant excessively to help compensate for their propensity to overheat. Lacking the protective proboscis of a snout, the dogs can also quite easily damage their eyes, and it makes me cringe to report that it's not uncommon for them to experience proptosis, or a prolapse in which—I'm sorry—the eyeball pops out of the socket. Most often this is caused by a collision or a fight, but it's been known to happen when pressure builds up in the head from something as simple as the dog's pulling too hard on a leash or chain. I know, yikes.

Why would we breed a dog that has breathing problems, can't reproduce naturally, and has eyes that sometimes pop out during walks? In the case of bulldogs, it's because they were originally bred for the sport of bull baiting, which pitted dog versus bull, and the architecture of the face was specifically engineered to allow the dog to be able to clamp down and hold on to a thrashing bull without hampering its ability to breathe. The folds on the dog's face channeled the bull's blood away from the eyes and off the face like tiny viaducts. The breeding problems come from the head's size, which is disproportionately large compared to the body and makes it impossible for a baby bulldog to pass through the birth canal of a female. That, too, is functional; putting the bulk of the dog's weight in the front and giving it a short, stout body was a protective measure that prevented a bull from breaking the dog's back by thrashing violently.

I feel slightly guilty reporting any of this, because bulldogs are actually wonderful dogs with great temperaments. People absolutely adore them, and they adore people. But it seems a little disingenuous to paint a picture of the purebred-dog world at its most elite level and ignore the fact that in the process of making these wonderful animals we've also kind of screwed them up.

Bulldogs actually aren't the only dogs that have trouble mating. According to our old friend Dan Rice, in his *Complete Book of Dog Breeding,* toy breeds have major issues, too. "The muscle mass in some tiny breeds is so undeveloped, and skeletal construction is so delicate, that males lack the physical strength, athletic ability, and endurance necessary to mount and breed a female," Rice writes. "Likewise, some females are so frail they can't support the weight of a male. The teacup-sized toy breeds are especially subject to those kinds of conformational breeding problems." Considering their short legs, he writes, "it is little wonder that dachshund, basset, and Welsh corgi males occasionally require assistance when attempting to breed."

To further complicate basset hound breeding, Rice reports, "many females have an apron of fat and loose skin that drapes downward over their vulvas, effectively preventing normal, unassisted intromission (male penis introduction into the vaginal tract)."

All that said, nature is one powerful bitch herself. Dr. Rice goes on to relate the story of a long-haired dachshund who utilized his tunneling prowess to dig his way out of his fenced yard and into one next door, where a tantalizing golden retriever in estrus roamed free—after all, who's afraid of a little dachshund? Oops—she got knocked up.

With that in mind, anything seems possible.

I feel the need to state here that I didn't meet a single person in a year of attending dog shows who didn't care deeply about his or her breed; these are people who work tirelessly and methodically to weed out genetic problems. Legitimate breeders, the kinds of people who breed and show the dogs you see at conformation events, are the first line of defense in maintaining healthy stocks. That's the reason we had shows in the first place. But it's an ongoing challenge.

The problem lies in the process—the way you create a breed is by interbreeding related animals to magnify desired traits, but that's a messy business, because you're also concentrating undesirable traits. In the words of McDowell Lyon's *The Dog in Action:* "Our domestic animals are handicapped by the fact that we force the parts upon them and preserve the bad along with the good. The animals of the wild, as complete species, have been more fortunate because of that great selection process known as the survival of the fittest."

Historically, the way you minimized flaws was to eliminate any diseased or otherwise inferior dog from the breeding program at the first sign of trouble. Today there's the added help of DNA testing and the ever-increasing knowledge of dog genetics provided by the Dog Genome Project, ongoing at the National Institutes for Health. Like the Human Genome Project, the DGP aims to locate and map genes, in this case canine genes—good and bad—so that a simple blood test can identify which dogs are carriers.

The first dog (a female boxer) was sequenced in 2005.[*] *Canis familiaris,* they found, provided a handy subject for genomic study, because the species has been broken down over time into breeds with gene pools that are then closed off, allowing for subsets of traits to be maintained within those populations. By looking at a specific breed of canine, the Dog Genome team can identify and study disease, behavior, and morphology, and in a relatively small number of genes. Initially this had little to do with dogs at all; the point was to help humans.

"If you look at the top ten diseases in dogs," the project's Heidi Parker told me, "all but one are top-ten diseases in humans as well. The only one dogs get that we don't is bloat." (Bloat, as we shall see soon, is

---

[*]The boxer was chosen for its relatively low level of heterozygosity. It has chromosomes that are very similar, making it easier to map than, say, a poodle, which has more variation.

serious business.) Dogs, she said, "get all kinds of cancer," plus epilepsy, diabetes, and heart disease. This would probably be the case with most animal species, she notes, but the difference is that most animals in the wild don't live long enough to develop problems like cancer and heart disease, both of which are closely related to aging. "The other thing about dogs is that they're getting medical care—they get diagnosed."

The dog genome map has been in place for over five years now, and additional breeds can be mapped in about a month. Whereas the first map cost $1 million, today it's more like $10,000 a pop. Increasingly, Parker and the team (led by Elaine Ostrander) are racing their human equivalents to uncover gene mutations that lead to problems. Because the genomes are so similar, the discovery of a mutation in dogs will often help lead to that same discovery in humans, and vice versa.

One area of close study for all breeds is the identification of markers that indicate disease. "The development of disease, a lot of it comes from recessive traits being amplified by breeding dogs too closely related." This can be eliminated, Parker says, by looking at dogs' ancestral trees to make sure there isn't excessive crossing.

G enerally speaking, the Australian shepherd is considered to be a healthy breed. While dozens of diseases can afflict it, only a couple are pervasive. The most serious is epilepsy, and there is great hope of discovering a gene for this that could be identified using a DNA test. But we're not there yet.

Few people have better perspective than Jeanne Joy Hartnagle, who, as the breed's de facto historian, has watched Aussies change over the past half century. "There is a pretty limited gene pool," she told me. And epilepsy was a new concern, one that hadn't been an issue in the past. "Unfortunately, it's a huge problem now." What happens when a few dogs that happen to be carrying hidden genetic flaws do really well in the show ring is that those flaws can be spread, because a successful dog's sperm is in demand. In some cases this is due to a lack of scruples

("People did not give good disclosure," is how Hartnagle puts it), but often it's just that the breedings happened when there wasn't "as much information as genetics." Either way, "That unfortunately got into the breed."

All responsible breeders test for a number of heritable problems. To help prevent hip dysplasia—a growing plague in many breeds, especially German shepherds, Labrador retrievers, and most large, working dogs—hips are X-rayed and evaluated by the Orthopedic Foundation for Animals (OFA), which assigns a particular dog a rating. Only dogs with "good" or "excellent" ratings should be chosen for breeding. Puppies have their eyes examined at eight weeks for eye defects, and those that are cleared are registered with the Canine Eye Registration Foundation (CERF).

Jack is CERF-"clear" and OFA-"excellent"; the only slight tick on his file is in the area of drug resistance. Another common issue among Aussies—as well as other herding dogs, like collies, Shelties, and German shepherds[*]—is that there exists in the breed a resistance to certain drugs, especially those containing ivermectin and loperamide (which is the key ingredient in Imodium). Dogs carrying this Multi-Drug Resistance gene (known as MDR1) are unable to flush certain toxins out of their brains and can suffer neurologic damage. Generally it's not a serious problem and is easily uncovered using an over-the-counter genetic test. Three results are possible: "mutant-mutant" (meaning highly drug-resistant), "normal-normal" (A-OK), and "mutant-normal" (mildly resistant). Jack is mutant-normal, meaning that he probably shouldn't be given dewormers containing ivermectin (Heartgard, for one), or antidiarrheals like Imodium, but they're not going to kill him either.

Being a responsible breeder, Kerry is always up front about such things, but this problem is one that doesn't really concern her. "I don't consider it a big deal at all."

---

[*]Which would indicate that this problem goes way back.

· · ·

The BBC swatted at the purebred hornet's nest with its special entitled *Pedigree Dogs Exposed,* which premiered in 2008 in England, the country that invented dog shows and reveres them to this day. This somewhat overwrought, not-exactly-nuanced documentary focused exclusively on the problems of purebreeding, which the narrator called "the greatest animal-welfare scandal of our time." Even more hyperbolic was the head vet for England's Royal Society for the Prevention of Cruelty to Animals, who said, "We're breeding them to death."

These types of exposés inevitably focus on extreme examples, and the most wrenching sequence in the BBC doc dealt with a neurological problem found in certain Cavalier King Charles spaniels, which are sometimes born with skulls too small for their brains (described by the narrator as "wedging a size-ten foot into a size-six shoe"). Dogs with this problem suffer from painful seizures that can be cured only by brain surgery that opens the skull to relieve swelling.

Most likely, the special suggested, the problem traces back to a few stud dogs that were overused in the 1950s. The implication is that sometimes the dogs that breeders think are best are not actually the best ones to breed, and the RSPCA vet Mark Evans has no qualms about singling out what he sees as the root of all problems plaguing purebreds: joint problems in Labs, an enzyme deficiency in springer spaniels, Westies "beset by allergies," German shepherds with sloping rears that cause them to be described by critics as "half dog, half frog."

"The cause is simple," said Evans. "Competitive dog showing." (The man wields a mean sword of inflammatory rhetoric; he also calls the Crufts show "a parade of mutants.")

One man you will inevitably see quoted if you dive into the matter of the ethics of purebreeding is Dr. James Serpell, director of the Center for the Interaction of Animals and Society at the University of Pennsylvania. And sure enough, there he was in the special. Serpell isn't antipurebred per se, but he pops up in the BBC doc to raise the point that dogs were first bred for function, "which caused the evolution of modern breeds." That paradigm shifted in the mid–nineteenth century, he pointed out. "Because dog breeding becomes a sport, and the idea of perfect arises."

The most outrageous claim in the film is the suggestion that the Kennel Club (the AKC of the UK) is an outgrowth of the eugenics movement, the now-disgraced idea of purifying the human race through breeding, which reached its awful apogee with Hitler. Lest we miss the insinuation, the narrator actually calls the Kennel Club "a eugenicist organization."

This is the problem with emotional arguments. When you care the most, you say the dumbest things. Animal-rights people typically come from a good place—they care about animals. But they also tend to make gross generalizations and oversimplify things.*

European countries have been quite active in legislating protections for purebreds. Tail docking, for instance, is now banned in England. To help compensate for this, breeders have quickly managed to breed the trait for a naturally docked tail from corgis into other breeds, like the boxer and the Aussie. (It takes only two or three generations.) The Swedish Kennel Club has banned mother-son and father-daughter breedings.

One of the most progressive changes is the movement to curb the number of times a sire can be used to stud. As I said, no one sets out to create dogs with problems—quite the opposite, in fact—but because the nature of judging dog shows is that it's subjective, it is possible that a top dog (or dogs) can become great champions despite having flaws (visible or not). As suggested by the example of the Cavaliers, a few stud dogs carrying the wrong genes can start a cascade of damage that pours over a breed's genetic tree.

---

*This works both ways, of course. I saw a lady at one dog show wearing a T-shirt that said BOOBS with each O being red and exaggeratedly large and printed over a breast. There was a line through both, and inside those O's the words PETA and ASPCA. She announced plans to sell them and expected sales to be brisk.

The most haunting cases involve problems that lurk undetected in a dog's DNA. In 1968 a German shepherd named Canto von der Wienerau sired a number of litters and then died suddenly at just four years of age. The cause was hemophilia A, and because males of his litters had already been bred many times over by the time he died, that gene was shotgunned around the breed, and every subsequent case of this disease is traceable to this one dog. (Thankfully, the defect has largely now been curbed. Score one for responsible breeding.)

The winner of the 2003 Crufts show, a Pekingese named Danny, was engulfed in controversy after being accused of having a face lift; it turned out that he'd had surgery for a throat infection caused by a genetic flaw. He was bred eighteen times, so the flaw lives on.[*]

Here in the United States, the AKC's Frequently Used Sires program requires that any male bred more than seven times, or three times in a year, submit to a DNA test—though the reason has more to do with ensuring that the dogs come from proper stock than eliminating sires with flaws (the rule states that it is for "genetic identity and parentage verification").

One problem is that no one knows how many times is too many. The club that oversees German shepherd breeding in Germany has put a cap on the number of times a dog can stud in a single year, but that number is eighty, and probably it's still too many. In England the basenji gene pool got so shallow at one point that a single sire was responsible for 80 percent of the puppies born; certainly that's too many.

I t's hard to argue with the feeling that some fault in this matter lies with owners and handlers who've come to accept as normal the covering up of flaws. "Handlers can finish and show dogs that are not necessarily the best representatives of their breed," said Mary Stine, a show vendor I met who worked for five years as an AKC field rep. "Then

---

[*]To give you an idea of how far genes can be spread, the top stud dog of all time in the United States was the English springer spaniel Ch Salilyn's Aristocrat, who sired 188 champions. That's just champions—so figure hundreds more puppies beyond that.

people think they have something special, and they breed it." This is particularly bad, she said, in the case of a dog that "you do things to to make it look good."

Stine said she once attended a Shetland sheepdog grooming seminar and watched people put powdered lead in the dogs' ears to make them droop. "Some will have their ears surgically broken by a vet. They will have teeth fixed; they will have coats dyed."

She recalled the case of a "rather famous terrier handler some years back" who was on his way to show a dog when an unexpected conflict arose. He passed one dog off to a fellow handler and raced to another ring, forgetting to tell the new handler that the dog he'd given her was still wearing corrective braces in its mouth. When the judge put the dog up on the table, the mouthpiece fell out and hit the surface with a thud. It nearly cost the fill-in handler a suspension. "It wasn't illegal to have that in the dog's mouth outside the ring," Stine says, because "it wasn't a permanent appliance." There is a line there, whether or not you can see it. "It's really crazy."

Stine used to own and show Belgian Tervurens, and the breed that is still near and dear to her heart currently has a major genetic issue with the dogs' "tail set." The standard dictates that a Tervuren carry its tail "with the body"; at rest it should go below the hock. But in many of them today, Stine says, the tail curls, "almost like a husky." And in many top dogs, "there's a really gay tail* that's dominant." Because it's dominant, any dog carrying that tail is "going to plaster that all over his puppies." She says she's seen puppies come from dogs like this with "beautiful low tails," and in those cases "you know it's been done"—she means surgically altered.

"One time I had a dog like that. She had a terribly curly tail," Stine said. "I literally had a judge tell me, 'Go get her tail fixed and come back out.' I was like, 'Okay.' I didn't. A breeder told me you can always do it and say she got her tail slammed in the door."

---

*A tail that curls forward, toward the dog's head.

Let me point out that Stine is definitely not anti–dog show. She makes her living selling purebred-dog products at dog shows. She's just seen everything, and like most of the people playing this game (one hopes), she wants to think that these issues are anomalous. Or at least not common. Except when they are. "When I was showing, I got to know all the dogs I showed against," she said. "I realized there were moments when I had the only honest dog in the ring."

She said she considered certain questionable tactics herself, but thought, "'If I do this, isn't it fake? I cheated.' That's always been my philosophy. I have no problem with chalk and good shampoo. But when I wash him off, he's still gonna be the same dog."

On the other hand, the end result of breeding done well is that we wound up with wonderful animals like Jack and Tanner and Rita, and all the other cool and interesting dogs that share our homes and workplaces. One of my favorite things in the course my research was reading about the almost impossibly diverse array of jobs that dogs have been bred to do.

"At various times, and in different places, domestic dogs have served an incredible variety of different behavioral roles," reported James Serpell in the introduction to his anthology, *The Domestic Dog*, "including security guards, burglar alarms, beasts of burden, weapons of war, entertainers, athletes, fighters, lifeguards, shepherds, guides, garbage collectors, and instruments for detecting truffles, drugs, dry rot, explosives, and estrous pheromones in cattle. As hunting aides they have been modified behaviorally (and physically) to assist in the capture or retrieval of everything from rodents and small birds to lions and kangaroos, and of course, since time immemorial, they have also employed their social skills to provide us with affectionate and reliable companionship."

Since Roman times they've been at our side in combat. The Soviet Red Army had more than sixty thousand enlisted dogs that wore uni-

forms and were given the rank of corporal. This canine corps is credited with saving the lives of at least seven hundred thousand wounded
soldiers—by delivering medicine to the field and even dragging them
to safety on sledges. Soviet war dogs also detected mines, carried more
than two hundred thousand messages to the front, laid twelve thousand kilometers of cable, and even served as saboteurs—at least once.
A dog named Dina is said to be responsible for bombing a Nazi train
in Belarus. On the flip side, a collie named Dick was responsible for de-
activating over ten thousand explosives in the course of World War II.

We're still finding new uses for them. Dogs are being trained to
"smell" cancer on patients.* Italy employs a corps of three hundred Lab-
radors, Newfoundlands, and golden retrievers that serve as lifeguards
on the country's beaches—leaping into action in some cases from helicopters, boats and Jet Skis. Anatolian shepherds are being raised on
ranches in Namibia with the express purpose of keeping cheetahs out
of the flocks and thus out of ranchers' gun sights. (Similar work is being done with komondors and wolves in the American West.) In places
where vampire bats are a plague on cattle, dogs have been deployed to
listen for their approach with their keen hearing and then prompt the
cattle to move, because the bats won't attack a moving target, and certain tribes in the Brazilian Amazon use dogs to warn them of poisonous
snakes on trails. A team of eight dogs employed by the Montana-based
Working Dogs for Conservation are now sniffing out invasive species

---

*And also a growing number of other disorders. A favorite story of mine is the one about
Kiko, a Jack Russell in Michigan who chewed the toe off his drunken owner's foot and
was hailed a hero for it. Nutshell: Jerry Douthett, the owner, went out drinking, came
home, and passed out, only to wake up and see that Kiko had eaten his toe. (The story I
read about this event includes one of my all-time favorite sentences: "Most people don't
get drunk enough not to wake up when their toe is being eaten.") What happened is that
Jerry had an undiagnosed case of type 2 diabetes that had killed the nerve endings in
his toe. The dog was drawn to the sweetness of the high sugar content in his blood (being released through a wound). When Douthett went to the hospital, horrified, doctors
discovered that he had type 2 diabetes, the same condition that had killed his brother.
They amputated what was left of the toe and began treatment for a condition he didn't
know he had. Kiko was not a freak but a hero. Which Douthett came to appreciate, but
not totally. "I now sleep in shoes," he told a reporter.

across the West.* One of the best known and most useful residents of New York City in 2011 is Roscoe, a beagle prized—and advertised on TV and in newspapers—for his ability to detect bedbugs.

Breeds have come and gone over the years, for the most part evolving into new ones but in some cases disappearing entirely. A few lost out to fashion and the whims of popularity, while others were obviated by technology. For instance, writes Jane Brackman in an article from *Dogs Today:* "Tumblers, who mesmerized prey by 'winding their bodies about circularly, and then fiercely and violently venturing on the beast,' disappeared when guns came into widespread use. Turnspit dogs, who made a living running on a wheel to turn meat so it would cook evenly, received their pink slips when technology improved cooking methods."

As far back as 1950, McDowell Lyon was wondering if, instead of perpetrating Old World abilities, maybe we should be updating our dogs. "Perhaps we should breed our dogs for modern conditions, even to sprawling with a highball on a chaise-longue atop a penthouse roof," he wrote. The joke is only funny because it's not that far-fetched.

---

*They're so good that they've even detected an invasive species that conservationists weren't yet aware of. Called Dyer's woad, it's a member of the mustard family. A story I read about these eco-dogs cited a keen sense of smell as the most important attribute, but it also said this: "The dogs are selected for intelligence, high energy and a tendency to be obsessed with toys, all traits well-suited to the company's reward-based training." Maybe I should forward Jack's résumé.

Jack wasn't always a beautiful exemplar of his breed. For a few weeks between six and nine months of age, he entered an awkward teen phase during which Kimberly worried he might not have a future as a show dog after all. *Photograph by Kimberly Smith*

Any show dog has at least a few humans behind him. Here, two of Jack's primary supporters—his owner, Kimberly Smith, and his breeder, Kerry Kirtley—work with him at a show in California.

Before she was in thrall to Jack, Kimberly adored a very different pet— Eric, the quarter horse she owned and competed with for three years.

Jack—pictured here with his handler, Heather Bremmer—broke out at the 2010 Westminster Kennel Club show. He won First Award of Merit out of a field of more than fifty of the world's best Aussies. *Photograph by Infocusbymiguel.com*

Promotional ads for show dogs are a critical factor in a larger campaign, and serve the same purpose as those advertisements movie studios place for Academy Award prospects.

Rita, one of the top Chesapeake Bay retrievers in America, shares some of the spotlight with her friends Jack, Tanner, and Nacho.

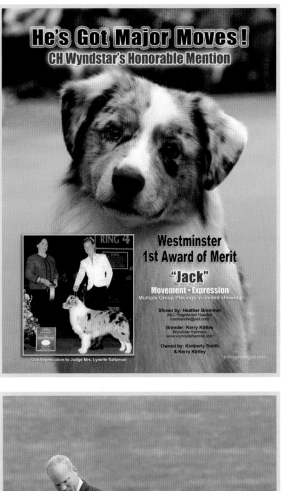

Jack's first-ever ad, which appeared in *The Canine Chronicle* a month after his breakthrough appearance at the 2010 Westminster show.

The nearly unbeatable Beyoncé, America's number one Australian shepherd, with her handler, Jamie Clute.

The famous show dog pose—known as "the stack"—isn't natural, and many dogs have trouble learning it. This led to the invention of Happy Legs, a tool that teaches dogs the position.

The parking lot outside a dog show is a temporary city of RVs housing handlers, owners, and dogs. Here, Kerry Kirtley works with Jack during the 2010 ASCA national in Waco, Texas.

Roommates—and first-time parents—Jack and Summer.

The products of Jack's first litter, with Summer, were adorable and spunky—none more so than the sole blue merle, the one Kimberly named Little Jack. *Photograph by Kimberly Smith*

Heather's husband and handling partner, Kevin Bednar, with Nacho the bullmastiff at the 2010 Eukanuba AKC National Championships.

Jack's friend Rita (aka GCH Cabin Ridge's Mega Margarita), who for a time was the country's top Chesapeake Bay retriever bitch. *Photograph by Heather Bremmer*

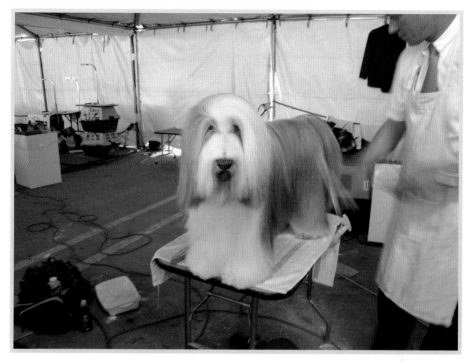

Dominator of the herding group: Roy (aka GCH Tolkien Raintree Mister Baggins), a bearded collie-slash-Gandalf-look-alike.

Heather's top dog, Tanner the Bernese mountain dog (aka GCH Blumoon Tanzenite V Blackrock).

At the end of the day, he's just a dog—and a very athletic one at that. (Also pictured: Jack's favorite toy, the blue Frisbee.) *Photograph by Kimberly Smith*

CHAPTER TWENTY

Delaware and Beyond: The Slump Begins

· ·

If it's not fun for the dog, it's not fun for you.

—DAVID FREI

· ·

In the northern realms of the East Coast, where we're slave to the seasons, the first of May marks a major transition, as the shows move outside, graduating from the smelly claustrophobia of overstuffed auditoriums full of dog hair and sawdust into the far more spacious environs of fairgrounds and stadiums, which come with their own unique problem: the possibility of inclement weather.

Jack's first outdoor show of the year was in Bear, Delaware,* a rural town a half-hour south of Wilmington. The coastal air didn't do much for Jack; he went zero for three over the weekend, clearly not at his best for a number of reasons. Heather thought his coat was lackluster; Kevin said he seemed a little worn down, that for the first time it seemed as if Jack "missed his mom"; and Kimberly said he was prob-

---

*A town that, in one of those strange bits of random happenstance, is the birthplace of the only purebred dog I've ever owned, Percy the English setter.

ably just sick, as well as tired from all the action he'd been enjoying back home.

It could have been any of those things, or perhaps a combination of all of them, but it might also have been something else: During Jack's absence Halle left Kimberly's to finish out her hoped-for pregnancy at Maggie's, because having her around was proving too much of a distraction for Jack, especially with Kimberly away all day at work. So when he came back from Delaware, his girlfriend was gone.

Jack was always exhausted after a weekend of showing, and his normal routine was to almost immediately curl up and sleep when he got home. Not this time. Poor, tired, ailing Jack searched every inch of the house for Halle—starting with the obvious spots like the kitchen floor and the tile by the fireplace, then checking the cage and the laundry room before moving upstairs to both bedrooms, where he made sure to double-check in closets and under the beds. He cried at the basement door, so Kimberly let him go downstairs, and then he cried at the back door, so she let him outside. But everywhere Jack looked, he found only empty space.

At 4:00 A.M. the first night, Kimberly woke with a start at Jack whimpering. He didn't have to pee—he wanted to go check to see if Halle had come home. Like a scout on patrol, Jack would "go to the basement, go to the door, go to her cage, and look outside." For two days he repeated the ritual every few hours, and then finally, recognizing the futility of his efforts, he just gave up.

I imagine if you let Jack choose between a handful of breed wins or a few weeks of furious lovemaking, he'd choose the latter, so even if the breeding didn't work out, it would be hard to call the past several weeks a total disappointment. It's all in the eye of the beholder.

Kimberly was disappointed, though, and felt as if Jack's string of losses had to be because of Halle. On top of that, of the ten days when Halle was sharing his home, Jack spent six of them showing. "It was a lot for a young dog to go through," she said.

I spent much of the late spring tethered to Brooklyn, awaiting the arrival of my own offspring, due anytime. And for those weeks while Jack and I were lost in our own respective reproductive activities, I kept track of his progress almost entirely via e-mail with Heather and Kimberly. Both agreed that Jack had lost some appetite and as a result his coat was suffering. You often hear show people talk about their dogs "blowing coat," which is something of a catchall term for a dog's fur being in a less-than-perfect state, typically either growing in for winter or thinning out for summer. Jack wasn't blowing coat, but he was probably lacking a little in nutrition. And nutrition, Heather kept telling Kimberly, is critical to coat.

Both Heather and Kevin were also increasingly concerned with Jack's fitness. It's something each of them can easily assess by touch—by feeling his muscle tone in the way that judges do—and by his performance on training runs with Kevin, who takes the dogs out for nightly bike rides when the gang is on the road. And on the first night in Delaware, Kevin could barely get Jack to run a mile. Heather informed Kimberly that "he was as bad as a mastiff," a breed not designed to run for miles the way an Aussie is.

Kimberly couldn't believe that that last part was true. Jack had always been a good athlete, for whom running came naturally. And when he returned to Pennsylvania, she decided that the only explanation was that he was ill. She was always worried that Jack's frenetic personality and his stoic tendency in the face of discomfort could cause her to miss cues that a problem was afoot. Jack was hard to read, she said. "He's so hyper all the time that even if he doesn't feel good, if he's in that cage all day long and you let him out to groom and potty him and show him, he's going to be so excited to be out of that cage." She had long worried that she might not know if something was really wrong until it was very far along—maybe too far along.

The next round of shows took place in Jack's backyard, in Bucks County, and boy, was that an eventful few days. For starters, an epic storm blew through Pennsylvania, bringing with it torrential rain and powerful wind gusts that threatened tents and Pomeranians alike.

"It was insane. It was horrific," Heather said when I called for a recap. "They took down tents because they were blowing over. Rings blew away in fifty-mile-per-hour winds. When we were in the ring on Saturday with goldens, posts were snapping. I could barely walk. I don't know what they did with toy dogs. They should have canceled the show."

But instead the show went on. And weather only fueled the chaos in the team's camp. Delays built on delays, and conflicts arose. Compounding troubles, in Kimberly's estimation, was a deep field of Aussie specials in better shape than Jack, plus an unfocused handling team that brought along too many dogs carrying higher priority (because Jack's precise standing in the hierarchy remained undefined). Twice over the weekend, Kimberly was poised ringside to show Jack herself should no handler arrive, and both times Kevin swept in at the last second and took the dog into the ring with no prep. Having Kevin was better than resorting to an unfamiliar substitute, but it wasn't the same thing—when it comes to Jack—as having Heather. But the only way to ensure having Heather was to sign a contract.

The situation only worsened as the month went on. For one thing, a new dog—Nacho the bullmastiff, who had an owner with ample disposable income—had signed on as a fully committed contract dog, pushing Jack further down the ladder. And this made Kimberly begin to question the wisdom of signing a contract for Jack, should the one Heather kept alluding to ever actually appear.* In theory she and Kerry had recently decided they'd finally sign one, but the way things were going in May, they instead began to discuss whether it made sense to commit to anything if Jack wasn't going to get priority.

---

*To be fair to Heather, the complications for this included the following: (a) The year was well underway, and priority largely established already. (b) She was trying to find a way to accommodate Kimberly's limited finances without violating her policies, as well as her loyalties to other owners. (c) Kimberly changed her mind often.

The way Kimberly understood a handshake deal she and Heather had first discussed at Edison was that if she and Kerry were to sign a year contract, the commitment would give Jack priority—a priority that was then never really defined. Kimberly's opinion on the matter was prone to regular swings, and on some days her frustration with Heather—which she would always qualify with the phrase, "Now, I love Heather, but . . ."—caused her to reconsider the whole arrangement, even though we all knew there was no one else she'd trust as much to handle her dog. Heather, on the other hand, seemed to feel she was regularly going out of her way to accommodate Jack—which, to be honest, she was—and that the situation wasn't actually any closer to the resolution she wanted: a signed contract that would lock Jack in for a year, and all that this implied.

As a man in the middle conversing with both camps, I could never discern exactly where the real problem lay, and I felt it was often in a simple lack of communication. I began to feel like a child in a marriage of passive-aggressive parents who loved each other but couldn't ever exactly agree on anything.

"Honestly, I'm not totally averse to changing handler if I have to worry about who is showing him and if they are going to make it to the ring," Kimberly wrote to me in an e-mail. "Don't get me wrong . . . I love Heather and Kevin. I have no desire to go anywhere else. But why would we sign a contract? We'll go show to show and take our chances."

She was even wavering between paragraphs.

"We're gonna win more with Heather than with a less experienced handler"—which she was viewing as the alternative. "Heather has the face. But if she can't commit, maybe we're better off with someone who has only five dogs."

Heather and Kevin are on the road almost nonstop, and when they do happen to be home, they're mostly either unpacking from the last trip or cleaning up, then preparing and repacking for the next one. When I managed to catch Heather on the phone a few days later, she was just back from the Bernese Mountain Dog National Specialty in Wisconsin, where they'd done ten consecutive days of showing from 8:00 A.M. to 5:00 P.M.—and to 10:00 P.M. on a few of the longer days. The high temperature over those ten days was forty-two degrees, and Heather is not a cold-weather person. What's more, it rained. A lot.

How was she doing? I wondered.

"Tanner left. He's gone. I wish he was here, There's not a whole lot I can do about it," she said. And then added, "I would not have chosen to send him." A large part of this was self-interest. Heather loved Tanner, more than any other dog—the Bernese mountain dog was her first breed—and she loved to win, which Tanner did often. But Heather said she was also a little worried about having such a valuable dog shipped to Europe and entrusted to the care of someone she'd never met. She trusted Dawn, who was both client and mentor, but still had her doubts.

Heather said that she and Kevin would be taking only a handful of dogs to the next show, on Long Island, where I planned to join them for my first show in six weeks, since my son, Charlie, had been born, on Cinco de Mayo. They were traveling light because they'd be leaving straightaway for a two-week vacation in Cabo San Lucas, Mexico. "We're very much in need of a break," she said, and it would be hard to argue that point.

I asked about Jack.

"Jack's not been doing anything at all," she said. "It just sucks. I mean, it happens. It's not one thing. It's a combination. A lot of these judges we'd never shown to before. When you start a dog out, there are a billion judges you haven't shown to," she said, the implication being that judges are predisposed to favor dogs they're familiar with; it's the same logic that drives the thriving vanity-ad business and the reason you rarely see a dog explode onto the scene its first year and shoot to the top of the rankings. It's possible we all read too much into Jack's early success, and I wasn't the only one starting to think maybe we were in for a long year.

She also mentioned Jack's fitness and nutrition. "I know Kimberly's working on getting him into better shape and getting his coat back. He was out of shape a little bit and out of coat a little bit, and you add all that up."

There was also the breeding. "He was a little stressed in Delaware."

Heather took some issue with the way the breeding was handled, saying, with a barely disguised tone of disappointment, "She called and told me Jack and Halle were together for three hours in a room. I said, 'You need to separate them!' Honestly, dogs can die from that. Male dogs can die." (There are worse ways to go, one supposes.)

Lastly, there was the matter of the competition. "There's definitely been some nice Aussie specials competing." This was a trend that seemed likely to continue.

"I definitely think the bitch is beatable," she said, meaning Beyoncé. "But Jack needs to be perfect. That's a dog that's been out campaigning for a while now. It's like showing against Tanner. Jack's still at the beginning-beginning stages."

CHAPTER TWENTY-ONE

Oyster Bay

Grooming is natural: wild dogs and wolves do it all the time; but the methods they use are basically limited to licking one another.

—JANE AND MICHAEL STERN, *Dog Eat Dog*

Oyster Bay is one of the crown jewels of the Gold Coast, a stretch of rolling, sylvan, extraordinarily pricey terrain along Long Island's North Shore. This is *Great Gatsby* territory, a land of spectacular century-old estates with brick-and-wrought-iron gates opening onto private lanes that wind off to gigantic mansions not visible from the roads. And on this, the second-to-last weekend of May, Oyster Bay is home to the Ladies Kennel Association of America's 114th all-breed dog show, at the Planting Fields Arboretum.

Heather and Kevin were to leave there directly for Newark Airport, where they'd disembark for Cabo. They left the trailer at home and brought only the Chevy Astro van, plus a small coterie of dogs, including both Jack and Summer, whom Kimberly planned to test against the show's relatively small field of Aussies. In total, there were just 558 dogs entered, and seven Aussies, including only one other class bitch, which meant that Summer stood a great chance of getting her first-ever AKC point.

The team set up their tiny camp a hundred yards from the blue-and-white tent where the dogs staged for the ring and just across a split-rail fence from a giant RV representing the International Canine Semen Bank, now accepting deposits. I arrived in time to see Summer trot into the ring for her dog-show debut, with Heather on the lead. The dog ably performed a down-and-back and then—just before stacking— proceeded to take a dump right in front of the judge, who was clearly irked but managed to overcome her repulsion and award the class to Summer anyway.

Heather saw me giggling and shook her head as she handed me Summer's leash. She informed me that Summer had crapped in her crate and again when they'd walked her prior to the show. "I've never seen a dog shit so much," she said, and it momentarily stunned me to hear this petite, meticulous young woman in pastels swearing openly in such patrician environs.

Jack was also ringside, waiting his turn. With just seven Aussies, including two specials, he stood a pretty good chance of breaking out of his slump, and sure enough he did just that, taking the breed in a matter of moments over the only real competition, a very unusual- (and cool-) looking red merle bitch with a red spot over her eye.

With such a small pack of dogs to look after, Kevin and Heather seemed especially relaxed, and I'm sure the thought of an upcoming two weeks of tacos and margaritas didn't hurt. During outdoor shows the handlers stage at their vehicles, and because there weren't many dogs to groom, mostly there was time to sit around and talk. And both were still concerned with Jack's fitness.

As a model of what good dog musculature should be, Kevin said to imagine Nacho, the new bullmastiff special. He wasn't there on Long Island, but I had a good picture of him in my mind—like any great bullmastiff, he looks to have been carved from a solid rock. He was all muscle. When I noted this, Heather said, "He didn't use to be." In the beginning Nacho could barely finish a mile on the roads. "I had to drag him to the finish," Kevin said. "Now he can do a mile and a half, no problem."

"The trouble with Jack," Heather said, "is that he spends all day in a town house. Nacho has a personal trainer"—pause a second to take that in*—"who his owners hired to bike, swim, and run him into shape." She looked at Kevin. "You need to have a talk with Kimberly later."

O n Long Island there was a light breeze and a whiff of spring growth; it was pleasant in a way that indoor shows weren't, and there was something graceful and sporting about the soothing rustle of paws in the grass.

Heather and Kevin had dressed in attire befitting the scene, Heather in a pink tank top and pastel floral skirt, Kevin in shirtsleeves and a pink silk tie. They would easily fit in at a polo match or a yacht club. Aside from Jack, the only other special in the van was Rita, and she, too, was having a rough month. She'd gone a few weeks without a win and had lost her standing as the country's number-one Chessie bitch. Her luck didn't turn in Oyster Bay either, and with Heather on her leash (in hope that she'd sway a judge known to prefer young female handlers), she lost again.

Each show I found myself obsessing over a new breed, and on Long Island it was the Dandie Dinmont terrier, which has the dual attraction of an odd name and an odder look. Named for a character in the Sir Walter Scott novel *Guy Mannering*† and recognized by the AKC since 1886, the Dandie Dinmont is, like most terriers, a vermin exterminator that, according to several online advisories, should not be trusted with small pets such as hamsters, gerbils, or rabbits. Mostly what I like

---

*He also has a personal driver, but that's not as ridiculous as it sounds. His owner, Emi Gonzalez, is bound to a wheelchair and can't drive.

†It is the only breed named after a fictional character, in fact.

about it is its head of hair: The dogs appear to be wearing curly white barristers' wigs atop their crowns, and combined with what the breed standard describes as "large, soulful eyes," they ooze personality and look more than a little like cartoon characters brought to life.

DANDIE DINMONT

Speaking of compelling characters, there was a large black, brown, and white void in the camp now that Tanner was off gallivanting around Finland. While Heather still wasn't totally on board with the idea, she was happy to report that his track record as a stud dog had improved dramatically over the past weeks. "Tanner got his act together. He just got eight bitches pregnant," she said, then corrected herself. "Or at least six."

I made a mental note to share that news with Kimberly. There was hope for Jack yet.

Things looked good for Jack at the group ring, too. The judge who'd be judging the Aussies the following day pulled Heather aside as she walked out to the ring and told her that "he's a really nice dog." A woman standing to my right spotted me talking to them and noted, "He's got such a cute face."

I'd have thought he had a shot at a Group 1 in Oyster Bay if not for the presence of the bearded collie Roy (aka Ch Tolkien Raintree Mister Baggins), the number-two herding dog in America, and a top-ten dog overall. In the end Roy didn't win the Herding Group; a puli—a dog that looks like a head of Rasta-man dreadlocks (and was once used in a Bud Light commercial as exactly that)—did. Jack took a Group 4. Which was hardly a bad day at the office and would at least help put an end to his backward slide in the rankings.

D og showing is not recession-proof. Participation had dropped in both 2009 and 2010, and the AKC did not take this lying down. In May the organization made two major announcements. The first: that it was going to open certain competitions—in particular, obedience and agility—to mutts. The second was the creation of an entirely new title, "Grand Champion."

Nobody seemed totally certain what this meant or how it would even work, and that would include Heather. Apparently, in addition to the regular Best of Breed and Best Opposite ribbons, judges could give out additional citations at their discretion, and these ribbons equal points that tally toward the title of grand champion, which seemed to be primarily a clever effort to keep more dogs out longer after they finish their championship, thus helping to stem the tide of declining entries.[*]

It was quite possible that the grand champion title would catch on. For one thing, the AKC incentivized it by stating that all grand champions would be invited to the year-end Eukanuba National Championship in December, an event that otherwise invites only the top twenty-

---

*Just after Oyster Bay, the AKC issued a press release announcing the first-ever grand champion. The headline was WEIMARANER, STOLI, LEAVES PAW PRINTS IN AKC HISTORY BOOKS AS FIRST AKC GRAND CHAMPION. It went on to explain that "a four-year-old Weimaraner named GCH Monterra's Best Bet, MH, affectionately known as Stoli, completed the title requirements to earn the newest AKC title at the Coronado Kennel Club all-breed dog show on May 18, 2010."

five dogs in each breed. But at this point Heather had yet to even bother studying up; to her it was just marketing.

Since things were so relaxed, we got to talking about bad dogs. Heather told me that she and Kevin had only ever fired three dogs—the first being a white Newfoundland (a gigantic breed) that used to shit in his crate and roll in it (repeatedly). Kevin would walk him for an hour at each show, trying to encourage him to move his bowels, but the dog refused. Instead he'd walk around for an hour, then wait until he was back in his crate, where, like clockwork, he'd shit. Heather, who tends to delegate the walks to Kevin, or to whoever's assisting them, at first assumed it wasn't being done right, so she walked the dog herself— for an hour!—and nothing happened. Then she put him in the crate, whereupon he took a giant dump.*

The second dog fired was a Berner who shit in his crate and, Heather said, "tried to eat you when you cut his nails." The third, another Bernese, was also a prodigious crate crapper. The lesson here is obvious: Heather will not tolerate a dog that can't control its bowels.

Among current clients the Cardigan Welsh corgi Thor was in danger of making the list—he'd shit not only in his cage but also lately in their house. "On my carpet!" Heather said, and glared at Kevin.

"I left him for like fifteen seconds!" Kevin responded.

"A minute, fifteen seconds—two seconds. It's too many," Heather snapped back. "What is our rule?"

Their rule, for the record, is that no dog is to be left unattended in the house until he or she has been proven to be trustworthy. Whereas many handlers let their dogs run relatively free and have houses that you would not want to enter without wearing scrubs, Heather and Kevin require that all client dogs go through a trial period wherein

---

*Some handlers will address this problem by "matching" the dog. This involves wetting the heads of two or three paper matches, then inserting the matches (sulfur end first) into the anus. According to Pat Hastings's *Tricks of the Trade*, "This is usually just enough of an irritant to stimulate the dog to eliminate in order to expel the matches. The sulfur is nontoxic and almost always works. If matching fails, however, the next thing is to try suppositories for infants."

they are given a tiny section of the house to roam freely. (This tiny section is floored in linoleum and easily cleaned.) If a dog doesn't soil it, his universe is expanded slightly. Still, most dogs are not to be trusted. Jack was one of only four dogs to have free rein over the house. Which spoke volumes about how much she trusted him, because Heather really does not like mess.

"People always claim their dog is 'mostly housebroken,' and almost always that means—not really," Kevin said. A prospective client had recently come by with a King Charles spaniel, and Heather's first question was, "Is he house-trained?" Oh, yes, replied the owner, who was then to leave the dog for a trial visit. As she was about to go, the owner handed Kevin a bag of diapers.

"What are these for?" he said.

"When he's in the house, he wears them in case he has to go," she answered.

"So he's not house-trained!" Heather howled. They were not currently showing a Cavalier King Charles spaniel.

The relaxed weekend seemed set to culminate on a high note for Jack, as all signs pointed to an excellent shot at a Group 1, which would land him in the Best in Show ring for only the second time all year. He easily won the breed again, and the male judge who'd be handling the group not only loved Heather (according to both Heather and Kevin) but had gone out of his way to compliment Jack the day before. Kimberly was giddy at the possibilities, and I felt myself getting excited that finally momentum might be tipping in Jack's favor. Maybe, just maybe, he could win a dog show.

I should have known better. With thirty minutes to spare, Heather went to retrieve Jack to groom him for the group and discovered a problem: He'd had the runs in his crate. Since Jack would rather burst than have an accident, Kimberly was immediately concerned. "No wonder he wanted out so bad," she said, and took him for a short walk.

She returned with news that he'd had more diarrhea—lots more—and Heather seemed especially serious as she urged Jack onto the table. He seemed not right. It's hard to say exactly what that looks like, but he was maybe a step slow and his ears hung lethargically. She felt his belly, and an expression of worry creased her face. I'd never seen this expression. "I think he might be bloated." At Heather's instruction she and Kimberly pressed on Jack's belly simultaneously, and vomit sprayed violently from his muzzle.

Heather was suddenly panicked. "I think you need to get him to a vet, and tubed, immediately!" she said, and began to run off. She turned around to see us still standing there, a little stunned. "You should be in the car!"

Kimberly, as the owner of a dog whose never-flustered handler was suddenly panicking, turned white. She ran to her car, rushed Jack into his crate, and waited for Heather, who was now jogging from some distance away with a show steward in her wake. She was already on the phone with a vet explaining the situation as the steward attempted to explain to us the location of the clinic, supposedly less than a mile away.

The car's GPS, naturally, directed us in an utterly ass-backwards manner, around the park the long way so that one mile turned into three, then four, then five, and the tension in the car rose as what was supposed to be a two-minute drive stretched to ten. Compounding the stress, Heather was calling one or another of our phones every two minutes while Jack puked repeatedly all over the back of the car, and the whole interior smelled like shit, literally; it seemed, impossibly, as if the poor dog's digestive system was so distressed that it was working in reverse.

By the time Kimberly screeched into the lot of the local animal hospital, both she and I were beyond frazzled. Heather had instructed us to barge in and tell whoever greeted us to "tube him" right away without bothering to explain what that even meant. But this being Sunday, there was just one vet on duty, and he was with another emergency. No matter our obvious distress, the receptionists couldn't have been more nonchalant. "Fill out this paperwork," one said between chomps of her gum.

In retrospect I know why Heather was so freaked out. Bloat is the second leading killer of dogs, after cancer. The technical term is "gastric dilatation-volvulus," and it refers to a condition when there's an abnormal accumulation of air, fluid, and/or foam in the stomach and often involves a twisting of the stomach at the esophagus. The twisting stomach traps air, food, and water, which causes bloating, which causes a further spiral of nastiness, obstructing veins in the abdomen, leading to low blood pressure, shock, and damage to internal organs.

On an informational Web page titled "Bloat in dogs" is the bold-faced warning: **If you believe your dog is experiencing bloat, please get your dog to a veterinarian immediately! Bloat can kill in less than an hour, so time is of the essence. Call your vet to alert them you're on your way with a suspected bloat case.**

Heather wasn't overreacting.

After a nerve-racking fifteen-minute wait, during which Jack's condition seemed to improve while Kimberly's most certainly did not, the vet arrived. He was pleasant and had a reassuring demeanor. If Jack had been bloated, he said, he no longer was. X-rays showed only a colon full of gas. After pressing for any possible foreign substances Jack could have eaten—"A towel?"—he accepted the news that Jack's system had to be empty. Kevin and Heather don't feed the dogs on show mornings, so the most he could possibly have ingested was some bait.

Factoring in all that, the vet suspected that Jack was suffering from bad gastrointestinal distress and hooked him up an IV to rehydrate him without causing stomach upset and also gave him some Pepcid and an antibiotic, just to be safe. When Kimberly informed the vet that Jack was prone to upset stomachs, he recommended that she add probiotics and acidophilus to his diet. "If it's recurrent, it could be triggered by stress," he said, and told her he thought it was fine to send Jack home.

His shot at the group, and Best in Show, had unfortunately long since passed.

CHAPTER TWENTY-TWO

Freehold

Dogs are a vortex of a powerful emotional force that bubbles up out of its ancient wellsprings and engulfs not just the dog but the dog's people.

—JON FRANKLIN, *The Wolf in the Parlor*

A few days later, I checked in on the patient. "Jack is doing well," Kimberly reported. "He's on a new diet—he loves his potatoes! I'm still giving him the diarrhea meds in the morning. He's asking for his walks. My vet supports the diet change and says that his stool was fine other than being soft. A better diet and managing stress is the prescription for now."

Kimberly was feeling so confident about his health that during Heather's absence she planned to show him herself at the upcoming shows in Freehold, New Jersey, hometown of Bruce Springsteen. She seemed more nervous about Halle, who was in her third week in Pennsylvania and was scheduled to go for her ultrasound tomorrow. "Hopefully, the vet will see that she is pregnant and is having a big litter," she said. An X-ray would follow on June 20, "and that's when we should definitely see puppies." Given a good result, the puppies would arrive within weeks.

I started to make mental plans to be there for the birth and for regular visits to Jack's first brood, to watch for the first time in my life as puppies grew into dogs.

But a day later bad news arrived. The ultrasound was negative.

Kimberly was gutted. And "Kerry is beside herself," she said. By this point, she figured, Kerry had invested well over a thousand dollars in the attempted breeding, "if not twice that. I keep thinking maybe the ultrasound is wrong. Maybe it was too soon? Wishful thinking. I'm so depressed!"

Already worried about Kerry's flagging interest due to Jack's recent inconsistency in the ring, Kimberly was bothered anew about what this blow meant to her dog's once-promising year. "It's how little she's saying that really concerns me." As for trying again, she didn't know what came next. "We may not get another shot."

I told her not to take it so hard, or at least not so personally. "It's not your fault."

"That is true, but he's my dog, and I feel somehow responsible for his not getting a live tie. He did try his little heart out, and they had tons of opportunity." She sighed. "Oh, well. Need some luck this weekend. Bring all you have tomorrow!"

I did her one better than luck. I brought Charlie, my three-week-old son, as well as his mother (who continued to be a very good sport), to the grassy expanses of East Freehold Park, on a hot but not humid Friday afternoon.

Kimberly told me to meet her at the grooming table, near the entrance and in the shadow of a row of Porta-Potties. To see one woman grooming a single dog in the shade of a tree was quite different from the bustling scene around the typical setup, but this is how most people experience showing a dog: occasionally, and by themselves. Owner-handlers with a single dog (or maybe two), it's worth noting, make up the bulk of entries at most dog shows.

"The main reason I'm showing him is, why not?" Kimberly said. "If I don't do well, they'll blame it on me. And if he does, kudos!" Really, she also felt she couldn't afford to stay away and lose valuable points. "I don't want him to fall out of the stats. You can't win if he's not showing. The more you're out there, the better your chances are in the rankings."

I'd long mused that having a child and having a dog are similar—both dogs and children are wild and messy and difficult to reason with. But walking around a show with a baby just reinforced the notion that the products marketed to these creatures are remarkably similar. There are toys, sunscreens, solar shields, and plush beds. I bought a squeaky dog toy shaped like an alien for Charlie, and at one point Kim borrowed one of Charlie's poo bags—for disposing of diapers in public places—to clean up after Jack. You even talk to dogs and babies the same way. There's lots of "Good boy!" and "No!" delivered in either stern barks or singsongy chirps, all of which I recently learned is an evolutionary phenomenon innate to humans known as "parentese." The canine equivalent is called "dogese," and it sounds virtually identical.

With a week of days blurring the memory of the bloat scare, Kimberly was coming to regret the missed opportunity of the previous Sunday. "Honestly, after he got rid of diarrhea, I think he would have been fine," she said. "So I was kicking myself, because we would have gotten a group placement. I'm so scared Kerry is just gonna bail."

Among the nineteen Aussies on hand, six were specials, all males, including Striker, always a formidable foe, and Tuck, a nice black tri owned by Kimberly's friends Steve and Kathy Ostrander and bred by Tom Gerrard, another local Aussie breeder-handler who was one of the few men active in the breed. Tom had beaten Jack a few times over the past month.

Kimberly did fine with Jack—if you were watching and didn't know her, you'd never think she was nervous (which she was) or not at all accustomed to handling (which she isn't). Jack stumbled at one point when something momentarily distracted him, but overall he looked good. Maybe he still wasn't quite in shape, or maybe he was slightly out of coat, or maybe it's just that Kimberly wasn't a professional handler in a ring full of them. Whatever the reason, Tuck won. And then won again the next day. On Sunday the winner was a black tri that looked fat and out of shape—that one stung extra hard—and on the final day, Monday, Striker took the breed.

Kimberly's e-mail recap to Kerry played up the positives while noting her own deficiencies as a handler. "Well, we didn't win but I felt better about our effort today. I didn't start off so hot." She had, she said, forgotten to pick up her number until the ring steward gently reminded her. "And I didn't have Jack's front feet set perfect," and by the time she realized it, the judge was upon her, and "it was too late to fix. It wasn't horrible. When we did our down and back we got lots of compliments from the Judge. He said 'You surprised me, young lady, your dog is a beautiful mover.' I'm feeling more and more confident each time we show."

Kimberly had noted that all the winners were big, mature dogs—emphasis on mature. And the matter of age was increasingly of note. Tuck was a year older than Jack, as was Striker. Kimberly told me that Tuck's owner, Kathy, put it best. "She said all of a sudden he came into himself. That's what Kevin and Heather keep saying about Jack. He's doing good, but they think he'll really come into himself at two and a half years or three. They still maintain that this could be a good year, but next year would be the ultimate year for him. I tell you—Jack looks a world better than he did the last couple weeks. The breeding, the showing, I don't know. He was not well."

But on the final day of May, she had bad news, and as usual it arrived via short e-mail. "Kerry is reconsidering the financial arrangement."

CHAPTER TWENTY-THREE

Ludwigs Corner

You have to understand, going into a show, that it is all bullshit. These judges are people you wouldn't ask how to cross the street, much less which is the best dog in the ring.

—JANE HOBSON, HANDLER, AS QUOTED BY JANE AND MICHAEL STERN, *Dog Eat Dog*

Kimberly's experiment as dog handler was not a tremendous success. She and Jack went 0 for 7 at the shows in Springsteen country, and the experience led to an insight that wasn't exactly a surprise. "Looking at my competition the last two weekends, I find that there is no point in my showing him," she told me. It was, I realized, a good experience despite the disappointment, because after a few months of waffling over their relationship Kimberly had a refreshed appreciation for Heather. "Specials must have a handler," she said emphatically.

One undeniable truth was that the quantity and level of competition had risen—and the only reason anyone could figure was that the AKC's Grand Champion project was working exactly as it had been designed. More champions were coming out more often, many from retirement, unable to ignore the dangling carrot of a flashy new title to add to the résumé.

Heather and Kevin, meanwhile, returned tanned and rested in late June to Ludwigs Corner, Pennsylvania, in the western suburbs of Philly. There, 1,393 dogs came out for the hundredth annual Bryn Mawr Kennel Club show.

Ludwigs Corner is best known for an annual horse show, but the same ground is perfect for dog shows and the sea of RVs they attract. And somewhere in that sea was the summer version of the setup. The setup, warm weather edition, is basically two parts—a white box truck modified to accommodate dogs and a nice trailer that serves as home for the grown-ups. The box truck is a Ford E-450 Super Duty, kitted out with heat, air-conditioning, and extra ventilation. (Coolest spot in camp is in the truck; it's icy, and powered by "like a ten-thousand-dollar generator," according to Heather. If Kevin needs a break on a hot day, he sometimes hides out inside.) When parked at shows, tents are stretched out from the vehicles to shade the grooming area and a series of four or five portable ex-pens that the various dogs cycle in and out of for potty breaks and fresh air. It looks quite a bit like a football game tailgate, with dogs.

Heather and Kevin's setup is never hard to find. It's always close to the exit, so that when the weekend is finished, they can easily depart without risk of getting stuck in RV traffic. On the final day of a show, Kevin will begin to pack up in late morning, and by midafternoon only the absolute essentials remain.

Indeed, in Ludwigs I found Kevin and the crew as close as possible to the action, right across a small culvert from the rings. As I strolled up, Heather was just taking Jack out for grooming.

How's his coat? I asked. Kimberly had been complaining that he looked "awful," so I half expected that Jack would appear naked or mongrelly or as if he'd just returned from ten days at Bonnaroo.

"Not bad," she said. "Kimberly's a little dramatic, as you know."

The day's show had fifteen Aussies entered but only two specials in the ring of Judge Brian Meyer, a strapping, handsome fellow in a green blazer, a light green shirt, a green tie, pleated khakis, and brown leather shoes. I had no doubt that he also excelled at golf.

Australian shepherds are always grouped with other herding dogs, so I'd spent a lot of time watching breeds like corgis and Australian cattle dogs (which are low-slung and mutty-looking and could pass for dingoes*) and pulik, which appear to be levitating when they run. They look like land speeders with dreads.

And the more time I spent around Aussie people, the more normal they seemed. There's jealousy and some obsession in the community, sure, but there's also a noticeable lack of weirdos, at least as far as I could tell. I watched some nervous parents lead their young dogs out into the ring, and it was quite apparent that these were undisciplined puppies; they ambled around a bit aimlessly at times and were prone to breaking stride and cavorting at inopportune moments. A predominantly white fluffy dog hopped around, and then a black tri was a little stubborn, and damn if it wasn't sort of cute, like watching six-year-olds run the bases backward at T-ball.

Judge Meyer was taking the physical part of his examination very seriously, meticulous with his inspections no matter the quality of the dog. This is the way it should be, of course, but usually isn't. Judges are on tight schedules and will often move quickly through an exam of a dog they can tell isn't one of the best. It's not the kind of thing you'd notice if you hadn't attended a lot of dog shows, but six months into my tour of the conformation world I was starting to notice these sorts of nuances. In the case of Judge Meyer, I actually caught myself nodding dismissively when he asked the owner of a dog with badly splayed legs to run down and back one more time.

A little after 10:00 A.M., the Best of Breed dogs joined the class winners, and just as Jack was about to make his first circumnavigation of the ring, Heather pulled him out of line and into the corner. What was wrong now? Oh, dear, he was squatting. And then crapping. She motioned me over. "Can you tell the superintendent we need a cleanup?"

Meyer somehow missed the incident and gave the breed to Jack, and

---

*Which themselves could pass for mutts.

as we left the area, a cowboy approached. He was authentic-looking, the kind of guy you'd encounter at the rodeo, and thus seemed totally out of place in this quiet, affluent corner of Pennsylvania.

"I just wanted to say that I don't know anything about dog show-ing, but I knew as soon as I saw him that that was the best dog," he said, pointing at Jack.

Heather thanked him.

"I'm looking for a dog, actually. But more working stock. Anyway, my opinion means squat, I'm sure, but that's a beautiful dog."

I gave him Kerry's number and said good-bye. Once he was out of earshot, Heather handed me the lead. I should have known by now to not expect anything resembling a celebration. "He was so bad." In ad-dition to the poop, he was, she said, marking compulsively with urine. "He started doing that in Long Island." That was when Halle was in heat, and it made sense that Jack's instinct would be to mark his terri-tory. Recently Summer had come into heat, so the little guy was prob-ably still defending his turf.

"Go put him in the ex-pen," Heather snapped, and ran off to her next dog.

That afternoon I saw a familiar face back at the setup: Trader, the Akita who'd been banned for allegedly snapping at a judge, had been reinstated and had reclaimed his spot in the truck. Tom Bavaria, Trader's owner, was happy to report that his dog had been cleared of all charges and had returned to competition with a bang, beating a field of three specials (which he said "was a lot for Akitas"), most notably a largely black dog that was the number-one Akita in the country.

Other than Dawn, Tom is Heather's longest-standing client. Along with his wife, Anne, he has been showing dogs for more than twenty years but took a long break after 1996, when his son was born, to be a dad. Instead of dogs, he said, "we did baseball and all that." Back before his parenting hiatus, Tom said, he handled his own dogs, but by the time he returned to shows, in 2004, the situation had changed. It was, he said, no longer tenable to handle your own dogs if you had aspirations beyond merely winning your dog's championship. "It's impossible for an owner-handler to get out of the group," he said, if one can even get in the group. "I can finish my own class dogs, no problem." He had, for instance, brought an Akita puppy to Ludwigs and had won with him. "But I cannot get a group placement anymore. And Trader is probably the nicest dog I've ever had." To give such a good dog his due, he felt he had no choice. He hired Kevin.

Akitas are not an especially deep or competitive breed, so Trader was at that point the nation's tenth-ranked Akita despite missing two months. "In all honesty, the best Akita in the country is probably sitting home right now because the owners don't want to deal with this shit," Tom said. "A shitload of dogs finish"—because finishing is what's important for breeding. "But few stay out. That's why they came up with Grand Champion—more money," he said with a smirk. "Your dog's a champion? Great. But is he a *grand* champion?!"

CHAPTER TWENTY-FOUR

Do Dogs Actually Like Dog Shows?

Show dogs should learn that being a show dog is fun and a game—just as herders, retrievers, and go-to-grounders have a good time at what they do for work.

—ANNE ROGERS CLARK, LEGENDARY JUDGE, HANDLER, AND BREEDER OF POODLES

People who dislike dog shows tend to argue that the practice is cruel, and I admit that before I attended one, I wondered if the dogs were just unhappy participants in their owners' vanity project. But after spending a single day with Jack, the answer seemed obvious: Jack loved showing.

"Oh, my God, they love it," said Stanley Coren when I reached him one afternoon at his home in western Canada. "They love the attention; they love the treats." Few people have obsessed more on the topic of canine happiness than Stanley Coren, a semiretired psychologist at the University of British Columbia, in Vancouver, who made a name for himself studying "handedness"* before moving on to chronicle dog smarts in a series of popular books that has made him a sort of Freud of the canine mind.†

T hey enjoy two things," he said. "The first is that they're social animals, and they're surrounded by dogs. Also, a dog gets lots of one-on-one attention—and lots of treats." Which is important, because "a dog's mind is food-focused. The other thing is, they get extra care. They're groomed and brushed and stroked. Most dogs take that sort of thing as attention, as a form of affection."

It's also fun. "Dogs do tend to look at a lot of this as play as much as anything else. And there's reward in there for the dog. Whether it's through the mouth or the brain."

I actually called Coren because I was thinking about thinking. Jack was always impressing me with his intelligence—or what I perceived to be his intelligence—and I kept hearing myself tell people that he was the smartest dog I'd ever met, without really even knowing if I knew what that meant. What was clear to me was that Jack had an aptitude to learn things and a desire to show that off. Beyond that he seemed to have a need to interact with humans, and in a way that went far beyond the playful give-and-take we have with our family dogs.

"You have to understand that there are really three types of intelligence," Coren said. "The first is instinctive intelligence—what a breed was bred to do. Aussies were bred to herd." Using this measure, he ex-

---

*As in, being right- or left-handed.

†Actually, Freud himself may have been the Freud of the canine mind. His chow chow Jofi sat in on the doctor's therapy sessions, features prominently in his work, and is said to be the basis for much of the early days of pet therapy. He's not my favorite best friend to a historical great, however. That would be Peps, the Cavalier King Charles spaniel belonging to the composer Richard Wagner, who reportedly could not write music unless Peps was sitting on a particular stool—awake and alert. Wagner would watch Peps's reaction to new compositions played on the piano and would decide whether they were good or not based on the dog's facial reactions.

plained, "you can't really compare the intelligence of a retriever and a sight hound. It's apples and oranges." I assumed that Jack would be good at herding, but I'd never seen him try it, so this one wasn't so helpful.[*]

"The second type is adaptive intelligence. That's really what the dog can learn to do for itself. And that varies a lot within breeds. Take the Lab—it's the seventh-brightest dog in dogdom. Somewhere along the line, you're going to hit a dumb Lab." This can be measured scientifically, he said, using direct intelligence tests. "I developed twelve of them based on the kinds of things we use for testing preverbal children."

Third is the type Coren used in his famous project ranking the breeds from most to least intelligent (or vice versa) based on a questionnaire he sent to the people he felt were most qualified to make such a judgment: dog obedience trainers. Coren sent his test to every accredited trainer in North America, and nearly half of them responded, making the statistical sample quite satisfying to a scientist like himself. It remains the most thorough study of its kind ever done. "This is working and obedience intelligence. It's really the equivalent of school learning. How much he can learn from training and how well he returns to it. It has the component of good adaptive intelligence. These things can be affected by personality factors and emotional stability.

"The Australian shepherd, for example, has some border collie in him and some other collies, too. That should make him a fairly bright dog, but part of the problem with the breed is that they tend to be quite emotional. They're easily distracted and sometimes get very worried or fearful, and that makes them perform less well." He likens the problem to a human with test anxiety. He might be very smart, but when put in front of a test he freezes up and can't perform.

In Coren's experience Aussies do better in more reactive situations,

---

[*]He was "instinct-tested" as a puppy to determine whether he had the genetic drive to herd, should the need ever arise, and he passed.

where they don't have time to overthink things—in particular, your athletic pursuits like agility and fly-ball tests. "What I consider to be intelligence is the mixture of those three things. Every dog has an instinctive intelligence." But one of the breeds Coren owns himself is the beagle, a dog that most people would call smart. And yet, according to one definition, it is not. "The chair you're sitting on is more trainable," he said. "They score seventh from the bottom in working and obedience intelligence."

The Australian shepherd lay smack in the middle—number forty-two. "I'm speculating that they don't do as well in the obedience ring because they're so easily distracted." I told him that Jack was something of a Jekyll and Hyde. He had moments where he was hugely distracted, but when it mattered—when a person he respected (Kimberly or Kevin or especially Heather) asked him to perform, he did.

"The ones who are spooky are going to be spooky about anything," Coren answered. "But the ones who are good are incredibly remarkable. If you've got a good, solid, well-socialized Aussie low in reactivity, then you have a dog who can compete as well as any dog in the top ten."

Conformation is a skill, explains Coren. "There are learned components to conformation, and a good handler can bring that out. The handler learns what a dog is capable of doing, and the dog learns what the handler wants in order to get the treat. Handling is a skill. It is a partnership."

There are three things that determine how well a particular dog does in conformation. There's his physical perfection as judged against an ideal, which we have discussed previously. There's how well a dog follows orders, and behaves as directed by his handler. This part is fairly simple, and yet even the good ones screw it up sometimes. Then there's the more ineffable quality of personality. It's what Billy Wheeler was getting at with the terriers. Does the dog have a spark? Different breeds express that spark differently: Dobermans stare intensely;

dachshunds have a playful bounce; miniature pinschers prance about like tiny Clydesdales. Jack has spunk. He is alternately charged up and obedient, and the fact that you're never quite sure which version you'll get makes his character compelling.

Australian shepherds love to show off. The dogs are tireless workers when employed in their traditional job and were selected to be bred for exactly this reason. It also makes them first-rate performers. Jack will sometimes do tricks spontaneously when he's bored, or maybe hungry, in the hopes that Kimberly—or anyone else who might have treats or at least effusive praise—notices.

The most famous Aussie trainer of all time is surely Jay Sisler, an Idaho farm boy who came of age in the 1940s. Sisler was an aspiring Pony Express racer when a horse stepped on his leg and broke his ankle. While recuperating, he entertained himself by training his two Aussies, Stub and Shorty. The two learned all kinds of tricks and became famous when a promoter paid Sisler ten dollars to bring his act to a local rodeo. Soon Sisler was one of the world's most famous animal trainers, and he and his dogs toured with Roy Rogers, playing to packed arenas, including Madison Square Garden. The dogs went on to star in several films, most notably the Disney movie *Stub, The Best Cow Dog in the West*, featuring a famous scene in which Stub chases Slim Pickens and rips off Slim's pants from behind as he tries to scramble up a tree.

Sisler followed no established training philosophy; he made things up along the way. His idea was that dogs should be taught only one thing at a time, and slowly. He would work his dogs daily, but only for fifteen or so minutes at a time. There was no leash, no punishment— rather, he used praise and pancakes, prepared daily for his breakfast by his wife, Joy. Sisler himself wasn't a breeder, but his dogs were so smart and adept at training that they were popular studs, and so they were all part of the breed's founding stock.

Fortunately for posterity, someone uploaded outtakes of Sisler's grainy old home movies from the 1950s to YouTube and, because there'd been no sound track, added in some Irish fife music plus pop-up comments that replace Sisler's commentary, lost in the transfer. We see, among other nifty tricks, his dog Queenie "walk" across a field on her hind legs, three dogs jumping rope simultaneously (one in front of Sisler and two behind), two dogs on a teeter-totter, dogs pretending to have an injured leg, a dog doing a handstand, one dog standing on hind legs balancing atop another's back, two dogs playing leapfrog, and—Sisler's big closer in the rodeo act—two dogs balancing on hind legs atop a bar/broomstick that itself is balanced on Sisler's belt buckle.

You'll also see Sisler's pet greyhound, which could jump as high as his shoulder and do forward rolls. Plus, all the dogs "tucking him in" under a sheet, then getting "into bed" themselves, and, finally, toward the end, an extended sequence of a monkey in a cowboy hat riding an Aussie that is racing around a course with jumps, in the snow.* I can't say for certain that Sisler was the progenitor of this now-familiar but resolutely popular Internet meme of monkeys riding animals, but he had to have been one of the first. He even taught one dog to do laundry—which is impressive but something you'd want to resort only to in a pinch. The dog, lacking thumbs, has to use his mouth to do the work, and it's awfully slow.

How smart is Jack, on the scale of dog intelligence? That depends how you define smarts. But you'll rarely find a description of Australian shepherds that does not include the word "intelligent," which surely stems from the dog's purpose—in order to herd sheep, a job it is bred to do independently, an Aussie must be able to react quickly and make decisions on its own, without allowing for the input of humans. They're also highly adept at following direction, as is immediately clear if you do happen to see one working cattle or sheep in conjunction with a human, and very willing to take orders. That makes them, theoretically, easy to train. And that, I believe, is what most people think of when they think of dog intelligence.

*The grainy film makes it difficult to ascertain the monkey's enjoyment level.

Jack's vocabulary initially struck me as very impressive—by the time he turned two, it was approaching a hundred words, and that seemed like a lot, though I didn't have much to compare it against. It had been more than a decade at this point since I'd lived with a dog, and the last one I'd lived with, the wild mixed-breed Whitney, was utterly untrained. So my baseline for dog obedience was pretty low.

Dogs are often said to have the mental capacity of a two-year-old child,* and if you use that comparison, a hundred words more or less seems about right. From two on, children build vocabulary at a frenetic rate, picking up an average of ten words a day throughout adolescence; according to studies, the average educated, English-speaking child in the United States will have a vocabulary of at least sixty thousand words by the end of high school.

Dogs plateau far sooner. A two-year-old dog is a mature dog—not at peak maturity in every breed, but the brain by that age is as developed as it will be. There are competing claims for all-time-smartest dog, as measured by breadth of vocabulary. For years it was thought to be a border collie in Switzerland named Rico, who knew more than two hundred specific toys by name and could retrieve them on command. The magazine *Science* studied Rico and found that his owners used operant conditioning—which is the fancy psychologist's term for positive reinforcement—to train him. They would present the dog with a new toy, say its name, and allow Rico to play with it. They'd then add it to his quiver of toys and ask him to retrieve it. If he brought the right toy, he was given food; if not, he got bupkes.

Worried that Rico was benefiting from owner cues—what scientists call the "Clever Hans effect"†—researchers put the objects

---

*I would probably add that this equivalent also extends to exuberance, hyperemotionality, and ability to simulate the effects of a tornado indoors. Neither dog nor child seems to be able to subdue emotion in the name of propriety. There is no propriety. There is only following orders. At least in the case of the dog.

†Named for a famous horse that was supposedly able to add and subtract but actually turned out, after a publicity barrage, to be picking up on subtle body cues given off by his trainer when he reached the correct answer.

in a different room and found that, sure enough, Rico retrieved correctly nearly every time. They declared that his vocabulary was "comparable to that of language-trained apes, dolphins, sea lions, and parrots."

Scientists attributed at least some of his aptitude for learning "novel words" to his herding nature (which provides high motivation, or "drive" as Aussie people like to say) and also the fact that "dogs appear to have been evolutionarily selected for attending to the communicative intentions of humans." Layman's translation: The ones that learn best were kept as pets and not used as ingredients for dinner.

A few years back, an even cleverer border collie surfaced, also in Europe. Betsy knew more than three hundred words, most of them names for toys. And, like Rico, she showed a remarkable ability to learn new words quickly. But Juliane Kaminski, a cognitive psychologist at the Max Planck Institute for Evolutionary Anthropology, wanted to use Betsy to test a more radical idea: that dogs had learned the particularly human ability to employ symbols, to let one object represent another. She asked Betsy's owner to show the dog a picture of an object she'd never seen before (the example in a *National Geographic* article on the experiment is a "fuzzy, rainbow-colored Frisbee") and then tell her to go find it in a room that held multiple toys. Betsy returned with the Frisbee.

When Kimberly first hired Heather, she wanted to be sure her new handler appreciated the aptitude of this special animal. She typed up and printed out a sheet with a few important notes. For instance, that he was "100% housebroken," he "does not chew other than some toys and he has never taken food," and "he loves empty bottles and will steal caps, but he doesn't eat them, he just chews them to pieces." Most important, "He's very routine and loves to be with people." She finished by noting that he has "a pretty big vocabulary, and I thought if you were familiar with it, it could make your time with him easier or more enjoyable." The following dictionary of Jack's terms was attached. (It has since expanded greatly, by the way.)

VOCABULARY

The ever-growing list (as of September 2011)

SIT	BISCUIT
DOWN	SHAKE (*will do both paws*)
STAND	HIGH FIVE (*both*)
STAND UP	TOUCH
COME	OFF
HERE	UP
STAY	YES
WAIT	FIND
SETTLE	LEASH
LEAVE IT	TREADMILL
GIVE	BIKE
WATCH	RIDE
WITH ME	WALK
KISS	OVER
HUG	PLACE
IN	TARGET
OUT	TABLE
OUTSIDE	TURNAROUND
POTTY	TWIRL
GO PEE	HANDSTAND
BIG POTTY	BACKUP
HUNGRY	FOOT UP
BREAKFAST	ALL ON
DINNER	OUT
SCOOBY	JUMP

TUNNEL	GO
TIRE	WHERE
WEAVE	EASY
UPSTAIRS	GET READY
DOWNSTAIRS	TELL ME
FRAME	QUIET
BACK	KENNEL UP
HOLD	SUMMER

TOYS

Toys : Most toys come and go, and Jack can learn the name of a new toy very quickly, sometimes in a matter of minutes—especially if he likes it a lot.

FRISBEE—*the all-time favorite.*

DUCK

BALL

ROPE

BABY

CHICKEN

TIRE

BURGER

BOTTLE

SANTA

FROG

HOMER

MONKEY

She added this note: "I never fight him or take a toy. He will put it in your hand if you ask him to GIVE *and* you don't participate in his teasing you to take it he will nicely give it."

One final interesting thing about Jack's intelligence is that he doesn't require reward in order to learn additional tasks or words. He seems to have the ability—indeed, the desire—to do it for praise alone, for the simple satisfaction of proving his own smarts. Given my recent interactions on the playground circuit, I'd say Jack is at least as bright as the average two-year-old. Which one of these animals possesses more enthusiasm, on the other hand, remains up for debate.

CHAPTER TWENTY-FIVE

New Paltz

All dogs smile, which is to say their faces become pleasant
and relaxed, with ears low, eyes half shut, lips soft and
parted, and chin high. This is a dog smile.

—ELIZABETH MARSHALL THOMAS, *The Hidden Life of Dogs*

Ludwigs, Pennsylvania, hadn't been an especially large show, but
in comparison, the Wallkill Kennel Club's show in New Paltz,
New York, was a middling affair. A mere 574 dogs and their human attendants had set upon the grounds of the Ulster County Fairgrounds, in
the foothills of the Catskill Mountains. I arrived a few minutes before
Jack was to enter the ring with a small group of Aussies, including just
three specials, and Heather looked a trifle annoyed with me. "Maybe
you should stay away," she said as I approached the setup. "He's a little
wild." It was not a surprising request at this point, but it wasn't just because she didn't want me to get Jack riled up. Someone else had already
achieved that result. "The rottie's in season."

More temptation was not what young Jack needed, and yet he was
now sharing a truck for the weekend with a rottweiler bitch in heat.

I slinked away and picked a spot behind some people in the ring's most distant corner. Kimberly wasn't able to make the show, and when I'd spoken to her on the drive up, she was still fretting over the state of his coat, but neither patchy fur nor rampaging hormones were enough to dissuade the day's judge, who worked swiftly in the thickening summer heat and picked Jack over the small field that notably included Bentley, the blue merle he hadn't beaten in months.

I met Heather just outside the ring and asked her if my hiding place had been adequate or if Jack had noticed me while he was in the ring. She flared her nostrils, squinted her eyes, and made a little nod of her head that I interpreted as "Follow me." Once out of earshot of the ring and the judge, she stopped. "Never ask me if he saw you." Okay, I said, confused. To intentionally signal a dog from outside the ring, she explained, is a trick known as "double handling" and is illegal, though oft deployed. "Discreetly," she said. She understood that in my case I actually meant that I was trying to avoid Jack's glance, not capture it, but the point of double handling is that some handlers use friends or associates positioned strategically in order to get an inattentive dog to look in a specific direction (straight ahead during the stack, for instance) or to use toys or lures to excite an otherwise lethargic animal.

Nowhere is this handling trickery more brazenly deployed than at a German shepherd specialty show, I learned, where it is a common sight to see people running around the outside of a ring, flagrantly signaling dogs by clanging a cowbell. In Germany double handing is such an ingrained component of shepherd shows that organizers have given up trying to deter it and instead will now set up, using ropes, a second ring outside the actual competition ring to allow room for all the running and whistling without fear that the whistlers might run into and over spectators. In American all-breed shows, on the other hand, double handling is a bit stealthier. But, as is the case with chalking and other grooming fixes that are technically frowned upon, Heather admitted, "Everyone does it."

Around lunchtime black clouds rumbled in over the Shawangunk cliffs that loom over the hippie hamlet and brought a torrential downpour of the type that could ruin a bichon's perm. It blew through with high winds but no lightning, causing only a half-hour delay during which the show's handlers didn't even bother to stop blow-drying their dogs. Jack, meanwhile, was going nuts—drooling madly outside the group ring—and when Heather left him for me to watch on a friend's grooming table (which, being raised off the ground, at least kept him stationary), he repeatedly managed to get his head stuck to the metal grooming pole because of a new and stronger magnet that Kimberly was using in his ear correctors.

Jack is, I told Heather upon her return, the world's spazziest show dog.

"That should be your book title," she said.

It might be the subtitle, I replied.

A bit after 2:00 P.M., the ring steward called the Herding dogs into the group ring, and Jack and Heather fell in line behind a blue merle collie and two spots ahead of Roy, the bearded collie handled by Cliff Steele that was having one hell of a year. He seemed to win every show I attended. The judge paid Jack some close attention, hesitating extra long as he paused to give him one last visual study on his final walk-by, but no dice. The Herding Group 1 went to Roy. That freaking beardie was shaggily lolling his way across the circuit, piling up medals.

As Jack was the only one of their dogs to qualify for the groups, Heather and Kevin were finished early, with a whole afternoon ahead of them. I suggested we celebrate this rare moment of downtime by having a beer, and Heather shook her head. "We don't drink at shows," she said. "I'm responsible for people's animals." This is something I didn't know about Heather (or Kevin), but I did understand her rationale. "Believe me," she added, "not everyone feels the same way."

So most handlers drink?

"Oh, yeah." And the way she said it implied that this wasn't all they were doing.

Weed?

"Yep. I'm so naïve, though." Heather explained that now she's regularly spying other handlers, who shall remain nameless, sneaking off the show grounds to "get high," but that for years she was totally oblivious to the fact. She said she finally caught on a couple years into her full-time life on the circuit when Kevin pointed out a group wandering into the woods and said, "What do you think they're doing out there?" Kevin knew exactly what they were doing out there. His wife, however, was somewhat scandalized by the news.

She patted me on the shoulder. "So there you go—keep an eye out for people walking into the woods."

D ay two of the Hudson Valley Cluster brought more people, more dogs, and far better weather. Having taken along the family for a weekend in the country, I spent the night at a nearby inn and arrived at the show plenty early, with ample time to let Jack bounce and vibrate and otherwise get past the greeting stage of his excitement curve.

A new owner, showing his Nova Scotia duck-tolling retriever for the first time, noticed Jack licking my face from the grooming table and asked Heather what seemed like an obvious question: How is the temperament of this friendly, handsome dog?

"Good," Heather answered. "Too good."

What did she mean by "too good"? the man wondered. This sounded counterintuitive.

"It means he wants to jump all over you and show it," she said, and gave an example of how this isn't a positive thing in the context of his job as show dog. In the previous day's breed ring, the judge finished his inspection and said, sweetly, "Aren't you a handsome boy?"

"That's all it takes for Jack," Heather said. "But you can't tell a judge not to talk to him."

He's a show dog in spite of himself, I chimed in, and realized that, too, might work as a subtitle.

"Oh, boy. Last night was fun," Heather said, meaning that it was not fun at all. The rottie was now "in full standing heat," which meant she was biologically primed to be bred. This is hardly the kind of thing any male dog can ignore, and so it wasn't just Jack who'd been agitated. "Nacho was howling all night, too. Then Trader started in. All three boys were going nuts. At one point I thought, 'Am I ever getting to sleep?'"

Jack's fate on this day lay in the hands of Mr. Victor Clemente, a man in rectangular metal-framed glasses with a ring of gray hair and a wisp of bangs that fell onto his forehead.

Two dogs who'd been beating Jack lately were entered—Bentley and Player, a nice, sturdy blue merle with a pretty face and a thick coat. The more I saw Jack around other Aussies, the more I realized that he always stands out (in most cases it's fair to say that he leaps out). If you're a judge looking for the "perfect" Aussie, you might opt for a typey black tri, and that often happens. Structurally, Jack is sound—he is a textbook Aussie—but the first thing you notice about him is that he looks unique. And I imagine some judges are drawn to that while others shy away, opting for a perfect black tri instead.

What was also increasingly clear was that none of the other Aussies gave off the electricity that Jack did, which was—again—both bad and good. All around the ring, the other Aussies were calmly relaxing. I watched Jessica Plourde bait Bentley playfully, allowing him to jump around and enjoy himself; it's something Heather would never dare do with Jack.

In the ring it was hard to get a read on Mr. Clemente and his mustard blazer. He took a hard look at Ben and Player and seemed only to glance at Jack, which was fortunate, because once the judge turned his back, Jack broke trot and leaped into the air. But by the time Clemente was looking at him again, stacked in line, Heather had Jack settled. Clemente took a long time to consider the line of dogs. A class dog, a red merle, seemed to be getting the hardest look, but in the end it was Jack again. And as Heather hurried off to another dog in another ring, she handed me the lead, patted Jack, and said, "He was a very good show dog today."

Which just goes to show how little I still knew about reading his behavior.

CHAPTER TWENTY-SIX

Jack and Summer

. . . .

When breeding a young bitch for the first time, it is often best to use a proven stud dog.

—DAN RICE, *The Complete Book of Dog Breeding*

. . . .

Sometime between New Paltz and the first of July, catastrophe struck back home at Kimberly's. Summer was in full-blown heat, and, having just spent weeks unsuccessfully copulating with Halle and then a few days in a truck with another bitch in heat, Jack was absolutely out of his mind with doggy lust. He was, in Kimberly's words, "whining like crazy, panting, drooling, and not eating a thing." He was losing fur and dropping coat, and, to make matters worse, the object of his affection, if that's what you'd call it, had absolutely no interest; she was clinging to Kimberly for protection.

Kimberly was living in a prison of hormonal dogs, going about her home life on edge as Jack chased a potential mate whose only defense was to use Kimberly as a human barrier. So frustrating was the experience that the only way Kimberly could relax was to partition off the front room with a gate and keep Summer penned in.

Then one afternoon my phone rang. It was Kimberly.

"You have to promise me you won't put this in the book," she said, and the fact that you're reading these words means that she later recanted. "Jack raped Summer."

That was one way to get my attention.

What seemed to have happened was that Kimberly—with a tight grip on Jack's leash—had gone to retrieve Summer from the front room to take her to the yard to pee, and in the instant that her guard was down and a portal opened, Jack went mental and, Kimberly said, "knocked me on my ass—well, actually on my hands and knees into the gate."

Stunned, she watched in slow motion as Jack seized his moment of freedom, and "in the sixty seconds it took me to get up and walk to the living room, they were tied!" Kimberly panicked, which panicked Summer, who, having never mated before and being unsure how to react, dropped to the floor and attempted to roll over and shed the frantically humping dog latched onto her backside. But dogs tied are tied, and there was really no escape for her. So Kimberly called out for Taylor, who never heard her cries, and righted the dogs to an appropriate position, then held on and attempted to comfort Summer until it was over. "She kept trying to hug me and climb in my lap," Kimberly said. "Poor baby! Damn Jack!"

She was embarrassed, she told me—"mortified, and so worried about Summer." The dog, being only just over a year, was, in her opinion, "way too young and too little for this." (According to the AKC, however, a bitch need only be eight months.) What's more, Kimberly had recently decided that the two wouldn't ever make a good mating pair—mostly because Summer's legs were too stubby, and while Jack's legs were a fine length, they weren't so long that he'd likely cancel that flaw. She had even begun to consider having the bitch spayed.

Nothing about the situation was good, in her estimation. Having heard of a "morning-after pill for dogs," Kimberly located it online, only to read that it wasn't 100 percent safe. And so she resigned herself to her fate and had already told Kerry, who she said was surprisingly supportive—though probably at heart at least a little upset at the news. If Jack had been successful with Halle, the puppies would have been due any day.

This was a complication no one could have planned for.

CHAPTER TWENTY-SEVEN

Bel Alton

. . . .

In how many other sports can a rank amateur—with a little
luck and a lot of work, or vice versa, walk right in and have
at least a chance of defeating the top pros?

—BO BENGSTON, *Best in Show* (THE BOOK, NO RELATION TO THE
FILM)

. . . .

The Charles County Fairgrounds in Bel Alton, Maryland, were
home to the Blue Crab Cluster, which ran over the Fourth of
July weekend. And a total of fourteen Australian shepherds had gathered in Ring 3 for assessment by Judge Walter Sommerfelt. It was a
small field with one dog casting a giant shadow—Beyoncé. America's
top Aussie had traveled north in pursuit of points, and as the judge conferred with his steward, she stood calmly, her shiny black hair perfect
as always, while her handler, Jamie Clute, warmed up in his camel-hair
jacket with a series of exaggerated neck rolls.

Mr. Sommerfelt had a round face, salt-and-pepper hair, and a trim
mustache, and I caught him staring at Beyoncé like a teenager in love
as the low, lithe dog circled the ring on legs that moved so fast they
seemed to blur. It was beyond obvious that Sommerfelt liked her, as
so many judges had before, and the result was never in doubt. He gave

the breed to Beyoncé, Best of Opposite to Bentley, and a Select ribbon to Jack, who celebrated the completion of his day's work by jumping on the judge when he walked by to enter the results in his book.

The following day Jack's judge was to be Terry DePietro, a recently retired schoolteacher from New Jersey who wore a floor-length floral dress and a straw Kentucky Derby–style hat. As she and Heather had known each other for years, I asked for an introduction and told DePietro that I hoped to catch up and talk a little about her job once she'd finished with the day's assignment. We met for some lunch in the judge's lounge, one of the few air-conditioned places on the grounds.

A dog had been disqualified earlier in the day, and I'd hoped De-Pietro might know why. She did not; the rumor was either too new or just that, a rumor. The most common disqualification, she said, was the one that had befallen Trader: aggression toward the judge. "If they try to bite you," she said, "they're done." And not just that—the dog is suspended from all showing and must apply for reinstatement, which involves a number of hurdles, including a critical test. The dog must appear before three separate judges, she explained. "If he can stand and be inspected by all three, he can be reinstated." (This is one judging assignment that seems unlikely to be sought after.)

The other thing that will get a dog booted is alteration of its appearance, and there is no grayer area—pun only sort of intended—in dog showing than this one. According to the letter of the law, you can't alter a dog's appearance in any unnatural way. This would apply to extreme procedures such as cosmetic surgery or the use of implants, as well as to simpler, wildly common practices such as the use of chalk and hair spray—the AKC rule book states that "no foreign substances" may be used. So if you were going by the book—and no one does—much of what takes place openly on grooming tables would be illegal. There is not a poodle or bichon in the ring that hasn't been coated in hair spray, nor a white dog that hasn't been chalked.

DePietro, like all judges, is well aware of the particulars of dog-show grooming. And she's pretty tolerant, so long as the exhibitors don't overdo it. "If I pet the dog and the powder goes up everywhere, he's out," she said. She's not at all tolerant of more extreme cheating—such as the use of false teeth. It's also not unusual for people to use rubber bands to straighten a dog's bite, she said.

Some cheating is very difficult to uncover. Sporting dogs, for instance, are supposed to have a "two o'clock tail set," meaning that the tail dangles just a little above the dog's topline. But many, and especially those goofy, happy, goldens, carry their tails high; it's just how they turn out, and you can imagine that we humans selected them that way at some point because it was cute. But it's not to the standard. And to compensate, some devious owners will cut a muscle in the tail, causing it to drop. This kind of thing infuriates DePietro. "What's the point of finishing that dog? All of its puppies are going to have that tail in the air."

Other deceptive practices that are difficult to detect would include the dyeing of hair (to make black dogs blacker, especially poodles), the tattooing of eyelids (because brown ones can be a flaw on dogs that should have black), and the insertion of prosthetic testicles into a monorchid dog,[*] as well as surgery to "correct" droopy ears or tails. In England judges were warned before the 2010 Crufts show to be vigilant especially for dye jobs, and there is even talk of testing hair samples of suspect animals. Judges will also sometimes pat a poodle's topknot to check for the use of hairpieces to enhance the pouf.

Sue Vroom, one of twelve AKC field representatives, told me that the important distinction for altering a dog's appearance is between a "foreign substance"—which can be grounds for an excusal—and a "change of appearance," which is a disqualification. The former is temporary and would be a case where the judge decides that the handler has used an "unacceptable substance" (e.g., chalk or hair spray) that

---

[*]The most common brand is called Neuticles, by the way, and its primary target consumer is the man who wants to neuter his dog but worries about what this says about his own masculinity. The same company also makes PermaStay prosthetics to help keep a dog's ears erect.

"would diminish the judge's ability to evaluate the natural characteristic of that dog." An excusal basically means, "Get out of my ring, for now." The dog would be done for the day, but the handler is certainly welcome to go give him a bath and come back the next day. On the other hand, a disqualification for change of appearance is one for permanent alteration—things such as adding a prosthetic testicle, or an eye, or teeth or a bridge, strings in the ears, or the removal of the third eyelid. A disqualification is permanent for the dog, and the handler is also subject to suspension and/or fine.

The AKC rule book also explicitly prohibits "cosmetic surgery," but this rule is not always clear-cut. One discussion in the forums of the online magazine Dog Press revolved around a "big-winning mastiff" that had leg surgery to correct a torn ligament. This seems fine—an injured dog should be fixed, right?—but the breed community was divided, because it was unclear if the injury was accidental or genetic. On another forum I found a discussion over the removal of "hanging nipples" on Great Danes; a vet had recommended it for the dog's comfort, but the reaction of responders was unanimous: Doing it will get your dog bounced.

The rule is this: "A dog is considered changed in appearance by artificial means if it has been subjected to any type of procedure that has the effect of obscuring, disguising or eliminating any congenital or hereditary abnormality or any undesirable characteristic, or that does anything to improve a dog's natural appearance, temperament, bite or gait." (Even if these surgeries were critical to the dog's health, I should add.)

The rules then go on to list eleven "procedures that would in and of themselves be considered a change in appearance by artificial means and make a dog ineligible for shows." The list includes the following: trimming, removal, or tattooing of the third eyelid (nictitating membrane—the transparent third eyelid that Vroom was talking about earlier); the insertion of an eye prosthesis; correction of harelip, cleft palate, stenotic nares, or an elongated soft palate resection; any procedure to change ear set or carriage other than that permitted by the breed standard; restorative dental procedures, the use of bands or braces on teeth, or any alteration of the dental arcade; the removal of excess skin folds or the removal of skin patches to alter markings; correction of inguinal, scrotal, or perineal hernias;* surgery for hip dysplasia, (osteochondrosis), patellar luxation, and femoral head resection; alteration of the location of the testes or the insertion of an artificial testicle; altering the set or carriage of the tail.

That last one is different from tail docking, which is one of a few artificial changes that the AKC is just fine with. The others are the removal of dewclaws,† if permissible by the breed, and debarking, which involves the partial removal of the vocal folds to cease or soften a dog's bark.

The most egregious example of cheating I heard about came up well into the writing of this book, when a Google News alert pointed me to a news story almost too shocking to accept. An Illinois man was arrested after a Chicago dog show in December 2010 and accused of drugging a top Siberian husky named Pixie, handled by none other than Jessica Plourde, Bentley's handler. Plourde apparently noticed that her dog was unnaturally sluggish, and when a witness reported seeing this man—whose girlfriend owned and handled a rival husky—feeding Pixie suspiciously, Plourde alerted officials and rushed the dog to the vet, who pumped her stomach and found both Benadryl and a drug called Protonix in her stomach. The man was charged with misdemeanor animal cruelty, but was later acquitted due to lack of evidence.

Like most Saturday shows, the next day's brought a far larger field, and Heather was showing three different golden retrievers, one

---

*Umbilical hernias are okay, however.

†A vestigial digit that sometimes appears on the far inner paw, where it joins with the leg, and can be thought of as a canine thumb. Only sight hounds still really need them.

of whom, Brad, turned out to be a notorious figure in the camp. Brad's claim to fame was that he gets so excited when he's on the grooming table that . . . well, he gets about as excited as a male dog possibly can. Kevin happened to look over the first time Heather was grooming him, and he did a double take at the sight. "I was like, 'Heather, what did you do?!'"

Brad's owner Diane Petruzzo, maker and seller of beautiful, hand-beaded, kangaroo-leather show leads (including Jack's) under the name Cane D'Oro, laughed when this story was recounted. It was just something she'd come to deal with. "Once he was fully groomed and ready for the ring, I was like 'Oh, no – he's dripping! We may as well let him finish.'" There was no further detail given. "What can I say?" she said unabashedly. "He thinks he's a stud."

Speaking of excited, Jack was hardly any calmer, despite the lack of rottweilers in heat. "He's a bad boy," Heather said. "He does not need another thing to be excited about." She gave me a look. "You need to train your dog"—lately she had begun to call him that in my presence, especially when Kimberly wasn't around.

It was hotter on Saturday, and a huge airplane-propeller-size fan blew beside the ring presided over by Thomas Feneis, who wore khakis, a short-sleeved oxford, and a white ball cap; a cell phone was clipped to his belt.

Jamie Clute had ditched the camel hair in favor of a blue suit that made him look too slick for the surroundings and also overdressed, considering it was ninety-five degrees out. Jamie, I decided, had an air about him, as if he assumed that the result was preordained, and I guess you could hardly blame him. Beyoncé had lost only a handful of times in 2010 and was not only the top Aussie but also the number-three Herding Dog as well as the twenty-second-ranked all-breed dog in America. She was nearly unbeatable.

Once he or she is on a dog at that level, Heather explained, a handler can't help but be confident. Jamie's schedule was simple, because after two years of showing Beyoncé he knew all the Aussie judges. He could simply scan down a list of judging assignments—which are available months in advance—and say, "This guy gave me a Group One, this guy gave me a Group Three," and so on. He most likely never faces an unfriendly judge except in the case of a late substitution, and if he felt bad about his chance there, he'd probably scratch the dog. The more you win consistently, Heather said, the more you can bend the odds in your favor. That's basic strategy, sort of like hedging your bets in poker.

Joining Jack and Beyoncé in the ring was Bentley—who had flown past Jack in the rankings and was now just outside the top five—plus two class dogs and a red merle special I'd not seen before. Stacked in line, it was Jack, Beyoncé, then Ben, all three looking like the class of the field. Our boy seemed good: calm, alert, undistracted by rottweilers. And then he pooped.

Heather sensed it coming and stealthily maneuvered him into the corner farthest from the judge, into a spot that was not in the dogs' trotting path. I slinked over to the corner and found her, nostrils flared.

"It's becoming a bad habit," she said. "Bad!" she hissed. "You are going to get in big trouble."

Oh, well. Beyoncé won anyway. Jack got Best of Opposite.

Heather stomped out and slapped the ribbon into my hand, along with Jack's lead. "It drives me nuts, because it looks like I don't take care of my dogs," she snapped. "You saw him. He was out for like ten minutes," walking around before the ring. "He tried to go on the down-and-back." She sighed. "It started when Kimberly showed him."

No one expected Jack to beat Beyoncé, at least not at this point. But the fact that Jack had spent a long weekend losing to the most dominant Australian shepherd in years only temporarily obscured the reality that he was losing more often than not. By the time the crew rolled into Bloomsburg a week later, it was hard to deny that Jack was in a slump and that tensions surrounding his situation had never been higher. Heather was frustrated with his condition and with Kimberly's apparent lack of focus on working to improve it, not to mention her tendency to wait until the last possible minute to decide whether or not to send Jack to a particular cluster. Kimberly was frustrated with Heather's persistent badgering and in the rising costs of the campaign. And Kerry, way out in California and hearing both sides, was frustrated by the entire situation.

More than halfway into a year in which the goal was ostensibly to chase rankings, it was increasingly clear that Kimberly still viewed Jack as pet first, show dog second, and in Heather's eyes the only way to fulfill his potential and make Jack great was to reverse that emphasis.

It's important to realize here than even a bad Jack isn't a bad dog, and against average competition he was still capable of winning. Often, on bad days, he did exactly that. But when top dogs were entered, average Jack wasn't enough. And having such potential unrealized drove Heather nuts.

CHAPTER TWENTY-EIGHT

Bloomsburg

I have a prejudice against people, even very small children, who are afraid of dogs.

—KONRAD LORENZ, *Man Meets Dog*

Among the 1,011 dogs entered at Bloomsburg, Pennsylvania, were sixty Dogues de Bordeaux,[*] which seemed likely to be all the Dogues de Bordeaux in America, plus just a single smooth fox terrier, albeit a very special one. It was Dodger, the top-ranked dog in all the land, sharing our turf for the first time.

On the show's opening day, Jack lost the breed to a dog none of us had seen before, even though Judge Roberta Davies seemed to like him. She awarded him a Select, and the resulting point put him over the halfway point toward his grand championship. Heather, despite her growing frustrations with the situation as a whole, actually seemed satisfied for the first time in a while. "I thought he was a great show dog," she said.

Perhaps part of this was because any drama surrounding Jack was subsumed by a larger matter: Nacho the bullmastiff had quit the team.

---

[*] A French breed best known for the prodigious drooler that starred as Hooch alongside Tom Hanks in *Turner and Hooch*.

"He wanted to be number one on the truck, and we couldn't promise that," Kevin explained. He and Heather, unlike some handlers, weren't willing to allow clients to bid against each other for status, and when Nacho's owner gave them an ultimatum—make Nacho Kevin's number-one dog or she'd go elsewhere—they stuck to their principles. Rita had been there first.

In happier news, one of Heather's favorite clients from the past was back. Mr. B was a flat-coated retriever (picture a thinner, shaggier black Lab) and even in a room of happy dogs his joie de vivre stood out. During the time when Heather showed him to a top five ranking in his breed, Mr. B was the team's "pet dog" and the only animal allowed to sleep in the travel trailer. Recently he'd unretired in order to pursue his grand championship, further proof that the AKC's marketing gimmick was working exactly as planned.

"That damn grand championship," Kimberly said upon hearing this explanation. "Bringing everyone out of the woodwork." She'd been attributing some of Jack's struggles to the deluge of "retired" specials who'd reemerged to add the honor, and though I suspected there was some truth to that, I also thought that having so much success in Jack's early days skewed Kimberly's sense of what's normal. Your average dog doesn't just roar out of the gate as Jack had.

Tanner, meanwhile, was still bouncing around Europe piling up ribbons. He'd just finished his Latvian championship, according to a Facebook post, and his return to the United States kept getting pushed back.

"Why stop there?" Trader's owner Tom said, teasing Dawn, who'd come out to a show for the first time in over a month. "Why not Estonia and Lithuania?"

"Stop making fun of my dog's itinerary," Dawn cracked.

What does it take to get your Latvian championship, exactly?

"Not much, probably," Tom said. "Just show up."

I joked that a virtual championship was next: You just e-mail photos of your dog and its title shows up a few weeks later, like a diploma-by-mail.

"It already exists," Rita's owner, Cindy, said. "It doesn't mean anything, but you can do it."

Ever the cynic, Tom picked up an issue of *Dog News* and waved it at me, the implication being that legitimate show dog owners were already buying ribbons. "It's not like we're not doing it already. This," he said, pointing to a flashy advertisement, "is just one step away."

I f anyone needed a reminder of what greatness looked like, it was there, in plain view at Bloomsburg: Dodger, America's top dog. Dodger was handled by Amy Booth, a thin, attractive Michigan resident in her early thirties who'd been a champion junior handler under the name Amy Rodriguez before she married the pro handler, Phil Booth, and formed yet another formidable husband-wife all-breed team. With her streaked blond hair and extremely tan skin, Amy looked superficially like an easy person to dislike. But, Heather said as we watched the smooth fox strut into the Terrier Group, Amy was actually one of the nicest handlers in the business. What's more, she not only handled America's top dog, she also bred him. It was hard, then, to root against her.

Or for that matter Dodger, a sprightly guy who hopped up and down, always keeping his tail erect, and then stood dead still when he needed to. Some of the terriers in attendance were lackluster—there was no pep in their step—but that wasn't an issue with Dodger, who sparkled.

Dodger was only three and already had sixty-nine Bests in Show in his year and a half of showing. She'd put sixty-eight on his grandfather over his life, Booth told me when I approached her during a break and introduced myself. She was, she said, in a hurry, but was gracious in blowing me off. Even now, after so many wins, she seemed grateful to have her dog complimented. Because she'd also bred him, her pride was especially evident. "He's a beautiful dog and he knows it," she said. "That helps."

Like Jack, Dodger is both beautiful and unique. Most smooth fox terriers have a mix of white and black on both head and body, but Dodger is fully white from tail to neck, with a black head. It looks as if someone popped the head off a white dog and replaced it with another from a black dog—like when you see a primer-red door on an old VW.

"White must predominate," she said when I asked if this was as unusual as it seemed to me. "But for some reason my dogs keep coming out this way, with the black head."

Does he win every time?

"Not every time," she said, and laughed, as if I'd asked a very naïve question. "He wins Best in Show about fifty percent of the time."

Later I watched dog and handler head into the group ring, and when her time came, Amy put Dodger on the table (like most terriers, the smooth fox is inspected on a table) and baited him, though he didn't seem to need it. He stood as if posing for an old daguerreotype—his body didn't so much as quiver. His head, though, was alert and engaged with the judge. Inspection completed, Amy plucked him up by the chest and plopped him on the ground, where he trotted away at her side. He was a funny mover, with a very particular gait. He listed left ever so slightly, and the legs didn't bend in his trot. The movement reminded me of Sony's old robot dog, AIBO.

To no one's surprise, Dodger won the group, and when I noticed a woman at ringside looking especially proud, I sidled over, hoping it was a co-owner or backer. She was, she told me, just Amy's best friend.

I said that I liked him. "He's a rock star," she said.

After the show I was curious to check the math and to see if a 50 percent win rate was as impressive as it sounded. I asked the one person who I knew would know the answer and would get it quickly. "My records show thirty-eight Bests in Show in eighty-one starts this year," Billy Wheeler told me. This was actually "well behind previous number-one dogs," he said, and went on. "This has been a very competitive year. The top four are quite close. I would not be surprised to see the Peke [Malachy], boxer [Scarlett], or Irish setter [Emily] overtake

Dodger before the end of the year." A facet of that is simple math, he explained. "The Sporting, Working, and Toy dogs have a built-in advantage, collecting two and a half times the number of points for a group win than the Terriers do on average." (There are more breeds, and thus dogs, in those groups.)

Wheeler said that part of that advantage was nullified by clever strategizing on the part of Amy and her husband, Phil, who Wheeler said have been carefully seeking out shows where terriers were entered in larger numbers and where wins would pile up points for the rankings. That likely explains their sudden appearance in Bloomsburg.

Wheeler said that he was disappointed that a chorus of naysayers was coalescing against Dodger, led by a faction within the smooth fox community that felt he wasn't even the best representation of the breed out there. Remarkably, another smooth fox—Adam, from California—was also in the top ten all-breed rankings. "There are those 'experts' who think Dodger is not a great smooth fox, but from where I sit, he is a great show dog," Wheeler told me. "He is only two shows away from breaking the breed record. Apart from number nerds like me, no one remembers who was a top dog five years ago, but every regular Joe who enters a show ring knows who the all-time winner in his breed was."

I made a note to test this on the Aussie people, because, thanks to Tom Grabe, I knew the answer: It was Flapjack.

CHAPTER TWENTY-NINE

August: All Is Not Lost (Yet)

Some dogs are natural-born show dogs, and some aren't.
Some you have to pull everything out of them.

—PAT HASTINGS

I got married the first weekend in August, so I can't be sure if I was
just distracted or if Jack wasn't showing much. In truth it hardly
mattered. When he was showing, he wasn't winning. Two more clusters came and went, and Jack was zero for both weekends. Dejection
was the prevailing mood.

The final weekend of August brought twenty-six all-breed shows
in ten locations over three time zones, including the three-day show in
Middleburg, Pennsylvania. If ever there was a slump buster, it had to be
Middleburg, which is sleepy even in dog-show terms. A mere 633 dogs
had come to this remote town, whose few attractions include a lovely
valley, a duck pond, and an Acme supermarket. Among the nine Aussies, only Jack was a special. Surely here was a show he could dominate.

Due to some crossed signals between my understanding of the

schedule that Kimberly had sent me and an especially swift judge, I actually missed Jack's ring time.

"Did you see that?" Heather asked when I found her back at the setup.

I did not, I answered. But I could tell by her expression that the news was bad. Jack had lost, to a class dog, and not even a good one. The slump continued.

"So that wasn't good," she said, and sighed. "I was pulling out clumps of hair—clumps! He's got a lot of leg anyway, so when his coat is thin, he looks even leggier. . . ."

And the behavior?

"The behavior wasn't great. I got more out of him than he wanted to give. Still, he should have won." She shook her head.

It's impossible, really, to say why a dog stops winning all of a sudden, as seemed to be happening to Jack. Certainly the very top dogs never seem to hit any prolonged rut, but I don't think Jack had yet to get on the type of roll that top dogs get on—where winning is more a right than an expectation. It's the difference between being the Yankees and the Tigers. For one team, the expectation of winning is so common and deep-rooted that you don't worry about the occasional loss, or even a string of them (an unlikely occurrence, of course). For the other a streak of wins is more surprising, and still thrilling, and you're always a little nervous for the moment when it's going to end. Because it will. The Yankees, though, weren't always the Yankees. (Take a look at the late 1980s and early 1990s, for instance.) And Beyoncé wasn't always winning 80 percent of her dog shows.

Heather told me that in Tanner's first year he went weeks sometimes without a breed win, and earlier in the summer Rita, too, was hardly winning at all. For most of the other dogs in the truck, dogs who cycled in and out—who over the long haul are the bread and butter of a handler's business—just a few breed wins, or even achieving a championship, is a life's work. So it's important to keep things in perspective.

Surely the situation at Jack's home wasn't helping. The unplanned tie from earlier in the summer had resulted in Summer's pregnancy, and her belly was swelling by the day. Most of Kimberly's attention had shifted to preparing for the imminent and unexpected brood. An X-ray revealed the skeletons of six tiny dogs on board.

Whether or not he understood what was going on, Jack's home routines had been disrupted, and suddenly he was no longer the focus of attention. Kimberly had cleaned the carpets and rearranged the furniture to turn the front room into a whelping salon. She'd ordered a whelping box and had put together a first-aid kit with all the birthing supplies recommended by Kerry. Her final preparations included a crash course in how to set up and run a live puppycam and installing a gate across the room's entry to keep Jack from meddling.

With Tanner in Europe, Heather seemed to be hungry for a consistent winner, and Jack's sudden tumble through the rankings had her a little discouraged. She and Kevin both made it a point to tell me they thought he wasn't looking his best.

I told Heather I thought that he'd already been out of coat once this year.

"He was."

Aren't they supposed to do that just once a year?

"They are. I think she should get him checked out. Could be his thyroid."

Could it be fatherhood?

"Could be anything. Stress. Diet. She's also been playing Frisbee with him, and Kevin noticed his topline is off." Kevin thought it was raised in the middle, or "roached," which indicates a bowed spine. "It didn't use to be that way." She paused. "We used to get him adjusted more often."

My day was an hour old, and it was already a bummer. I needed a boost and found it in the town's one claim to fame I'd neglected to note. It is the home base, and show, for Dottie Davis, aka the Candy Lady. If Middleburg's show were known for nothing else, this fact alone would make it worthy of attention in a book about dog shows.

There is a good chance that if you attend a dog show in the Mid-Atlantic region of the United States, along the I-95 corridor, you will find Dottie Davis manning the table outside whichever ring is hosting the largest dog breeds. You will know her by her warm smile, her eyeglasses on a chain, her carefully tended helmet of gray hair, and especially by the two or three ever-filled plastic tubs of candy that sit on her table. A self-described "little old lady with a hearing problem," Dottie wears hearing aids at home but never at a dog show. "There's just too much interference," she told me.

Before Dottie was the Candy Lady—by my estimation the most sacred and beloved individual on the dog-show circuit, East Coast edition—she was Dorothy Davis, physician's wife, high-school English teacher, and a breeder of Great Danes.

Dottie's official job is as ring steward, a critical position in dog-show logistics. A typical show will have eight or ten rings operating simultaneously during the Best of Breed portion of the schedule, and over the course of the morning and early afternoon, some ten to fifteen breeds will cycle through each and be judged swiftly, in segments, escorted by a rotating cast of handlers, some of whom will appear in the ring with different dogs in the same breed. The armband, then, is perhaps the most critical piece of equipment in the entire apparatus, because if, for instance, Heather Bremmer should come through with two or three Bernese mountain dogs in the course of ten minutes, the only way the judge—and by proxy the official record and the AKC—will know which is which is by the armband affixed to her bicep by a rubber band.

Dottie's job is first to call the dogs, by class, into the ring at the assigned time and then to note which armbands are present and which have decided not to show up (scratching is very common). Once the judge has made his or her decision and marked it the judges' book, Dottie keeps a watchful eye on both the book and the clock. She also sets up the ring a half hour before the show's start and makes sure that the judge is consistent in his or her methods. If the first dog enters from the left and is made to run around the ring in a circle, and then on a diagonal, all dogs must follow the same pattern.

Dottie no longer exhibits dogs herself. At home she was down to a single Dane, a ten-and-a-half-year old bitch named Milano (or Ch Dee Dee's Milano of Usonia, if we're being formal). Milano is so named because she comes from one of the last litters Dottie bred, one in which all puppies were given cookie-themed names. Most breeders theme their litters, to help ease the stress of coming up with so many names.

"One was Snickerdoodle, another was Teddy Grahams, and so forth and so on," Dottie explained. "I went to the grocery store and looked up and down the cookie aisle and picked the ones I liked." Her favorite litter theme was probably the "liquor litter." From that batch she kept Dee Dee's Absolut Gibson, named for a cocktail she enjoys when tippling.

If you know anything about Danes, you know that the dogs have relatively short life spans, and so ten and a half ("and going strong!") is exceptional. Dottie attributes that in part to an improvement in the understanding of one of the breed's most common killers: bloat. You'll remember bloat from Jack's scare out on Long Island, but it is a relative plague upon Danes and other massive breeds, as well as large animals like horses and cows. "We have learned what the very first signs are," Dottie said. "If they have nonproductive vomiting, you better get that dog to a vet immediately." Vets will typically then open the dog up and tack the stomach to the rib cage, preventing future twisting. "My last two Great Danes—the last one lived to eleven and a half—were both tacked." And she attributes their long lives to that.

Dottie's vet happens to be a former student of hers from Southern Columbia High, a school outside Bloomsburg where she taught English for thirty years. Before that she was a nurse for ten years, and also a mother to five children, and she didn't actually get around to dogs until she'd raised the kids "to a degree that I could get out of the house."

Her husband, who died five years earlier, was a family physician and then later a doctor at a renowned local hospital. One thing he wasn't was a dog-show person. "I tell everybody he wasn't the greatest husband, he wasn't the greatest father, but he was one helluva good doctor. And that was his life," Dottie said without the slightest hint of regret. "Dogs were my life. And we tried very hard not to interfere with each other. We were married fifty-four years, and he came to one dog show. But he was incredibly supportive. When I bought one motor home after another to carry the dogs, he never balked at all. And he loved the dogs. But dog shows—no."

Dottie didn't set out to become a dog-show person. (I've found that with the exception of people who were born into the life, it wasn't a childhood dream for most.) She had always admired a Great Dane owned by the head of her school's English department, and when the time was right, she sought one out from a friend. "I'd only ever had one dog, a boxer, and that wasn't quite big enough for me. That's why I went to Great Danes—they're plenty big enough."

That first Dane, a bitch named Penny, came from a show home, and so it was kind of inevitable that Dottie would end up showing. She discovered quickly that handling wasn't her thing. "I wasn't comfortable in the ring," she explained. "For three years I was president of the Pennsylvania Council of Teachers of English, which encompasses forty thousand teachers. I could get up in front of them and it didn't bother me one ounce worth. But put me in a ring with the dog and I was a freaking nervous wreck."

Dottie got her start in stewarding because she thought she might like to judge, and every judge must steward while pursuing a provisional license. That was fifteen years ago. "I can help sixteen times as many people by stewarding as I ever could by judging," Dottie explained. "When you judge, you have Winners Dog, Winners Bitch, and Best of Breed. Those people are your best friends. And everyone else thinks you did a real shitty job. And do I need that at my age? I don't think so. I think I have found my niche."

She certainly doesn't miss breeding Great Danes, "which is honest-to-God hard work." For two weeks a breeder of Danes has to sit with the puppies twenty-four hours a day, almost literally. "You can't leave the bitch with the puppies, because she'll lie on one and kill it. Not intentionally, but they're just too big. So what you have is a mattress beside the whelping box, and you live there. Every three hours you take the puppies out of the box, bring the mother down, put her in the box, put them on her, let them feed, take them out, take her out, clean the box again, and put them back in. You do that every three hours for two weeks."

Because being a ring steward is just a step—an annoying step for most ambitious types—toward becoming a judge, Dottie is surely one of the (if not *the*) most experienced stewards around. "I think I'm real close to the oldest. I'm seventy-eight. I'm so close to eighty you can spit on it."

She doesn't travel alone, or even drive, to shows anymore. She shares a motor home with Doug and Kris Cash. Doug is chief of police in another Pennsylvania town but moonlights as the Guy in Charge of Parking. He is hired by the local kennel club to manage the flotilla of RVs and box trucks that descend upon the local fairground/convention center.

Dottie doesn't count the number of shows she stewards in a year, but for most of the year it's one weekend on, one weekend off. In the summer, though, she packs the schedule; it could be four weekends a month. The truth is, she could work every weekend—she's particularly valuable, as she works both the breed ring and the group ring, where mistakes are common. Because handlers work with multiple dogs, they're constantly putting on and pulling off armbands, and it's easy to show up with, say, a Great Dane while wearing the number of a Doberman. Dottie's job is to check the dog against the number in the catalog. "It's kind of important what I do, and I take great satisfaction in doing it right." She also makes sure the judges record their decisions. And, of course, she keeps the candy bowls stocked.

Dottie can't remember exactly how long she's been supplying sugar to America's dog shows, but the story goes back at least as far as the early 1970s, when she realized she was bad at handling and hired a professional to work with her Danes. Like many handlers, hers used liver to bait the dogs, and also like many handlers she stored this bait in her mouth when it wasn't in use, and one day she came out of the ring with pursed lips and said, "Do you have anything to take this liver taste out of my mouth?" Dottie didn't, but that would be the last time she was unprepared to deal with such a crisis. She arrived at the next show with a package of the green gummies known as spearmint leaves and put them out in a little container.

"They went within fifteen minutes," Dottie recalled. "So I increased the number"—and then also the kinds of candy—"from spearmint leaves to orange slices to cherry slices to little black bears," all of them gummies. If you sell only white cars, no one asks for black, but as soon as you offer white and black, someone wants yellow, and next thing you know, you're selling cars in ten colors. Requests poured in. Not everyone was satisfied with gummies. "Somebody wanted chocolate, so I started bringing chocolate. Now I don't do chocolate in the summer"—it melts and makes a mess of her bowls—"but any other time of the year there is a container of chocolate and a container of gummies."

Dottie now arrives at shows with a rolling suitcase full of candy bags bought from one particular Giant supermarket near her home. She's such a voracious consumer of bulk candy that she has the cellphone number of the candy's distributor, in case the store is running low. For a three-day weekend, Dottie spends about a hundred twenty dollars on candy, which just about cancels out the thirty-five to forty dollars she earns per day for serving as ring steward (not to mention gas and food).

Occasionally someone slips her a twenty, she's received "innumerable thank-you notes," and the idea of a donation box is often raised. "The AKC would have a stroke," she said, and laughed. "And not only that, they'd want either a cut or the whole thing."

Money, though, has nothing to do with it. "I not only enjoy doing it—they so enjoy having it," Dottie said. "I'm retired; my children are all over the place, I'm seventy-eight years old. Why not spend the money I have? If I didn't have the candy, I might as well not go."

Only one question remained. What is the Candy Lady's favorite candy? "I'm not a candy person," she said, then qualified her answer. "But every once in a while, in the middle of a long afternoon, I'll eat one of the mini Milky Ways."

The following day's array of Aussies was even weaker—it was a rough-and-tumble, snipey field that an in-form Jack would have trounced easily. Only a single dog looked worthy of him—or of the him I still had in mind: a red merle that won Winners Dog out of the classes. Figuring it couldn't hurt to mix things up, Heather sent Kevin in with Jack, and the experiment backfired badly—he galloped into the ring and hopped onto Kevin in plain sight of the judge. A man, Kevin later told me, "who doesn't tolerate misbehavior."

With his thinner coat, Jack did look tall and leggy; from the front he was fluffy enough, but the back looked like another animal entirely. A motley-looking black tri bitch won, to great applause (she was apparently a hometown girl), and the Best Opposite went to the red merle. Once more Jack was shut out.

Back at the setup, Heather and Kevin didn't even bother to mask their disappointment. They were in agreement that they didn't want to keep showing a lackluster dog, and the truth was, I think, they'd have kicked him out of the truck sooner if not for me and my notebook.

"I have homework for your dog," Heather told me. "Write this down." This was her prescription:

1. Twenty to thirty minutes of biking five times a week.
2. He needs to get his thyroid checked out.
3. He needs to get on a supplement for his coat.
4. A chiropractor should be adjusting him twice a month.

She and Kimberly had already discussed giving him a break from shows. "If he just goes away for a month, then comes back the same, it's a waste," she said. "But this could be an opportunity. There's nothing wrong with the dog. But right now he's in terrible shape, and it starts with conditioning."

She pointed out that she was not trying to pick on Jack. In her capacity as dog coach-manager-trainer, she gives instructions to any client who's got an out-of-shape dog, and as proof she asked a Bernese owner sitting nearby if she hadn't been right when she'd asked the woman to have her dog lose some weight. "I thought that was crazy," said the owner. "But she dropped twenty pounds and we started winning."

"It's one thing to lose to good dogs, but we're losing to crappy dogs," Heather said. "And that's not good for anyone."

I promised to relay this information but pointed out, again, that Jack wasn't actually my dog. Kimberly lived two hours from me and was about to be caring for a houseful of puppies she never planned to breed. She was more than a little distracted.

Heather shrugged. "It's like seeing the doctor—you can either listen to what he says and get better or ignore it and don't."

Kimberly, as I'd suspected, wasn't entirely receptive. Her first response was that Jack is just fragile, and she seemed to be taking Heather's criticisms personally—as parents of troubled schoolkids often take teachers' observations. "I know Jack, and he can be emotional," she told me. His hyper persona, she explained, tended to mask any signs of stress, but she could tell that he wasn't his usual self. She was certain the puppies were the cause of it.

She said she'd been finding clumps of hair around the house and assumed they came from Summer. "Pregnant dogs drop hair right and left." But when she roused Jack from a nap on the hassock for a recent bath, she noticed that the hassock was covered in hair. "He's always had the nicest, easiest, most cooperative coat. It's nice and smooth." She was clearly upset that her dog was not in great shape. "I'm going to get him back to where he was."

She insisted that he "hates" the Taste of the Wild food that Heather prefers, but she admitted that the Purina FortiFlora—a dietary supplement for digestive problems that Heather had insisted upon—was working. It hardened his stool.

And she refused to give up Frisbee—"He loves Frisbee"—but said that she would schedule adjustments with the chiropractor to correct his topline, which she admitted was looking rounded and out of form.

She also planned to get back to what she called the basics. "Sometimes I think when a dog is losing is that much, you overthink the answers. My plan is to work on the diet. Work on the coat. Work on the mind. He needs to be happy. I want to take him back to agility. He loves agility."

Her pride was definitely wounded, and she was pulled in two directions. On the one hand she worried that showing a dog in bad shape would reflect poorly on her and Heather, as well as Kerry, as Jack's breeder. On the other hand, she was worried that taking him off the circuit for too long would damage his reputation and the progress he'd made on his focus by working with Heather. "I want him happy and feeling good again," she explained. "I want to get him back to how he was before."

I was getting the sense that she might be dancing around something here; it just seemed like she'd at least sort of decided to give up on him. And that Kerry, who had the most to lose by having a dog from her kennel show poorly, was also thinking the same thing.

Kimberly's words, though, said otherwise. "What I want to do more than anything is redeem myself with my peers. I think he's been out too long not looking good. He does not look like he used to. So let's take him away for a little bit. Work hard on what we can control, get back to where he's stunning in the ring."

As proof that she wasn't giving up, Kimberly said she'd decided to send Jack to the Australian Shepherd Club of America Nationals in Waco, Texas, in October, and that she was "talking to Heather" about the year-end Eukanuba AKC National Championships, which

is open only to the top twenty-five dogs in each breed or to any dog
that achieved its grand championship. At this point, however, neither
of those was a certainty.

"I really think if we give him a proper break and don't rush him
back, he will come out smoking again," she said. "He's a young dog."

CHAPTER THIRTY

Hey, Puppies!

Being a parent is tough. If you just want a wonderful little
creature to love, you can get a puppy.

—BARBARA WALTERS

Jack spent Labor Day as he'd spent most of his first few weeks
off—at home, alternately sleeping, running, playing Frisbee, seeking out toys, frantically observing action outside the house (in particular the comings and goings of his favorite neighbor, Garth, a Yorkshire
terrier), and harassing Summer and his first brood of puppies. No one
can ever truly know if a male dog is actually aware that he's sired a
litter, and you wouldn't tend to make any inferences based on Jack's
behavior toward the six sightless lumps living in a homemade wooden
whelping box in the front room of his house. Certainly he was curious,
even more so after his former mate nipped at his nose every time he
poked his head into the box.

The puppies came, in the end, right on schedule, with signs of labor starting at 9:15 P.M. on August 26. On back-to-back days, Kimberly
had stayed up most of the night, compulsively checking Summer's
temperature, and by 7:00 A.M. of the morning of the twenty-sixth, it

had dropped a full two degrees in twelve hours, signaling that labor was imminent. Allowing herself only short breaks for food or to use the bathroom, Kimberly sat vigil at the whelping box, and at 10:00 P.M. she noticed a pool of liquid; Summer's water had broken. After two hours of contractions had produced no puppies, Kimberly called her vet and was told to bring Summer in as a precaution, so that they could try to speed things along. (The worry being that a puppy could be stuck in the birth canal.) At 1:35 A.M., after a calcium shot, the first puppy emerged. It was a red merle boy, and "he was gorgeous," Kimberly said.

As things seemed to be progressing nicely, the vet sent them all home to let nature finish the job. Three more puppies came by 4:30 A.M., and then labor stalled. Kimberly called the vet and was told to give it time, and two full hours later the last two emerged, with the sixth and final puppy taking the longest of all. "That one took a little work," Kimberly said, "but she is breathtaking." As she did with each, Summer licked the pup's face clean, swallowed the placenta, and nudged it toward her teats. Confident they were all healthy and breathing, Kimberly finally headed to bed at 9:00 A.M., and when she left the room, she looked back and smiled. All six were nursing.

I saw the puppies for the first time just two weeks to the day after their arrival. They were tiny, furry, adorable things that were already starting to develop personalities. In order of appearance (on planet Earth), they were:

1. Cork, a red merle boy so named, according to Kimberly, "because he got stuck and held up the process."
2. Little Jack, or LJ, a blue merle with a "silver coat" and black eye paint, named for his resemblance to Papa.
3. Breeze, a black tri girl named "because she came in ten minutes" and because of the expression "summer breeze."

4. Bodi, a big black tri boy who was already active and friendly at two weeks, despite having no sight or hearing and only limited smell.
5. Jackson, a red merle boy. Get it? Jack's son.
6. Patience, a black tri girl who finally came twelve hours after Cork's emergence from the womb and who Kim had been told to beware might be stillborn. Hence her name.

I picked them up, but only briefly, and they squeaked so quietly that it was almost inaudible. At this age puppies can be handled, though it should be kept to a minimum. By four weeks, when they've entered what trainers call the "early socialization phase," it's actually quite important to handle them often and to start broadening their horizons. A dog in its second month needs to be exposed to all manner of stimuli, in particular those things you'll expect it to encounter, and be unfazed by, later—other pets, farm animals, and especially things that move but are not alive, such as fans, sprinklers, vacuums, and cars. You also need to show them that people won't always look like you, and that's okay. The dog-psychology expert Stanley Coren notes, "As a person, you recognize that children, men with beards, men or women wearing hats, people in floppy raincoats, people wearing sunglasses, senior citizens, and people with canes, crutches, or wheelchairs are all humans. To a dog, however, each of these appears very different, moves differently, seems larger or smaller, with odd outlines and perhaps unreadable expressions."

At this stage in Jack's puppies' lives, when they still resembled guinea pigs more than dogs, it was also a little early to know which ones might develop into show dogs like their dad. Breeze was the only puppy born with what appeared to be obvious show imperfections—the white on her ear wasn't necessarily a disqualification, but it was an indicator that she wouldn't be show quality. "The others are at least show quality in terms of markings," Kimberly was happy to report.

Jack's slump had caused him to plummet in the rankings, and the hiatus wasn't going to help. As of August 31, he was barely hanging on, at number twenty, and there were just a handful of options in October for him to even attempt to win points and solidify his spot in the top twenty-five by the first week of November, when the qualification period for Eukanuba closed. That marquee show had been on Kimberly's wish list, and a goal of Heather's, since Jack first started showing promise back in January. It was, other than Westminster, the most important and prestigious show of the year.

"We fell four places, from sixteen to twenty, in the last thirty days," Kimberly told me. "We need to hold five places in forty-five days! Gonna be really, really close." There was, of course, one wild card: If Jack could achieve his grand championship, finally, that, too, would qualify him for the show. By this point he had more than enough points for that title, but only one of the three required majors. "If we can get two majors," she said hopefully, "He'll be a grand champion."

CHAPTER THIRTY-ONE

Deep into the Heart of Texas

She doesn't know how lucky she is. Her first-ever show dog and she gets this?

—SPECTATOR AT THE ASCA NATIONAL SPECIALTY, IN WACO,
SPEAKING ABOUT KIMBERLY AND JACK

The plan, as much as there was one, had been for Jack to take September off to grow coat, lose flab, and get his mojo back, but the nature of show entries (which require a decision weeks in advance) and her ongoing consternation over whether to take Jack to the ASCA Nationals in Waco (which would cost a bundle) meant that Kimberly entered Jack in only a single weekend of AKC shows between mid-August and October. With all the excitement over the puppies, the time had just flown by.

The cluster at Wrightstown, Pennsylvania, was the first time Heather had seen Jack in over a month, and she declared the weekend "phenomenal." Facing the year's deepest field, Jack took the breed the first day over ten specials, including, as Kimberly pointed out, "that beautiful bitch Aster"—the country's number-two female and the third-ranked Aussie overall. The next day he went Best of Opposite to Aster, and "it could have gone either way," Heather said. As she told Kimberly, "There's no shame in that."

Jack's harshest critic seemed satisfied that his sometimes reluctant owner had followed her instructions. "I think she stopped Frisbeeing him, so his topline looks better. His coat is coming back in, and surprise—she's giving him Dyna-Coat again. Everything I told her to be doing, she's finally doing, and it's coming all together. It's just a little frustrating that she didn't do this before."

Heather wasn't quite ready to declare him 100 percent back—to the level he'd been at Westminster, which was Heather's high-water mark for Jack—but she was pleased. He could still use a series of adjustments, she noted. "But I'm a lot happier. Let's just say that. This is why people pay us to do what we're doing. Part of it is the guidance of it. I want him to be successful, too."

As parents of an athlete often hunger for the approval of his coach, so did Kimberly seem to be buoyed by Heather's enthusiasm with regard to Jack. Hearing a handler she obviously respected speak so positively about her dog, particularly after the lows of late summer, was enough to reenergize Kimberly, and as September turned to October, she was back to believing that Jack needed to pursue his destiny as a show dog.

Kerry, too, seemed to be feeling good. Other than directing the wheres and whens of breeding, she hadn't asked for much in return for sharing the burden of Jack's costs. But she'd made it clear, on and off throughout the year, that she hoped Kimberly might bring Jack to the ASCA Nationals in Waco. Though Kerry often enters AKC events and recognizes how important that is in a dog's overall value, she is at heart more of an ASCA person. This isn't unusual among Aussie breeders, because it is where the breed was truly born, and in California especially, Kerry was active in ASCA; she was even a judge.

"I think if we can get him to Nationals, we can kick some ass," she told me in August, and when Kimberly finally agreed at the end of September, Kerry was thrilled. She admitted, after that fact, that she'd paid his entry fees months before, just in case.

Because Jack wasn't an ASCA champion[*] and because the organization does not recognize AKC titles (or vice versa), the experience at Nationals would require starting over. As an unfinished dog, Jack would have to win a class in order to have a shot at Best of Breed, and at the Nationals even the classes were stacked with top dogs. For the main event, the actual National (which takes place on the final day of a week of shows), Kerry had considered her options and entered him in Open Blue Merle instead of Bred by Exhibitor, because the latter, she said, was the hardest of all to win; it was where breeders introduced their future stars. And though Jack was very much Wyndstar's future star, Kerry wanted to maximize her chances and avoid as many of the best young dogs as possible.

Being a good and dutiful husband, Don drove Kerry's RV two days across California, Nevada, Arizona, and Texas in convoy with another RV filled to the brim with the Churchill family—Kerry's good friends and frequent buyers of her dogs—while Kerry flew in and hopped a cab to the event's site. By the time she arrived at the Waco Fairgrounds, her shade tent was up, her ex-pens were out, and the RV was hooked up to power and comfortably chilled. Don, however, had already flown home to take over care of the brood.

K imberly and I were to fly in the same evening, from Newark. Which is how I found myself at the Continental Airlines PetSafe desk at 7:30 A.M. on a Thursday, preparing for my first cross-country commercial flight with a show dog.

There are easier ways to do it. One of the top dogs of 2009, an affenpinscher named Taser, traveled largely by private jet. But he was owned by the family that had invented the nonlethal weapon made fa-

---

*Which has a point system similar but not identical to the AKC's.

mous in a thousand episodes of *Cops,* so there you go. There's also Pet Airways, a start-up out of Delray Beach, Florida, that is America's "first pet-only airline." Pet Airways operates a single nineteen-seat twin-engine Beechcraft to fly its cabinful of pets to and from nine U.S. cities. Says the Web site: "On Pet Airways, your pets aren't packages, they're 'pawsengers!'"*

For the proletarian crowd, it's commercial aviation or a very long drive. So we left Jack in the hands of a friendly woman at the Continental desk, who passed him on to a porter, who wheeled our boy off on a cart along with a black Lab, six beagles, and a mutt with the raspy bark of a dog who'd had his bark softened via vocal-cord surgery.†

By the time we finally located Continental's cargo office on the other end, in a far corner of the Dallas–Fort Worth Airport's sprawling plot, Jack had been on the ground for two hours. Kimberly was understandably worried that he'd be scared and in dire need of a pee, but when we pulled up in a cab, there he was, walking happily in the grass out front along with an airline employee. "He's beautiful. I was hoping you wouldn't show up," the woman said, half joking. "We've eaten, we've watered, and we've peed on everything possible." She patted him on the head. "Good luck, Jack."

Driving with a loose Jack is never easy, and on Kimberly's advice I attempted to placate him by stopping at Wendy's for chicken nuggets. This worked, for approximately the two minutes it took him to devour all twelve of them. Then he resumed his efforts to distract me from the task at hand, driving, by repeatedly sneaking up and thrusting his nose under whichever arm was resting on the window ledge or center console. "He's a noodge," Kimberly said, and laughed at me.‡

---

*Perhaps Jerry Grymek is consulting?

†The procedure is known as bark softening or debarking and has been banned in the United Kingdom and some other European countries.

‡Kimberly has her own car quirks. She doesn't like seat belts. "I was in the rare accident where not wearing one saved my life," she says, and she's never worn one since.

Jack is also agitated by turn signals—or perhaps the more ac-curate way to describe his relationship to them is that the sound excites him greatly—and if you are driving him in a car with GPS, you'd best mute it; either sound will induce an incessant, high-pitched, excited whine. Kimberly's son first noticed this quirk when Jack was a puppy, and the dog has never outgrown it. Her best guess at an explanation is that he's come to associate the sound of the turn signal with the act of stopping, at which time he can get out and do something more interesting. But I am subject to my own habits and was unable to override a lifetime of driving behavior to appease the quirks of a dog. Over and over the pattern repeated itself: I would click the signal to turn or change lanes, Jack would whine, and Kim-berly would say, "See, I told you." Fortunately, most of the drive to Waco is a ruler-straight strip of interstate highway. I picked the fast lane and stuck with it.

The thirty-seventh annual ASCA National wasn't expected to be one of the bigger editions of this yearly event. Still, it attracted at least five hundred and maybe as many as a thousand Aussies to the plains of central Texas. No one could say for sure what the precise num-ber was, because unlike the AKC's Aussie National, which is primarily a conformation event, the ASCA National is more of an all-arounder, and many dogs were double- and triple-entered in events that included herding,* obedience, agility, and conformation. No matter the number, it was easily the largest number of Australian shepherds that would gather in one location in 2010, and to see them all assembled on a single fairgrounds was to glimpse a startling array of colors and variations even within the four basic styles of dog.

Despite the sea of RVs parked around the grounds, most owners who attend the National stay in hotels and keep their dogs in horse

---

*Which itself is three separate events of increasing difficulty: ducks, sheep, and cattle.

stalls in a vast barn where livestock is housed and judged during fairs. It was easily the size of a Walmart, this barn, filled with row after row of stalls, each housing one kennel's worth of dogs—and in the case of some especially frugal folks, even the owners themselves, who'd pitched tents on the loamy dirt and straw floor. Which kennel, exactly, was which was revealed by decorations; the door and outer walls of the stalls were festooned with posters, placards, ribbons, trophies, and, often, a bowl of gratis candy.*

"You're gonna see all types here," Kerry whispered as she led us on a tour of the barn. The primary division, she said, was between "big, overdone dogs" and "skinny dogs with very little coat." The former were bred and groomed for conformation, and this would include Jack. The latter were "Aussies looking like Aussies are supposed to," if your idea of an Aussie is dog that works for a living on a farm. Kerry said that at the USASA national—that's the AKC specialty for Aussies, where Beyoncé was the two-time defending champion—you'll see "great big pouf balls"; here the predominant style was a "rangier" dog that looked as if it had wandered through some briar patches on its way over from the ranch. Working people tend to think conformation dogs are too big and soft and wouldn't know a sheep from a Bedlington terrier; some conformation people consider working dogs to be scrawny mutts.

"Jack's too AKC, I think," Kimberly fretted as we walked past stall after stall of dogs like this. "He looks so different. That could be good or bad."

The more we surveyed dogs in the barn, though, the more I realized that dividing the animals into just two basic types was a vast oversimplification. There was, in fact, great variety among the dogs—and not just the variance between the larger, more heavily coated AKC-type dogs and the leaner, working-type ASCA dogs. There were dogs with more "stop" (the flat spot where snout meets skull) and others whose

---

*The spirit of Dottie reaches far!

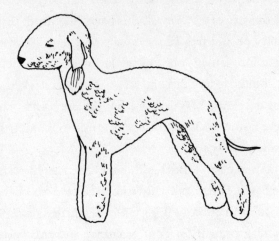

BEDLINGTON TERRIER

foreheads were on more of a slant. There were skinny dogs with dalmatian markings and no brown or tan, one completely black dog that was almost wolflike, and many "bicolors," which are fully acceptable, I learned, in both AKC and ASCA but which I'd never seen before because they wouldn't stand a chance at AKC shows. Just when I thought I knew everything about Australian shepherds, I realized I knew nothing. ASCA and AKC will likely never merge, and a hundred years from now it's sadly possible the two dog types may have diverged so wildly that they'll no longer look like the same breed.

An AKC show catalog is pretty straightforward. Some of the names might seem ridiculous, but there are only a few titles to dress them up with. The vast majority are prefixed only by Ch (and now GCh). The ASCA catalog, on the other hand, is a regular alphabet soup. Because so many dogs pursue titles in multiple events, the dogs' names are surrounded. Working titles come at the front, followed by the Ch, then the dog's name, then after it come obedience and agility titles, and the end result is listings that look like lines of Korean War–era code. For instance, this one, pulled at random from the Waco show catalog: ATCH-II Ch Zarra's Lone Star Cowboy CD GS-N-OP GS-O-OP GS-E-SP JS-N-SP JS-O-SP JS-E-SP RS-N-OP RS-E-SP. Your eyes would glaze over if I explained every letter in detail, but the sum of it is that ol' Lone Star is a champion in agility and conformation and has multiple titles in obedience and stock. He is a very well-rounded dog.

Perhaps the most coveted title at the ASCA National is the Most Versatile Aussie, or MVA, and it is awarded to the dog who does best in all four major categories: conformation, stock, agility, and obedience. This requires that a dog be pretty enough to be named Best of Breed, fast and nimble enough to complete agility courses, obedient enough to follow complicated and nuanced commands, and brave and experienced enough to herd ducks, sheep, and cows.

An ASCA show is also the only place you'll see spayed and neutered dogs competing in conformation, warranting separate categories for "altered" (fixed) and "intact," and the only place you'll find the 1970s singing sensation Toni Tennille—one-half of the 1970s sensation Captain and Tennille—a stalwart of the southwestern Aussie community who'd arrived in Waco in a black Chevy Suburban to enter her altered Aussie bitch in conformation; her Captain (and husband), alas, had stayed home in Arizona.

I t's not unheard of to see professional handlers at ASCA events, but it's certainly more exception than rule. Most dogs are handled by their owners. Jack would be no exception. Had Kimberly given her enough notice, Heather could probably have been available to come to Waco, but this type of special service would have cost fifteen hundred dollars for a day of her time, plus travel expenses. Heather and Kevin do handle at several AKC national specialties a year—the Bernese mountain dog show is a major event on their calendar—but no other breed in their truck has a rival organization that would stage its own specialty show. And since ASCA handlers tend to be owners (or at least breeders), the option wasn't even considered. There was no discussion. Kerry would handle Jack.

Which is why, on the morning of the week's first preshow—there are three of them building up to the National—you'd have been hard-pressed to find anyone in Waco more nervous than Kerry. The previous night she had spent a half hour on the phone with Heather talking strategy and was now working from a page of hastily scrawled notes, some of which were illegible. Those she could read, she repeated aloud until they were firmly etched in her memory:

1. Don't let him get into a match of wills—he will try to test you.
2. Don't let anyone play with him near the ring.
3. No baby talk. No praise—specifically no "Good boy."
4. He responds well to "with me" (which means heel) and "back" (take a step back, especially during a free stack) and a "tch-tch" sound that works in place of food when baiting.

I n the end Jack wasn't awful for Kerry, but he wasn't great either. He mostly cooperated fine on the movement portions but fidgeted during the stack. Still, he made the cut and was given fourth out of twenty-three dogs, good enough for his very first ASCA ribbon and hardly a bad showing.

Kerry, however, wasn't at all satisfied. She exited the ring swiftly, with her head down, her lips pursed, and her dog on a very short leash. ASCA was her realm, and she wasn't used to having a dog from her kennel misbehave on her watch. I told her that compared to what I'd seen at some shows, Jack had actually been pretty good for her. "Pretty good is not what I want out of this boy. These are important people, and they are paying attention." Between those lines lies the explanation for why the ASCA National is such a big deal to Kerry. It is the one and only time in a given year when all (or nearly all) of the top breeders and kennels come together to scout dogs for breeding. If Jack impressed, his stock as a stud dog would rise.

The judge really liked Jack, Kerry said, but he also noticed every misstep. "He told me he was a beautiful dog. He also said, 'He a young dog. His feet are all over the place.'" That snub stung. "I wanted to say, 'First Award of Merit at Westminster.'" She brushed a wisp of red bangs from her forehead. "But I didn't. You can't say that."

For the second preshow, Kerry changed strategy. She preferred the judge working in Bred By Exhibitor and so entered Jack there, against even stiffer competition. And again he took fourth. For an ASCA unknown, these were encouraging results. At the least it said he belonged. But he could be better.

"Kerry is disappointed," Kimberly whispered as we watched her lead Jack out of the ring. And then added, as if I hadn't spent the past year attending shows with her, that the results didn't affect her. "I'm not that competitive."

The main reason Heather has always badgered Kimberly about keeping Jack in competition week in and week out, rather than entering mostly shows convenient to his owner's schedule (because his owner likes to have him home as much as possible), is that she thinks he gets better as his comfort level increases. Over a cluster of shows, Heather says, Jack always improves.

Except in Waco. Jack's third and final preshow before the National was a fiasco. Going into it, his prospects seemed good. The judge, according to Kerry, "was really into cutesy." And, Kimberly said proudly, "it's hard to get a more cutesy face than Jack's." To avoid distracting her dog, she said this from our hiding spot, behind a woman with a walker in a hallway adjacent to the ring. In an exception to Heather's theory, Kimberly had a feeling that Jack's willingness to work with Kerry was about to regress. She had, as owners do, an intuition about her dog, and it told her that Kerry had gotten as much cooperation as she had so far only because Jack had been jet-lagged. But now, with two solid nights of rest under his belt, Kimberly feared trouble. "I think he's going to be the Jack I expected him to be yesterday."

And her maternal instincts were spot on; out in the ring, Jack was giving Kerry fits. "He's being so bad," Kimberly said only seconds after the start, and her spirits sank as her dog failed to make the cut. Already she was working out a justification. "I think Jack's the kind of dog who will tell you when he's had enough," she said, then suggested that this was precisely what had happened in Middleburg, when Heather's patience finally broke.

Kerry was downtrodden. She never knew what hit her. When the judge, a young woman no older than thirty with the countenance of an owl, dismissed Jack, she whispered to Kerry, "At least you can take him outside now."

"He and I have some work to do," Kerry said as we all headed for the RV. Kimberly was sullen.

After the frantic action of the preshows, the actual National was a slow and tedious affair. With so many classes (tris, merles, puppies, bred by, etc.) and each class multiplied by four (for intact dogs, intact bitches, altered dogs, and altered bitches), it was one bunch of Aussies after another cycling through rings in front of judges for hours on end. The room, which had been bustling and congenial during preshows, was quiet and tense, with almost no barking. Only when dogs were placed would a burst of applause break out, then quickly cease.

No one expected Jack to actually win Best of Breed, the ASCA National's equivalent of Best in Show. To do that would have been a stunning upset; he'd have to first be selected as the best blue merle male, then the best blue merle overall, then Winners Dog over all the various class winners, then finally be picked over all the top ASCA specials in America—dogs already known to ASCA judges. It was beyond a long shot. Possible, but fantastic.

Out in the blue merle ring, though, Judge Jasa Hatcher seemed to like Jack, who went about his job capably and with verve, as if he'd been working with Kerry for months. As was increasingly the case, he seemed aware of the heightened import of what was going on. He was a totally different dog from the one we'd seen before, and when Kerry led him on his first run around the ring, so perfect was his cadence that there was no tension in the leash, which hung limply from her hand. Hatcher, a blonde in her late thirties who was easily the most attractive judge I'd seen all year, watched with a smile.

When she reordered the dogs for placement, Hatcher put Jack second and seemed to be at least considering the idea of bumping him to first when she signaled for one last go-round, at which time spectators gathered about the ring began to cheer for their favorites, and Jack, hearing applause, broke from his trot. Hatcher did not miss this. She looked hard at the line, and instead of bumping Jack up she moved him down, to third—and that's how they finished.

"Ah, shoot! He heard the cheers and he broke at the wrong time," Kerry said, annoyed but not angry. It was, however, an especially ill-timed mistake. The second-place dog in any class, she explained, can actually still qualify for the main event, Best of Breed, because if the winning blue were to go on and be selected Winners Dog, the second-place dog from his class would be called in to compete for Reserve Winners, which offers another chance to advance. When I shrugged and said that this sounded far-fetched, she shook her head. "Oh, no. It happens." And sure enough it did that very afternoon, when Winners Dog and Reserve Winners went to the first- and second-place black tri males.

Still, Jack's lack of purple ribbons did not make the trip a failure. "A lot of people want to know who he is," Kerry said, and her aspirations in bringing him halfway across America were at least partly fulfilled. By the time he left, important people were paying attention.

CHAPTER THIRTY-TWO

Bloomsburg (Again)

> It is certain that the dog is not just like one of many other
> animals, but rather a creature of humans, an artificial
> animal, which has been shaped in its behavior and
> appearance according to human desires.
> —VILMOS CSANYI, *If Dogs Could Talk*

You know you've been on the dog-show circuit a long time when you start repeating locations. And in early November, I exited Interstate 80 for the Bald Eagle Kennel Club's 76th All-Breed Dog Show and found myself, for the second time, in Bloomsburg, Pennsylvania. If you look at a dog-show calendar, you'll find this isn't an unusual occurrence, and if I hadn't had a new baby at home and had been more diligent in my attendance, I'd already have repeated a couple of locations at this point. West Friendship, Maryland, for one, was on Heather and Kevin's schedule three separate times in 2010.

My return to Bloomsburg coincided with a Komondorok Club of America National Specialty and was also special because it was to be the first show attended by Jack's progeny. Puppies under six months are actually forbidden inside dog shows because their immature immune systems put them at a heightened risk of disease; they're also kind of a huge distraction, for people and dogs.

Already, just ten weeks into their short lives, Kimberly's hope that this accidental mating would yield a brood of future stars was beginning to dim; nearly all the puppies were displaying flaws that would likely preclude them from being show quality.* Even Little Jack, a beautiful blue-eyed rendition of his father, was looking imperfect.

Kimberly pointed to a dime-size smudge of brown on his head. "Believe it or not, that rules him out," she said. It is what Aussie people call "running copper" and means that a gray or black spot also contains brown. There is no such thing as a coat that is too mottled or haphazard, but within that pattern the spots themselves must be pure.

I asked about Jackson, the red merle with aquamarine eyes. He, too, was beautiful.

"White ear."

Breeze?

"White on her ear."

Bodi?

"No neck."

That left only Cork and Patience, a black tri with perfectly symmetrical markings. Aesthetically she was flawless, except that she was very small, and if her mother was any indication, that wasn't likely to change. According to the standard, an otherwise perfect dog shouldn't be faulted for being small; in reality, everyone knows that judges do it anyway.

Kimberly had brought the puppies to have them evaluated by Heather, and also by Kristin Elmini, an acquaintance of Kerry's who had bred Jack's father, Honor. She'd come out because she knew that the judge liked her pretty red merle, Dallas—a three-time Best in Show winner who won the breed at the Garden in 2007—so she'd brought

---

*Though, as we've learned, it's impossible to know anything for sure at such a young age; they could also grow up to be beautiful, perfect dogs.

him out of semiretirement to rack up some easy wins toward a grand championship. (He was, as it turns out, also Jack's uncle.)

It began to sprinkle as Kimberly took the puppies out of the back of her Subaru wagon in sets of two to show to Kristin. They were larger than pugs and had reached a stage of maximum cuteness—the precise point at which puppies look most like stuffed animals come to life.

"I see a lot of Jack in them," Kristin said. "The Mill Creek and Kaleidoscope lines* are very strong." She pointed to the tinge of tan on LJ's crown. "You'll get that—and also the long ears," which she pointed out on Jackson. "That's Kaleidoscope."

"Jack produces beautiful heads," Kimberly said proudly.

"That's Mill Creek," Kristin pronounced, with the knowledge of someone who'd spent a lifetime in the breed. Her opinions were concise and swiftly issued. LJ's ear, she thought, was not a major concern. If Kimberly was worried about whether to sell him to a show home or a pet home, there was always a third option: "You can bite the bullet and hold on to him and hope it grows out. Honor was very light in color. I'll have to pull some puppy pictures for you." She was also not that worried about the white on Breeze's ear. "You can always clip and dye it."† As the black-and-white dog pounced on LJ's back, Kimberly laughed. "She has Jack's eyes and brains—and his fire."

"I don't like her shoulder," Kristin said as Kimberly walked the puppy down and back. "She has a short back. It's cute, but she'll probably overkick, like Player. He has a lot of rear angulation. That's Kaleidoscope."

She pointed to Jackson in comparison. "See how he has a much better shoulder? Hers was straight." She picked the merle up and plopped him on the tailgate. "Feel here," she said, grabbing Kimberly's hand and directing it toward the pup's shoulder. "Put your thumb here." Kristin

---

*Two very well-known and respected Aussie kennels. Mill Creek produced Honor, Jack's father.

†An act that would be, of course, illegal.

was a font of knowledge, her head filled to bursting with nuances of the dogs' pedigree. "How are the bites? We have Cole* in there. He can produce overbites." She stepped back and took Jackson in. "I like this puppy—a lot. Every one of the puppies has a really nice, correct rear."

The littlest, Patience, was next. Her size was deceptive, Kimberly said. "She's a brute. She's piss and vinegar. She has Daddy's attitude."

"That's good. I'd rather not have to drag it out of them," Kristin said. "That was Honor's weakness." She lifted the puppy and felt her neck, topline, and back. "Very balanced between front and rear. The thing I don't like is that she has a lot of space between elbow and chest. That's where I would fault her—I'd like more here," she said, palming the dog's delicate chest.

I caught myself thinking that I'm glad we don't do this with our human children to determine which path their lives should follow: *Your son has a great face, but his shoulders are too narrow for science. He'll have to work in sanitation.* My face must have reflected it.

"I pull puppies apart," Kristin said matter-of-factly. "I don't say, 'This is your next Best in Show bitch.'"

Herding puppies is at least as difficult as herding cats. Every time one was returned to the tiny ex-pen Kimberly had set up in the grass, at least two others spilled out. "You need ten hands to handle puppies!" Kristin said, and grabbed LJ by his scruff. "This puppy I like." She reached between his legs. "Do you have both your nuts, too?" She confirmed that he did and set him down. "I like this puppy a lot. You put this puppy down and he's just right on."

"He's real independent."

"That's my kind of puppy."

He looked a lot like Jack—but with blue eyes.

"Who's left? The big boy?" That would be Bodi.

"He has no neck," Kimberly said, preempting what she assumed would be the obvious criticism.

---

*Another prominent sire.

"I *own* no neck," said Kristin, meaning in her line. "I bred to a neck like a giraffe. You can fix that in a generation."

Right then Kevin appeared. He and Heather were just back from a set of shows in Puerto Rico, and judging by the tan there must have been time in the schedule for sunbathing. He hadn't seen the puppies in a month. "Is that Little Jack barking?" he said. "Of course!"

Heather joined the party and wasted no time in pronouncing that she liked Patience the least. She said, "I don't like that one," over and over as the puppy walked down and back. "She would be my pet dog." Bodi, though, was improving in her estimation.

Puppies are certain to draw a crowd, and the chorus of critics grew as Belinda Rhoads, owner of Bentley (now ranked seventh) also entered the fray. She liked Jackson and Breeze, the latter for her size. She shrugged. "I like a doggy bitch. I like a big bitch."

We were far from a quorum, or any kind of consensus.

"I like all the boys," Heather said. "Which says a lot about Jack. It's easier to get nice girls. For an oops litter, it's a really pretty litter."

The following day was a wet one, and a rainy day makes for perilous conditions for white dogs—or even white-footed dogs. Imagine how the komondor people felt.

There are few dogs more unusual-looking than the komondor, which resembles a sheepdog with dreadlocks. And that's precisely what it is. Bred in Hungary to protect flocks from wolves and bears and any other animals that might want to snack on sheep, the komondor is a large and independent-minded dog known for being both tough and brave.

KOMONDOR

The dreadlocks on a komondor—which are actually known as cords—are right there in the breed standard, and, as is the case with human Rastas, are never cut; they last a lifetime, or until the dog retires. Why does a sheepdog need dreads? As should be very clear by now, apparently quirky purebred-dog quirks rarely if ever turn out to be quirky at all. The dreads are intended to make the dog look like a sheep, so that a wolf/bear/thief won't notice the dog there and will sneak up on the flock and then—oops—get a very unpleasant surprise. This surprise is critical when you think about it, because a bear that sees a dog might not be intimidated at all. But a bear that thinks he's strolling up to snack on some sheep will likely be scared out of his tiny bear mind when one of those sheep rears up, barks, and bites him on the ass. Like most guard dogs, komondors* are very lethargic and seem docile—until they're not. You would be wise not to fuck with a dog that is bred to protect sheep from bears.

---

*The fancy Hungarian plural is "komondorok." Dog people prefer this, while Webster's Dictionary opts for "komondors."

If you've been to some dog shows, you might have noticed the other breed with dreads, the puli.* I asked a woman in a purple kilt standing with two komondors if it was just bizarre coincidence that humans bred two dogs with Jamaican haircuts, and she said no, that wasn't coincidence at all. The puli is also Hungarian, and the two breeds work in concert. While the komondor protects, the puli herds.

There are many reasons you would want to think deeply before adopting one of these impressive dogs. For one thing, they weigh up to 125 pounds and like to tackle people. So there's that. Show owners must also go to great lengths to grow and maintain their cords—to keep them dry and free of urine stains. Every time a dog needs to go out, it is wrapped in tarps and bungeed up like a backyard BBQ in winter; the dreads on top of the head are hidden behind an oversize shower cap. And with all the mud outside, they were having to be extra vigilant in Bloomsburg.

Marlene and Joseph Horvath of New Egypt, New Jersey, are known "the Kilt Crew" because they wear kilts to every show, and because of that they are as recognizable as their dogs.

"It is a high-maintenance breed," Marlene told me. "I kick myself for not getting a wash-and-wear dog." The Horvaths own seven of these impressive animals and currently have two others staying with them. Marlene said the cords grow four inches a year and that it takes six to seven years for them to grow fully. Once the mats begin to form, you use a special tool to split and shape them. There is some trimming, and it requires a three-hour bath to soak them for cleaning, then another twenty-four hours to dry completely. For this reason, she said, "my retired dogs are shaved."

One of her dogs, an older bitch, was resting in a crate, and when I leaned over to say hi, she was up in a blur and barking. I recoiled. WOW. OKAY. Yikes.

"They're livestock guard dogs," Marlene said. "A lot of people think

---

*Or "pulik" in plural.

they're big, safe, fluffy guard dogs. You're standing next to me, I'm her mom, and she doesn't know you." She smiled. "They're a wonderful, wonderful breed to guard your family. But they need a *lot* of socialization."

Though Hungarians get credit for komondors, the breed is actually far more ancient than that, thought to have originated in Mongolia with tribesmen who wandered all the way to Hungary and then settled there. When Hitler invaded Hungary, the breed was almost wiped out, because the dogs were so fierce that the Germans had to shoot them in order to get into homes.

Dare I ask: Are they okay with kids?

"*Your* kids," Marlene said. "Your kids' friends you have to be careful with. If the kids are roughhousing, they could think the kids are in trouble." In which case the dogs are likely to do what they do— which is pounce and pin the target to the nearest flat surface. Joseph Horvath said that a dog owned by a friend, a dog he knows well, recently pinned him against the wall and held him until the friend arrived and told the dog to release him. The breed standard, according to Marlene, says to "heed their warning bark, or they may attach themselves to you," which would be a euphemism for "will pin you to wall."

Komondors rest eighteen hours a day, Marlene said, because they never really sleep soundly. In guard dogs at least some senses must always be attuned for trouble. "But they're lightning fast," Marlene said. "They'll go from lying down to on top of you in five seconds.

"Size doesn't matter to them," she went on. "If they think one of their family members will be hurt, they'll go after whatever it is." She recalled the story of a woman who fell while handling her komondor in the breed ring. Another handler, acting on instinct, rushed to help her. "And everyone else froze," she said. "They all yelled, 'Stop!' Her dog had put himself between her and everyone else. She had to tell him it was okay so people could come help out."

The only resident of her house who doesn't respect them, she said, is her three-pound Pomeranian. "He's a tough little cracker. When they play with him, he'll bite their nose."

In addition to nine komondors and the Pomeranian, the Horvaths have a vizsla, a kuvasz,* and five birds (plus three children). This is probably not the quietest house on the block. "The birds are louder than the kids," Marlene said. "They talk. They know the dogs by name, and they tell them to shut up and be quiet."

The fact that one special withdrew hardly mattered for Jack, who looked good and showed well but lost anyway as Dallas took the breed for the second straight day. And Kimberly was beginning to accept the hard lesson about too much too soon. Because Jack had won so often in his early months, she'd come to expect winning; subsequently, when he didn't win, she tended to channel her disappointment in counterproductive ways—by getting frustrated and wavering about her willingness to pay money for shows if she couldn't count on winning. By November she was managing her expectations better. "Jack is an exceptional dog," Heather explained. "And when he was a class dog, he won all the time *because* he's exceptional. But now he's a special." At this level, "they're all exceptional."

It wasn't a totally lost weekend; there was always an upside. And the upside in Bloomsburg was the arrival of Mandy, the show-dog chiropractor.† Mandy Armitage lives outside the charming Delaware River town of New Hope, Pennsylvania, and is another celebrity on the circuit. If your dog is having back or neck or leg problems—or just generally seems out of sorts—you get in touch with Mandy, and for twenty-five dollars her magic hands will get down to business. She works seven days a week and has a sympathetic husband "willing to take care of my kids." (She has two.)

Heather, like most handlers, is a firm believer in Mandy's skills, and

---

*Those are also Hungarian breeds.

†The correct term, according to Mandy, is "chiropractitioner."

she continued to state in unambiguous terms that as long as Jack was her responsibility, she wanted him to have regular adjustments. Early in the year, he'd seen Mandy at least every other week; over the summer, though, the frequency slipped. By Bloomsburg he was definitely in need.

Because Kimberly had already left to take the puppies home, Heather told me to go meet Mandy by the truck, where Jack was napping in his crate.

"Hi, Jack!" Mandy said as he shot up from his slumber and began to wiggle and then thrash with excitement. "Jack, stop." She fixed him with a stare. "Let's walk him."

Within a few steps, she suspected he might have to poop. He'd gone three times already, I told her. "Stress," she answered, and thirty seconds later he popped a squat and left a steaming pile in the grass. Mandy patted him on the head. "Good boy!" she said.

"Now he'll relax," she pronounced, and began to push on his side and topline, not firmly but not softly either. Jack stood there looking unbothered.

Mandy's mother, father, and brother are all chiropractors, and she followed suit. "Only I hate people. I prefer animals." Mandy's card reads VETERINARY CHIROPRACTITIONER,* which she compares to a dental practitioner. She is certified in Veterinary Orthopedic Manipulation. "Vets give me the right to do this."

I had distracted her from her work with my questions, and Jack began to wander off. "Jack!" she yelled. "Hang out, dude!"

There are, somewhat surprisingly, "quite a few" people like her out there. "But I'm probably one of the few that uses my hands." Most veterinary chiropractitioners, she explained, use something called an activator; "it looks like a gun with a doorstop on the end. What they do is, they tap the vertebrae, and it's supposed to make all the muscles jiggle and then relax. Then the bone goes where it belongs. I don't find that always to be true. . . ."

---

*Who have certifications, but not licenses.

Jack had begun to whimper a little. "I know, I know," she said, and moved her hands to his head, where she commenced another series of adjustments. "Let me get your head on right. I know. Hi! It's me, isn't it? Did you just get it?" She soothed him with some baby talk, and he began to settle a little. "Come here, Jack. Let's finish you. Right here. Stop. Jack!"

Don't be offended, I told her. The only person I knew who could consistently make him stand still was Heather.

"Now, that's good—stop! Stay. Okay, now we're getting some- where." And then, "No rolling in the dirt!" She coaxed him up. "Now you're okay, I know."

He showed little sign of settling.

"Actually, in about ten minutes he'll feel drunk," she said. This par- ticular adjustment "gives them a head rush. That's what brings their fo- cus in." Then to Jack, "This is your spot—let me fix it. This flattens out your topline." The roached back is a common one among show dogs, she said; fortunately, it's easily corrected.

What causes it?

"If I knew that, I'd be a billionaire and I'd do this for free." But it's not just dogs who need this, she said. "Everybody's goes out of whack. I get adjusted at least once a month."

She finished up and gave Jack a belly rub. "Where does Jack go?"

I pointed out his crate, and she returned him to it.

Mandy's business isn't exclusively for dogs. She sees cats and pigs, as well as goats and horses. "Horses are a little harder on my body," she said. "Cows are the worst, especially after birthing if they can't get up. It's hard for me to move a hip if they're lying down. My father was taught to use the rubber-mallet-and-two-by-four method. I have a two- by-four wrapped in lambskin so it's nice and padded. I line it up and DOINK! it with a mallet." This knocks the dislocated vertebra back into place.

"I have a group of chickens I work on," she continued. "Their necks go out. Have you ever seen a chicken breed? It's like rape. They grab the female's neck. I had an ornamental chicken come in that got raped by a rooster. It twisted her neck so bad that her eyeball was looking up. She was so relieved, the next day she laid an egg."

Mandy does have limits. A zoo recently asked her to work on an elephant, but she refused. "All I could picture was myself getting hurt. And then many other clients would be upset."

Even before she was certified, Mandy used to observe and study her mom's work. "I think the body always knows where the vertebrae should be, but sometimes the muscles won't let the bones align. The body responds to movement, to age, to environment, to stress, or to chemicals. I help the body maintain balance."

So what exactly did you just do to Jack? I wondered.

"I moved"—and she looked up and counted on her fingers—"two, three, four, eight different bones. It's very fast, very quick, very effective. The faster I'm in and get it done, the faster they get back. Watch, he'll be out cold in fifteen minute. They sleep like babies."

Mandy explained that she knows how the skeleton is supposed to feel, so she feels along the spine for muscles that seem wrong and manipulates them to slip bones back into their proper places. "Some I have to move harder than others. With Jack we've gotten to the point where I don't have to fight with his body."

So it just feels as if a bone is out of place?

"I am feeling muscles, and they sometimes feel like a rubber band or a hose. Depends on which muscle is reacting. I work five layers down below their structural muscles—those are spinal muscles. I do knees, hips, toes, whatever. My lure coursers and racers"—meaning the speedy sight hounds—"they need their pasterns* done. A lot of the sight hounds flex at the pastern stop. Not all dogs use it." One of her most unusual clients is a weight-pulling dog, a thirty-five-pound pit bull capable of moving three thousand pounds on a sled. "He came in to see me because he was stuck at eleven hundred pounds. But eight months later

---

*Dogs walk on their toes, essentially, and the pastern is the elongated area between the foot and the joint. The foot flexes at the pastern joint.

we've now broken three thousand. I think he's close to being number one."

Then there's the Chihuahua with no front legs; it stands up on its hind legs and runs around. "If I didn't see it, I wouldn't have believed it. I put it down in my office, and the lady said you have to catch it. It took off across my office and looked like a flying squirrel. It was just this Hail Mary flying across my office. What it does is push itself up, using abdominal muscles, and then goes."

Great Danes put on weight so quickly—six pounds a week when they're young—that "they end up getting very knock-kneed. I palpate the socket. I've got ways to fix many things. Agility dogs will come in because they can't hit a jump right. It's their eyes. I can work an eye nerve that controls depth perception."

How?

"It's in the neck. Every bone in the spine feeds a nerve that goes to somewhere in the body. One of my favorite ways to describe chiropractic is to think of a garden. It's required to have ten gallons of water every day. And your well has a hose that feeds the garden. If you put a rock on that hose, eventually the garden could wither and die. Let's turn to the dog. The brain is the well and the spine is the hose. When the vertebrae move, it's called a subluxation—that's the rock. Their body's the garden. I remove the rocks off the hose. That's all I do."

Jack's situation was that he was playing too much Frisbee, she explained. "He would get his rear tucked under and leap up in the air. He'd rock his hips, so his topline had to come up—cause and effect. It's called a roach. If you play Frisbee, keep it low. What I don't want is for him to jump up and twist. It throws the body off."

Mandy has no time for doubters. "People who say, 'My dog doesn't need it'—that's ignorance. I have found one dog in all my years doing this who didn't need it, and I did not charge the owner for touching her dog."

Business was booming, Mandy said. And she'd never felt healthier.

"Because I'm balanced, I haven't been sick since I had my nine-year-old. I don't get colds." Adjustments, she said, aren't just physical. They're therapeutic. "You flush out, you go to bed, and you feel great. It's amazing the things that chiropractic does."

By this point another client was waiting. It was Claudette, whose bloodhound Benny was one of Kevin's specials last year. (He's the one who descends from the dog owned by Christopher Guest's character in *Best in Show*.) These days Claudette was more of a part-timer, and she'd brought one of Benny's sons, Solo, for a test run—and, since she'd spied Mandy, also an adjustment. Claudette told me Mandy had worked wonders on many of her dogs. For Benny, it helped him fight his tendency to drop his tail in the ring.

"A lot of the dog-show stuff is not natural to them," Mandy said. "We're asking them to stand in a position that's not comfortable." She recalled the case of one of Claudette's bloodhound bitches. "She didn't want to poop. She hadn't gone in like two or three days."

Claudette nodded. "Mandy came over, did her magic-fingers thing, and said, 'Go for a walk, and she'll go in about five minutes,'" she recalled. "Five minutes later she went."

I was with Mandy to this point; in fact, I was ready to sign up all the pets in the neighborhood. Then things got a little metaphysical.

"I've done a phenomenal amount of stuff to understand them," she said, meaning the animals. "And what's happened is, I can hear them. Like Jack—he came out and he was a little weird. I knew what to do because I could hear what he was saying. I could feel what he felt."

Did she mean like Reiki* for dogs? I asked, intending it as kind of a joke.

"I'm through Reiki three," she said.

---

*A Japanese relaxation technique popular with the dream-catcher crowd that seeks to manipulate a person's "life-force energy."

It works?

"Wonderfully. What a difference it has made."

I was quietly absorbing that fact when Claudette tapped me on shoulder and pointed into the truck, at the crate, where Jack had fallen sound asleep.

CHAPTER THIRTY-THREE

Philadelphia

Remember, folks, he's a show dog. He loves the applause.
—WAYNE FERGUSON, CHAIRMAN OF THE NATIONAL DOG SHOW AND
EMCEE OF THE EVENT

On November 19, at 2:34 P.M., I was at lunch with the director of communications for the American Kennel Club when I felt the buzz of my phone vibrating in my pocket. While my lunch companion excused herself to go the restroom, I glanced at my phone and found the following message from Kimberly, who had sent it to both Kerry and myself:

> Jack finished his Grand Championship today by going Best
> of Breed over the number one and number three Aussies in
> the country! Wooohoooo!

First off, this was awesome news. It meant that Jack had finally gotten the elusive major that would complete his grand championship and that he had beaten the unbeatable Beyoncé in the process. Second, it turned out to not totally be the case. He did beat the country's number-one and number-three dogs—one of whom was Beyoncé—but there

were only ten dogs entered, so it wasn't a major after all. The fact that
these ten dogs included many of the best Australian shepherds in America, gathered in Philadelphia for one of the biggest shows in the country, didn't change that fact. It was a huge win, but Jack still wasn't a
grand champion.

The next day I joined the party in Oaks, Pennsylvania, where the
Kennel Club of Philadelphia was staging its annual cluster of shows that
culminated with the self-proclaimed National Dog Show Presented by
Purina, and taped by NBC to be broadcast on Thanksgiving.

"We will have America's top dogs," Wayne Ferguson, the Kennel
Club's president, told a local reporter. "A win at Philadelphia is considered one of dogdom's best."

The National Dog Show is probably the third-most-important show
in the country after Westminster and Eukanuba, and it is as famous as
it is thanks solely to a Eureka moment on the part of NBC Sports executive Jon Miller. Ten years ago Miller's wife brought home the movie
Best in Show, and he loved it. He was taken, he said, "with how enter-
taining the whole concept was," and when he got to work, he assigned
an intern to find out what the second-oldest dog show in America was,
thinking that surely Westminster was oldest. The intern came back
with surprising news: Westminster was the second-oldest show, and
the oldest was one the Kennel Club of Philadelphia first staged in 1876.*

Miller called Ferguson, recruited Purina as a sponsor, and convinced his bosses to try a bold experiment: to air a dog show after the
Macy's Thanksgiving Day Parade. The company's research department
expected the show do at best a 2.0 rating. It got a 7 and had a total audience of more than 19 million.

A decade later the show is a fixture on Thanksgiving Day and has
attracted an average of 18.5 million viewers. And some of that success
is owed to its hosts, Westminster's David Frei and his color man, John

---

*It has not, however, been held continuously ever since, which is why Westminster can
claim to be oldest.

O'Hurley, the host of *Dancing with the Stars* (as well as the actor who played J. Peterman on *Seinfeld*). When his friend Jon Miller called him with the offer, it was utterly out of the blue. "I answered the phone, and on the other end I heard WOOF-WOOF," O'Hurley told me. "And that's how it started."

Ten years and two bestselling dog books later, O'Hurley says he's "right in the middle of the dog world," but that first year he was "a total neophyte." O'Hurley was the perfect foil for Frei, and made his mark with quips like, "When the judge picks through hair on an English sheepdog and finds only one eye, it's the wrong end."

O'Hurley is still funny, playing the role of rube to Frei's straight man, but he's increasingly a dog man himself. One of his books stars a Maltese of his that lived to twenty—"One of the oldest dogs on record and a little drill sergeant until the end."

If you are among the millions of Americans who tune in for the National Dog Show while picking turkey threads out of your teeth, you probably think it's a haughty affair. Staged by the experienced TV sports operators of NBC, it has the look of a black-tie ball that happens to feature dogs. There is flattering light, purple bunting, and oversize vases of flowers. The reality is a little less velvety. If you pulled back on those cameras, out of the ring, over the low blue walls emblazoned with the logo of Purina, past the spectators, and through the thick black curtains that turn day into night—because it's daytime, despite what it looks like—you'd find yourself in yet another large, charmless convention center. In this case the Greater Philadelphia Expo Center, in an office park just down the road from Valley Forge.

The National Dog Show doesn't actually even happen until Saturday, but dogs and handlers arrive on scene Wednesday to primp for a four-day cluster that often attracts many of the nation's top dogs;* a win on Saturday, after all, means national TV exposure.

---

*Though, surprisingly, none of the top three all-breed dogs for 2010—Dodger, Malachy, and Emily—were entered. They were all in Columbus, Ohio, where the setter was a surprise winner on day one of the four-day weekend in Ohio's capital city.

Jack's surprise win over Beyoncé, unfortunately, came on the first day, Thursday, which didn't diminish it in any way. It just didn't lead to TV. To get that he'd need to repeat the miracle over the weekend.

Kimberly arrived with some surprising news. She'd managed to get rid of most of the puppies. Two were in "pet homes" in Pennsylvania, and on Saturday she'd drive four more to the airport to ship off to Kerry, who had prospective homes for them out west. That left one. She had decided to keep Bodi.

She was still giddy from the previous day's win. It was a highlight to take down Beyoncé under any circumstances, even if Jack had missed a major—and the grand championship—by a single absentee dog. Entries were too low on Friday as well, so to complete the title, Jack would have to beat Beyoncé again on either Saturday or Sunday.

Philadelphia is big in every way. The show is one of only six benched shows left on the dog-show circuit, making it popular with spectators, who swarm the floor ogling dogs. Unlike Westminster, which packs dogs into rows that barely allow room for spectators to pass one another without elbowing the dogs in the snout, the Philly show has the largest footprint of any dog show I'd visited. It wasn't cramped at all.

Heather led Jack into the Aussie ring, and he took the first position in a line of eight lovely dogs. Kimberly said she was so certain in advance he'd have no chance that she didn't even stick around to watch Jack's win. She left early to try to beat the traffic.

"I thought maybe Beyoncé was out of coat," she said when Heather told her about the win. "Heather said, 'No, she looks phenomenal.'"

And she did—Beyoncé did have a coat befitting her name, shiny and thick and lustrous. Jack, too, was looking great. The white of his ruff shone nearly as much as hers, even without the contrasting black hair.

Kimberly and I were watching from behind a pole, trying to stay out of Jack's vision, and I was startled by a voice over my shoulder. It was Mandy.

"How's he doing?" she asked.

"He beat the number one dog, who's number one by like a billion points," Kimberly said.

"Heather told me," Mandy replied. "But she said he's still not right. She had a list of things for me to work on." That Heather, never satisfied.

Our grandfatherly judge was thorough. He was clearly not just going through the motions. Beyoncé's movement was zippy—she wasn't electric, like Jack, but she was confident. When running, her legs glide and nearly float.

Not surprisingly, she won, with Best Opposite going to Jack. For once no one was disappointed. "He was actually better today than yesterday," Heather said to Kimberly, and then she gave me a disapproving look. "You missed yesterday. Beyoncé has lost like five times all year"— out of nearly 150 shows.

I said that I couldn't believe they'd beaten such a dominant dog and then didn't win, let alone place, in the group. Heather admitted that she'd made the mistake of thinking this very thing and saying it out loud, thus jinxing herself. "Nothing's for granted, Josh. You just never know. Put that in your book. You just never know."

After beating Jack on Friday, Beyoncé went on to win the Herding Group over a top-notch field of dogs that included Roy, the shaggy Gandalf look-alike that was still dominating America's herding dogs. (He was in his second year as the country's number-one herding dog, in fact.) Winning a group early in a show cluster has some unstated benefits, primarily that the dog is on display twice more for all the judges, who gather for the groups and Best in Show in a special section with padded seats, snacks, and champagne. It's unusual for a dog to win a group, go on to compete for Best in Show, then lose the following day in its breed. And this didn't happen to Beyoncé. She won the breed on Saturday, solidifying her appearance on national TV and validating Jamie Clute's rare trip north.

It was hard for Kimberly to fret much over that. Jack showed well and got Best Opposite (again) over several other top specials. And Beyoncé was pretty much a snowball rolling downhill at this point.

For TV the groups were given extra pomp. A color guard trotted out for the National Anthem, and then the *Chariots of Fire* theme played as the dogs stacked. Jamie had changed into a dark suit for the occasion and was joined in the ring by both Heather—sparkly under the lights in a red sequin blouse, with a Pembroke Welsh corgi named Panda—and Kevin, who was working for the first time with a Norwegian buhund that was the only dog entered in its breed,* as well as a who's who of top handlers, including Michelle Scott, Ernesto Lara, and Greg Strong, who seemed to find himself into at least a couple groups at every show.

Kennel Club president Wayne Ferguson worked the PA. "Herding dogs have the sole purpose of moving livestock from one place to another," he told the crowd from a seat at the table next to the one where O'Hurley and Frei talk for TV. "There are twenty-four breeds and varieties in the Herding Group."

You'll hear Ferguson if you're watching along on TV. He's the Voice of God, intoning in a deep baritone the breed facts that precede each dog. For instance, that "the briard served during the First and Second World Wars, carrying ammunition to troops," that the bearded collie is "a masterful escape artist that thinks fences are for climbing," or that—as Jamie trotted out with Beyoncé—that the "Australian shepherd is not a dog of Australia at all but an American invention. This is an active, super-intelligent breed that lends itself well to training."

Beyoncé received an enormous cheer, probably the biggest yet, as she whipped around the edge of the unusually large ring with her tongue dangling ever so slightly out of one side of her mouth. It was apparently propitious; she won the group, again, and Jamie stood smugly grinning at the center of the traditional handler scrum, where, upon

---

*If your only goal is to get on national TV, once, and other plans have failed, you could always show up at the National Dog Show with a rare breed.

the completion of every group, disingenuous handshakes and hugs are exchanged.

Three groups later the pomp began anew as the seven group winners reassembled for Best in Show. Joining Beyoncé were the Irish setter, the boxer, the Scottish deerhound, the American Staffordshire terrier, the schipperke, and the affenpinscher, the latter with the Mexican superstar Ernesto Lara on his lead. This was a new arrival from Europe, having dominated the show circuit there, and was widely expected to become one of America's top dogs in 2011.

"Folks, a Best in Show at the Kennel Club of Philadelphia is one of dogdom's greatest achievements," Ferguson said as a nervous titter in the crowd filled the air while Judge Paula Hartinger mulled her options. Australian shepherds don't win major shows often, but it wouldn't be a total shock for Beyoncé to win either. The 2007 winner was an Aussie named Swizzle, and Beyoncé certainly had momentum on her side.

Hartinger surveyed the dogs, stacked like statues, and proclaimed, with great verve, "It's the Irish setter!"

For Clooney, as this particular setter was named, it was his first-ever Best in Show, and it was also kind of a big surprise.

John O'Hurley, it should be noted, called it. "Every year I put my finger on which I like the best," he told me. "I've been rooting every year for the Irish setter. That, for me, is the prettiest of dogs. And for the life of me, I couldn't understand why it hasn't won Best in Show."

Clooney, he said, was just a "gorgeous setter. To me they represent what a dog show is about. When you watch that dog come into the ring, the hair, the strut—it flows beautifully. It's a beautiful representation of what I feel a show dog should be."

Kimberly and Jack probably should have quit while they were ahead. Sunday was the final day of the cluster, and it was bound to be anticlimactic anyway. Heather and Kevin found themselves with a deluge of dogs and a major scheduling snafu. Show superintendents don't build the schedule with overtaxed handlers in mind; they try to be considerate when possible, but there's no way for them to predict the problems of a handler who has too many dogs. And in Kevin and Heather's cases, they had four Bernese mountain dogs—including Tanner, who'd finally returned to his old life on Dawn's farm and to his place at the top of the pecking order—to show in the same ten-minute window that contained Jack and the Aussies.

If the show had been on schedule, there was only a seven-minute cushion between Tanner and Jack. And the show wasn't on schedule. It looked for most of the morning as if the best-case scenario was that Kevin would show Jack, and that's what happened.

Kevin led Jack, whom he hadn't handled in months, out to meet his judge: Christopher Tilghman Neale—a tall, dapper, fellow in a brown suit with a copper tie and matching pocket square. He had the hair and the air of a man you'd see at the yacht club. Neale was a gawker. He stared intensely at the dogs as they stacked—and Jack was cooperating gamely—and then stared intensely again the whole time they were moving, locked on each dog like a spotlight until it reached the far side, at which point he spun around and pointed to the next one.

He pointed to Jack. Kevin began to run, and Jack followed for a few steps and then, for whatever reason, jumped straight up onto Kevin's back. Kevin snapped the lead, but this only encouraged Jack, who then jumped on his front. Any doubt remaining that there was a magic to handling—or that Jack was still a difficult dog—vanished there. If Jack could steal a Best Opposite after that mess, it would be a miracle. And he didn't.

This was very frustrating for Kevin, who is an excellent handler who just happens not to have the rapport with Jack that his wife does. But it wasn't necessarily a reason to worry. Jack's propensity to drive Heather nuts was precisely the reason she has always believed in him. Once she told me that you can have a mediocre dog with tons of personality or a phenomenal dog with no personality—"and the mediocre one will win ninety-nine percent of the time." Jack was not mediocre, and he certainly didn't lack personality either.

The only encouraging news of the day was that Jamie Clute wasn't going to bring Beyoncé to Eukanuba. "We won last year, and the judges suck," he told me when I intercepted him returning from a cigarette break to resume grooming a giant schnauzer. Instead he would chase points until the year's end. "We're the number-five herding, and I think we've got a shot at number three." He still wasn't sure whether he'd retire Beyoncé after Westminster "or come back and go for number-one herding dog" in 2011.

When I got home that night, I went online and pulled up Beyoncé's record. According to InfoDog, which lists only shows produced by the superintendent organization MB-F (so maybe half of the events entered), the bitch had won the breed in sixty-six of the seventy-three shows she took part in. That's not quite as good as the five losses Heather had guessed at, but it was a 90 percent win percentage, which seemed pretty astounding. In addition, she won the Herding Group twenty-three times (31 percent of the time) and had four Bests in Show. This information put Jack's win earlier in the week in a bit more context. The simple act of beating Beyoncé, even once, seemed all the more impressive. It was another very fine line for his rapidly expanding résumé.

CHAPTER THIRTY-FOUR

A Quick Lesson in Poor Sportsmanship:

The Battle for (and Insanity over)

Number One

Whoever is winning at the moment will always seem to be invincible.

—GEORGE ORWELL

Any actual tension between Jack and Beyoncé existed only in my mind. The truth is, Beyoncé was running unopposed on a platform of dominance, and once Jamie won the breed at the National Dog Show and stormed on into the Best in Show ring, he'd probably long since put the blue merle that had beaten him Thursday out of mind. Aside from the occasional ringside shit-talking, Australian shepherd people are generally a pretty genial bunch.

That certainly wasn't the case in the smooth fox terrier community. As the show season cruised into twilight, Dodger was locked in a race for America's number-one dog with Malachy the Pekingese, a race that looked almost certain to go down to the wire. The dogs' handlers were jetting around the country piling up points, avoiding each other whenever possible, and switching spots at the top of the rankings numerous times. But that wasn't Dodger's only fight. A vicious battle had erupted in his own breed, as fans and supporters of the other smooth, Adam—himself a top-ten all-breed dog (registered name GCh Slyfox Sneak's A Peek)—barked and nipped at Dodger's record with increasing ferocity. And one of the places they did this most loudly was in the comment section of Billy Wheeler's Dog Show Poop.

Every time Wheeler reported on a Dodger win, anonymous commenters would commence yapping. Their argument was that Dodger wasn't even the best smooth fox in America, so he couldn't possibly be the best dog overall, and it was based on a couple of factors. One, that Adam had won the National Specialty, which supposedly rewards the country's top smooth fox but in the end is, like all shows, just one judge's opinion. And two, that depending how you did your math, Adam actually had more breed points, so that Dodger might have been the number-one smooth in all-breed rankings, by winning more big shows with higher entries, but he wasn't the number-one smooth among smooths.

Things got so nasty that Wheeler, who had recently endured heart surgery, had seen enough. He felt the need to respond and, after reading one anti-Dodger comment too many, wrote a post titled "A Public Response to Anonymous Commenter." Here's what he said:

> Perhaps it is my current medical state that makes me so intemperate. I think that breeders/owners who snipe at a dog of their own breed who is doing exceptionally well are doing a disservice to their own breed, the dog game at large, and, unwittingly, to themselves. There are forces all around us that would like to put an end to this sport. We should be rallying around the top winners in our respective breeds, not fighting within the family. It is probably not as damaging

within the Smooth Fox community as it is in some of our rarer breeds. In a rare breed, this type of selfish behavior is genocidal.

The Smooth Fox family is lucky to have two such worthy dogs out there representing their breed. I believe both have been touted in these pages many times. BUT the dog that is your breed's face to the public is of paramount importance to your breed. For you to claim that Dodger is not the Number One Fox Terrier is an argument that isn't likely to be well understood or accepted by the average dog lover.

While I celebrate breed specialties as family reunions where narrow interests can be indulged for a few days once or twice a year and breed aficionados can debate the fine points of the standard, I am somewhat suspect of using breed points. One specialty win can give an owner the specious legitimacy of claiming their dog is Number One because of the opinion of one judge. In this instance we have two dogs, winners of their 2009 & 2010 National Specialties, respectively. That was the opinion of two judges. Dodger has won over 200 Terrier Groups. I'm not sure how many judges were involved, but it was way more than two. I believe both Team Dodger and Team Adam know I love the Smooth Fox breed and I love both dogs. I know that most of my readers know I love the dog show game. I would be bored silly if every Smooth Fox looked exactly alike.

So, I invite you to write enthusiastic comments celebrating every time any Smooth Fox or any other Terrier or any other breed that you fancy is mentioned in these pages, but understand if you want to tear down your own house, do it somewhere else.

Wheeler posted that on a Saturday night, and then, the next evening, posted the results of the weekend's biggest shows, in Maryland, where Dodger won Best in Show on consecutive days, putting himself firmly back in the top spot on the rankings.

I reached out to Wheeler to dig a bit further into what was causing all this, because this level of internecine fighting was so foreign to the world I'd been inhabiting with Heather and Kevin's dogs.

Wheeler said that for me to really understand the conflict required a quick lesson, starting with the "reality that the smooth fox is the quintessential show dog." Westminster's first-ever Best in Show winner, in 1907, was the smooth fox terrier* Ch Warren Remedy, a dog that also won the following two years. Smooth fox terriers, Wheeler pointed out, had won Westminster thirteen times, more than any other breed. "There have been smooth fox among the top winners for more than a century. That's over a hundred years of jealousy, debating over the standard, and know-it-alls telling us what the perfect smooth fox should look like," he wrote.

SMOOTH FOX TERRIER

---

*Prior to that year, there was no BIS awarded.

When I was doing my research, I found and read a book called *Champion of Champions,* published by Random House in 1950. Its subject was Nornay Saddler, "a pert and precise smooth-haired fox terrier" who became the world's most famous dog.

We meet Saddler on page one on the day of perhaps his greatest triumph, a win at the 1941 Morris & Essex Kennel Club show, when he defeated 3,480 dogs to win his fifty-sixth Best in Show, eight months after retiring (for the first time). "His four feet fairly twinkled as they spurned the ground, much like those of a trotting horse sailing down the straightaway," wrote author Don Reynolds, whose pen often runs purple. "The life of this little dog had touched and influenced the lives of many humans and he had gained a measure of fame denied to all but a few of his kind." He was, Reynolds wrote, "a dog which became the canine marvel of our age."

Little Saddler hailed from Nottinghamshire, England, born in 1936 in the mud during a torrential rain—and Reynolds wasn't about to pass on the chance to point out the symbolism in that event, seeing as how the word "terrier" comes from the Latin word *terra,* meaning "earth." He quotes one of the most colorful and illuminating descriptions of the terrier's function, written in 1570 by Dr. John Kays, founder of Caius College at Cambridge University. Terriers, Kays wrote in a passage that infuriates my spell-check, "creepe into the grounde, and by that meanes make afrayde, nyppe, and byte the Fox and the Badger in some wort, that either they tear them to pieces with theyr teeth beyng in the bosome of the earth or else hayle and pull them perforce out of their lurking angles, dark dongeons, and close caves, or at least through coneved fear drive them out of their hollow harbours."

Our boy Saddler made his show debut at seven months, in front of a judge who proclaimed him "the loveliest terrier I have ever seen," and he won his first Best in Show a week later. His English owner quickly sold him for the then-astronomical price of one hundred pounds to an American, Jim Austin of New York's Long Island, and put the little dog on a freighter, where he came down with distemper and nearly died.

Saddler got off to a rough start in America, finishing dead last at his first show and then again at his second, but the minute Jim Austin hired a professional handler, his "luck" turned. Saddler won the breed at his first Morris & Essex, then the biggest show in the country, and never stopped winning. He went 19 for 19 in the smooth fox ring in 1937, with six Bests in Show, and just kept pouring it on in 1938. At that time the record for the most Bests in Show by any dog was thirty-two (held by an English setter) and on October 8, 1938, Saddler won his thirty-third, in Wilmington, Delaware.

Saddler became a celebrity, and a radio host created a stir by estimating his value at a hundred thousand dollars,* causing Jim Austin to hire a private security guard to accompany the dog on his travels. "Saddler was photogenic long before the word was popular," Reynolds reported, and said the famous dog grew so accustomed to traveling in Pullman luxury rail cars that he would summon the porter by pushing the button with his nose and then order himself a roast-beef dinner. He was only the second animal ever profiled in the *New Yorker* (the racehorse Man o' War was the first), and also appeared in the *Saturday Evening Post,* and *Town & Country.* When the war broke out in Europe, Austin donated Saddler's . . . um, services, and the little dog humped his way to twelve hundred dollars for the British war effort. The money went to buy a fighter plane—named the *Dog Fighter*—which shot down eight Nazi planes. "I sink my teeth into Adolf with this $1200 I earned myself through stud fees," said a promotional ad featuring little Saddler.

Saddler's story was fascinating—here I was thinking Jack was colorful!—but it also helped me, in retrospect, to understand at least a little why smooth fox people were so crazy.

I couldn't seem to determine if either Dodger or Adam was related to Saddler, but considering that at one point during the 1950s sixteen

---

*And this was long before India's maharaja of Pithapuram, a collector of smooth fox terriers, made Austin a blank-check offer that was politely declined.

of eighteen class winners at the National Specialty came from him, it's not hard to imagine they've both got at least a little Saddler on board.

Wheeler said that it wasn't just that half of smooth fox people preferred Dodger and half preferred Adam. "We have a third of the folks who like Dodger, a third who like Adam, and a third that don't like either," he explained. And the fact that any of them were using math to back their emotional arguments was only complicating matters.

"The debate over who is the number-one fox terrier is an inside-baseball argument. There are different ranking systems in the dog world. Some people only count all breed points—i.e., the number of dogs defeated regardless of breed. This system penalizes terriers and favors dogs in the Sporting, Working, & Toy groups"—which tend to have far larger numbers within each individual breed (because many terriers are quite rare).*

"Some people prefer the breed points—i.e., only the dogs of the same breed defeated are counted. This system favors those breeds which rarely get noticed in the group or BIS competitions—e.g., Canaan dog, Japanese Chin, or Tibetan spaniel.

Clearly I'd asked the right guy. The system, Wheeler pointed out, also favors volume,† and fortunately for me he had run all the math. "The number-one dog last year, the Scottie Sadie, competed at more than 150 shows. Dodger has already done more than 120 shows. Adam has done something over 80. Dodger has won BIS 42 percent of the time, Adam has won BIS 25 percent of the time. Dodger has won 89 percent of the Terrier Groups he appeared in, and Adam had won 80 percent of the groups when he won the breed. Dodger won the Na-

---

*He provides an illustrative example of how this all works in practice: "The number-one dog in 2007, a giant schnauzer, was often unopposed in the breed and never had to face more than twenty-five other dogs in the group. Nonetheless she accumulated on the average three times the points of the Terrier Group winner, because she was able to defeat the Doberman or boxer that had to fight dozens others in their breed."

†He suggested that a fairer model was probably the cat-show ranking system, which allows each cat's owner to choose only its top one hundred judges and use those points. Note to self: *Show Cat*, the book!

tional Specialty at Montgomery County in 2009, Adam won an Award of Merit." Nearly every result seemed to favor Dodger, which was a bummer for Adam, because it seemed likely that in any other year he'd easily be the uncontested number-one smooth. (Which might explain why his camp was so frustrated.)

Adam's biggest claim to the smooth fox crown was the fact that he won the specialty in 2010, but even that has an asterisk. Dodger's team skipped it, Wheeler said, because "they did not think the judge was favorable." To add a final dash of confusion, "Adam skipped the all-terrier show in Long Beach, in June, which Dodger won, for the same reason."

Pushed for a conclusion, Wheeler told me this: "Both Adam and Dodger are wonderful show dogs, but I have no problem saying that I think that Dodger is the better show dog." And then hedged his bets with this: "Is he the better smooth fox? I'll leave that to those that think such things are important."

In a follow-up he noted that my interpretation of momentum—that a show dog on a winning streak can't be stopped because no judge wants to look dumb—wasn't as simple as it seemed. Momentum simultaneously creates a backlash from the competition, which can work the politics to help build opposition. He said, in fact, that Dodger's owners asked him "not to make a big deal about him closing in on the all-time breed record, because they feared that there would be a movement to keep him from getting the record.

"By the way, how can anyone claim that the all-time breed winner (and he is only three years old) is not a great representative of the breed? A breed which, as I have pointed out, is the epitome of the show dog?"

Beats me.

CHAPTER THIRTY-FIVE

Go West, Young Jack

Now tell me, which of these dogs would you like to have as
your wide receiver on your football team?

—FRED WILLARD, AS BUCK LAUGHLIN, IN *Best in Show*

A few minutes before 8:00 A.M., the PA inside the Long Beach
Convention Center clicked on and a man's voice interrupted
the thrum of the room. "Welcome to the eleventh annual AKC/
Eukanuba National Championship," he said, and then "The Star-
Spangled Banner" was sung, live, by a man in an ill-fitting suit. Blow
dryers did not cease for the occasion, but at least most people stopped
and removed hats and stared toward the singer, or toward where they
thought he might be. Depending where a particular handler was sta-
tioned, that might be hundreds of yards and thousands of dogs away.

Outside, the Long Beach Convention Center had been draped in hot
pink—the official color of Eukanuba, the pet-food manufacturer and title
sponsor whose marketing dollars have paid off so well that the brand is
now shorthand for the event, in the way that Kleenex is for facial tissue.

For the 2010 edition of the invitation-only show, some twenty-five
hundred dogs from forty-nine states and forty countries had arrived to

compete for $225,000 in prize money, the year's largest purse, and the second-most-coveted all-breed title after Westminster. A show dog's career can be made by a Best of Breed ribbon at Eukanuba, to say nothing of a group win or placement, and in some years the competition draws more top dogs within each breed than even Westminster.

Jack's qualification had nearly gone down to the wire. But when the closing date for entries rolled around, a month before the show, his late surge had kept him in the top twenty-five and secured his place in California. Which was fortunate because Kimberly's fallback—that Jack would get in via his grand championship (for 2010 only, the AKC invited all grand champions)—didn't pan out, as Jack remained a major short. Nonetheless, this one-time provision explained how there were thirty-one Aussies entered. And the glaring absence of Beyoncé meant that every one of them had a chance.

The two-day National Championship didn't begin until Saturday, but the convention center began filling with dogs on Wednesday, when the so-called Dog Hair and Eggnog Cluster of preshows took place. Since Kerry lives only an hour or so north of the site, she had driven down that morning to enter another of her dogs—a less accomplished red merle named Bailey—and to stake out a prime RV spot close to the center's back entrance, as well as a swath of space for grooming inside the professional handlers' tent out back. For the duration of the preshows, she shared that space with Karen Churchill and her daughters, all three of whom were competing in juniors.

Karen, who we'd gotten to know quite well in Waco, was the first familiar face I spotted on Friday, when Kimberly and I arrived to scout the venue and the other top Aussies that had come early for the practice. She pointed us to a couple of the top West Coast dogs that we'd never seen back East and in particular singled out a red merle. It was Rowan, the red tri who'd stolen Jack's win at Westminster. "That's your competition," she said, but added, "I think Jack will do well."

"It all depends," Kimberly said, failing to finish the thought. "Wait until you see him with Heather. She brings out the best in him."

What Kimberly didn't add was that circumstances had conspired to seriously complicate things for Jack, who had a tenuous hold on proper ring etiquette even at the best of times. The lesser of the two complications was that Kerry wanted to show him at a nearby ASCA show on Saturday, less than a day before his breed competition at Eukanuba. The more problematic issue was that Halle had come back into season and was currently occupying a crate in Kerry's RV, awaiting her former mate. "Did you tell Heather?" Karen asked when the subject was raised. "Maybe you shouldn't."

Appearing for the first time at Eukanuba were the AKC's six newest breeds, including the Mexican hairless dog, the Xoloixcuintli; the bluetick coonhound (the state dog of South Carolina); and my new favorite breed of the weekend, the Norwegian lundehund.

LUNDEHUND

Lundehund means, literally, "puffin dog" in Norwegian, and it's an apt name for this breed, which has what must be the single most specific raison d'être in the stud book. To quote the breed standard: "The dog was used to wrestle and retrieve live puffin birds from the crevices of steep vertical cliffs." And not just any cliffs—the cliffs of the island of Værøy and its neighboring isles in the Lofoten Archipelago, north of the Arctic Circle. Because of its remote habitat and extremely isolated gene pool (other dogs were banned from the islands), the lundehund is considered by some to be the oldest purebred dog breed on earth. These facts alone make it awesome.

But the lundehund is a fascinating little creature* for so many other reasons. Physiologically, lundehunds are polydactyls, meaning they have bonus toes—a minimum of six on each foot, instead of the typical four, and in some cases as many as nine—to aid in climbing. On the bottom of the foot, the lundehund has a single elongated pad that serves as a brake when it's descending cliffs. The dogs also have a unique shoulder structure that allows their front legs to splay out 90 degrees to the side of the body, enabling them to grip both sides of a crevice. What's more, their ears can close either to the front or the back, to block out any debris that could fall while the dogs are spelunking. Finally, the lundehund is the only breed with an intentional ewe neck† that can turn 180 to either side, or straight back, enabling the dog to touch its forehead to its back—which is both functional and a cool party trick.

The lundehund hardly needs more color, but its backstory is the capper. The dog came about as close to extinction as a breed can come without actually disappearing from the earth—twice!—when, during World War II and again in the 1960s, distemper nearly erased the population. In 1963, the lundehund's nadir, just six remained in the world, creating what biologists call a population bottleneck. But under

---

*And it *is* little, standing just thirteen to fifteen inches at the withers.

†The "ewe neck"—conformation jargon for a neck that bends backward more than 90 degrees—is a major genetic flaw in any other breed.

the careful stewardship of a Swedish geneticist, the breed was nursed back to viability, and today there are at least fifteen hundred around the world*—two of whom had come to compete in Long Beach.

Meanwhile the back-and-forth race for the year-end number-one ranking grew tighter by the day. The top three dogs—Malachy, Dodger, and Emily—each took a Best in Show at the West Friendship, Maryland, shows, where Jack scored an elusive major, nearly cinching his grand championship in his last outing before heading to Long Beach and where, in the third of three shows, Malachy had beaten a group of six that included Tanner, in his first Best in Show group since returning from Europe.

In attendance that day, Dawn had let herself think for a second that her dog had a chance at his long-sought-after Best in Show, not knowing at the time that some of the country's top-ranked dogs were also in the ring. "The judge looked at him close," Dawn said when we ran into her and her husband, Newell, at the team's grooming setup. "Then the judge fell on him—*on him.*" And Tanner being Tanner, a good, obedient, happy old lug, he didn't budge. "He just stood there, so still. And at the end she looked over at him and was thinking, 'I like you. You're a good boy. But . . . there's that Pekingese. I gotta give it to the Peke.'" Here she paused to set up her punch line. "My son asked if it was a nice dog. I said, 'It's a bedroom slipper!'"

To which Heather added, matter-of-factly, "That dog might win the Garden."

Malachy snatched another Best here in Long Beach, at the preshows, while Dodger jetted down to Savannah, Georgia, and took one himself. All three of the top dogs were entered in Long Beach, but no one yet knew whether Dodger would come to California to face Adam on his home turf.

During a lull in the action on Friday, Kerry decided to give Jack a go at Halle, but considering their struggles during the summer,

---

*Good news unless you're a puffin.

she first stopped and picked up an artificial-insemination kit "just as a backup." And it was a good thing, because the two still couldn't seem to connect. "He's trying his little heart out, but he can't hit the target," Kerry said from her extremely front-row seat on the floor, where she was simultaneous raising Halle's rear and trying to direct Jack's aim. After ten minutes of fruitless air humping, Jack backed off, panting, and Kerry performed the AI.

Saturday was an off day, so Kimberly and Kerry took Jack a few miles up the coast to Rancho Palos Verdes for the ASCA show. On the surface it made little sense—to risk upsetting Jack's delicate psyche for a small show on the eve of a huge one—but Kerry had a broader canvas in mind; she wanted to expose Jack a bit more to her West Coast peers, and though Heather and Kimberly both quietly felt it was probably not the greatest idea to mix signals by putting the lead in Kerry's hands the day before one of the biggest shows of the year, they both went along with it, because it was important to her. "If Kerry wants to do it, she's earned that right," Heather told me.

ASCA shows tend to cluster in a single day, so that there's one show in the morning and one in the evening. This saves money on location rental and travel for participants and makes sense when you're talking about small fields. For the morning show, Jack was one of only eight intact class dogs and the only entry in Bred-by-Exhibitor, meaning he was guaranteed to be participating for Winners Dog points unless he peed on the judge.

Ringside, we met the Churchill clan, as well as their friend Jessie, who had brought Jack's full brother, also named Jack. He was a big, fluffy black tri with a strong family resemblance—he, too, had a handsome, blockish head. In comparison to our Jack, he seemed calm, though Jesse said he's actually anything but. "We call him Jackrabbit because he loves to jump." Like his father, Honor, I said. "Yep," she said. "Jump up, spin. Jump up, spin. Jump up, spin . . ."

Kerry put Jack on his show lead and took him away for a few minutes of practice. "Have a firm hand," Kimberly said. Just as Jack is unwilling to follow the direction of anyone he sees as a playmate—a group that would include myself, Kimberly, and (at least if Philly was any indication) even Kevin—he seemed to be giving Kerry fits now because he associated her with breeding. If the frantic attempted humping of her leg, back, and arms was any indication, he was blinded by hormones and viewed her as a potential girlfriend.

"You pissant," Kimberly said, almost under her breath, as she watched Kerry attempt to get Jack to stack. "He can't keep his feet still." Indeed, he was a live wire. "She's nervous, and he can feel that on the lead. You give him too much and he might misbehave. But act too tense and he feels it and can't move. It's such a fine balance."

A conversation taking place at the truck next door temporarily distracted me, as one woman broached the subject of "Elliot's semen" with her friend. Apparently someone was flying a little fast and loose with the poor boy's seed. "I said, 'Don't you waste that on just any old bitch!'"

Meanwhile, in the ring, the judge was in no rush. She had the dogs circle once, twice, then a third time, asking for a stack in between laps two and three, then again at the end.

"This is ASCA," Karen Churchill said when she heard me scoff at the pace. "These are breeders. They really know the breed." And around they went, again.

"She's trying to give it to him," Karen said, meaning Jack's nephew Click, at the end of Jesse's leash. Jack, by this point, was over it. He'd grown bored of the whole thing, and his behavior worsened noticeably the longer the judge dragged things out. He lost to his nephew, and by the time Kerry had returned to the grooming table, she was so frustrated she could barely speak.

Things went slightly better at the second show, even though Jasa Hatcher, the blond judge who'd bumped Jack at the last minute during the Nationals in Waco, was an hour and a half late. Kimberly was extra nervous as Kerry headed back for round two. Foremost, I think, she was worried that Kerry wouldn't like her dog and that the whole point of this exercise—to expose him to other kennels that might want to breed to him—could blow up in their faces.

The key with Jack is always not to panic and to let him think he's in charge. In his best performances, Heather once said, it's almost as if he is leading her. And sure enough, once Kerry relaxed a little and gave him a bit more lead, he trotted nicely around the ring, freezing into a perfect stack. "Right there he looks beautiful," Karen said. Truthfully, he deserved the win, but Jasa gave him Reserve Winners instead.

Kerry at least was smiling again when she walked back.

"Congrats on close but no cigar," said one rival owner.

"Kerry, does that dog not have an off switch?" said another.

She smiled at both and put him in his crate. "I'm just happy he didn't hump my leg."

B ack at the convention center, things were off to a good start, as Kevin and Rita won the breed at the Chessie ring. "I like the way this weekend is going!" Dawn howled as she wrapped Cindy in a big hug. Rita's win meant that she and Kevin would be on TV—ABC airs Eukanuba on tape, a few weeks later—and if anyone deserved some success, it was Cindy, who had long since exhausted any disposable income she had to show her dog. "They don't know this, but I took out a twenty-thousand-dollar home-equity loan to pay for this," she said when I congratulated her later. It was a surprising revelation, but not an unusual one among dog-show patrons, who forgo vacations for years in support of their hobby. (One Belgian Malinois owner-handler I met told me she had *never* taken a vacation—not one day, in more than thirty years of working, was given over to anything but her job, breeding, or dog showing.)

After some discussion of Jack's lack of focus, it was decided that the best plan to ensure he would be okay for the morning was to have Kimberly take him down the road to the Hilton, to share a room with Cindy and Rita, rather than have him spend another night whimpering in a cage within sniffing distance of Halle. But first Kerry wanted to take another shot at breeding.

Considering that Jack managed to sire a litter of puppies with Summer in a single frantic moment after knocking over his owner, it was obvious that the problem wasn't just that he was inexperienced. If he did it once, you have to think, he could do it twice. Especially if he didn't have to rush.

Kimberly took a position toward the driver's cabin, where Kerry had built a makeshift mating platform with a collapsed crate and a folded-up blue tarp so that Jack was standing a few inches higher than Halle. (Because maybe the problem was height.) Kimberly held the lead tight around her increasingly frantic dog as Kerry backed Halle in front of Jack, who immediately began to hump away even before he was in position and continued to thrust wildly as he jumped up and mounted her—his front paws locking her back legs as tightly as if he were clinging to a cliff's ledge.

Kerry, who had one arm around Halle to help calm the nervous dog, reached under to attempt to steer Jack's aim. And then—bingo, a tie. Kerry hugged the dog. "Good boy, Jack. You're not on my shit list anymore."

"Let's help him over," she said as Jack began to step gingerly with one leg, which Kerry lifted carefully over Halle's back so that the two dogs could assume the bizarre and unromantic position of a tie in progress.

"So this means the week before Westminster we should have puppies," she said. "I hope Don doesn't have plans." She could barely contain her happiness over the event, however, as the weight of so much time and money spent on the failed attempts back in the summer fell away. "I'm just thrilled. After all we went through . . . I can't believe it all worked out now," Kerry said. "He came out for this show"—something that was very much in doubt until recently. "She came into season."

Seventeen minutes later Jack began to tiptoe and test whether the doors were unlocked and it was safe for him and his penis to disengage, and then . . . liberation.

Kerry put them into crates; both dogs were ready for a nap.

"Now that's done. We gotta focus on getting him ready for tomorrow," Kerry said. And with that he was off for his bath.

The big day broke with some fresh drama. The night before, on the walk to the arena to see Rita show in the Sporting Group, where she looked great but failed to place, Heather had asked Kimberly if she'd talked to Kerry about being ready to handle Jack, "just in case." This was the first time this issue had been raised, and it was a shock to Kimberly, considering she'd flown three thousand miles, spending money she didn't really have, to see her dog compete with Heather on the lead. Kimberly's reply, she told me the next morning, was, "We may as well scratch him. And that's the last thing anyone said about it."

Cindy overheard the two discussing this potential crisis and, with Kimberly's permission, later raised the issue with Dawn and Georgeann Reeve at the hotel bar. And after reviewing the logistics, they all agreed that Heather was being unnecessarily fretful. There was plenty of breathing room in the schedule for her to show Jack and still make it for Tanner's ring time.

Heather wasn't wrong to worry—she's protecting her investment and best client—but the reality was still hard for Kimberly to swallow, especially since it was Heather who'd encouraged her to enter Jack in the first place, saying over and over to both of us that "it could be your only chance." (She was technically right. It was possible that Kimberly wouldn't show Jack in 2011, and even if she did, and was again only half committed to the cause, there was no guarantee he'd qualify.)

As the morning unfolded, however, the tension subsided, and by the time I headed to the grooming area to check up on the team, Heather was finishing up Jack before heading out to Ring 9 for the Best of Breed competition.

Ring 9 turned out to be gigantic—easily the size of one that would typically be used for groups. And the judge presiding over Ring 9 was

Mrs. Roberta Davies, last seen in Bloomsburg, where she'd liked a less fit Jack but had not given him the purple Best of Breed ribbon.

Judge Davies wore a flowing blue tunic-y shirt/dress that draped amply over a set of matching pants. She was a tall, regal woman, with a short, brown, Bieber-esque coif, delicate ovoid glasses, and excellent posture.

Ten dogs had scratched from the event, so the actual number of entries at call time was twenty-two, including at least four of the top ten. Notably absent was Beyoncé, and I remembered what Jamie had told me about the judges for this event. He'd said the judges were bad, by which he didn't mean they were actually bad at judging, but rather bad for him. Which was to say he was fairly certain that Davies wouldn't choose Beyoncé. (This is very common handler strategy.)

Back at the ASCA Nationals in Waco, one of the country's top breeders had told Kerry that she, too, was skipping Eukanuba because of the judging; the result, she'd said, was a foregone conclusion. At the time Kimberly and I took this to mean that Beyoncé was a lock to win, but Kerry cleared that up in the opening moments of the breed competition when she told me that another breeder who'd skipped the event had also said that the outcome was preordained. She pointed to a specific dog—a red merle named Reckon, handled by his breeder, a famous and very successful figure in Aussie circles—and said, "Watch, that's your winner." The judge, rumor had it, was close with that dog's owner and was known to like this dog. And whether or not that was really true, it helped explain all the absent dogs.

The giant ring helped lift spirits. It was great for Jack, Kimberly noted, because as handsome as he might be, his greatest quality is his movement, which isn't best displayed until he's able to work up some speed. Heather was also thrilled.

Judge Davies went through the line, carefully watching each dog's down-and-back and nearly its entire run around the ring. Jack was toward the end of the line, the last male before the five bitches entered, and I positioned myself so that when Heather stopped, I was there.

She was beaming. "He's showing a-*maz*-ing," she said. "Maybe the best ever. I hardly have to do anything." This was fairly insane news, that the same dog who'd nearly humped Kerry in the ring, who'd been distracted for much of his time in Long Beach by the pull of his loins, could suddenly snap into Show-Dog Mode. But such is the mysterious method of Jack.

Once through the entire field, Judge Davies began her cut. The first dog chosen? The red merle, Reckon. She pointed to the corner of the ring. She walked on and picked out another dog, then another, and then Jack, then moved to the spot where they had assembled and began to reorder them. Reckon stayed up front. When she got to Jack, her choice was swift, and she placed him just behind Reckon, but with space for the bitch who would slot in as Best of Opposite Sex.

Tension built as Davies added two more dogs and shuffled more, still not moving Reckon or Jack, who was stacked in line as if stuffed. "Wait—it's not over," said a friend of Kerry's, and yet it sure felt like it was. And then it was. "Best of Breed," Davies said to Reckon's handler. "Best Opposite," she said to the bitch Pebbles. And then, "One, two, three, four, five," to the Award of Excellence winners, number one going to our boy Jack.

"Freaking honorable mention," Kimberly said, referencing Jack's pedigree name. "It's a curse!" And then she smiled. Third (and really second) was the same result as Westminster, and either of them—let alone both—was a great honor. Rowan, the dog who'd beaten Jack at the Garden, failed to get any notice here, and considering that Reckon didn't show in New York, you can make a case that Jack was now the most successful Australian shepherd in America across the top shows, other than Beyoncé. (Throw in his Best of Opposite at the National Dog Show and the case is even stronger.)

"I can't believe this is the same dog," Kerry said. Heather, meanwhile, was so happy and proud of both herself and the dog that she was almost bouncing.

"Of all the dogs I've ever showed—ever—he's the hardest dog I've ever handled," she told me. "One day he's phenomenal—the next day he's a mess. If he was like this every day, I could take him to the top five easily, maybe number one."

One mystery that will bother her forever, because it can't be solved, is what exactly turns Jack on and off. "Something about the big shows," she said, puzzling over some possibilities. Could it be that he's the canine equivalent of an athlete who can motivate for only the biggest games—who, in sportscaster parlance, plays up (or down) to the level of his competition? "At big shows like this, he sees the competition and is just like, 'I got this.' But then at a small show—he's like, 'Eh.'" In her fifteen-plus years of handling, Heather said, she'd never had a dog like Jack, who snapped in and out of focus to such extremes. "We just need to figure out what we did," she said, having no idea, of course, that the reality of what had been done (the breeding, the extra shows) was the exact opposite of what we would have done if we were really trying to optimize Jack's performance.

She looked at Kimberly. "What did we do?"

I'd be remiss to buzz on past Eukanuba without noting that the dog that beat Jack—a dog that had recently arrived from a successful run in Italy but was basically unknown in the United States—would go on to win the Herding Group[*] in front of thousands in the Long Beach Arena that night. And that out of a field that included two favorites for Westminster—Malachy the Peke and Banana Joe the affenpinscher— plus Adam the smooth fox (Dodger never showed)[†] and two other top-ten dogs, Reckon would then go on to become the first-ever Australian shepherd to win Best in Show at Eukanuba.

---

[*]In which Roy the bearded collie was the overwhelming favorite. Not only was he the country's top herding dog by a mile, but the group judge was one of the original breeders of beardies in America.

[†]So much for resolving that argument.

This could be spun as an encouraging thing for Jack. He lost out to the dog that went on to win the second-most-important dog show in America. Would he have won it, given the same chance? We'll never know. It was even easier to spin it as a good thing for Aussies, no matter how you feel about any politics that played into Reckon's success. "It's a good advertisement for our breed," Beyoncé's owner, Sharon Fontanini, told me later. "It breaks the glass ceiling for Eukanuba and shows that judges could and should put Aussies up for big wins." With Westminster looming, it wasn't hard to sense the hope in her voice.

CHAPTER THIRTY-SIX

Wildwood: Once More, with Feeling

The curtain rises on a vast primitive wasteland, not unlike certain parts of New Jersey.

—WOODY ALLEN

At least for 2011, New Jersey's most popular beach town was not expecting another wallop from a winter storm. The previous year's historic nor'easter was still so resonant that some people actually skipped 2011's cluster of shows in fear of the memory, and an intrepid businessman was hawking T-shirts that said I SURVIVED THE BLIZZARD OF 2010 in the lobby of the convention center.

The four-day cluster had grown to five days for 2011, and Jack was back with Heather and Kevin for his first shows since Eukanuba. He'd spent the holidays, and the month of January, putting on some pounds and also picking on Bodi, who, being a puppy, was prone to repeating the same mistakes. Foremost among them, nibbling Jack's food. Secondly, being a subordinate unaltered male in the same roost as a female. When Summer began to exhibit signs of coming into season,

Jack's territorial instincts revved up, and Bodi was often cowering from his snarls.

Speaking of reproduction, out of California came word that Jack's second litter had arrived, inconveniently, while Kerry was at a business conference in Phoenix, so Don was there to shepherd the always messy arrival of eight puppies (actually nine; the last was stillborn). The litter contained six boys and two girls and included three blue merles and five black tris. There were no red dogs in the litter.

I hadn't seen Jack in weeks, and my first glimpse of him was a familiar one: his white, gray, and black form quivering atop a grooming table as an irritated Heather worked over his coat. She spied me from a distance and intercepted me in the walkway. "He's a little excited today," she said. "So can you go hide?"

Kimberly would be missing all five days of the Wildwood cluster while at a wedding in the Dominican Republic. Her BlackBerry wasn't able to send e-mails, but she was able to receive them and get to the Internet (as well as make calls), so she tended to check in periodically via Facebook.

So far Jack was 0 for 2. He'd been Best Opposite on Wednesday, having beaten the two big specials—Bentley, now the country's number-two Aussie, and Tuck, the black tri that had beaten him on several occasions in early 2010 before his owners, Steve and Kathy Ostrander, had decided to take him off the circuit—but lost to a puppy bitch out of the classes. On Thursday he took Select, to Bentley.

Tuck, by the way, was back as of January 1, and not just back— the Ostranders had hired Heather to handle him, and he was to be her top Aussie after Westminster, because Kimberly had made a decision: Rather than fret about money and blame immaturity for Jack's inconsistency, she was going put him away for at least a year. It was, she said, a surprisingly easy decision to come to. She felt that a year of growth was good for his body and mind, and it would give her time to save some money to do it right, should she opt to consider a full campaign for him in 2012 (ideally, with some backers). Within days Tuck was signed on; slots in the truck do not stay open for long.

This being a new year, and the run-up to Westminster (which dog people pretty universally call "the Garden" in the same way the AKC National Championship is "Eukanuba") Heather and Kevin had the complete retinue of animals in tow for Wildwood.

As the big dogs of 2010 prepared for their Garden finale, a whole new set was building steam for 2011. Close to home, Tanner was off to an excellent start. Back-to-back Working Group wins gave him two more shots at his first-ever Best in Show—one of his team's main goals for 2011. He didn't win either time, but his mere presence in the final seven against some of America's top dogs—including Roy the beardie,* Walker the toy poodle, and Banana Joe the affenpinscher—was impressive.

Having been away from shows myself since before the holidays, I wondered how it would seem, but watching the Aussie ring from a semi-obstructed view spot behind two women and a trash can, I still found it easy, even with weeks of distance, to pick out a bad dog from afar. I could also sense Jack's edge; nervous electricity practically radiated off him. Heather was feeling it, too, and she ran him down and back outside the ring, giving his lead a few hard upward yanks until he settled into a text-book run. Aesthetically speaking, he was in pretty good shape—his coat was thick and shiny, and if you were to nitpick (or ask Heather), maybe his only issue was that he could stand to lose a pound or two.

Stacked first in line, Jack looked distracted, as if he were daydreaming of Halle B, but not so totally absent as to upset the judge who was giving him the hands-on inspection. Even with his ears twitching in search of trouble, Jack was laser-focused on Heather, who swiftly regained her mind meld over him, even with eight weeks of distance between them. Jack, however, is always one unexpected distraction away from a breakdown, and a burst of applause next door in the Doberman ring caused him to start to jump just as Heather was beginning the down-and-back. She sensed it immediately and with no sign of fluster

---

*Yes, him again.

stopped him, yanked his lead, turned him 360 degrees to hit reset for dog and judge, and restarted the run.

I often found myself comparing Jack's edge with a top dog like Bentley. Granted, Ben was older—by nearly two years—and he was on a full-time campaign and thus out every week without fail, but I'm still pretty sure that, all things being equal, Ben is always going to seem more composed; in contrast to Jack, especially, he's a wax figurine.

That's a good thing if you're his handler, Jessica Plourde; you never have to worry about him, say, jumping on the judge. But it's Jack's edge that makes him potentially very special. Terriers and poodles always (or nearly always) seem edgy, and they consequently win a ton of ribbons. If Jack could consistently harness that sparkle—and Kimberly could find someone to pay for a campaign—I think he could make a run at number one. (Ben, for instance, had never beaten Jack at a big show, like Westminster or Philly.)

But this judge preferred Ben and gave Select to Jack, again. Tuck left unrewarded, but Steve and Kathy, two of the nicest, most cheerful, salt-of-the-earth people you'll ever meet, took it well. They had a whole year to look forward to.

One owner who wasn't quite so accepting of her fate was Cindy, whose dog Rita had lost her spot in the truck. The plan all along had been for Rita to retire after the Garden in order to (hopefully) get pregnant and so that Cindy could begin to repair her decimated finances. But Kevin had recently broken the news to her that Nacho, the bullmastiff, was back as his number-one dog for 2011 and the number two in the truck, behind Tanner. "I had a meltdown last week," Cindy told me. "He called to tell me there could be a conflict at the Garden. I'm in debt because of this dog. I live alone, and half my salary goes to this," she said. "I called all my friends, and they said, 'You know what? You need a break. Take some time off.' They're right."

Tom and Anne were also in Wildwood, with Trader, plus a young Akita bitch and a pair of corgis. I asked Tom if he was going to special Trader for 2011.

"Not this year," he said, wiping away sweat with his tie, which bore the hand-painted profile of a corgi. "They asked me if I wanted to be the number-two working dog in the truck," a complicated and expensive proposition considering that Nacho's owner, Emi Gonzalez, could afford not only to campaign her dog but also to commission for him custom clothing and accessories (all of it with chili-pepper accents) and hire a personal driver to transport him back and forth across states. "I don't want to have to bid on that," Tom said. "Nacho's owner has more money—and Trader's not even three yet. I'll wait and see what happens after Tanner retires."

His plan for now was to take it show by show; if the schedule looked friendly, he'd enter. But only then. "Because if Tanner and Nacho win"—and all three are in the Working Group—"who takes Trader into the group ring? He's not the kind of dog you can just hand off to someone else."

One thing was clear, and probably pretty true all over the room: Kimberly was not the only owner with handler concerns, or economic realities, to consider.

D og shows involve many lulls, which is why all-breed handler setups tend to serve as home bases for the many owners who gather there, socializing and eating meals together while waiting for their dogs' ring times. I had come to enjoy these gatherings, but I also liked to take advantage of lulls to walk around and observe the many other corners of the culture. By Wildwood, though, I'd long since browsed all the tinctures and treatments and potions at the holistic-products booth as well as the full line of Chris Christensen shampoos and coloring products, and the mailboxes and sweaters and pendants at Wags Incorporated, so I found myself wandering in search of some neglected corner I'd overlooked. I found it in the person of Jennifer Vawter.

Jennifer is the face behind the International Canine Semen Bank (ICSB) RV I'd been seeing around at shows but had been too shy to penetrate. (Har, har.) In Wildwood I found her seated on a stool at a booth in the building's foyer, studying her latest sample under the microscope. Jennifer has jet-black hair and dramatic bangs and on this occasion wore black boots and a dark, lace-adorned dress under her white lab coat; the overall vibe was a little goth.

I asked her how she would sum up her job. "Breeders come by with dogs, and I collect the semen and freeze it for future use in their pedigree." I did not ask how that semen was collected here, in this very public setting, and I didn't need to. But her husband explained it anyway. "The running joke is that it's a very scientific process." Here he paused for a giant smirk that portends a punch line. "Remember high school?"

The necessity of frozen semen has already been discussed in these pages. And ICSB is a business founded by an Oregon scientist named Carrol Platz[*] to collect and store samples for the nation's breeders. When a client needs a sample, ICSB will retrieve and ship it overnight in large canisters filled with liquid nitrogen. The sample itself is about the size of a ChapStick; the canister that keeps it cold looks like an old milk container and weighs thirty pounds. Once semen is unfrozen, it can live inside a bitch for up to three days, and over that period more and more of the sperm cells will awaken and resume their life's work— swimming like hell upstream in search of the target.

Jennifer said that the samples will stay viable "indefinitely" in ICSB's freezers, where they are stored, as they were shipped, in liquid nitrogen, which maintains a constant temperature. "I know of forty-five-year-old semen that's produced thirteen puppies," she said.

Jennifer is a great advocate of freezing any champion dog's semen, and that's not just because it's her livelihood. "The reason I got started in this is because I lost a four-year-old dog unexpectedly to Lyme disease." This particular dog finished his championship in record time and before that had won group placements out of the classes. He seemed destined for greatness. "I didn't collect and freeze him because he was

---

[*]Carrol is a man and had an incredible last name for this career.

so young," she said a little wanly. "I had his whole life to do it. Then he got a rare form of Lyme and he was dead in twenty-four hours. It set my whole breeding program back five years."

Before she masturbated dogs for a living, Jennifer was a dog groomer, but she gave that up to go into business with the founder of ICSB's Delaware franchise, a man named Lee Jones. When Lee died suddenly five years ago, she was left with a choice: take over or let it be sold. "I felt an obligation to help his wife keep the business going," she said. Lee's wife stayed on to help. She oversees storage and treatment. "I do this end of it," Jennifer said, and then added, utterly deadpan, "I'm pretty much the hands-on."

(Un)fortunately, I had just missed a collection from a schipperke, which I imagine is a job requiring steady fingers rather than a whole hand. Jennifer put on a thick rubber glove that stretched to her elbow and looked like something a superhero might wear, then reached into a cooler full of dry ice.

Most reproductive vets, she told me, collect in long "straws" that hold the entire ejaculation in one tube that is all unfrozen at once. ICSB's clever method is to freeze the semen in pellets that can be portioned out into a number of tiny test tubes and then unfrozen for each breeding in a specific quantity determined by the density of sperm.

To make the pellets, Jennifer placed a bar of dense metal about the size of a brick and covered in centimeter-long pins on the dry ice—she referred to it as "this doofatchet"—where the metal reacted with the ice, burning tiny holes in the surface. The noise was surprisingly loud; it sounded like a cell phone vibrating on a hollow plastic tabletop. Using a very fine-tipped dropper, Jennifer then deposited tiny gloops of semen into those holes and then set a timer that beeps when they're frozen.*

Jennifer can approximate the density of sperm cells and uses that

---

*Dry ice starts out as a gas, rather than a liquid, which is why it's perfect for freezing—it doesn't contaminate the substance. This is very similar, I should note, to the way Dippin' Dots, "Ice Cream of the Future" since 1987—and in Chapter II since November of this year— is made.

number to estimate how many pellets are required per breeding. In this case the schipperke's sample yielded seventy-seven little sperm balls, and she knows from experience that this breed requires 75 million sperm cells per milliliter for a successful breeding (a number based largely on weight). "That's average for a small dog." For the smallest dogs, your Yorkies and Chihuahuas, it's more like 50 million. With a mastiff you need 250 million.* "It's all a number thing." She recommends clients store six to eight breedings, but some keep upwards of fifty or sixty. "I recommend keeping twice what you're realistically going to use. Leave room for error."

The genius of the pellets is that they can be thawed in batches, and the samples aren't just useful for breeding. Semen is an excellent source of DNA, and often Jennifer will thaw and dispatch pellets to labs for newly developed genetic tests. "With Portuguese water dogs"—and this is true of all breeds, really—"they're always coming up with new genetic tests. Even if a dog is dead, you can thaw a pellet and see if he's a carrier of [now-common genetic health problems like] cardiomyopathy." If your dog tests positive, you don't breed him. Simple.

She thawed one pellet so that she could analyze its motility under the microscope. "Whoo-hoo! Take a look." It was a busy little scene in there, sperms wiggling wildly, and it struck me that this might make a cute cartoon.

Was there at least a private room for the collection? I wondered.

She pointed to the curtain.

Do you set the mood?

Her partner fielded this one. "Sure, whisper sweet nothings, play a little doggy porn . . ." He seemed to take great delight in the mechanics of his wife's profession and left me with the story of introducing Lee, the founder, to a friend of his who happened to be a prominent judge. "So they shake hands, and Lee says, 'I should tell you that I jerk off dogs for a living. You never know where that hand has been.' And the judge

---

*She also sometimes has to be the bearer of bad news. "I find males that are too low, and slow swimmers, and males where everything's dead. Not often, but in some breeds more than others."

looks at him and says, 'Well, I'm a rancher, and I inseminate cattle, so you never know where that arm has been.' It took a lot to shut Lee up," he said between guffaws. "But he was speechless."

I found Tom and Cindy outside the ring watching Jack and Heather take on Tuck and Kevin and six other dog-handler combos. Tom, I guess, hadn't watched Jack much before—at least not in the recent past—and he was puzzling over Jack's topline, which seemed to slant down ever so slightly. Cindy thought it could be Heather's styling; she often poufs up the hair on his rump with hair spray, but that wasn't the area Tom was referring to. "See the black spot?" he said, meaning a patch of color just past the midpoint. "It looks off."

Not to the judge, who gave Jack the breed. But when Heather came out to hand Jack to me, Tom pointed it out and said that to him the topline looked imperfect.

"It is," Heather answered. "He's roached. He looks better after an adjustment." That didn't bother her. What did was his behavior, which wasn't improving. "He's just so bad." Better than yesterday? Considering the lull in his show schedule, it wouldn't be surprising for Jack to need a couple days to regain his composure. "Worse," she said. "Maybe the same. Tell Kimberly her handler isn't getting paid enough."

In the group, however, Jack was a different dog. "Look at him," Cindy said. "He's so focused on her." The edge from earlier was gone, and he stacked perfectly, despite all the dogs and people and activity. The judge seemed to like him and picked Jack along with five other dogs in her first cut, but that's it—there'd be no group placement.

I told Heather I couldn't believe that this was the same dog I'd watched in the morning, a dog that had won despite looking as if he might leap upon and commence humping the judge. "So much better," she said. "So much better. He's always better in groups. I do think maybe he doesn't take it seriously unless it's big."

For this to be true would require a level of understanding—of quantifying importance and allocating his attention selectively—that seems impossible for a dog, but, having watched it happen time and again, I couldn't totally discount it.

O n Wildwood's final day, Judge Lydia Coleman Hutchinson picked Tuck. This was disappointing, sure, but I also felt happy that Steve and Kathy, who in a month would be committing thousands of dollars a month to handling and travel for Tuck's campaign, would at least end the weekend on a high note.

Kimberly packed Jack's things and was gone within a half hour. But it was only 10:00 A.M., a little too early to leave. How could I make best use of my time? And then I saw him, enjoying a rare moment of rest: Kaz! With Westminster on the horizon, it seemed like a good time to finally meet Kaz Hosaka.

It would be impossible to choose the best dog handler working today—attempting to assign a value to such a mystical art is impossible—but one man who is always in the conversation is Kaz Hosaka, the master poodle craftsman.

Hosaka was newly started in the business in his native Japan when the legendary handler, breeder, and judge Anne Rogers Clark and her husband discovered him while judging a show. At that time he was working with a Doberman. "I had never showed a poodle in my life," Kaz, who is very friendly and speaks excellent, accented English, told me. "Never groomed one either. And of course I didn't win nothing [in their rings]." But after the show, he said, Mrs. Clark called him and said, "If you want to become a professional dog handler, you should come to the United States and I'll teach you how to show dogs."

So at the age of nineteen, and speaking no English, Kaz packed up for the United States, moved in with the Clarks, and studied the art of poodles. "They said I was terrible at that time but they liked my hand when I was touching dogs. That's why I came to this country and worked for Mrs. Clark for many years."

Thirty years later Kaz is unequivocally the top poodle groomer and handler in America. How long did it take him to become good?

"Still I am not good," he said.

You're the best there is, aren't you?

"People think so, but I don't think."

How could you be better?

"If I get new glasses, I can see better." He laughed heartily. "Still I'm not comfortable with it. Still I'm losing lines,* and that's why I ask my assistants, 'What do you think?' every time I groom a poodle. They watch every day, and they know if it doesn't look right. I need a third eye to help. Otherwise you start losing lines." He took a breath. "I will always get better. I will never be perfect."

Hosaka travels the East in a box truck with two assistants, both of them young Japanese girls summoned from the homeland to learn the way of the poodle as he did three decades ago. "I think learning never ends," he said. "Especially with poodles. It is very important, this grooming the hair and trimming. Also, we have to show good—and this breed is not easy. Poodle is not easy."

Poodles—America's ninth-most-popular breed—can be quite independent. The Poodle Club of America says that "the poodle is 'a person' and expects to be treated as one."

"Basically they are a one-person dog," Kaz explained. "Everyone says poodle have wonderful temperament. I don't think so."

Then why do you love them so much? I asked him.

He smiled wide. "To be honest, I love to win dog shows. That's why I came to this country. It took me twenty-three years to win Best in Show at Westminster. I guess I'm lucky. Everyone tries hard. And I have seven group firsts and a Best in Show."

When Kaz won the Best in Show in 2002 with Spice Girl, it was

*This is Poodle Art Talk, and I interpret it this way: When Kaz is shaping the poufs, he sees through the hair and pictures the lines around which he must trim. A handy parallel could be found in the line attributed to Michelangelo in which he says that he carved away at marble until he "freed the figure inside."

his third appearance in the final seven. He has since won three more groups, but still lacks a second title. This year he had his work cut out for him. His main dog, a white toy named Walker, was good, he said, but not great, and the Toy Group was stacked with David Fitzpatrick handling Malachy and Ernesto Lara on Banana Joe.

"My big hope is I get third behind them," he said.

The reason he'd spent three decades perfecting the style and care of arguably the most difficult breed in the show is simple: "I like to win dog shows, and in order to win dog shows I have to groom better than other dogs, trim better than other dogs. I work very hard for that."

It must be frustrating, then, when he loses to, say, a pointer, a dog that requires no grooming whatsoever. "Sometimes I get so mad after Best in Show," he said. "Because no matter what happened, I have to wash them, every night." That's because three times a day—before breed, before group, and before Best in Show—Kaz hair-sprays his poodle. And because that's not good for a dog's coat if left in, "we have to take it out. So every night we wash it."

Kaz is also a firm believer in a daily brushing. Every day he and his assistants brush every dog in the kennel back home in Delaware—currently that's about twenty dogs, though it's sometimes closer to thirty. Now, brushing a toy poodle isn't bad—it takes about five minutes. But Kaz doesn't just have toys. For Wildwood, in fact, he had three standards—and those take twenty minutes or a half hour. And after the brushing you have to apply bands to all the long hair to keep it from tangling and then add a topknot on the dog's head.

"This breed we have to crimp, we have to trim, we have to grow coat." With a shih tzu, another seemingly complicated grooming job, "the most important thing is growing coat. You just trim the edges. Cutting is everything. We do crimping, growing coat, trimming—and the style. It's the most complicated.

"To me the poodle is challenge. I can see a picture and know which handler trimmed it. And people probably know, 'That's Kaz's dog.' To me it's art."

Poodles under a year can have what is called a "puppy cut," which is basically minimal grooming. After a year, though, the dogs must be trimmed into one of two patterns:* Continental, which is mostly naked on the back half, or English saddle, which Kaz describes as "party pants and pom-pom." Each of these cuts can take hours—"an hour if you're good"—but it's the maintenance that really takes time.

"If it's early in the morning, I cannot sleep. I have to wash the night before, after Best in Show"—which he's often in. "Everybody knows I'm the last person usually at shows." That's why when he's finally done, Kaz likes to cut loose. A friend of his told me if I wanted to break the ice with him, I should come bearing Hennessy and then added, "You should see that man play beer pong." Maybe my greatest dog-show regret is that I didn't.

Every year after Westminster, Kaz retires the previous year's special. He was about to say good-bye to Walker. But already there was a new one in the wings: Sugar Baby, the granddaughter of his Westminster winner, Spice Girl. Kaz bred them both, and also Spice Girl's mother, who won the group at the Garden.

"Sugar Baby—I think she's the best mini I've ever bred," he said. "But she doesn't know it yet." Part of the thrill for him is to turn an unknown into a known. "I like the people to look at a dog and say, 'Nah.' Then a month after, it's, 'Wait a minute, she's pretty.' Then six months later, 'Wow, that's beautiful.' I can change people's mind. I love that."

When he first showed Walker, he says, nobody liked the dog, especially after his 2009 special, Vicky, was so highly regarded.

And Spice Girl: Was she the best ever before this one?

"Spice was the most difficult dog I ever showed."

Stubborn?

"No, shy. She's so moody. Sometimes she showed great, sometimes

---

*These are far from the only cuts you'll see in the world's poodle homes, mind you. For a laugh do some Googling around. The dog's coat makes it a living topiary, and people have not missed out on the possibilities.

no. It's amazing we won the Garden. She was perfect in breed, perfect in group; she showed excellent." But in the Best in Show ring, he said, live on TV, she saw the cameras and "got nervous. She dropped her tail."

Kaz isn't just a groomer, of course. He's a handler, and he was prepared. "I had her very favorite toy." He pointed to a much-bitten, heavily chewed white cell-phone squeaky toy in his grooming tackle box. "I used it outside with Spice Girl. But never at dog show." At Westminster, however, he had a hunch he might need a wild card and carried the toy in his pocket. "I knew she was going to spook. I have twenty seconds to show her, and I was the last one in line. I hold her, beg," and then just before the judge—and camera—turned to him, he played his card: He showed Spice Girl the toy.

"She's like 'WHOO!' Then I give her favorite food, chicken." (Also not something he typically does in the ring.) "And after that she held her head up, her tail up. Perfect."

The Garden was the next stop for Kaz, and for me. It would be my second—and for the purposes of this book, last—show and Kaz's thirty-first.

His big hope for this year was Walker, and Kaz patted the dog gently, his various pom-poms tied back into bands. "He will retire next week," he said, repeating himself.

Nearby his dutiful assistant groomed a class dog. His only goal on Sunday was to put a point on this young bitch, and, once prepared, he carried the dog off toward the ring like a man carrying a delicate little sculpture—carefully moving her so as to not muss the poufs.

CHAPTER THIRTY-SEVEN

Last Stop, Westminster

We're the same every year. We're having a dog show.
What becomes different is what dogs are going to be the
big dogs.

—DAVID FREI

Westminster has always been a media magnet, but it got a gigantic boost in 2008, when Uno the beagle won Best in Show. Uno is "by far" the most famous winner in the twenty years that David Frei has been affiliated with the show, he told me. All Westminster winners become celebrities, at least for a day or two, until the news cycle churns on past, but Uno took the fame to a different level. The Best in Show winner was, for the first time ever (or at least the first time in the mass-media era), not some froufrou canine prom queen but just a regular old dog.

Uno hadn't been a favorite, but he was a top beagle, and when he got into the Best in Show ring, "He did things in the ring that happen with great show dogs," Frei said. Most famously, he did what beagles do—"he bayed at the right time." It's pretty unusual to hear a top show dog bay or bark or vocalize in any way, so when one does, it's actually quite charming, especially when that dog seems to be doing it not as an act of defiance but as a performance. The only similar incident Frei could recall was in 2004, when the Newfoundland—a black bear impersonator of a dog named Josh[*]—"barked at the right time and the crowd went nuts," Frei said, noting that, "I think the crowd loves it when a dog acts like a dog."

Uno's owner Caroline Dowell preferred not to travel; she lived on a 200-acre Texas ranch that doubled as a beagle rescue and was far too busy tending to dogs in need. And a falling-out with Uno's handler left Frei as the beagle's personal PR rep and wingman. With Frei on his lead, Uno became the first show winner ever to make an official visit to the White House (at George W. Bush's invitation), the first to ride on a float in the Macy's Thanksgiving Day Parade, and the first to throw out a pitch at a major-league baseball game, something he did twice, in St. Louis and Milwaukee.[†] Uno walked the red carpet at Matthew Perry's charity event in Santa Monica and hung out with Snoopy.[‡] "Everybody wanted a piece of him," Frei said.

Much of this travel was possible because an executive of Midwest Airlines at that time was a dog-show enthusiast, and Uno was given special dispensation to fly in the cabin, in his own seat. He was even issued his own ticket (Frei keeps one in his desk as proof), and during one trip the computer—having no way to know that "Uno Frei" was a dog—selected him for special screening, and the TSA agents, in a rare moment of security-line levity, wanded him just for fun.

Once Uno had set a precedent of firsts, finding new ones quickly became difficult. The trailblazing of the 2010 winner, Sadie, involved both the legitimately novel (she was the first Westminster winner to "ring" the bell to open the New York Stock Exchange) and the more

---

[*]Obviously my favorite winner of all time.

[†]The answer to your question is this: Frei threw the ball and Uno fetched it, then bayed to delight of the crowd.

[‡]Costumed version.

prosaic (she was the third dog ever to visit the Empire State Building's observation deck). She had recently gotten pregnant—pardon, in whelp—and seemed to be, at least as far as anyone can recall, the first defending champion to get knocked up and miss the chance to come back as ambassador for promotional opportunities and morning-show drop-ins.

Some of my favorite products of the Westminster PR blitz emerge from the dog stories unearthed by David Frei and his team and printed out for distribution in the pressroom. The 2011 mix included a gluten-detecting Beauceron whose owner is so allergic to glutens that she can be ill for weeks if she even so much as eats something cut by a knife that was previously used to cut a product containing them; an American Eskimo dog that has been taught to carry out household tasks—for instance, turning down the bedsheets at night—for a former air force fuel-systems mechanic with a debilitating arm condition; and a Great Pyrenees who guards a herd of goats from coyotes and bears on the owners' farm in Missouri's Mark Twain National Forest.

From the category of heartwarming tales of animal survival, we had Lola the Afghan hound, born of a bitch flown from Germany to Ohio to breed. The owners were preparing to take her to the airport for her return trip when she escaped out the front door and was on the run for six days, a period in which she was both hit by a truck and run over by a car. Found injured on the porch of a stranger's house, the dog survived—along with the puppies gestating inside her uterus, one of which became Lola. A Shetland sheepdog named Uber was also lucky to be around; bitten four times by a copperhead snake, the dog was so close to death that the vet had begun to discuss the matter of euthanasia with his owner. A last-minute blood transfusion saved his life, and, completing the made-for-TV story, the medical bills were paid by people around the country who sent donations through a Facebook page set up to raise money.

Among 2011's more colorful human stories was an animal trainer from SeaWorld (showing a Belgian Malinois), a Florida high-school teacher who teaches a canine science program and raised money to bring some of her students (as well as her Norfolk terrier, Happy), and Brigadier General Rhonda Cornum—billed as a "war hero" on a press release—handing out the show's first morning. It wasn't hyperbole. Cornum was shot down over Iraq while serving as the flight surgeon on a search-and-rescue operation sent to locate a downed pilot and then captured by forces loyal to Saddam Hussein.

Cornum is now based at the Pentagon, where she oversees soldier fitness for the army, and in her spare time she shows both horses and dogs (Gordon setters, primarily). "I starting showing dogs long before I was in the army," she told a smattering of journalists in the pressroom while petting the large black-and-tan dog that would later join her in the ring. Cornum was making her first appearance at Westminster since the 1970s. "I can't honestly say why I like to show dogs," she said. "I just really love them, and I'm really proud of them, and I want people to see them, and I guess that's how you do it."

She thought she was the army's only moonlighting dog handler, certainly among those operating in the Pentagon's executive suite. "I say I'm demonstrating a good balance in my life," she said with a smirk.

It seemed inevitable that someone would ask an inane question, and indeed one writer wondered, "What's harder, dog shows or the army?" The ex-POW, surprisingly, didn't scoff or blanch. Rather, she considered it seriously and answered quickly. "Oh, I think dog showing is much harder," she said, and it was obvious she wasn't kidding.

W estminster is always nuts. As a benched show, at which all dogs and exhibitors have to be in the building from 11:00 A.M. to 8:00 P.M., cramped into the walkways underneath the stands at Madison Square Garden, it would be stuffy and crowded without the spectators. But with tens of thousands of fans sharing two-thirds of the normal space (because of ongoing renovations), it was downright claustrophobic.

Twenty-four hours before, this same building had hosted a hockey game, and less than a day after the event concluded on Tuesday, the Knicks would be back in action. In the span of four days, the surface of the "world's most famous arena" would be transformed from ice to Astroturf to basketball court.

"How's our boy?" I asked Heather as I saw Jack on the table being blown dry.

"He's doing great," she answered.

"He seems calmer."

"That's because I sent everybody away."

"I can take a hint," I said, and headed off to find Kimberly.

Kimberly showed up in New York with a deep tan and a new boyfriend. I'd met Tom Gerrard at the ASCA Nationals in Waco, where his dog Yoshi earned Premier status (a rough equivalent to Award of Merit, which helped him finish the year as the fifth-ranked ASCA Aussie in America), and I knew his name and dogs from Aussie chatter at shows and on Facebook. I recalled Kimberly telling me in Texas that because he was a single man in good shape and had recently split from his wife, he was a hot commodity among the female free agents in the Australian shepherd community. And here he was, on her arm.

I liked Tom, a friendly machinist who lived in a modern wood house on seven hilltop acres in Pennsylvania and pursued two vastly different hobbies in his free time. He played guitar in a rock band and bred and showed Australian shepherds. And sitting there with him, I appreciated his deep knowledge of the breed. Perusing the show catalog, he helped handicap the field for us, pointing out certain kennels and pedigrees that were formidable while discounting others. "I don't even know why this dog is here," he said about one.

A 1:00 P.M. ring time slowly bled over to 1:15 and 1:30 and then 1:45 as our scheduled judge, a Maryland veterinarian named H. Scott Kellogg, ran extremely late in a nearby ring. Dogs and handlers stood patiently at ringside, slowly withering in the heat and lights but unable to sit or lie down for fear of mussing coats that were meticulously prepped. Every few minutes Heather would spritz Jack with water.

A man walked by hawking show programs, tossing off one clever breed-specific adaptation after another: "Get your dalmatian diary! Get your directory of dachshunds! Get your Tibetan terrier Torah! Get your Labrador library!"

Finally, at 1:50, Mr. Kellogg wandered into the ring and his steward called the dogs, which he surveyed and then split into three groups— two sets of males and one for the bitches. Jack was in the first set to be judged.

"I feel just like I did last year," Kimberly told me. "I'll be happy to make the cut."

As thirteen males trotted around and stacked up on the far side, a woman to my left was joyful at the sight. "Look how many, Marion! And they're all so wonderful."

Jack was seventh in the line, and while he wasn't jumping on any-one (yet), he did look edgy. If you didn't know what you were look-ing at, you might assume that Heather was ignoring him, but I'd been watching these two long enough so that it was hard not to pick up the signs of tension—she gave his lead a tug and bent over to hiss in his ear as she brushed along his topline. Nothing she did there was even remotely cruel, but an experienced handler will almost never openly reprimand a dog in the ring, especially not in a ring with hundreds of eyes trained on it.

"He's a handful," Kimberly said. "He's hot. She's really gotta work him."

Jack's movement, though, was fluid, and the only obvious sign that his focus was wavering came at the end of the go-round, when he leaped up into Heather's chest, a playful moment that caused the entire section to burst out in laughter.

Aesthetically, he looked great; his coat was as full as I'd ever seen it. "He's maturing," Tom said, and I heard him commenting on Jack's feet, which he said were round and compact. "That's how feet should be. They're just right." The woman next to me concurred. "He looks like he has on nice soft slippers. And look at that butt! So cute."* In the stack he was statuesque, his gaze locked on Heather, and the woman was impressed. "I don't know anything about how this works, but he's the only one out of all of them who knows how to stand there."

Mr. Kellogg surveyed his options seriously, never varying from his stock pose: bolt upright with his hands clasped at his crotch. And he must have agreed, because Jack was the first dog selected for the cut, and as Heather led him out to await the second cut, Kimberly exhaled and sat back in her seat. "Now I can be happy. He made the cut."

"Which one is yours?" a woman asked her, and, upon hearing, said, "Congratulations. He's beautiful."†

Six of the nine dogs in the second group were blue merles, including Bentley and Spooner, Summer's sire. And in my opinion Jack looked better than all of them. Ben made the second cut, as did Striker, the red merle we'd run into often early in the year. He then vanished from the circuit; it turned out he'd been showing in Italy and had returned only recently as an Italian champion.

Striker made the final group, along with Jack and Bentley and all three of the bitches, one of whom was Beyoncé, so formidable at this point that only two of the twelve females that entered the show even bothered to show up.

It may have been bias at work, but at the Garden I was underwhelmed by her. She was a pretty dog, with a beautiful coat, but her movement, to me, wasn't as elegant as some of the others', including Jack. Mr. Kellogg barely gave her a look and spent most of his time deciding whom he liked best out of Jack, Ben, and Bodi, a black tri we'd seen in Waco and at Eukanuba. In the end he picked Beyoncé anyway—leading me to believe he'd made that decision from the outset and was really just focusing on filling out his card. In a surprise, Bodi was awarded Best

---

*Eavesdropping in a dog-show crowd yields many gems. For instance, the woman behind me commenting on shar-peis: "They snore and they have stomach issues. It's like living with my mother."

†Not Jack's son.

Opposite, and Jack, Ben, and Striker all got Awards of Merit—meaning that Jack ended his year the way it started and also kept alive his streak of finishing thisclose to the top at every major event.*

"Can't complain about the last five he picked," Tom said.

Ben's owner, Belinda Rhoads, came by and hugged Kim. "My goal was to make the cut," she said as the two exchanged congratulations.

"Mine, too!" Kimberly squealed.

On the floor, Heather looked our way, smiled, and gave us a thumbs-up.

W estminster is a swan song for many dogs. A more natural coda to a career might seem to be at the end of a year, when the rankings restart, but Westminster is so important that it makes for a natural finale, especially if your dog can provide a joyous one. The 2011 show, for instance, was the end for Walker the toy poodle, who won his variety but did not place in the brutal Toy Group, and for a whole host of dogs that appeared on the evening telecasts, where Frei acknowledged one retirement after another. Dodger chose to retire before the show. "He retired as the number-one dog in the country," Frei told me when I bumped into him in the media room. (The smooth fox was in town, however, to receive the Winkie for Show Dog of the Year.)

I told him I suspected this meant that his team didn't like the judge.

Frei smiled. "You've learned a lot. I think they were worried Dodger wouldn't win his breed." And that would be a pretty bad way to end a career.

If Jack never showed again, I don't think Kimberly would have regrets. He began 2010 unknown, a young male taking his very tentative first steps as a show dog, and despite the ups and downs—with entire months skipped for various reasons—he ended the year with more impressive ribbons than any Australian shepherd not named Beyoncé. He was—and always would be—a well-decorated show dog.

---

*Which Kimberly and Kerry, half joking, would refer to as the "Honorable Mention" curse.

I wasn't convinced, however, that he was done. Kimberly some-times talked about 2012 and beyond, and she was increasingly pointing out how her dog was finally maturing. His second impressive Westmin-ster had caught the eye of some wealthy Brazilians who'd been looking to campaign an Aussie back home. One of them, a slick cattle rancher in a cashmere scarf who also "has hotels," had come by to pet Tanner, and later his handler also made an appearance. Heather was certain they'd agree to take Jack to Brazil for six months, finish his championship, and make him that country's number-one Aussie, then send him home to Kimberly and pay for a full American campaign in 2012.

"This is a fantastic opportunity," she told me. "I think she should consider it."

Whether Rita would be joining Jack in retirement was increasingly up in the air. She'd won another Award of Merit, and Cindy, interviewed by her breed's magazine the *Morning Call,* looked as proud as I'd seen her. Rita had, unfortunately, lost her status as Kevin's top dog to Nacho, whose owner, Emi, arrived with buttons and postcards and was thrilled to see him notch an Award of Merit of his own. He was off to such a hot start in 2011 that it seemed possible that both he and Tanner would be in conten-tion for America's top dog in their respective breeds—meaning that Kevin and Heather would be facing off over and over in the Working Group.

The Garden, however, wasn't Tanner's show. When Trader took Best Opposite in the Akita ring, Tanner was the only one of the regular dogs not to leave with a ribbon.

"The only dog that didn't win was the number-one dog," Dawn said. "The big loser is Tanner." She was taking it well and was in very good spirits, as always. "You know what I told Georgeann? I said, 'Guess what—there's another dog show, next weekend.'" She slapped me on the back and went off in pursuit of a glass of wine.

In the end the Best in Show wasn't Malachy (though he was in the final seven) or Emily (who wasn't) or Beckham the cocker spaniel or Adam (who added one last splash of kerosene to the smooth fox fire by winning the Terrier Group the day after Dodger picked up his Winkie) or Roy, the beardie, a dog I found myself pulling quite hard for, if for no other reason than I'd seen him win 4 bazillion Herding Groups. No, when our Italian judge, Paolo Dondina, was handed a microphone, he announced to the crowd in charmingly broken English how happy he was to be there and how humbled he was "by the quality." He walked toward the seven dogs. "The winner of best in show is . . ."—and he held that pause and veered left toward Roy, only to say—"the deerhound!"

David Frei had told me that foreign judges were unpredictable. So in that sense this was refreshing. It seemed possible that he actually, objectively, chose the best dog in the ring. Still, the deerhound? It looked so . . . smelly.

DEERHOUND

People in tuxedos converged upon the dog, Hickory, and her handler, Angela Lloyd, and both seemed a little shell-shocked when they faced the media a half hour later in the pressroom, along with the judge. Frei introduced them and noted that Lloyd had been named Best Junior Handler here in 1998. When a reporter got things started by observing that the dog didn't seem terribly interested in those of us assembled in this small room on the second floor of Madison Square Garden, Lloyd replied, "You guys don't look like a bunch of squirrels and deer."

The judge was asked what he'd seen in the dog.

"I think she was beautiful," he said. "Not only great showmanship, in great show condition and feeling the type like we want to see. This one feel perfect with the standard, in all the ways. Is very well balanced, beautiful head, ears, everything is okay, and the handler did a marvelous job with her." He looked at the dog the way he might at Carla Bruni. "Now she's had enough, probably because she's not used to the press. And probably she's tired, usually."

He wasn't ready to step out of the spotlight just yet, however. It reminded me, more than a little, of Roberto Benigni accepting his Oscar for *Life Is Beautiful*. "I'm a hound person, I had Afghans, whippets, Irish wolfhound. I never own deerhound, but this is my dream. Like Walter Scott said, if I remember, he say, 'This animal, he has to be not from this world; is like to be in the heaven.' And I feel the same way. I'm very happy and honored to have this special and super deerhound to judge and to put over other six top dogs. Was not an easy win. Because all the others were Best in Show winners in any case. If this one had to be choose, because only one can be choose, all the others please me a lot. I found the standard of the dogs and the presentation absolutely superb. And what can I say, I am in the heavens."

Lloyd was asked what that moment felt like, to be the handler of the dog named Best in Show at Westminster. "It takes a minute to sink in," she said. "You question whether you heard it correctly. You play it again in your head."

And Hickory—was she also over the moon? Surely she'd been

dreaming of this moment since she was just a little deerhound, frolicking in the Virginia leaves?

"Hickory is overwhelmed," Lloyd said as the dog writers scribbled. "She showed like she's never showed before. She was solid and steady. Even with all the lights and cameras and the noise and spotlights. She came right through it." She gazed affectionately at the dog that seemed to be trying to hide behind her. "I thought she was worthy before."

Lloyd said that it was difficult to prepare for an event like Westminster, held under the lights in front of a crowd of thousands. "You really can't duplicate it. You have to have faith in the fact that the dog trusts you and knows you're not going to put her in a situation that will hurt her in any way. This was her first time under the spotlights. She was curious—I felt it on the lead when we first began, but I think she felt I was very excited and just went with it. She handled it perfectly."

Adding some nice punctuation to the moment, Lloyd noted that this was to be Hickory's last show, too. "She's done." The deerhound would be returning to her owners, on a Virginia horse ranch, to become a mother, producing a new generation of show candidates when she wasn't harassing chipmunks and woodchucks.

The finality had not escaped Lloyd. She said she'd probably most miss the "nudge in the middle of the night" when Hickory would approach the bed and bump her handler's body with her nose just to say, "Hey, I'm here."

"I think that all dogs are easy to love," she said wistfully. "But sometimes you find the ones where everything clicks. She is certainly one of those dogs. We've been through a lot together." She swallowed hard. "That builds bonds."

The next day I got an e-mail from Billy Wheeler, asking if I'd enjoyed Westminster as much as he had. He told me that Hickory's win wasn't actually a big surprise at all and that if the dog hadn't been felled by bloat that had cost her twelve weeks of showing, she'd have been a top-ten dog. He said he was "delighted with her selection." He was far less happy with the "Smooth Fox Terrier people."

"I have seen more bitter campaigns, but not many," he wrote to me. "Dodger's Camp thought I favored Adam and Adam's Camp thought I favored Dodger. As a journalist that kind of makes me proud." I asked if there was at least some resolution in his mind over Dodger's legacy. In fact, he said, the opposite was true. "Dodger ended up Show Dog of the Year and he did set a new record for Smooth Fox Terriers, no minor feat for such iconic show dogs. However, he won no marquee show, and boycotted all the major ones, Montgomery County, Eukanuba, and Westminster (he did win the Group there in 2010). As such, his place in history will be as the breed record holder, not among the great show dogs of all time."

Dodger, then, was to be no modern-day Nornay Saddler.

Wheeler went on to say that he was disappointed, though not surprised, that Beyoncé failed to place at the Garden. "But at least she won the breed."

He asked me if Jack would be continuing, and I said it didn't look like it. He was surely going to be out of the picture for 2011. "I look forward to seeing your book," he said. "I hope in the process, we have made a dog-show junkie of you."

I closed the message and considered that. Had they? Not in the sense that I had any plans to continue stalking America's dog shows on my own, at least not regularly, nor did I envision any future in which I would own a show dog. But I was undeniably changed by the experience. Whereas the longing for a pet dog in my life over the previous decade had been only very occasionally conscious (most often after I'd spent a weekend in the country with my brother's yellow Lab, Zoe, a sixty-pound dose of Prozac), I noticed it growing more and more palpable, manifesting itself as a kind of restless itch whenever I departed the company of the kinds of dogs I longed for—happy, active dogs like Zoe or Jack, especially, but even when I played tennis at my local park, where I often see a guy from my neighborhood walking a Bernese mountain dog that always makes me think of Tanner.

Once they hear about this book, people inevitably ask me if I own a dog.

I've always thought I would, but years have gone by and I haven't. Now I know I will, and my wife and I talk about it more and more, agreeing that the right time is probably when our son, Charlie, is old enough to shoulder at least some of the responsibility and to learn a little about life by caring for something else—like, maybe, one of Jack's kids. Wouldn't that be something?

CHAPTER THIRTY-EIGHT

The End. For Now. (Maybe?)

> It is as if once a dog loves you, he loves you always, no matter what you do, no matter what happens, no matter how much time goes by.
>
> —JEFFREY MOUSSAIEFF MASSON, *Dogs Never Lie About Love*

The last time I saw Jack at a dog show, it was in the benching area under Madison Square Garden. The team's setup was empty, except for the dogs—Jack, Tanner, Rita, Trader, and Nacho—each one sprawled out and asleep despite the ongoing clamor of the show, which had begun its transition for the night session, for the groups and Best in Show. Heather and Kevin had gone back to the hotel to change and rest. Dawn and Georgeann were off drinking wine. And Kimberly and Tom were having a steak dinner out on Thirty-fourth Street.

Jack lifted his head when I walked past, and I stuck my fingers through the crate's bars. He sniffed them and promptly returned to resting. I then ventured off to the media room for a couple hours, and by the time I thought to check back, the whole crew was gone—having packed up and loaded the dogs onto carts and joined the throng that lined up at the arena's exit ramp, waiting for security guards to open the doors to the outside at eight, when the benching period was officially over. Where just an hour before there had been rows of yapping dogs, now there was only empty space.

Tom and Kimberly took Jack outside, and the three of them walked a few blocks through the buzz of Manhattan at night to the car, then loaded up and drove home to Pennsylvania, into a new year with a more uncertain schedule.

Heather and Kevin were packed up and out of the Hotel Pennsylvania by seven in the morning and would enjoy a rare succession of nights in their own bed before loading up the truck and heading out to the next shows, so numbed by the repetition and rhythm of the dog-show circuit that short of winning a Best in Show at the Garden, a show like Westminster happened and then faded into memory the same as a podunk weekend in Bloomsburg. By the following Thursday, the setup was reconstituted in Suffern, New York, and the only notable difference in the camp—other than the weekend's new day-rate dogs—was the absence of Jack and the appearance of Tuck in his place at the end of Heather's leash.

Within a few weeks, Tom had begun to practice handling Jack, with the goal of finishing his ASCA championship. He also capitalized on Jack's absence from the circuit to take his own champion boy, Yoshi, back out to AKC shows, where he occasionally met—and sometimes beat—Heather and Tuck. It hadn't even been two years since Yoshi and Jack had first met, in the ring in Bloomsburg, at Jack's first AKC show with Heather, when Kimberly and Tom were just two Aussie owners who admired each other's dogs.

At home in the town house and also when he and Kimberly were staying with Tom in the country, Jack struggled a little living alongside other intact males—first picking on his maturing son, Bodi, a smaller and younger dog who was easy to dominate, and then also facing off with Yoshi, who was nearly as large and four months older. That didn't go so well, and during one spat Yoshi caught Jack by the face and tossed him aside, leaving a puncture that led to an abscess that led to "a quarter-size bald spot on his show side" that Kimberly and Tom spent a good month treating and draining.

That was the last time Jack and Yoshi were allowed to play together. Instead one would get to run with the pack of Aussies that roamed Tom's verdant property and then be crated while the other one got his turn. Boys will always be boys.

Accepting that she couldn't really keep two male dogs, Kimberly made the difficult decision to place Bodi with the treasurer of her agility club, Kruisin' Kanines—where he stood a good chance of earning many performance titles*—and had come to terms with the likelihood that the unplanned pairing of Jack and Summer wasn't going to yield top-quality dogs. Their offspring had Jack's beautiful head and decent movement, but nearly all of them got Summer's short legs. Kimberly also spent the spring fending off Kerry's pleas to take one or two of the puppies from Halle B, five of which Kerry was thinking might be show quality. One, which she'd been calling Ricky, looked like a good candidate to become Jack's first champion son—especially after he took Best Puppy in Show at two different ASCA shows. "Breeding is all a big long waiting game," Kimberly said. "No one really told me that, but it takes so long." Then she added a common refrain: "You just don't know."

Out at the AKC shows, Tanner, Nacho, and Trader were all winning so often that the situation was causing a recurring problem—three dogs in the Working Group but only two handlers to show them. In those instances Trader was the odd dog out, and rather than put a substitute handler on him, Kevin and Trader's owner, Tom, had decided to withdraw the Akita instead. By midyear Tanner and Nacho were both the country's top dogs in their breeds, and Trader, competing in a smaller breed, was entrenched in the top five himself.

---

*Which was nearly as good as having one of Jack's puppies earn his conformation championship. "You want a stud dog that can have both performance and conformation," Kimberly explained.

Even Tuck was doing well, but Sharon Fontanini had decided to keep Beyoncé out another year, and because of Jamie's determination to overtake Roy as the country's top herding dog, she was showing up more and more north of the Mason-Dixon Line, where bigger shows bring more points. And when Beyoncé wasn't casting her shadow over the Aussie ring, Reckon—the Best in Show winner from Eukanuba—would often swoop in for a day or two and take the breed ribbons. If Beyoncé retired to be bred after 2011, as everyone expected, Reckon was likely to step in as the country's top Aussie.

And Rita? Rita won almost every show through April and was back to being the country's top Chessie bitch, but once she had enough points that qualification for Eukanuba and Westminster seemed certain, Cindy took her off her medication, and when she went into heat in June, Rita left Kevin. For the first time in two years, Cindy didn't have a large bill bill to pay to her handlers every month. Her vet tested Rita's progesterone daily and, one Thursday, gave Cindy the green light. She left work, packed a bag, and set out for Illinois, stopping only to sleep four hours at a rest area in Ohio.

Once there Rita bred to the top-ranked all-breed Chessie in America, a male named Moose who was owned by Lawrence and Diana Lentz, of Mundelein, Illinois. The Lentzes were, Cindy said, nothing like most of the other Chessie people back east. They were "absolutely lovely people" who put her up for the trip in their lake house, and the trip wasn't just pleasant, it was fruitful. A few weeks later, a scan confirmed that Rita was pregnant and in late August, two puppies—one male, one female—were born. Despite her late start at motherhood, Rita was excellent at the job, and Cindy planned to keep whichever puppy looked most promising once they matured.

Freed from Heather's rules, Kimberly took Jack off his supplements, temporarily gave up on his coat maintenance, and let him return to his favorite activity: Frisbee. He was, at least for a while, enjoying just being a dog, and the photos she sent me of him chasing his blue Frisbee sure were a sight. In one he is jumping so high that his upper torso has left to the top fame of the photo, and a second dog jumping below him is already high enough that you can't see the ground. "He's going to be great at agility," Kimberly said, and she was already pining for titles in that discipline, a whole other realm of AKC competition that is smaller but no less fervent and competitive than conformation. She planned to reenroll him in lessons.

Kimberly made a point, however, to keep doing Heather and Kevin's schedules, and the assembly of these meticulous Excel documents required weekly phone calls that could sometimes last up to an hour. "You talk to Heather an awful lot for someone who's not showing your dog," Tom told her. This was, of course, at least a little calculated. No matter what she said, Kimberly had no intention of retiring Jack, and despite the ups and downs of their relationship over the year, her respect for Heather only magnified with time. Kimberly had no doubts about who she'd want on her dog if and when the time came to return him to the ring. She found herself missing not only the competition, but also the camaraderie that came along with it. The community that formed around the setup, she realized, was as addictive as the wins.

"Jack's kind of on the back burner a little bit right now," she told me. But not forever. She'd even briefly considered sending him to Canada with Heather, to pick up his Canadian championship, but when Steve and Kathy decided to send Tuck, she decided to wait another year—the idea was to beat up on Canadian dogs, not compete with other quality dogs from the United States. Instead she and Tom were considering a trip north of the border themselves.

The thought of Jack's scraps with Yoshi had even caused her to consider something radical. "Now, if those Brazilians wanted to take him for a year, I'd probably consider it."

She had, I reminded her, dismissed that outright as recently as Westminster.

"He wasn't being a dick."

Very quickly she realized what she'd said.

"He's always going to be my boy. He's always going to be my bud."

He'd just have to learn how to adapt to sharing his roost. Because over the Fourth of July weekend, Tom proposed and Kimberly accepted. It was only a matter of time until she sold her town house and moved to the house on the hill where her two dogs would make it seven Australian shepherds under one roof, with plenty of room to grow. Maybe, sometime soon, this would become the birthplace of Jackpot Kennels, with Jack as the founding stud dog of the line.

Kerry was thrilled to hear the news, that the woman she'd introduced to her beloved breed would be marrying a man who was already in the thrall of Australian shepherds, and that the two of them, just maybe, could make for an East Coast outpost of Wyndstar—if not officially, at least as a good base for housing and showing future show dogs in the country's most competitive region.

Unfortunately, we learned in July, it probably wouldn't be Ricky. Because right at the six-month mark, Jack and Halle's star puppies' development as show dogs stalled. The two pups that Kerry had felt quite certain would develop into contenders—Ricky and his brother Caruso—both began to exhibit dental problems within days of each other. Caruso's was the less serious issue. He was, Kerry said, "level," which meant that his teeth didn't have the overlapping scissor bite required of the breed. There were finished dogs out on the circuit with the same problem doing quite well, she told me. But it was a fault, and as a judge and a breeder, she didn't want that fault in her line.

Ricky, she said, had an even more serious issue, and her voice sank as she explained that her favorite puppy—the one she called "Squishy-Faced Ricky"—was "undershot." What this meant was that he had begun to develop an underbite, and there was little chance of its correcting itself; if anything, the issue would probably get worse. The problem didn't seem to come from Jack's background, and he himself had perfect teeth, so likely it was just a bad pairing—or maybe just bad luck. In any event, it was a reminder that when it comes to breeding, you never really know.

This left only one dog with perfect structure, conformation-wise:

Pavi (for Pavarotti),* the one with the ugliest mug of all. "He has a rott-weiler face," Kerry said, and it wasn't a compliment.

Ricky, though, "he is just the prettiest. I love him." Finding that flaw had nearly wrecked her. "I wanted to cry when I saw it, literally," she told me. "I'm still sick about it. But this is this game."

The line went silent for a second.

"Hey, if you want a really nice, beautiful pet, I've got one for you."

---

*The pups had all been named for opera singers, sort of. Ricky was for Ricky Ricardo, because Kerry could only think of so many names.

ACKNOWLEDGMENTS

First and foremost, in the order I met them: Heather Bremmer, Kevin Bednar, Kimberly Smith, and Kerry Kirtley. Without the willingness of these four people to open their worlds—with virtually no questions asked—to a stranger from New York with a notebook, this book would have been impossible. Next, the rest of the owners of Team Brem-Dar, especially Dawn Cox, Cindy Meyer, Tom and Anne Bavaria, Steve and Kathy Ostrander, Emi Gonzalez, and Claudette Lyons, as well as their awesome dogs Tanner, Rita, Trader, Tuck, Nacho, and Benny. Also, Karen Churchill, Sharon Fontanini, Kristin Elmini, Carla Viggiano, Doug Johnson, Anna Morgan, Marlene and Joseph Horvath, and all the other dog owners and handlers who tolerated me and my relentless badgering over the course of a year. I might not have even gotten that far if not for Kim Estlund, a music publicist I'd known for years who revealed herself at a *Rolling Stone* photo shoot to be a breeder and handler of cocker spaniels, and provided both enthusiasm for my concept, and some initial introductions that helped get me started.

Billy Wheeler, author of the indispensable Dog Show Poop blog, very patiently answered about three hundred question-filled e-mails, and did so promptly. He was first described to me as the "Perez Hilton of the dog-show world," but that is wildly inaccurate; he's more like a human Wikipedia of dog-show knowledge, only with better sourcing.

Westminster maestro David Frei invited me to his office, twice, and also responded promptly to e-mails once he determined I was not a nutjob. He even took me to watch his Cavalier King Charles spaniel Angel do her therapy dog work at the Ronald McDonald House in New York—an experience that was both wonderful and heartbreaking at once. If you're looking for charities to support, might I recommend Angel on a Leash, the therapy-dog organization founded by Frei.

At the AKC, Lisa Peterson was a great help, even though I still get the impression that she's suspicious of my motives, as was the new librarian, Craig Savino, who got a tour of his newly inherited stacks while searching for the dusty nineteenth-century dog-show history texts I was after last summer. If you are ever looking for a rare dog book or an issue of *Komondor Komments,* the AKC's incredible library in New York City is an indispensable resource.

Dog-show personalities whose insight appears occasionally or often throughout this book include Jerry Grymek, Amy Booth, Pat Hastings, Terry DePietro, Jasa Hatcher, Tom Grabe, Ron Scott, and the poodle impresario Kaz Hosaka. Jeanne Joy Hartnagle and I played phone tag for months, but on the few occasions when we finally connected, she was a font of knowledge on the history and heritage of Australian shepherds. What she couldn't recall, Jo Kimes helped fill in.

Harder to categorize but no less important to this project were Dottie Davis (aka the Candy Lady), Perry Phillips (the dog-show photographer), Mandy Armitage (the dog world's chiropractor), Susan Catlin (aka Mrs. Happy Legs), Chris and Lisa Christensen (the czar and czarina of dog beauty products), Jennifer Vawter of the ICSB, Mary Stine, and John O'Hurley.

Scientists who were very patient with my layman's questions: James Serpell at the University of Pennsylvania, Robert Wayne at UCLA, and C. A. Sharp for her unbelievable knowledge of Australian shepherd heritage and genetics. Speaking of canine genetics, Heidi Parker at the

Dog Genome Project provided invaluable guidance. On the subject of doggy smarts, the psychologist Stanley Coren and Alexandra Horowitz, retired fact-checker, Columbia professor, and now bestselling author, helped me greatly.

The bands Sigur Rós and Explosions in the Sky provided musical inspiration (and via Pandora channels helped me discover some alternatives in the category of beautiful orchestral noise), and I could never have accurately recalled what many of the above people here said without the prompt, flawless transcription of Susan Gregory.

Laura Hohnhold, Jason Adams, and especially Gillian Fassel provided critical insight on flaws in the manuscript, and my agent, Daniel Greenberg, has been the loudest cheerleader of this project since I first mentioned the germ of the idea over Belgian fries at a lunch several years back. Mauro DiPreta bought this book and provided a keen eye and excellent support—until he abandoned me and took a new job before we were finished. Kidding! He got an excellent offer and wisely took it, which was a bit of a bummer for me, but ultimately not a bad thing, because it enabled me to befriend and work with the most excellent Denise Oswald, who shepherded me and the book through the stressful final stages of editing and production (that is, when she wasn't planning the Brooklyn Book Festival, bailing our her Irene-flooded basement, or attending Comic-Con).

I'd like to thank my wife, Gillian, and son, Charlie, for enduring my absences, accompanying me to shows, putting up with a year of arcane dog facts, and preventing me from impulsively adopting a puppy. We'll get one in due time. I love you both.

My father, David Dean, has been a champion of my work and a supporter of my career and life in general through the highs and lows. I can never truly thank him enough. Likewise, my brother and sister, Eric and Jennifer, have been supporters and fans and sometimes also bonus parental figures who never hesitate to dispense unsolicited wisdom, and my stepmother, Polly, really deserves a better descriptor because she is as much a family member as any of us.

Finally—and with a heavy heart—I'd like to take a moment to acknowledge my mother, who I'm very sorry to say will never actually read these words. My mom passed away quite suddenly a few weeks before I turned in the first draft, complicating the completion of this book in all the ways you can imagine. I miss her terribly, and it is difficult to have to accept that she'll never read my first book, but I can confidently say that it wouldn't exist without her. It was her gift for words and love of reading that made me a writer, and it was her strength in the face of tremendous hardship that still inspires me today—especially when I'm having a moment where things seem tough. In comparison to what she dealt with, my life is easy. May our bond in language live forever in these pages. I love you, Mom.

Finally, A Thoroughly Random Collection of Purebred-Dog Marginalia

I. DOG-SHOW LINGO

A partial list of useful terms.

ANGULATION:	the angle at which bones meet at joints—for instance, the shoulder or hip
ARTIST:	a judge whose preference is for aesthetics—comparing the dog against his/her mental image of the "perfect" specimen (the opposite of engineer)
BAIT:	any food or other object that a handler uses to get a dog's attention in the ring
BALANCE:	when all the parts of the dog, moving or standing, produce a harmonious image
BLAZE:	a white or colored strip on the center of the face and/or chest
CAMPAIGN:	the process of showing a champion dog in pursuit of further glory
COBBY:	short-bodied; a dog that is as tall as it is long
CROUP:	the lower back, just in front of the tail
DAM:	the mother
DOUBLE HANDLING:	the act of someone other than the handler getting a dog's attention in the ring to help the dog to show or look better
DUDLEY NOSE:	flesh- or liver-colored nose
DUMP:	to lose in the ring
ENGINEER:	a judge whose preference is for structure and how a dog is put together
FANCIER:	a dog-show person
FLYING TROT:	a fast gait in which all four feet are off the ground for a brief second during each half stride; highly sought after, rarely achieved

GAIT:	a dog's stride in the ring
HANDLER:	a show dog's trainer/coach
HEADHUNTER:	a judge who prefers a perfect head, to an obsessive degree, sometimes overlooking significant flaws in other areas
IN WHELP:	pregnant
LEGGY:	having too much leg, making dog appear gangly
NICK:	a breeding that produces desirable puppies
PACING:	moving both legs on one side simultaneously; a fault
SIRE:	the father
SPECIAL:	a dog that has already achieved its AKC championship and is being campaigned for breed rankings
STACK:	the correct posing of a show dog, when stationary, in the ring
TOOTH FAIRY:	a judge who has a predilection for perfect teeth
TYPEY:	having all the distinctive characteristics of a breed; not always good
WICKET:	a device used to measure the height of a dog at the withers
WITHERS:	the high point of a dog's shoulder, where height is measured

II. OFFICIAL STATE DOGS

Alaska can thank a kindergartner for the fact that it now has an official state dog. Paige Hill and her classmates at an Anchorage elementary school were so passionate about the idea that they lobbied all the way to the state legislature, where they testified. In May 2010, Alaska became the eleventh state to name an official dog: the malamute, naturally. Here are the other ten:

LOUISIANA: Catahoula leopard dog. Sometimes known as the Catahoula leopard cow-hog dog, and neither version includes actual leopard.

MARYLAND: Chesapeake Bay retriever. Named for the iconic bay and said to descend from two dogs saved from a boat that sank in the 1600s. Sensible enough.

MASSACHUSETTS: Boston terrier. Obviously.

NEW HAMPSHIRE: Chinook. Developed by a New Hampshire man who bred the dogs starting in 1917 to pull sleds, Chinooks got so rare by 1981 that only eleven survived. Things are much better today—the number is at least six hundred, and growing.

NORTH CAROLINA: Plott hound. This is an actual breed? It is, and it's named for a family of North Carolinians who developed the dog in the eighteenth century.

PENNSYLVANIA: Great Dane, chosen because one is shown in a period painting of William Penn that hangs in the state court-

house. When the vote was taken to select the dog, state legislators actually
voting by barking. This is true.

SOUTH CAROLINA: Boykin spaniel. A compact spaniel
bred in the early 1900s by hunters who
required a smaller retriever for hunting in the narrow channels of the Wa-
teree Swamp. A rare rival, then, to the
lundehund for most specific breed.

TEXAS: Blue Lacy. Herding dogs that are a
cross of greyhounds, scent hounds,
and coyotes. Most certainly not AKC-
recognized.

VIRGINIA: American foxhound. George Washington is said to have helped create this
breed from French foxhounds given to
him by the marquis de Lafayette.

WISCONSIN: American water spaniel. This hunting
dog is the only breed native to Wisconsin. In that sense kind of a no-brainer.

III. DOGS NAMED FOR PARTS OF
THE UNITED KINGDOM

All of the following are terriers: Cairn, Yorkshire, Norwich, Norfolk, Bedlington, Staffordshire, Manchester, West Highland, Sealyham, Lakeland, Skye, Airedale, and, I guess, the Border terrier, since it is named for the border between England and Scotland.

IV. REASONS YOU MIGHT BE DENIED A DOG

Breeders of purebred dogs are honest folk. They don't want you to own one of their animals unless you're really, truly a good match. Here are some of my favorite actual reasons I've seen or heard as to why you should not choose a particular breed:

1. Because corgis herd by nipping at ankles, they are considered bad dogs for runners. Also, they have very short legs.

2. While otterhounds can be good with children, a young otterhound is big and likely to be klutzy and may not be the best companion for a wobbly toddler or a frail elderly person.

3. Siberian huskies might eat your cat. And I quote (from a sheet handed out by the breed club): "While the Husky is normally gentle and friendly with people and other dogs, owners must be aware that small animals in and around the home such as squirrels, rabbits, birds and CATS, are potential victims of their strong predatory instinct. They are swift, cunning, and patient in their hunting skills." They also dig holes. If you have a proclivity for landscaping—don't buy a Siberian husky.

4. Owners of the extremely loyal vizslas joke that you'll never go to the bathroom alone again. Warns the official breed club for these Hungarian pointers: They can be "mischievous and destructive," and "they are notorious counter-surfers, trash robbers, paper shredders, refrigerator door openers and tree climbers."

5. Leonbergers are not for the weak or meticulous. "Even experienced Leonberger owners have had their wrists broken when their leashed Leonbergers took off unexpectedly after deer," warns the breed club. They

also shed "copious amounts of hair all year. When a Leonberger blows his coat, he sheds more than most dog owners can imagine."

6. Schipperkes love to wad things up—towels, shirts, paper. The end result, once wadded, said one owner, is known as a waddie. Not a dog for hoarders.

V. DOG NICKNAMES, A PARTIALLY COMPLETE LIST

Dog-show people like to talk in shorthand. An Australian shepherd is rarely that—it is an Aussie. You can go months without ever hearing the complete name. As this list shows, it doesn't take a poetic genius to come up with a breed's nickname.

Diminutive Category

ROTTIE:	rottweiler
RHODIE:	Rhodesian ridgeback
SHELTIE:	Shetland sheepdog
BERNER:	Bernese mountain dog
GOLDEN:	golden retriever
BEARDIE:	bearded collie
AMSTAFF:	American Staffordshire terrier
FRENCHIE:	French bulldog
NEWFIE:	Newfoundland
CHESSIE:	Chesapeake Bay retriever
SAMMY:	Samoyed
GRIFFS:	wirehaired pointing griffon
TIBBIE:	Tibetan spaniel
PYR SHEP:	Pyrenean shepherd

Elaborate Category

THE CHARLIE:	English toy spaniel
KING OF THE TOYS:	miniature pinscher (aka min pin)

THE SMILING DUTCHMAN:	keeshond
LITTLE CAPTAIN:	schipperke
THE CANINE FENCE:	Beauceron
THE MILK-CART DOG:	Bouvier
THE MUSTACHED LITTLE DEVIL:	affenpinscher
THE BARKLESS DOG:	basenji
POACHERS BEWARE:	bullmastiff
THE LITTLE LION DOG:	lowchen
THE DOG WITH THE SMILING FACE:	Samoyed
THE SILENT HUNTER:	Akita
THE TURNSPIT DOG:	Glen of Imaal terrier

VI. ON DOG SIZE

World's smallest dog: Boo Boo, a Chihuahua—4 inches tall, 6 inches long, 24 ounces

World's biggest dog: Giant George, a Great Dane—43 inches tall (tallest dog in history, by the way), 7 feet long, 245 pounds

❖

VII. BREED-SPECIFIC PUBLICATIONS

A partial list of the author's favorites and other notables.

The Lhasa Apso Reporter
The Spotter (dalmatians)
The Bulldogger
Boston Barks (Boston terriers)
The Bagpiper (Scotties)
The Pom Reader
Headlions (lowchens)
The Modern Molosser (all mastiff types)
Komondor Komments
Better Beagling
Doberman Digest
The Alpenhorn (Bernese mountain dogs)
The Third Eye (Ibizan hounds)
Tassels & Tales (Bedlington terriers)
The Courier (Portuguese water dogs)
Staff Status (American Staffordshire terriers)
Schnauzer Shorts
Great Scots (Scottish terriers)
The Bagpiper (Skye terriers)
Chin Chin Chat
Havanese Hotline
Just Frenchies
Pinscher Patter (min pins)
The Dew Claw (briards)
Border Lines (border collies)

BERGER PICARD (AKA PICARDY SHEPHERD): A herding breed euphemistically described as "rustic" (read: ugly) from the Picardy region of France, the BP had a moment in America thanks to the movie *Because of Winn-Dixie* and nearly went extinct between the two world wars. It is still largely unknown here, and a fact sheet handed out by fanciers includes this, one of the more confounding sentences about dogs I read all year: "Picards are often mistaken for another canine actor, the Wirehaired Portuguese Podengo Media, another scruffy looking rare breed." Also, according to the BP Club of America, the dogs, "with their crisp coats, were used to smuggle tobacco and matches across the Franco-Belgian Border. The tobacco would be put in goatskin pouches, hairy side up, and attached to the dog's shaven back."

BARBET: Also known as the French water dog. Currently in the process of applying for AKC recognition, this breed, too, was nearly extinct after WWII. It has thick woolly "hair," not fur, and comes with its own terminology. A male is a barbet, a female a barbette, a young male a barbichon, a young female a barbiche, a male puppy a barbichet, and a female puppy a barbichette. A barbet fancier, naturally, is a barbetier.

CIRNECO DELL'ETNA: An endangered sight hound that originated in Italy. The first one came to America in 1996—her name was Cy'rena Seta dell'Oro—from Slovenia.

PUMI: A Hungarian herding breed, like the puli as well as the mudi (which, come to think of it, is another breed I've never heard of)—the three were considered to be the same breed until the turn of the twentieth century. It is thought that the pumi came from breeding pulik (the black-haired dreadlock dog) with a terrier, which resulted in a narrower, longer head and a livelier attitude. Fewer than a hundred in the United States.

CESKY FOUSECK: A Czech gun dog that looks a lot like a German wire-haired pointer. Also, the rare breed most often mistaken for a winger on the Slovakian national hockey team.

BOERBOEL: A South African farm dog. Not to be confused with a boerewor, which is a tasty South African sausage.

❖

IX. ALTERNATE AND/OR DEFUNCT BREED NAMES

ALSATIAN: German shepherd

YE ANCIENT DOGGE OF MALTA: Maltese

FRENCH MASTIFF: Dogue de Bordeaux

TOY BULLDOG: French bulldog

GROENENDAEL, OR

   CHIEN DE BERGER BELGE: Belgian sheepdog

RUSSIAN WOLFHOUND: Borzoi

X. MOST WESTMINSTER BEST IN SHOW WINS, BY BREED

1. Wirehaired fox terrier, 13 wins

2. Scottish terrier, 8

3. English springer spaniel, 6

4. (Tie) Airedale terrier, boxer, Doberman pinscher, smooth fox terrier, standard poodle, Sealyham terrier, 4

5. Pekingese, pointer, miniature poodle, 3

XI. MOST WESTMINSTER BEST IN SHOW WINS, BY GROUP

1. Terrier, 45 wins
2. Sporting, 19
3. Working, 15
4. Non-Sporting, 10
5. Toy, 9
6. Hound, 5
7. Herding, 1

XII. A CURATED SELECTION OF T-SHIRT SLOGANS
OBSERVED AT DOG SHOWS

Crazy Dog Lady

Woof Is My Co-pilot

Money Can Buy a Dog, But Not the Wag of Its Tail

I Kiss My Dog on the Mouth

Who's Your Doggie?

My Indian Name Is Walks with Poop

You Had Me at Woof

Bitches Love Me

I Like Big Mutts

Your Dog Doesn't Know Sit

Run Fast, Bark Loud

Dog Hair. The Other Condiment.

My Kids Have 4 Feet

My Dog Isn't Spoiled. I'm Just Well Trained.

The More People I Meet, the More I Like My Dog

I Love Dogs. It's Humans that Annoy Me.

Husband and Poodle Missing. Reward for Poodle.

Checking Pee Mail
(drawing of dog sniffing tree)

It's All Fun And Games Until Someone Ends Up In A Cone
(drawing of dog with cone on head)

Holy Shih-Tzu

Pugs, Not Drugs

I Post Pictures of My Wiener on the Internet
(photo of dachshund)

I Trip Over My Wiener
(drawing of dachshund silhouette)